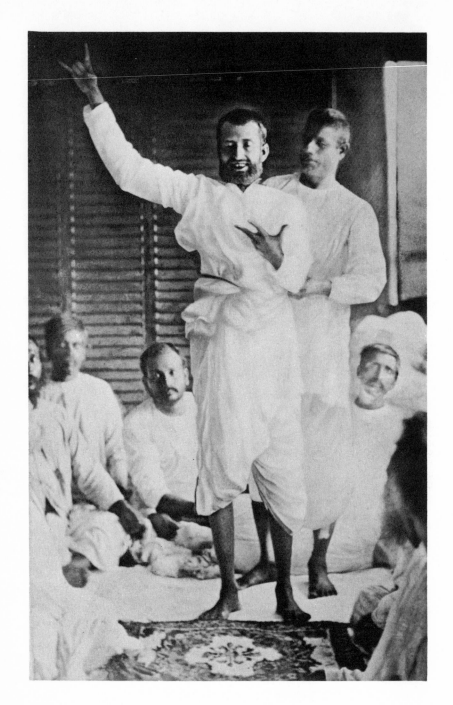

Ramakrishna in Keshab's house

Christopher Isherwood

RAMAKRISHNA
AND
HIS DISCIPLES

SIMON AND SCHUSTER
NEW YORK

FIRST PRINTING

LIBRARY OF CONGRESS CATALOG CARD NUMBER: 65-17100
MANUFACTURED IN THE UNITED STATES OF AMERICA

Readers interested in the subject matter of this book are invited by the Vedanta Society of Southern California to correspond with its Secretary, at 1946 Vedanta Place, Hollywood, California 90028.

This book is dedicated – indeed, one may say it dedicates itself – to Swami Prabhavananda, head of the Vedanta Society of Southern California, my *guru*, dear friend and literary collaborator for the past twenty-five years. It was he who asked me to write it, and who has helped me with his advice and encouragement throughout the writing.

I owe great gratitude to Swami Madhavananda, head of the Ramakrishna Order, who read the manuscript chapter by chapter as it was sent to him at the Belur Math in Bengal, and supplied me with most valuable corrections, added information and comments.

From first to last, I have had constant help from John Yale (now Swami Vidyatmananda). While in India recently, he verified many details, collected illustrations for this book and compiled the explanatory notes on them which are printed in an appendix.

Here, at our centre in Los Angeles, I must also thank Swami Vandanananda, Ursula Bond (Pravrajika Anandaprana) and the many other members of the group who have shared in the work of this project.

C. I.

September, 1964

Contents

Illustrations

ILLUSTRATIONS

I

The Story Begins

———

This is the story of a phenomenon.

I will begin by calling him simply that, rather than 'holy man', 'mystic', 'saint', or 'avatar'; all emotive words with mixed associations which may attract some readers, repel others.

A phenomenon is often something extraordinary and mysterious. Ramakrishna was extraordinary and mysterious; most of all to those who were best fitted to understand him. A phenomenon is always a fact, an object of experience. That is how I shall try to approach Ramakrishna.

Modern advertising has inflated our value-judgements until they are nearly worthless. Every product and person is said by its publicist to be the best. I want to avoid the competitive note here so I will say only this: Ramakrishna's life, being comparatively recent history, is well documented. In this respect, it has the advantage over the lives of other, earlier phenomena of a like nature. We do not have to rely, here, on fragmentary or glossed manuscripts, dubious witnesses, pious legends. What Ramakrishna was or was not the reader must decide for himself; but at least his decision can be based on words and deeds Ramakrishna indubitably spoke and did.

You will find a full bibliography at the end of the book. But I must also mention here the two great works which provide almost all of my source material. This book is really no more than an introduction to them, and I shall quote from them and paraphrase them throughout it. One is *The Gospel of Sri Ramakrishna* by M.; the other is *Sri Ramakrishna the Great Master* by Swami Saradananda. M. is the pseudonym of Mahendra Nath Gupta, the headmaster of a Calcutta high school, who first met Ramakrishna in 1882 and thereafter visited him regularly during the remaining four years of Ramakrishna's life.

After each visit, M. noted down everything which had been said and done in his presence by Ramakrishna and those who were with him. The result is a very big book, which is probably close to totally accurate reporting. Saradananda was still in his teens when he met Ramakrishna and became his disciple. It was not until many years later that he began to write the articles which accumulated to form *Sri Ramakrishna the Great Master*, a biography which covers all of Ramakrishna's life except its last few months. Although Saradananda did not begin his work until more than twenty years after Ramakrishna's death, there is no doubt of its authenticity. Many of those who had known Ramakrishna were then still alive, and Saradananda carefully compared his memories with theirs. *The Great Master* has also the value of having been written by a monastic disciple, who has actually shared the extraordinary experiences he describes. 'Nothing beyond my spiritual experience has been recorded in the book,' Saradananda once told a questioner. This seemingly cautious answer is in fact a claim so tremendous that it silences all suspicion of boastfulness; a man like Saradananda could not have made it unless it was literally true.

As for myself, it would be dishonest to pretend I am addressing you as an impartial biographer. I myself am a devotee of Ramakrishna; I believe, or am at least strongly inclined to believe, that he was what his disciples declared that he was: an incarnation of God upon earth. Nevertheless, I am not writing this book primarily for confirmed believers or unbelievers. The sort of reader I *am* writing for is the one who is not afraid to recognize the marvellous, no matter where he finds it; the sort of reader who is always on the lookout for a phenomenon.

I only ask you approach Ramakrishna with the same open-minded curiosity you might feel about any highly unusual human being: a Julius Caesar, a Catherine of Siena, a Leonardo da Vinci, an Arthur Rimbaud. Dismiss from your mind, as far as you are able, such categories as holy-unholy, sane-insane, wise-foolish, pure-impure, positive-negative, useful-useless. Just say to yourself as you read: this, too, is humanly possible. Then later, if you like, consider the implications of that possibility for the rest of the human species.

If you leave Calcutta airport early one morning on a west-bound flight, you will be able to have supper that night in Rome. If, instead, you take a car to Kamarpukur, Ramakrishna's birthplace, you will easily arrive in time for lunch. In the first case, you will have travelled well over four thousand miles; in the second, about seventy. Yet in one sense the shorter journey can be said to be the longer, because it takes you backward in time. Many of these Bengal villages have changed little in appearance during the last hundred years. And if Kamarpukur has changed more than its neighbours, it is in having become an international centre of pilgrimage with a modern temple dedicated to Ramakrishna. That is to say, it is less concerned with the possibilities of its future than with the great event of its past.

The houses of these villages are still mostly built of mud with roofs of straw thatch. Between them run narrow, winding lanes, unpaved, with open gutters on either side. There is still no plumbing, no electric light, no gas. Water must be carried into the houses from a well or tank. Washing of one's self and one's clothes is also done in a tank – which in India means an artificial reservoir or pond, fed by rain-water and, sometimes, springs, and kept clean by fish. Many of the villagers, like their ancestors, are rice-farmers, and they still use the ox or water buffalo for ploughing and as their beast of draught or burden. Trousers and other articles of city clothing are still unusual among them, but the men, and more particularly the boys, now often wear shorts because they are cheaper than the dhoti, the cloth which is wrapped around the waist like a skirt or looped between the legs. And the older girls now no longer veil their faces when in the presence of strangers.

Kamarpukur is larger than its neighbours, being in fact a group of three adjoining hamlets, Sripur, Kamarpukur, and Mukundapur; but it is not large enough to be marked on the map of India in any ordinary atlas. If you look northwest of Calcutta for Burdwan and then measure off a point thirty miles due south of that city, you will have Kamarpukur's approximate location. The villages of this district are scattered over a gently undulating plain. It is usual for a village to be protected by a grove of palms, banyans, or mangoes; so that in autumn, when the rice-shoots are green, it is a tropical island in a vegetable sea. In winter, when the paddy-fields are stubbly and dry and the dust of the red earth blows over the eroded landscape, it is an oasis in a semi-desert.

If you have never been in India, it may be difficult for you to picture such a village; as you must do in order to set the scene in your imagination for the first act of this story. When an American pictures to himself an old-fashioned village, he probably thinks of the ones which are still to be found in remote parts of England. He sees stone or brick cottages surrounding a church and a village green, on which there is also an inn. It is a congregational group; private homes arranged around the centres of communal worship, business, gossip, and sport.

The Bengal village does not present, like the English village, an outward appearance of order. It will contain a number of temples and small shrines, but these are not meeting-places as Christian churches are, because Hinduism is primarily a household religion and its rites of daily worship are mostly practised in each individual home. There is no inn or public eating-house here, because of the problems which arise from the caste-rules forbidding some people to eat in the proximity of others. The Bengal village has no central green or square; its meeting-places are the wells and the tanks, and only occasionally the temple precincts. Nevertheless, it has its own pattern of social order; a pattern more complex but more clearly defined than that of the English village. This pattern is based upon the caste-system. The members of each caste share the village between them, respecting each other's separateness yet living in interdependence.

The Western visitor to a Bengal village may be too polite to criticize, but he will probably think it dirty and primitive. He will object to the wanton exposure of garbage in the gutters. He will be shocked by the bareness of the houses, which are often furnished only with a single cot, a pile of sleeping-mats, and a trunk for storing valuables. He will be disgusted when he discovers that the kitchen floors are habitually rubbed with cow-dung.

The Bengal villager would not understand the Westerner's reaction to his method of garbage-disposal. Where else are you to put it, if not on the street? That, surely, is better than keeping it inside the house? If he could see the chamber-pots in old-fashioned English cottages, he might well be shocked. And he would certainly be disgusted to learn that the cottagers usually took only one bath a week and wore the same clothes for a week before they washed them. As for the bareness of his own house, he would prefer it to the clutter of their parlours; crammed with useless furniture and dust-catching draperies – yet without a single shrine! He would perhaps advise them to try cow-dung on *their* floors; it is an excellent antiseptic.

It must not be supposed from what I have written above that these Bengali villages are mere relics of an earlier age. Even when their appearance is unchanged, change *has* touched them, below the surface. The effects of closer contact with the cities, with the life of India as an independent nation, with public education and social medicine, are being felt, of course. Schools have come to the villages, and immunization shots. Nowadays, family ties are not quite as strong as they were; caste-rules, especially with regard to eating in mixed company, are rather less strictly observed. The slogans of democracy are beginning to be heard even in these intensely conservative communities; although, as yet, they do not sound very convincing in face of the villagers' profound inborn respect for hierarchy and tradition.

So much for the present. It is not our concern here. The question now to be answered is: what was Kamarpukur like in 1836, the year of Ramakrishna's birth?

In some respects it was more prosperous than it is today. The population was large and steadily growing, but everybody had enough to eat. More than sixty years had passed since the last major famine, which had killed nearly one-third of the people of Bengal. The health of the villagers was generally excellent; it was only later to be seriously undermined by the great malaria epidemic of 1867.

In addition to agriculture, they carried on various small industries. They made sweetmeats and ebony hookah pipes. On their handlooms they wove dhotis and towels, some of which were sold as far away as Calcutta. Passing close to the village, there is a road which runs south to the city of Puri and its famous Jagannath shrine; in those days, before the railroads, great numbers of pilgrims used it and these were potential customers at Kamarpukur's markets.

On the whole, life in such a village was happy. Poverty is a relative evil; and in this case it was widely shared, and prevented from becoming extreme by the helpfulness of your neighbours. As a community, Kamarpukur met one of the most important demands of the modern social psychologist; no one could feel rejected there. Everybody had his or her place in the caste-structure. The family recognized total responsibility for all its members, even the most distant. The old were honoured. Women were treated with respect. Children were indulged and petted by all. As we study the personality of Ramakrishna, we see in him the sublimation of the village child he once was; innocently secure in his love for his mother and his certainty of being loved. You cannot imagine a less frustrated childhood than his, or one less likely to produce conflicts and neuroses in later years. It will be important to bear this in mind when we consider the psychological states which Ramakrishna afterwards passed through.

The villager's sense of belonging was strengthened by his acceptance of Caste. This statement may sound paradoxical, since the caste-system implies a degree of rejection of certain individuals by others. But it must be remembered that the castes are not merely exclusive; they are also interdependent. They provide for a division of labour. Without each other's assistance, they could not exist.

The four main castes are: the *brahmins*, the *kshatriyas*, the *vaishyas* and the *sudras* – the priests, the warriors, the merchants, and the servants, to name them by their original functions. When the system was first established in India by its Aryan invaders, many thousands of years ago, a man's caste was probably determined by his occupation in nearly every case. But, with the passing of the centuries, Caste became a matter of hereditary social status, rigidly respected, and surrounded by a mass of restrictions and regulations designed to prevent caste-mixture. No amount of wealth could buy you membership in a higher caste, and intermarriage was absolutely forbidden. Meanwhile, the main castes were divided into sub-castes, corresponding to various trades and professions; but even these smaller and more precise categories have been broken down by the economic forces of modern life. Nowadays, a member of the blacksmith's caste is not necessarily a blacksmith.

The so-called untouchables are sometimes spoken of as a caste; but actually they are outside Caste altogether. When the Aryans settled in India they had to deal with various groups of people much less civilized than themselves; some were their own camp followers, others the local aborigines. If these people were exceedingly primitive – in their religious beliefs, their sexual habits, and their choice of food – then the Aryans did not admit them even to the lowest of their castes. And this state of exclusion, like caste-membership, became hereditary.

6

When the Christian missionaries came to India, they converted and educated many untouchables, and these converts could then enjoy social recognition, provided they moved to places where their background was not known. For this reason, many were to be found in the larger cities, including Calcutta. But untouchables, as a general rule, were rarer in Bengal than elsewhere; and it is possible that there were none at all in the Kamarpukur district in Ramakrishna's day.

From the standpoint of our democratic thinking, Caste is an evil since it makes men unequal. The present Government of India takes this view, as did the Hindu reformers of the nineteenth century, such as Keshab Chandra Sen, about whom I shall have much to write later. The Government's present policy is to abolish Caste by degrees, as public opinion permits; and the levelling process of industrialism is helping to do this quickly among the urban populations. It would be worse than reactionary – it would be ridiculous – to try to defend the caste-system as it is today. It has no future in our world. But we must understand what Caste meant to Ramakrishna and his contemporaries; and, to do this, we must consider its virtues. Its defects are uninterestingly obvious.

To understand Caste as an idea rather than as a system, we have to go back to the Bhagavad-Gita, which dates from about the fifth century B.C. and is still the most widely read work of Hindu religious literature. In the eighteenth chapter of the Gita, we find Caste presented as a kind of natural order. The four castes are described in relation to their duties and responsibilities, without any mention of their privileges. The typical member of each caste is presented as a certain kind of human being with certain capacities; and his capacities determine his duties. In Sanskrit (in which the Gita is written) the word used is *dharma*, meaning the particular duties, the way of life, which a man's nature imposes upon him. Great stress is laid upon the importance of following your own dharma and not trying to follow the dharma of another.

Considering the castes from this standpoint, the Gita tells us far more about their functions than we could learn from merely hearing their names.

The brahmin is much more than just a priest. According to the Gita, he must be the seer of the community; the man through whom its contact with the life of the spirit is maintained. In India, the religious

7

ideal has always been to obtain knowledge of the *Atman*, the divine nature within man, through direct experience; revelation has never been the property of a Church, as in the West. It is not towards any religious body but towards the individual seer, the knower of the Atman, that the community looks for an example to sustain it in its own struggles to gain enlightenment. That this enlightenment can actually be obtained by any individual – that the Atman can really be known in the sense of self-knowledge – is the fundamental proposition of the Hindu religion. Hinduism accepts the revelations obtained by mystics of other faiths – including those which recognize the authority of a Church or ruling body. And it accepts these revelations even when, as sometimes happens, they have been declared heretical by the ruling Church simply because they were not received through that Church's mediation.

How can the Atman be known? By meditation, and by self-disciplines which open the eye of the spirit. Therefore the brahmin must be chaste, austere, scrupulously truthful, compassionate towards all living creatures. His faith in the Atman must be based on direct self-know-ledge, not credulity. He may be a scholar and interpreter of the sacred books; but his interpretations must be drawn from his own experience, not merely from academic knowledge of former commentators.

The kshatriya is much more than just a warrior. The Gita expects him to lead the community in peace as well as in war. He must be a man of determination and courage; farsighted, generous, and com-petent to carry out his administrative duties.

The vaishya is not a mere merchant in the modern sense; in business to enrich himself. He is the provider for the community. He farms. He breeds cattle. It follows that he must not engage in activities which squeeze profits from others without really benefiting them. There is no doubt that the Gita would condemn much of what is considered legitimate business practice today.

The sudra is to serve the community, but not as its sullen slave. His service is an act of self-dedication. His reward is in the knowledge of his indispensability. Without his co-operation, the other three castes could not exist.

Having defined the respective duties of the castes, the Gita con-tinues: 'All mankind is born for perfection, and each man can reach it if he will only follow his own dharma.' Elsewhere in the Gita, this statement is amplified: It is not enough just to do your duty, you must do it in the spirit of non-attachment. To quote from the second chapter: 'You have the right to work, but for the work's sake only. You have no right to the fruits of work. . . . Perform every action with your heart fixed on the Supreme Lord. Renounce attachment to the fruits. . . . In the calm of self-surrender, the seers renounce the fruits of their actions, and so reach enlightenment.'

To act without attachment to the fruits of an act is to act without fear or desire; desire that a certain result may be obtained, fear that it may not – or vice versa, when it is a question of doing one's duty in the face of possibly unpleasant consequences. We are to perform every action as though it were a ritual, of which the value is symbolic. We perform this ritual to the very best of our ability, but without anxiety as to what its consequences may be. The consequences – the fruits of the act – we dedicate to God.

Ramakrishna was fond of saying that you could get the essential message of the Gita by repeating the word several times. 'Gita, Gita, Gita,' you begin, but then find yourself saying 'ta-Gi, ta-Gi, ta-Gi'. *Tagi* means one who has renounced everything for God.

Since the work proper to any kind of dharma can be done in this spirit, it follows that Caste is no barrier to equal spiritual opportunity for all. Actually, seven of the best-known saints of southern India were untouchables. Ramakrishna was himself a brahmin, but he had disciples from each of the four castes. In any case, when a man takes monastic vows, his caste-membership automatically ceases.

Caste is meaningless and indeed intolerable unless it is related to the ideal of spiritual self-development. Throughout the centuries when Caste was a vital force in Indian life, it appeared to everyone, high and low alike, to be an outward manifestation of the natural order of things – an order which existed in and by the will of God. To live your life in accordance with your caste-dharma was to evolve towards knowledge of Him. If your spiritual evolution went far enough, you would not be reborn after death but united with the impersonal consciousness of His being. If you merely accumulated good karma – that is, the merit of good actions – you would be reborn under more favourable conditions for reaching enlightenment in the next incarnation; into a pious brahmin family, for example. But, whatever sins you committed, however degraded the births which you consequently passed through, you would always ultimately get another chance to work your way upward. You did not fear permanent damnation, and injustice was unthinkable to you, since you did not believe in a judge, even a divine judge. Your reward or punishment was simply your karma, good or bad; and your karma was the direct result of your actions, in this or in previous lives. In either case, you had nobody but yourself to blame or thank.

Such was the religion which the British conquerors of India dismissed as the basest paganism! If you had asked them to be a little more specific in their condemnation of it, they would have replied contemptuously that Hindus are polytheists. I shall deal with the British and their prejudices later. This question of polytheism I must discuss right away.

A Christian believes in God in three persons – God the Father, God the Son, and God the Holy Ghost. He will hotly deny that he is a polytheist, explaining that his three persons are really one God, the Holy Trinity. The Hindu also denies that he is a polytheist, and for a similar though not identical reason. He sees the many gods as aspects of one central Reality or Godhead, which he calls *Brahman*. Brahman cannot possibly be described because it has no attributes, being the substratum of all attributes. Brahman does not act, being the substratum of all action; it simply is. Brahman is omnipresent. When it is spoken of as dwelling within any particular creature or object, it is called the Atman. But this is simply a matter of linguistic convenience: Atman and Brahman are one and the same.

In the West, most of us equate 'religion' with the cult of Jesus of Nazareth. Christianity offers us no alternatives. But the Hindu has a number of cults to choose from; he is at liberty to worship Shiva rather than Mother Kali, or Krishna rather than Rama. Or he may turn aside from all of them and prefer to meditate upon the absolute attributeless Brahman. Since he knows that Brahman's aspects may be infinite in number, he is obliged to recognize the gods of other religions also. The first Christian missionaries to India were disconcerted when their hearers readily agreed to accept Jesus as a divine incarnation but firmly refused to regard him as unique and give up their own gods in consequence.

The peasants of Bengal in Ramakrishna's day were no subtle theologians. They would have been incapable of formulating these

beliefs in words, but they understood them perfectly in spirit. Kamarpukur was full of shrines to various deities, to one or other of which
everybody paid homage. The life of the village revolved around the
annual religious festivals and performances of sacred plays. Even the
children in their games pretended to be wandering monks, imitated
the holy rituals, and acted out scenes from the tales of the gods.
These people were certainly not a community of saints; but religion
entered into everything they did and gave them a sense of order
and trust amidst the hardships of their lives. They trusted in God,
they were not afraid of life or unduly anxious about the future.
Much that we in our sophistication make complex seemed simple to
them.

Lest what I have just written should sound a little too sweet to be
true, I must now admit that the Bengal village sometimes suffered
under a most shameful kind of tyranny: that of the (comparatively)
big landowner. Such petty tyrants, when they arose, were all-powerful
in these remote places; the local law-officers were merely their tools.
It was not unknown for one of them to get away, literally, with
murder. Such a landowner was Ramananda Roy, a mean and vengeful
man who ruled over the village of Derepur, two miles west of Kamarpukur.

About 1814, this Ramananda was persecuting a poorer neighbour
and needed someone to testify falsely against his victim in the local
court. Ramananda wanted this false witness to be a man whom the
villagers respected and whose word would therefore be believed. So
he approached Khudiram Chatterjee.

Khudiram came of a brahmin family which was relatively well-to-
do; he had inherited nearly fifty acres of land in the neighbourhood.
He and his wife Chandra were pious people, ardent devotees of the
divine incarnation Sri Rama. (Sri, when applied to spiritual exemplars,
is a Hindu title of reverence, such as 'Lord' or 'Master'; it is also the
equivalent of 'Mr' in modern Indian social life.)

Khudiram knew very well the danger of refusing to perjure himself.
But – being the kind of man that he was – he did refuse; and Ramananda's vindictiveness was aroused against him. Soon afterwards,
Ramananda brought some altogether baseless charge against Khudiram,
and this time false witnesses were not lacking. Khudiram lost his case

and had to sacrifice all of his landholdings in consequence. He was ruined.

As it turned out, the story did not have a tragic ending. For Khudiram had a good friend in Sukhlal Goswami of Kamarpukur. Hearing with sympathy and indignation of the way in which Khudiram had been mistreated, Sukhlal now offered him a group of huts on his own property and nearly half an acre of rice-field as an unconditional gift. Nor did Sukhlal give away his worst land. Indeed this field was so fertile that it was known as Lakshmi-jala, the Meadow of the Goddess of Good Fortune. So it came about that Khudiram, Chandra, and their two children were able to leave Derepur and settle in Kamarpukur.

Thus, within a short space of time, Khudiram experienced two extremes of human conduct: Ramananda's vileness, Sukhlal's noble generosity. His reaction to both was characteristic. He nursed no hatred against Ramananda; he never forgot to be grateful to Sukhlal. But, though he was now among friends and though his family's subsistence was fairly assured, he was mindful for the rest of his life of the lesson he had learned. He did not lapse into false optimism. He remained keenly aware of the uncertainty and transience of the world's hopes and goods. More and more he turned his mind towards what is eternal and unchanging. He devoted himself increasingly to the cult of Sri Rama, his chosen deity.

As for Ramananda, he died without leaving any children. His land passed into the possession of strangers. And all the result of his greed and scheming was just this – that today the name of Derepur is still merely another name, known only to a very few, among all the villages of India.

2

The Birth of Ramakrishna

Soon after the move to Kamarpukur, Khudiram had the first of a series of spiritual experiences which were to be granted to him and to his wife Chandra during the years that followed. Since such experiences, in all their variety, are to be a recurring theme in this story, I will make some general remarks about them now.

When we use the word 'experience' in its primary sense, we mean – to quote the dictionary – 'the process or fact of personally observing, encountering or undergoing something'. That is to say, experience is valued because it is personal; being contrasted favourably with hearsay or the information got from newspapers and books. Experiences are held to be more or less important according to the intensity of their effect on the experiencer.

These two factors – the personal nature of experience and its measurement by intensity – are most significant when we come to consider the kind of experience called spiritual.

If someone tells me about an experience he has had in the world of ordinary sense-perception, I shall usually be able to decide whether he is speaking the truth or lying. I can do this because I can almost always relate the experience he describes to similar experiences of my own. And so his experience is of value to me. But if someone tells me about an experience in the spiritual world I shall probably be in doubt, because I have no similar experiences to which I can relate his. Unless, for other reasons, I have become convinced that this person will never lie to me, his experience will therefore be of no value to me. Many of my readers will know that sense of sad frustration with which one listens to some spiritual testimony one longs to believe in but can't, because the witness is so obviously dishonest. It is human nature to pretend to know a little more than you really do. But, alas,

13

how many pupils have lost faith because they caught their teacher exaggerating!

So – a little spiritual experience of your own is of more value to you than all the recorded experiences of the greatest saints. And, indeed, without that minimum of personal experience, you cannot possibly begin to guess at the magnitude of theirs.

A spiritual experience can only be properly judged by its intensity; the intensity, that is, of its after-effect on the experiencer. It is no use trying to decide whether or not a certain experience was spiritual by analysing its circumstances; these may have been produced by some quite external cause, such as sickness or the use of certain drugs. One should not ask oneself 'was my experience an hallucination or not?' but rather 'what has my experience left with me, now that it is over?' A true spiritual experience, even one of lesser intensity, must at least slightly affect the experiencer for the rest of his life.

But now I must try to answer the question: what is a spiritual experience?

The difficulty here is that the average reader's mind is apt to be confused by various ill-defined terms he has met with in books – such as vision, trance, psychic phenomenon, revelation, spirit message, etc. (Even such an authority as Roget's *Thesaurus* gives 'vision' as a synonym for 'hallucination'.) As the result of these vague definitions, the reader gradually comes to rely on Matter as the only reality and to think of Spirit as a shadowy and dangerous hinterland of deceptions and illusions. True, the modern physicist keeps telling him that Matter itself is a deception; the table is utterly unlike the thing we think we see and feel. But even this warning does nothing to alter his concept of Spirit. For, according to his mental filing system, what the clergyman tells him about Spirit is 'religion', and the findings of science and religion can never, he thinks, be reconciled with each other.

The Hindu religious philosophers of thousands of years ago were much more truly scientific in their outlook than most of us are today; and they drew no such crude dividing-line between Matter and Spirit. They explained the evolution of the universe as a projection of a series of coverings around the Reality which is Brahman. Brahman itself is pure undifferentiated consciousness; but each of these coverings represents a stage in progressive differentiation, by which the One becomes seemingly many.

14

This evolutionary process is said to be motivated by *Ishwara*. Ishwara is what most of us mean when we say 'God' – that is, God with attributes; loving, merciful, and just. Brahman, being the Absolute, is beyond all attributes and all action. It is Ishwara, Brahman united with its power, who creates a universe, sustains it, and in due course dissolves it again – for the process of evolution and involution is said to operate in an eternal cycle. To say that Ishwara is the creator is not to imply a dualism. For the power of Brahman can no more be separated from Brahman than the heat of fire can be separated from fire itself.

The power of Brahman is the basis of all mind and matter. It is called *Prakriti* or *Maya*; the terms are interchangeable. Maya is popularly supposed to mean 'illusion', but this is a loose and misleading translation. Maya (or Prakriti) can only be called illusory in a relative sense; namely that the universe which is made of it is impermanent and other than Brahman, the Reality.

According to Hindu philosophy, the evolutionary sequence is as follows. Prakriti projects *mahat*, the basis of the individual intelligence. Mahat projects *buddhi*, the faculty by which the nature of objects is distinguished and their functions are classified. Buddhi projects *ahamkara*, the ego-sense. Ahamkara projects the powers of perception and also the objects of perception; the subtle and gross elements, and the subtle and gross faculties with which we perceive them.

These coverings are therefore coverings of ignorance; they hide Brahman from us. The material universe which is known to our physical senses is the grossest manifestation of this ignorance, since it is the most outward covering, farthest from Brahman.

Matter and Spirit are not divided; they are interrelated. The former is evolved from the latter, and the difference between them is only one of degree. When the meditative mind turns in upon itself, following a line of involution in its attempt to reach Brahman, it becomes aware of this truth. Beneath the gross elements of the material world it encounters the subtle elements which are their essences. This is what is called the psychic world. Within the psychic world, we possess subtle bodies which are the essences of our gross elements. The psychic world exists superimposed upon the material world; but it does not normally make itself apparent to us or concern itself with our doings. It is, as you might say in the jargon of nowadays, on a different wave-length.

Our experience of the material world is obtained only while we are awake. Our experience of the psychic world may be obtained while we are awake or dreaming, and it may be produced by means of concentration or austerities or drugs. Beyond the material and the psychic worlds, the mind enters the world of spiritual experience. Such experience differs altogether from psychic experience. It can be recognized by its lasting effect upon the experiencer; psychic visions cannot transform a man's nature, no matter how startling and vivid they may be. Unlike psychic visions, spiritual visions are not generally variable. If you have a vision of Jesus, for example, he will appear to you just as he has appeared to other devotees; he will not necessarily resemble any picture of him you have made for yourself in your imagination. A psychic experience may cause you no particular emotion, or it may depress or terrify you; a spiritual experience will always be accompanied by great joy. During a spiritual vision, the experiencer loses awareness of his material surroundings; they become merged in light. During a psychic vision, the experiencer often remains fully aware of his material surroundings; and indeed the apparition itself is apt to appear in such a natural manner that it is at first mistaken for an ordinary human being or animal.

The highest spiritual experiences can only be known in that state of consciousness which in Sanskrit is called *samadhi*. Samadhi is a state quite other than that of waking, dreaming or dreamless sleep; it has been described as superconsciousness. In samadhi, a man knows his absolute identity with the Atman, which is his real nature.

The first of Khudiram's visions took place in the following manner.

One day, Khudiram had to go to a neighbouring village. On the way home, he felt tired and stopped to rest in the shade of a tree. It was a quiet place, and a soft breeze was blowing; he became relaxed in body and mind, lay down and fell asleep.

Spiritual visions which come to us in sleep are not like ordinary dreams; they can be better described as visitations, for they are much more vivid and memorable than the encounters of our waking life. In this vision, Khudiram saw Sri Rama, his chosen deity, in the form of a celestial boy whose body was green like a blade of young grass. 'I've been there a long time,' the Boy said, pointing to a particular spot in the middle distance. 'I had nothing to eat and no one to look after me. Take me back to your house. I want very much to be served by you.' At this Khudiram was greatly moved; he prostrated again and again before the Boy. 'Oh, my Lord,' he said, 'I am a poor man, and my devotion is weak. How could I possibly serve you in my hut? And if my service is unworthy of you, I shall lose your grace. Why do you make such a hard demand of me?' But the Boy reassured Khudiram, saying graciously, 'Don't be afraid. I shan't blame you for anything that's lacking. Take me with you.' Khudiram burst into tears of joy, and woke.

Looking around him, he now recognized the very spot which Sri Rama had indicated in the vision. And there he saw a stone lying which he knew to be a sacred *shalagrama* stone. Beside this stone, as if guarding it, a cobra was reared on its coils with hood expanded threateningly.

(The shalagrama stone is usually about the size and shape of a plum; it has one or more holes in it and bears certain markings by which it can be identified. Shalagramas are natural formations, and most of them are found in the River Gandaki, a tributary of the Ganges. It was not, however, so very surprising that Khudiram found this one in a paddy-field in Bengal, for the stones are regarded as emblems of Vishnu, and a wandering holy man might well carry one around with him to worship.)

Khudiram was still in the exalted mood of his vision. He hurried over to the stone without a thought of fear; and, indeed, by the time he had reached it, the cobra had disappeared into its hole. Khudiram brought the stone back home with him, performed the prescribed ritual of dedication and set it up in the household shrine to be worshipped daily. It was thus that he received the Boy of his vision as an honoured family guest.

Khudiram had not exaggerated when he warned the Boy that he would be poorly entertained. There were days when the household had nothing to eat. But, when this happened, Khudiram would comfort his wife Chandra, saying, 'Never mind – if Lord Rama chooses to fast, why shouldn't we?' And it was not long before their situation improved, thanks to the richness of the land Sukhlal had given them. It throve, despite Khudiram's unworldliness and his preoccupation with ritual worship. When Khudiram went to bathe in the tank, the villagers stayed out of the water, as a sign of their respect. And while Khudiram was admired, Chandra was loved, because she was so generous and so ready with her sympathy for all who were in trouble.

Years later, Ramakrishna said of his parents: 'My mother was the soul of honesty and sincerity. She didn't know much about the ways of the world, and was incapable of concealment; she said whatever was in her mind. My father spent most of his time in worship and meditation, and telling his beads. Every day, while he was praying, his chest swelled and shone with a divine radiance, and tears rolled down his cheeks. In his spare time, when he wasn't engaged in worship, he would make garlands for Sri Rama. The villagers respected him as a sage.'

It has been already mentioned that when Khudiram and Chandra moved to Kamarpukur they had two children. These were a son, Ramkumar, born in 1805, and a daughter, Katyayani, born in 1810. Twelve years after the arrival of the family in Kamarpukur, a second son, Rameswar, was born. These, with a second daughter, Sarvamangala, born in 1839, were to be Ramakrishna's brothers and sisters. But, for the benefit of those readers who find it difficult to keep many names distinct in their minds, I will say at once that only one, the elder brother Ramkumar, was to play any considerable part in Ramakrishna's adult life.

No close relative of such a figure as Ramakrishna can be without spiritual greatness. But, even in this family, Ramkumar was outstanding. He combined his father's deep faith with practical ability in worldly affairs; and as he grew to manhood he became their breadwinner. He was an excellent Sanskrit scholar, and had mastered the Scriptures so thoroughly that he was able to earn a living by giving advice to those who wanted some doctrinal point settled for them. He had also learned how to perform certain rites which are designed to ward off sickness and other misfortunes. In the course of his spiritual disciplines, he had developed psychic powers; he was able to foresee coming events and detect latent diseases in apparently healthy people. These powers he demonstrated dramatically on many occasions.

Once, for example, when Ramkumar was visiting Calcutta on some business, he went to bathe in the Ganges. While he was doing so, a rich man arrived with his family at the bathing-ghat. Since bathing in the Ganges is a religious rite rather than a mere act of hygiene, it is performed even by those who could wash much more comfortably in their own homes. And, in fact, the wife of this rich man was trying to preserve some of her domestic privacy; for she was sitting in a curtained palanquin which her servants carried right down into the water, so that she could take her bath inside it. Being a country boy, accustomed to the open, unashamed ways of village life, Ramkumar had never seen anyone bathing in this manner. As he looked in astonishment at the palanquin, he caught a glimpse of the lady's beautiful face between the curtains. Instantly, in a flash of his psychic insight, he knew that she would be dead by the next day. The knowledge overwhelmed him with sadness – so much so that he involuntarily murmured to himself: 'Such precautions about washing this body in private, today – and tomorrow they'll be bringing it back to the river, a corpse, for everyone to see!'

Most unfortunately, the lady's husband overheard Ramkumar's words. Terribly shocked and angry, he resolved to punish this young prophet of evil just as soon as his prophecy had been proven false. So, with outward politeness, he insisted that Ramkumar should return to their home with them. But that night the seemingly healthy wife fell suddenly sick and died.

Ramkumar also made a prophecy about his own wife – namely that she would die in her first childbirth. To his great relief, his wife remained childless for many years. But she did die, at the age of thirty-five, in 1849, in giving birth to a son named Akshay who will appear later in this story.

Like all pious Hindus, Khudiram loved to go on pilgrimages. In 1824, he travelled on foot all the way to the shrines of southern India; a journey which took a whole year. Again, in 1835, he set out for Gaya, in Bihar. At this time, Khudiram was sixty years old; but he was still lean and strong, and the hardships of the road meant nothing to him.

Gaya is doubly holy. The city itself is sacred to Vishnu, the preserver of the universe and the second deity in the Hindu trinity, with Brahma the creator and Shiva the dissolver. (Actually, this trinity personifies the three functions of Ishwara: creation, preservation, dissolution.) And, a few miles outside Gaya, is the traditional site of the pipal tree beneath which the Buddha meditated and attained enlightenment.

Khudiram stayed about a month at Gaya, worshipping at the many shrines in the surrounding hills and plains. He reserved for the last the most sacred shrine of all; the main temple which contains the foot-print of Vishnu. Here he made the offerings of boiled rice balls and powdered wheat or barley which are called *pindas*. Such offerings are regarded as tokens of reverence for one's ancestors.

That night, in sleep, he had another vision. He saw himself back in the Vishnu temple, making the offering, just as he had done that day. All around him were his ancestors, accepting his offering and blessing him. Then he became aware that these ancestors were them-selves worshipping the Lord, who was enthroned in their midst. The Lord looked affectionately at Khudiram, beckoned to him to approach, and said: 'Khudiram, your great devotion has made me very happy. The time has come for me to be born once again on earth. I shall be born as your son.'

Again, as in his earlier vision, Khudiram protested. The honour was too great. He was poor and unworthy. He begged to be excused from accepting it. But the Lord refused to accept his excuses. 'Don't be afraid, Khudiram,' he said. 'Whatever you give me to eat, I shall enjoy.' When Khudiram awoke, he felt certain that this was a divine revelation, and that the Lord of the Universe was actually about to be born into his household. He said nothing about his vision to anyone, left Gaya a few days later, and was back in Kamarpukur before the end of April.

On his return, he found Chandra in a strange radiant mood of love. Her concern for her neighbours was such that she could not take her meal until she was sure that all of them had eaten. If anyone had not, she wanted to share her own portion of food with him. She had the same guileless, trustful attitude towards all. It seemed that she could no longer think of anybody as being a stranger to her.

Chandra told Khudiram about the experiences she had had during his absence. 'One night, I dreamed that you had come home. The first thing I knew, you were holding me in your arms. I felt so glad! But then I saw your face – and it wasn't you. It wasn't a human face. It shone, like the face of a god. I screamed and struggled to get free; and then I woke up with a great start and I was alone in bed, shivering all over with fright! So then, after a moment, I asked myself: "Does a god ever appear to a human being in this way?" So I decided it couldn't have been a god, but some wicked man who'd come into the room for an evil purpose. I got up and lighted the lamp – but there was nobody there, and the door was still bolted from inside. All the rest of that night, I was afraid to go back to sleep. As soon as it was morning, I sent for Dhani and Prasanna and told them everything; and I asked them: "Do you think a man really came into my room? I have no quarrel with anyone in the village." But both of them laughed at me and scolded me. "You silly woman!" they said. "Has old age softened your brain? Better not tell anyone else about that dream of yours, or you'll start a scandal." So then I decided that it was only a dream, and that I wouldn't speak of it again except to you, my husband.'

A few days after the night of her dream – in broad daylight – Chandra had been gossiping with this same friend Dhani, who was the daughter of a neighbouring blacksmith. The two women were standing before a temple of Shiva – it is actually a small domed shrine, only large enough to contain half a dozen worshippers – right opposite Khudiram's home. (The temple is still there, today.)

'All of a sudden,' Chandra told Khudiram, 'I saw that the holy image of Lord Shiva inside the shrine was alive! It began to send forth waves of the most beautiful light. Slowly at first, then quicker and quicker. They filled up the inside of the temple, and then they came pouring out – it was like one of those huge flood-waves in the river – right towards me! I was going to tell Dhani – but then the waves washed over me and swallowed me up, and I felt that marvellous light enter into my body. I fell down on the ground, unconscious. When I came to myself, I told Dhani what had happened. But she didn't believe me; she said I'd had an epileptic fit. That can't be so, because, since then, I've been full of joy and my health is better than ever. Only – I feel that light is still inside me; and I believe that I'm with child.'

Khudiram now told his wife about his vision at Gaya, and assured her that her own visions were no fancies, but revelations of the great grace which they were soon to receive. So the two rejoiced together. And, as the months passed, it became known to everyone in Kamarpukur that Chandra was indeed pregnant, at the age of forty-five. It was noticed that this pregnancy made her remarkably beautiful; and the neighbours shook their heads, taking this beauty for a sign that she was fated to die in giving birth to her child.

Meanwhile, Chandra continued to have visions, with increasing frequency. Almost daily, the gods and goddesses appeared to her, or she heard their voices around her, and the tinkle of their anklets, or smelled their subtle perfumes. A great change had come over Chandra since her visions began. She no longer felt any awe of the gods. She loved them so much that they seemed closer to her than her own sons and daughter, and her attitude to them was now that of a mother. This was the tone in which she used to talk about them to Khudiram: 'Today, I saw a god riding on the back of a swan. I was startled, at first; then I felt sorry for him, because his face was quite red from sunburn. So I called to him and I said: "Dear little god, riding on your swan, your face looks burned by the sun. There's some cool rice in the house; I cooked it yesterday. Do come and eat a little, and refresh yourself before you go on." He heard me and he smiled. But then he faded away, and I didn't see him any more.'

These visions and their sequel have been received with disbelief even by some of Ramakrishna's greatest admirers in the West. Romain Rolland dismisses them indulgently as charming fables. Max Müller regards them as products of what he calls the Dialogic Process: 'the irrepressible miraculizing tendencies of devoted disciples.'

Now, the creation of legends is a natural mark of human reverence for what one feels to be greater than oneself. No reasonable person reveres the Buddha any less because his biography has been over-decorated with marvels. But the case of Khudiram and Chandra is different; and I think it only fair to point this out.

Legends may, and perhaps must, accumulate with the passing of generations, as one well-intentioned historian after another repeats a story with his own additions. But legends require time to grow. We are not dealing with legends here. We are dealing either with the truth or with lies. In this case, if a lie was told, it was told by those directly concerned in the situation at issue. It was told with deliberate intent. It was told by individuals who believed, or said they believed, that lying is the filthiest kind of impurity and the grossest obstacle to one's spiritual progress.

Max Müller is too tactful to speak bluntly, but he implies that Ramakrishna's disciples – including their chief spokesman, Vivekananda (whom Max Müller knew personally) – were responsible for thus falsifying the record fifty years later, after Ramakrishna's death. Their motive for doing this would presumably have been to prove that Ramakrishna was conceived in a supernatural manner and was therefore a divine incarnation, like Jesus of Nazareth. When we meet Vivekan-anda in the latter part of this story, we shall find him a highly sceptical young man with a western-agnostic education in Calcutta, who refused utterly to believe in the supernormal until he had, so to speak, banged his head against it. And even when Vivekananda's disbelief had been modified by personal experience, even when he had become one of Ramakrishna's most passionate devotees, he still discouraged blind faith in others, still urged everyone to find out the truth for himself. And, over and over again, he asserted that it really did not matter whether you believed that Ramakrishna was a divine incarnation or not. Can we accuse such men of lying?

According to Hindu religious custom, the room in which a delivery takes place becomes ritually unclean for ten days thereafter; anyone who enters it during this period must wash himself after leaving. The practical value of this restriction is to discourage outsiders from coming in and fussing around the baby at a time when it is very liable to infection.

Most families build a special lying-in hut, or set aside a room for this purpose which is apart from the main building. Khudiram's home consisted of four rooms only: the shrineroom dedicated to Sri Rama, Khudiram's bedroom, Ramkumar's bedroom, and a living-room. In the yard opposite the main hut there was a roughly-made shed of bamboo and thatch which was the kitchen. At right angles to this was another thatched shed. It was here that Chandra was to bear her child.

(The sheds have gone, now; and a memorial shrine has been built on the site of the second shed. Khudiram's hut still stands.)

Inside the second shed were a fireplace for boiling paddy and a husking-machine, a primitive apparatus for pounding the boiled paddy until the rice is disengaged from its husk. Two people are needed to work this machine; one of them makes the husking-hammer rise and fall by moving with his foot a lever to which the hammer is attached; the other keeps feeding fresh paddy into the hole beneath the hammer. In later years, Ramakrishna was to take the husking-machine as one of the many homely illustrations he used in his teaching: 'How are you to live in the world and yet be mindful of God? Take an example from the housewife. She's busy in so many ways at once!

With one hand she pushes the paddy into the mortar of the husking-machine, with the other she suckles her child; and meanwhile she's bargaining with a neighbour. But, all the time, her mind is fixed on a single idea; not to let the hammer of the husking-machine fall on her hand and bruise it. So, no matter what your worldly duties are, keep your mind fixed on Him.'

Chandra's labour pains began shortly before dawn, on February 18, 1836. The delivery was easy. Chandra had barely time to reach the shed, with Dhani's assistance, before the child was born.

Dhani later described a strange circumstance of the birth. Having done what was needful for Chandra, she turned to the baby and found that he had somehow rolled across the floor. He was lying among the ashes of the fireplace, still bloody and unwashed, without uttering a sound. As Dhani took him up and washed him, she marvelled at his beauty and size; he might well, she said, have been a child six months old.

Mindful of his vision after visiting the Vishnu temple at Gaya, Khudiram decided to call this third son of his Gadadhar – for Gadadhar, meaning 'Bearer of the Mace', is one of the epithets applied to Sri Vishnu. It was as Gadadhar that the boy grew into adolescence. Not until he was a young man at Dakshineswar was he first given the name by which the world was later to know him: Ramakrishna.

3

The Boyhood of Ramakrishna

———————

The art of astrology has been practised in India since ancient times; and today it is still customary to cast the horoscope of a newborn child. Khudiram was a skilled astrologer, so he was able to do this for Gadadhar. In later years, several well-known astrologers entirely confirmed his findings.

The horoscope was extraordinarily auspicious. It showed that Gadadhar would live in a temple, surrounded by disciples; that he would found a new institution for teaching religion, and that he would be revered for generations to come. All this was, of course, no more than a confirmation of the message received by Khudiram and Chandra in their visions. It might be supposed, then, that their belief in the divine mission of their son would now have been established beyond all doubt. Khudiram and Chandra were great devotees, and their faith was strong; but they were also parents, and they worried over their latest child just as much as any other couple in the village might have done.

Most of their anxiety proved to be groundless, however. This strange new guest in the form of a baby did not have to go hungry. Khudiram had a nephew named Ramchand, who lived in the town of Midnapur, not far distant to the southwest; and Ramchand was both well-to-do and generous. When he heard of Gadadhar's birth, he at once sent his uncle the present of a cow, so that a supply of fresh milk was assured.

And so it was whenever help was needed; helpers were not lacking. This was demonstrated when the time came to perform the ceremony of *anna-prasana*. Anna-prasana is a very important event in the life of a young Hindu child; it is the occasion on which he or she is given rice to eat for the first time – generally at the age of six or eight months for a boy, five or seven months for a girl. The child now assumes an identity. It is formally given a name. It is dressed in the best finery its parents can afford. It is crowned and, where possible, carried through the village in a palanquin, accompanied by musicians. It is sometimes taken into the temples and made to bow its head to the presiding deities. Finally, it is seated on a specially painted stool, and rice is given to it.

This ceremony can be performed in a very costly manner. But Khudiram, like other poor people, had to simplify it to its barest essentials. So he planned merely to offer rice to Sri Rama and invite only a few close relatives to share it afterwards. In every *puja* (act of ritual worship), the meal which follows the ritual is regarded as sacramental, since at least a portion of the food that is eaten has been first offered to the deity. Such consecrated food is known as *prasad*. To eat some of this prasad is as much a part of the worship as to participate in the ritual itself.

As a matter of fact, a wealthy friend of Khudiram in the village, the landowner Dharmadas Laha, had already decided to take charge of the anna-prasana for Gadadhar. But Dharmadas, to tease Khudiram, did not tell him this. Instead, he got the leading brahmins of the village to come to Khudiram and request that they might be his guests at the ceremony. Khudiram was in a dilemma. He could not possibly refuse the brahmins; and, since he had invited them, he saw himself compelled to invite all of his many other friends in the village. So he faced humiliation or ruinous expense; a choice which, according to the code of hospitality which prevails almost everywhere in Asia, could only be decided in favour of ruin. In his desperation, Khudiram appealed to Dharmadas, who now reassured him and undertook to provide all that was necessary. So Gadadhar's anna-prasana was celebrated in great style and a crowd of guests, from orthodox brahmins to beggars, were fed.

Chandra no longer had daily visions; perhaps this was because her preoccupation with the safety of her child kept her mind down to the material plane. But strange happenings still took place in the house from time to time. One morning, when Gadadhar was about seven months old, Chandra left him on the bed under a mosquito net and went out of the room to attend to her household duties. Some instinct, however, made her return shortly afterwards, and there she saw an uncannily tall stranger lying under the net, filling the whole bed. Gadadhar was nowhere to be seen. She rushed out to call Khudiram; but, when the two of them returned, the baby was back in its place, alone.

Meanwhile, Gadadhar grew. He was vigorous and healthy, never suffering from sickness of any kind. From his earliest years, he had a strongly defined character. He was lively, affectionate, ready to be friends with everybody. But, at the same time, he had a curious streak of obstinacy in him. Although his memory was unusually retentive, he absolutely refused to remember any of the rules of arithmetic. And whatever he was forbidden to do – flatly and without explanation – he would do immediately; and never lie or try to hide the fact that he had done it. He was also very restless; and, if he felt so inclined, he would simply run off and play. But Khudiram was patience itself, and he soon found that he could dissuade Gadadhar from doing things if he explained carefully to his son exactly why he should not do them.

For example – the big tank called Haldarpukur at Kamarpukur had two bathing-places, one for the women, the other for the men. Small boys like Gadadhar would often use the place reserved for the women, and make themselves unpopular there by splashing. An elderly woman told Gadadhar angrily to go to the men's place, adding that it was anyhow bad that he should see the women washing themselves. Gadadhar asked why, and got no clear answer; only a dark vague hint that something would happen to him if he did this. So, next day, he hid himself behind a tree near the tank and watched the women washing themselves and their clothes. When next he met the woman who had scolded him, he told her: 'The day before yesterday, I saw four women bathing; yesterday six, and today eight. But nothing bad has happened to me.'

The woman had to laugh, in spite of herself. She went to Chandra and told her the whole story. Chandra waited for the right psychological moment and said to Gadadhar: 'Nothing bad will happen to you if you watch the women bathing – that's quite true. But they don't like it; they feel insulted. And I'm a woman, too. If you insult them, it's the same as insulting me. You don't want to do that, do you?' Gadadhar at once promised not to watch the women any more.

At the age of five, he had to start school. School was held in a *nat-mandap*, a theatre-hall; this was a slightly raised platform, open on all sides but protected by a roof. It was used for plays and dancing. Classes were held early in the morning and again in the late afternoon, to avoid the midday heat. Gadadhar still disliked arithmetic, but he was developing a talent for drawing and clay modelling, and his memory easily mastered the songs, tales and dramas which were based on the Scriptures. He was a quick and brilliant mimic, and could imitate the mannerisms of anyone he had seen even once; but there seemed to be no malice in his mimicry, as there so often is. People were naturally drawn to him – not only his own schoolfellows but grown-up men and women. Among boys of his own age, he was always the centre of the group, the inventor of new games.

He was strangely fearless, even of those things which children are apt to fear most; the dark and the supernatural. He would go deliberately to places that were popularly supposed to be haunted by ghosts and ghouls. Khudiram had a sister, Ramsila, who would sometimes be possessed by another personality, so that she became entirely changed. Whenever this happened, the other members of the household would regard her with awe and devotion, believing that a god had entered into her. But Gadadhar showed curiosity rather than awe. When his aunt was in this condition, he stayed near her and watched her closely. 'I do wish,' he used to say, 'that the spirit that gets into Aunt Ramsila would come into me, too.'

His unusually strong constitution would seem to have been based upon an abnormal quality; an almost utter absence of body-consciousness. Body-consciousness is expressed in anxiety about ourselves; and this anxiety interferes with the natural unselfconscious functioning of the body. Thus, we undermine the health we are overanxious to maintain.

If Gadadhar was not at all a lonely child, he was certainly not dependent on the company of others. He would roam off happily alone and lose himself in the sense of Nature around him. It was thus that, at the age of six or seven, he had his first intense spiritual experience.

'One morning,' he recalled in later life, 'I took some parched rice in a small basket and was eating it while I walked along the narrow ridges of the rice-fields. In one part of the sky, a beautiful black cloud appeared, heavy with rain. I was watching it and eating the rice. Very soon, the cloud covered almost the whole sky. And then a flock of cranes came flying. They were as white as milk against that black cloud. It was so beautiful that I became absorbed in the sight. Then I lost consciousness of everything outward. I fell down and the rice was scattered over the earth. Some people saw this, and came and carried me home.'

As soon as Gadadhar had regained consciousness, he seemed to be as normal and healthy as usual. But Khudiram and Chandra were greatly concerned; they feared that their young son was becoming subject to fits. Gadadhar was too young to be able to describe to them clearly what had happened to him. He could only assure them that he had not simply lost his senses. In some manner which he could not put into words, he had remained inwardly aware, throughout his experience, and it had made him feel very happy. As time passed, and Gadadhar did not become physically ill, Khudiram was somewhat reassured. But he now inclined to the belief that Gadadhar had come under the influence of the evil eye; so he took the boy away from school for a while. Gadadhar was delighted. He had all the more time for play.

It was now 1843, and the season came around for the *Durga Puja*, which is Bengal's great autumn festival. Mother Durga is the personification of the Power of Brahman. Literally, the name means She who protects us from danger.

Khudiram had a standing invitation to attend the Durga Puja at the village of Selampur, which was the native place of his nephew Ramchand. Ramchand always celebrated this puja lavishly, feeding many guests. The festivities would last for eight days.

But, this year, Khudiram hesitated to go to Selampur, although he wanted to do so. He had not been well lately. He suffered from chronic dysentery and other digestive disorders; and he felt an instinctive unwillingness to leave home even for a few days. At length, however, he made up his mind to go. He would have liked to take Gadadhar with him; but he knew that this would make Chandra anxious. Since the incident of the black cloud, she hated to let the boy out of her sight. So, instead, Khudiram took his eldest son, Ramkumar.

This proved to have been a fortunate decision. For, just as the puja was coming to an end, Khudiram fell seriously ill. He weakened quickly, despite the efficient medical care which Ramchand was able to provide. On the last day of the puja he could barely speak. Towards evening, at his request, Ramchand and Ramkumar helped him into a sitting posture. Then Khudiram uttered the name of Rama three times, and so passed from them.

The pain of this separation was terrible for Chandra. Like any other pious Hindu wife at that time, she had not only loved her husband as a man but also reverenced him as her spiritual guide. Without him she felt lost in the world; she lived chiefly for the day when she would leave it and be with him again. Ramkumar now became the head of the household and responsible for its maintenance.

Although Gadadhar was so young, he too felt the loss of his father keenly. In consequence, he became more solitary and meditative, and also more consciously protective towards his mother. It was at this time that he began to visit the resthouse in the village at which the pilgrims used to stop on their way to and from the shrine at Puri. He listened to the talk of these men and shared their meditations. He brought them food, waited on them and watched them, seeing, with the candid eyes of a child, not only the good in some but the bad in others. Throughout his life, he loved to make fun of sham holiness and hypocrisy.

Sometimes Gadadhar returned home from these visits to the rest-house with his body smeared with ashes, according to the custom of those who have renounced the world. Once he appeared with his dhoti torn up and worn in three pieces, as holy men wear theirs. 'Look, Mother,' he cried, 'I'm a monk!' At this, Chandra became alarmed; for she had heard that monks sometimes persuaded quite young boys to follow them, out of eagerness for the adventures of a wanderer's life. But Gadadhar solemnly promised Chandra that he would not leave her; and the holy men themselves, hearing of her fears, came to her and assured her that they had had absolutely no intention of luring Gadadhar away from home at such a tender age.

About this time, Gadadhar had his second spiritual experience. At the village of Anur, about two miles north of Kamarpukur, there was a spot sacred to a goddess named Visalakshi (literally: the One with Large Eyes). The place was in the open fields, without any protective building around it; and there was a reason for this. The goddess

Visalakshi was thought to be especially partial to poor and vagrant people. The cowherd boys of the neighbourhood were her favourites. These boys used to take the copper coins and sweets which wealthier pilgrims had left as an offering; and this pleased and amused the goddess. There came a time, however, when a rich man built a shrine for Visalakshi. The offerings were now locked inside it, and the boys could not take them. The goddess, as a mark of her displeasure, made a huge crack in the surrounding wall. And whenever anybody suggested rebuilding the shrine, Visalakshi would appear to that person in a dream and sternly warn him against doing so.

One day, a party of women from Kamarpukur started off across the fields to visit this place and make an offering to the goddess. Gadadhar – or Gadai, as they called him for short – decided that he wanted to come too. The women were doubtful at first, knowing that this would be quite a long walk for a child; but they could not resist taking him with them, because he knew so many stories and was famed, even at that early age, for the extraordinary sweetness of his singing voice. 'Gadai has spoiled my ears,' one of them said of him, later.

And so they started out, laughing and singing with the charming, gay, little boy. But suddenly, in the midst of his singing, Gadadhar appeared to be stricken dumb. His body stiffened and became numb. Tears poured from his eyes. The women were dismayed. They thought he must have had a sunstroke. They brought water from a near-by pond and sprinkled it over him, but with no result.

Among the women was Prasanna, the widowed sister of the land-owner Dharmadas Laha. This Prasanna was a person of exceptional insight. She was one of the first to recognize greatness in the boy. 'Whatever you may say,' she told him, several years later, 'you aren't an ordinary human being.' But when she talked to him like this, Gadadhar would only smile sweetly and make no answer; or he would change the subject.

Prasanna now suggested that perhaps it was the goddess Visalakshi herself who had possessed the boy. So she and the other women began to address Gadadhar as though he were indeed the goddess. 'Oh, Mother Visalakshi,' the women cried, 'save us, protect us, look upon us with compassion!' Within a few moments, Gadadhar returned to normal consciousness. And, this time also, he was perfectly well and not even tired. The women felt reassured, and cheerfully completed their pilgrimage.

At the age of nine, Gadadhar went through the initiation-ceremony known as *upanayana*, which roughly corresponds to the rite of confirmation practised by Christians and by Jews. In the upanayana, the male child is taught a particular Vedic prayer, known as the gayatri, and invested with a sacred thread. He thus becomes a full participant in the Hindu faith. In Bengal, the sacred thread is given only to brahmin boys. Until a brahmin boy has received the thread he is not regarded as a brahmin, but merely as a sudra. Once the thread has been received, the boy is permitted to perform ritual worship; and he is obliged to observe strict rules of purity, truthfulness and diet. Thereafter, he is known as one of 'the Twice-Born', because he is held to have undergone a spiritual rebirth.

One act of the upanayana is that the boy – who has become, so to speak, a temporary monk – has to beg his food for three days, receiving these alms in a begging-bag. The person who first gives him alms is an important figure in the ceremony. Now Dhani, the daughter of the blacksmith, who had helped Chandra at the time of Gadadhar's birth, had long since begged Gadadhar that she might be the one to give him the first alms and be addressed by him, according to the custom, as 'Mother'. Gadadhar had promised her that she might have this privilege.

But when, just before the ceremony, Gadadhar mentioned his promise to his eldest brother, Ramkumar objected. For it was customary that the first giver of alms should be of caste-rank equal to that of the boy's mother; and Dhani belonged to the blacksmith caste. But Gadadhar insisted that he could not break the promise he had given, since an act of untruthfulness would make him unfit to wear the sacred thread. Dharmadas Laha was appealed to. He decided that the boy was in the right. And so Dhani's great desire was happily satisfied.

About this time there was a meeting of *pandits* (scholars who are learned in the Scriptures) at the home of Dharmadas Laha. The pandits had been invited there to take part in a *sraddha*, a ritual which is held in honour of a dead relative on the day after the period of family mourning is over. When they were assembled, a discussion began which developed into an argument. The pandits were arguing a complicated theological point, with considerable heat. And, since this was India, they had most of the village for audience–including even Gadadhar and many other small boys of his age. These other boys could hardly understand anything of what was being said; they giggled among themselves and imitated the excited gestures of the pandits. Only Gadadhar listened with great attention. After a while, he turned to one of the pandits and said: 'But isn't this the answer they're looking for —?' And, to this man's amazement, the ten-year-old boy proceeded to suggest a solution, convincing and clearly stated, to the problem which was being discussed. The pandit turned and told his colleagues what Gadadhar had said. All agreed – this *was* the solution. Astonished and awestruck, they gazed at the boy; and some of them took him on their laps and blessed him.

This incident is well authenticated. Years later, it was described to Swami Saradananda by Ramakrishna himself and by villagers of Kamarpukur who had themselves been present. Yet Max Müller has cast doubts upon it, simply because it resembles an incident in the life of Jesus of Nazareth. In the Gospel according to St Luke, chapter two, it is recorded that:

. . . his parents went to Jerusalem every year at the feast of the passover. And when he was twelve years old, they went up to Jerusalem after the custom of the feast. And when they had fulfilled the days, as they returned, the child Jesus tarried behind in Jerusalem; and Joseph and his mother knew not of it. But they, supposing him to have been in the company, went a day's journey; and they sought him among their kinsfolk and acquaintances. And when they found him not, they turned back again to Jerusalem, seeking him. And it came to pass, that after three days they found him in the temple, sitting in the midst of the doctors, both hearing them, and asking them questions. And all that heard him were astonished at his understanding and answers. And when they saw him, they were amazed: and his mother said unto him, Son, why hast thou thus dealt with us? behold, thy father and I have sought thee sorrowing. And he said unto them, How is it that ye sought me? wist ye not that I must be about my Father's business? And they understood not the sayings which he spake unto them.

Actually, the first point which should strike us in reading this narrative is the difference in character between the boy Jesus and the boy Gadadhar. Gadadhar would never have spoken to his parents in that way. Throughout his childhood and adolescence, he never once declared his true nature and his mission so openly – even when it was guessed at by others, such as Prasanna, or an old man named Srinivas who once took the boy aside into a secluded place among the trees, hung a garland around his neck and paid homage to him as if to a deity in a shrine.

If we do admit that there is a general resemblance between these two incidents, we must note in fairness that there are also similar incidents to be found in the recorded lives of Krishna, of Shankara and of Chaitanya; three of the greatest figures in the history of Hinduism. And since the cult of Krishna was flourishing long before the birth of Jesus, we must assume – if we take Max Müller's attitude – that Krishna's story inspired the biographers of Jesus, Shankara and Chaitanya to imitation! As a matter of fact, there are at least half a dozen important events in Krishna's life which have their counterparts in the Christian gospels.

That same year, as the time for the *Shiva-ratri*, the festival of Shiva, approached, it was arranged that a troupe of players from a neighbouring village should perform a religious drama, based on an incident in the story of Shiva, at one of the houses in Kamarpukur. A crowd of devotees would watch it, as part of their night-long vigil in Shiva's honour.

At dusk on the very day of the festival, the boy who was to play Shiva became sick; and the director of the troupe could find no substitute. It was feared that the performance would have to be put off. Some of the older villagers of Kamarpukur went into hurried consultation, and they decided that Gadadhar ought to play the part. Although he was so young, his looks were right for it and he knew many of the songs of Shiva which would be sung. At first, Gadadhar was unwilling. He preferred to stay and worship in his own home. But his friends persuaded him that his acting would itself be worship of another kind, for he would have to keep his mind on God throughout the performance.

So they helped Gadadhar to put on the make-up of Shiva as the ideal monk. His hair was matted, his body sprinkled with ashes, the monk's rosary was hung around his neck. He mounted the stage with slow, sedate steps and stood there motionless. At the sight of him, the audience was strangely awed; for the boy's face wore a smile of extraordinary beauty and his gaze was fixed as if in profound meditation. Involuntarily, some of the spectators began to utter the names of God, while others whispered to each other: 'How beautiful Gadai looks! Who would have thought he could play the part so well?'

But Gadadhar continued to stand there without moving, and now it was seen that tears were streaming from his eyes. The director and a few others went over to him and found that he appeared to have lost all external consciousness. The audience began to shout advice: 'Throw water on his face! Fan him! Repeat the name of Shiva!' A few grumbled: 'The boy has spoiled everything – now they'll have to stop the play!'

At length, the audience dispersed. Some men carried Gadadhar home on their shoulders. But, despite all their efforts, he could not be aroused from his ecstatic state until after the sunrise of the next day. Certain narrators of this incident even say that he remained outwardly unconscious for three whole days.

Throughout his life, Gadadhar was apt to be moved to ecstasy by watching performances of religious dramas. And, quite aside from this, he took a lifelong pleasure in mimicry, clowning and comic play-acting. Once, when he was in his early teens, he heard a neighbour named Durgadas Pyne boast that no man had ever seen the women of his household or their living-quarters, so strict was his enforcement of purdah. Now Gadadhar was so popular and so completely trusted that he was welcome to visit the wives and daughters of most families whenever he wished, although he was now becoming an adolescent boy. Therefore he accepted Durgadas Pyne's boast as a challenge, and told him: 'I can see everybody in your house and all the rooms in it, if I want to.' Durgadas did not believe him.

Some days later, Gadadhar disguised himself as a poor weaver-woman. Just before dusk, he approached the house of Durgadas from the direction of the market, dressed in a coarse dirty sari and cheap ornaments, with a basket under his arm and a veil covering his face.

Durgadas was sitting with some friends in the living room. Gadadhar introduced himself, saying that he had come to the market to sell yarn and that, through some misunderstanding, he had been left behind by his companions. He begged shelter for the night. Durgadas asked a few questions and then, perfectly deceived by Gadadhar's answers and his disguise, said: 'All right – go in and ask the women if they can find room for you.' So Gadadhar entered the women's quarters, where he sat and gossiped with the members of the family, charming all of them. Thus the whole evening passed.

At length, when it grew late and Gadadhar had not returned home, Chandra sent his elder brother Rameswar to look for him. Rameswar went to that part of the village where Gadadhar was usually to be found and shouted his name. From inside Durgadas Pyne's house, Gadadhar shouted back: 'I'm coming, Brother!' and out he hurried in his female costume, to meet Rameswar. Even Durgadas had to laugh at the joke against him.

Those were joyful days. The growing boy lived in a world of friendship, fun and play; and yet his nature became increasingly capable of spiritual insights and devotion to God. One moment he might be the liveliest in his group, the next he might be deeply absorbed. Speaking of this period later, Ramakrishna said: 'The women would put aside things for me to eat. No one distrusted me. Everybody took me in as one of the family. But I was like the bird of happiness. I used to frequent only happy families. I would run away from a place where I saw misery and suffering.'

Nevertheless, suffering was to touch his family again, and indirectly to alter the course of his own life.

Mention has already been made of the tragic fulfilment of Ramkumar's prediction that his wife would die in childbirth. This happened when Gadadhar was thirteen.

After the death of his wife, Ramkumar went through a period of acute depression. Memories of the past made it painful for him to remain in Kamarpukur. And the family was in serious money difficulties again. Rameswar, the second son, had lately married and was earning very little. Chandra was getting old. Gadadhar could not be counted on. Akshay, Ramkumar's motherless baby, was an extra mouth to feed. And Ramkumar himself was going deeply into debt. So he decided to leave the village and open a *tol*, a Sanskrit school, in Calcutta. Thus he hoped to be able, after a while, to help the others.

During the next three years, Ramkumar returned to Kamarpukur for short annual visits, in order to keep an eye on his family. He was particularly anxious about Gadadhar. True – the boy was a loving son to Chandra and a devoted uncle to little Akshay; he was pure-hearted, sweet-natured, devout and beloved by all who knew him; he could paint, and make images of the deities with skill; he was an accomplished actor and singer. He had founded his own theatrical company among the village youths, directing the plays and acting in them; it seemed that this might become his profession.

But Ramkumar, the schoolmaster, was not impressed. From his point of view, Gadadhar was frittering away the precious days of his youth, since he was not attending school and preparing himself to be a wage-earner and father of a family. Ramkumar therefore proposed that Gadadhar should come back to Calcutta with him, help him in whatever ways he was able, and study at the tol along with the other students.

Nothing could have been farther from Gadadhar's inclinations. To him, school was an institution which existed to instil worldly-mindedness into its pupils, to make them eager to acquire possessions and reputation. All such learning seemed to him to be a delusion and an emptiness.

Nevertheless, he accepted Ramkumar's offer. To leave his dear family and his native village, to go to noisy, overcrowded Calcutta, to attend this school – how could *that* be a step in his life's true direction? Apparently, it could not be. But Gadadhar had faith in God's hidden workings. And he loved his brother and was glad of this opportunity to help him.

The brothers left for Calcutta together. Gadadhar was then sixteen years old. Though Ramkumar did not know it, and though his own plans for the boy were very different, he was, in fact, taking Gadadhar straight towards the fulfilment of his destiny.

4

How Ramakrishna Came to Dakshineswar

In those days, the city of Calcutta was the seat of British rule in India and the main port of entry for the ideas and culture of the West. The changes that were taking place in India, for the worse and for the better, all had their beginnings there. In making the journey from Kamarpukur to Calcutta, Gadadhar had passed from the timelessness of village life into the very midst of contemporary history.

The year of his arrival, 1852, was only five years away from the end of an epoch in Anglo-Indian relations. In 1857 came the Mutiny. (Now officially called by Indian historians The First War of Indian Independence. I use the old offensive name with apologies; because it will be familiar to most of my readers.) The following year, the powers of the East India Company were formally abolished and the government of India was transferred to the British Crown. Thus the responsibility for what was done in India was placed directly upon the British Parliament and people. And thus, very slowly, events began to open up the long, bloody path which was to lead to independence.

Already, during the pre-Mutiny period, there had been much bloodshed in many parts of the land, as the process of annexation went relentlessly forward. In 1852, the British went to war with Burma for the second time and seized one of her maritime provinces. But all this violence seemed relatively remote from Calcutta itself, where the British had been peacefully established for more than seventy years. They had built an imposing European Quarter – 'a city of palaces', one contemporary traveller called it; while another was reminded of St John's Wood in London. Its architecture was predominantly neo-classical; the larger mansions had stately columns and massive porticoes, and their rooms were vast, airy and scantily furnished in order to lessen the heat. Here, the social life was elegant and excessively formal. The

38

high British officials rode around town in carriages with outriders; on their arrival at evening parties, servants would run ahead of them carrying flaming torches. Their families went to church and to the opera, their ladies drove out along the Esplanade and gossiped about each other, their sons played cricket. Despite the climate, everything was done to preserve the atmosphere of home. As for the Bengalis, they usually saw the insides of these palatial homes only in the capacity of servants. And even when some wealthy high-caste families were occasionally invited to receptions, it was scarcely on a basis of friendly equality. Only recently, British Calcutta society had been plunged into controversy because Lord Auckland the Governor-General had actually permitted forty-five Bengali college boys to appear in his presence wearing shoes! As the century advanced, however, many of these barriers were gradually broken down.

The British in India at that period must have seemed strange, paradoxical beings to any detached observer. They were imperialists with bad consciences. They were builders of bridges, roads, hospitals and schools – public benefactors who were nevertheless ceaselessly engaged in the piecemeal conquest of a nation. For the Indians, who did not want them, they sacrificed their health and their lives, going back to England prematurely aged, yellow-faced, on crutches, to die. Tens of thousands of them were buried in the country during the two centuries of their occupation. Many were altruistic, many were heroic, many were deeply devout and felt that they had accepted voluntary exile in this savage and unhealthy land in order to do God's work among the benighted. What almost none of them seem to have been aware of was that they were in the most religious country in the world; and in the presence of a spiritual culture which made their own sectarianism seem provincial indeed. Even Honoria Lawrence, wife of Sir Henry Lawrence, certainly one of the noblest and most dedicated Englishwomen in India, could write coldly: 'There is something very oppressive in being surrounded by heathen and Mohammedan darkness, in seeing idol-worship all around, and when we see the deep and debasing hold these principles have on the people, it is difficult to believe they can ever be freed from it.'

Gadadhar himself was destined to have little direct contact with the foreign conquerors of his country; but many of the Bengalis who visited him in his later years had become Western-minded to a greater or lesser degree; some had been educated in one of the British schools and had learned English. We find no bitterness in Gadadhar, at any time in his life, when he referred to the British – only a playful humour. Talking of the power of self-suggestion, he once said: 'If even a sickly man puts on high boots, he begins to whistle and climbs the stairs like an Englishman, jumping from one step to the next.' He used to speak of friends who had become influenced by Western ideas as 'Englishmen'; saying jokingly: 'Look at these Englishmen – they take the trouble to come here! That makes me sure my visions can't be all imagination.' What would Honoria Lawrence have made of this 'heathen', who once went into ecstasy when he saw an English boy in a park standing in an attitude which reminded him of the Boy Krishna!

It must not be supposed that the British met with nothing but subservience from the Bengali population. There were many Bengalis of determined character who were not afraid to challenge the authority of the foreigners and make themselves respected by them.

Such a one was a lady named Rani Rasmani. (She was not really a Rani – that is, the wife of a Raja; this was merely a nickname which had been given her by her mother in childhood. When she grew up, people went on calling her 'Rani', in recognition of her royally benevolent and commanding nature.) She had become a widow at the age of forty-four, inheriting an enormous fortune from her husband, Rajchandra Das; and she lived in the Janbazar district of central Calcutta. She was well known throughout the city and highly popular because of her generosity, courage and piety. By a paradox by no means unusual in India, this lady, who had not only the power of great wealth but also the best qualities of a great aristocrat, belonged to the sudras, the caste of the servants.

On one occasion, it is related, the British Government imposed a tax on all fish caught in the Hoogli – the most important, commercially, of the mouths of the Ganges. Many of the fishermen who were impoverished by this tax lived on the Rani's land, so they came and complained to her. The Rani told them not to worry and immediately went into action. For a large sum, she obtained a monopoly of the fishing-rights. The British agreed to this arrangement, supposing that the Rani planned to open a fishery and thereby supply them with tax-revenue without the difficulties of tax-collection from a large number of people. But no sooner had the Rani obtained the rights than she had chains hung across the river in several places, holding up the shipping. When the British protested, she replied: 'I bought these fishing-rights from you at great expense. If I now let ships pass up and down the river, they will frighten the fish and I shall lose a lot of money. However, if you'll agree to abolish your new tax, I'm ready to give up my rights. If you won't, I shall sue you in the courts, and you'll have to pay me damages.' The British had the good sense to recognize – with humour, one hopes – that they had met their match. The tax was abolished.

The Rani was an ardent devotee of the Goddess Kali; and in 1848 she decided to make a pilgrimage to Benares, which is regarded as the holiest city in all India. But, on the night before her departure, she had a dream in which the Goddess appeared to her and said: 'There is no need for you to go to Benares. Build me a temple here in Calcutta on the Ganges bank, and install my image in it. Arrange that I shall be worshipped there daily and offered food. I will manifest myself within that image and accept your worship.'

Such was the Rani's faith that she changed her plans immediately. She did not go to Benares. She purchased twenty acres of land from a Mr Hastie, an attorney of the Calcutta Supreme Court, alongside the river at Dakshineswar, which is about four miles north of Calcutta. Here, with the assistance of her son-in-law, Mathur Mohan, she began to arrange for the building of a group of temples within a temple-garden. This elaborate and costly undertaking was under way but still far from being completed at the time of Gadadhar's arrival in Calcutta.

Ramkumar's tol was in the Jhamapukur district of Calcutta, and it was there that Gadadhar now settled down to live with and assist his brother. Ramkumar was badly in need of an assistant, for he had much to do even to earn a bare living. According to custom, the teacher at one of these Sanskrit schools was not allowed to demand any set fee; he might only accept voluntary gifts from his pupils, and these were apt to be small. The only other compensation he could hope to receive was from the Government, at the time of the examinations. For each pupil who passed, the Government allowed a certain sum of money to the teacher, larger or smaller, according to the pupil's grade. This arrangement was not a fair one, for the teacher could hardly be blamed if he was not lucky enough to have brilliant boys in his school.

A secondary profession was open to Ramkumar; that of a family priest. Since only brahmins were allowed to perform the full ritual of worship before a shrine – even a shrine in a private home – the wealthier members of other castes were prepared to pay a priest to come twice daily to their homes. But the performance of these rituals took time which Ramkumar could ill afford to spare from his teaching. So he handed over all such duties to Gadadhar.

Gadadhar was an ideal assistant. Not only was he well-versed in the rituals, but he loved the work for its own sake. Most professional priests were apt to hurry through their duties; Gadadhar performed them with devotion. And he would linger on, after the worship was over, talking to the members of the families he visited and singing songs for them. Though he was now a young man, the ladies felt no hesitation in making an exception to their rule of purdah and appearing before him. His innocence and gaiety charmed everybody who met him. Soon he was as widely popular as he had been at Kamarpukur.

Ramkumar observed all this with mixed feelings. He did not forget that he had brought Gadadhar to Calcutta primarily in order that he might prepare himself for the responsibilities of life. Much as he needed Gadadhar's help as a wage earner, he did not shirk what he saw as his brotherly duty. He reasoned with Gadadhar, begging him to study. But, once again, Gadadhar showed his gentle but immovable obstinacy. He told Ramkumar that he saw no utility in a worldly education – in learning, as he put it, 'to bundle rice and plantain'. (Such were the gifts that pandits generally received for their services.) Ramkumar had not the heart to insist, for he loved his brother dearly. So he resigned himself to letting Gadadhar live his own life and to struggling on himself as best he could; trusting that a clearer path of duty would be shown to both of them before long.

In this manner, nearly three years passed.

Rani Rasmani was a woman who was accustomed to act boldly upon impulse, without pausing to worry about possible difficulties. But now, as the temples at Dakshineswar approached completion, she had to face a problem which, in the first excitement of her undertaking, she had chosen to ignore – that of her own caste-status. As a sudra, she was debarred from fulfilling what was now the ambition of her life – to offer cooked food daily to the image of her chosen deity in a temple which she herself had built, and to have holy men come and partake of the prasad. The rules of Caste on this point were complex and strict. A sudra, vaishya or kshatriya might offer fruit or other uncooked food before a shrine; but only a brahmin might offer cooked food. And only a brahmin might cook food that was to be offered. Furthermore, no brahmin might act as a priest or even partake of prasad in a temple which belonged to a sudra. To do these things was to become impure.

Thus the Rani began to realize that all her money and effort had perhaps been spent in vain. Desperately, she sent out letters to pandits who were expert in the interpretation of the *Shastras*, the scriptures which lay down the proper procedure for ritual worship. The answers she received gave her no hope. The pandits were all agreed. The Rani's wish, they said, could never be fulfilled.

In due course, the Rani consulted Ramkumar, whose reputation as a pandit was considerable. And from him, at least, she got a more encouraging answer. Ramkumar agreed in principle with his colleagues, but he made this suggestion: 'Let the Rani make a formal gift of the temple property to a brahmin. Let this brahmin arrange for the installation of the image of Kali in the shrine and for the cooking of the food that is to be offered to her. Then other brahmins will be able to take prasad at the temple without impurity.'

The Rani was delighted; and she at once followed Ramkumar's advice. She legally made over the temple property to her own guru (spiritual teacher), retaining only the right to act as his business representative in managing its affairs.

The work of building was not even yet quite completed, but the Rani fixed the earliest auspicious date for the ceremony of installation; May 31, 1855. Her eagerness was due partly to a dream in which the Goddess Kali appeared to her and told her to hurry. Kali identified herself with her image, which was lying packed in a box ready for the ceremony; she told the Rani that she could not endure being shut up any longer. It is said that, when the box was opened, the image itself was found to be covered with moisture, as though it had been perspiring!

The other pandits the Rani had consulted disagreed, however, with Ramkumar's solution of the problem, finding it to be too liberal.

In their view, the handing over of the temple property to the Rani's guru, in order that it might no longer be owned by a sudra, was little better than a legal trick. It would not necessarily make the temple prasad acceptable to a strict brahmin. And, in any case, a brahmin priest who officiated for a sudra and accepted the gifts due to a priest must be considered, from an orthodox standpoint, to have degraded himself. These opinions were not openly or positively expressed, for fear of the Rani's displeasure; but they were whispered around, and, as a result, the Rani found it hard to get any brahmins to come to Dakshineswar.

Her difficulties were largely solved by a brahmin named Mahesh, who was already employed by her on her estates. Mahesh was able to persuade his brother Kshetranath, who was a priest, to officiate at the temple of Radha and Krishna – one of the two main temples within the Dakshineswar compound. As soon as it became known that Kshetranath had accepted this office, other brahmins came forward who were willing to work as assistant priests or as cooks to prepare the food for the offerings.

But the more important temple, the temple of Kali, still required a priest; and the Rani wanted this priest to be a truly devout and learned man; one who would be both worthy and able to perform the very sacred installation ceremony. Naturally, she thought of Ramkumar. She therefore sent Mahesh with a letter to him. Mahesh was a suitable go-between because his native village was not far from Kamarpukur and he already knew Ramkumar quite well. Mahesh added his persuasions to the Rani's appeal, and Ramkumar agreed not only to officiate at the installation but to stay on as a priest at the Kali temple until a successor could be found for him.

The ceremony was duly held on the date the Rani had fixed. It was an occasion of extraordinary splendour and princely generosity. Many pandits had assembled, some of them having come from far distant parts in India, and each was given a silk wearing-cloth and a gold coin. The temples were lighted with innumerable lights, so that every corner was as bright as day. The singing of religious songs continued throughout the night. Hundreds of people partook of the prasad.

Gadadhar was present; but he did not take prasad. Instead, he bought some puffed rice at the market and ate it before walking back to Jhamapukur to sleep. Next day, he returned to Dakshineswar.

Ramkumar urged him to stay; but he would not do so. He went back to Jhamapukur and waited there for nearly a week, continually expecting Ramkumar's return. When Ramkumar did not come, he at length decided to go to Dakshineswar once more. It was then that Ramkumar told him that he had agreed to assume permanent charge of the worship of Kali, at the Rani's request. He was giving up the tol altogether.

Gadadhar objected strenuously. He reminded his brother that their father Khudiram had been very particular in these matters – never performing worship on behalf of sudras or accepting any gifts from them. Ramkumar – whose integrity was certainly above question and who genuinely believed that he was doing right – reasoned with Gadadhar about his scruples; but neither of them could convince the other. Finally, the brothers had recourse to a method of deciding questions which used to be very popular among country people. It is called *dharmapatra*, the 'leaf of impartiality'. 'Yes' and 'No' are written on pieces of paper or on leaves of the *vilva* tree, which are customarily used as offerings in the worship of Shiva. These are placed in a pot and a child is told to pick one of them. If 'Yes' is picked, Providence is held to have sanctioned the course of action which is in dispute. If 'No', it must be abandoned. In this case, Ramkumar's wish to stay at Dakshineswar was sanctioned by a 'Yes'. Gadadhar at once accepted the decision; but he still refused to eat the temple prasad.

'Very well then,' said Ramkumar, good-humouredly. 'Take uncooked provisions from the temple storeroom and cook them yourself with water from the river. Surely you believe that the Ganges purifies everything?'

Gadadhar did believe this. He already had a great devotion to the Ganges, the sacred river beside which he was to pass nearly all the remaining days of his life. He believed that even the least breath of the river breeze purified everything it touched. From this time on, he settled down at Dakshineswar. But he continued, for a long while, to cook and eat his food in a place apart from others.

Swami Saradananda in his book devotes some space to discussing this refusal of Gadadhar's to eat the temple prasad – no doubt because he was aware that non-Hindu readers might find it strange and apparently unreasonable. Was Gadadhar just being deliberately self-righteous – as young people sometimes are? Was he taking a mischievous enjoyment in showing himself more orthodox than Ramkumar, who had hitherto been his mentor? No, says Saradananda – and he draws a distinction between the attitude of Gadadhar and that of an ordinary religious bigot. The bigot is motivated by egotism, and his scruples are merely prejudices based on pride. The bigot prides himself on his obstinacy and therefore refuses to modify his views. But Gadadhar's attitude was based upon his unquestioning, selfless faith. He had absolute faith in what the Scriptures and his father had taught him; he did not presume to interpret these teachings or compromise with them in any way. Such steadfastness may look like bigotry at first; later on, it always shows itself for what it really is. For, as a great soul progresses towards complete spiritual illumination, he no longer feels the need for rules. They fall away from him, like supports which his mature faith no longer needs. We shall see how Gadadhar, in his later life, broke the rules of Caste many times. That did not mean that he denied the value of those rules for others.

1. Studio portrait of Ramakrishna

For notes on illustrations see Appendix

2. Ramakrishna at Dakshineswar

3. Sarada Devi and Nivedita

4. Sarada Devi

5

Early Days at Dakshineswar

In the main features of its appearance, the Dakshineswar temple-compound has not changed since the time of its completion, rather more than a hundred years ago. Today it is still one of the most impressive landmarks on that part of the Ganges. (Another is the Belur Math Monastery which is the headquarters of the Ramakrishna Order.) The view of Dakshineswar, looking upriver from the south, has now been blocked by a large metal bridge which connects the banks just below the temple grounds. But the devotee of Ramakrishna can take at least some satisfaction from the fact that this bridge, which used to be named after Lord Willingdon, one of the last viceroys, has been renamed the Vivekananda Bridge, in honour of Ramakrishna's great disciple.

Nowadays, the temple-compound is not as well kept as one could wish. The surface of the tiled courtyard is rough and broken. The gardens are no longer well cared for. Some of the buildings have been attacked by the rot which so easily takes hold in this humid tropical climate. Crowds of children and adults beg, try to sell you souvenirs or to take charge of the shoes which you are obliged to remove and leave at the entrance of the sacred precincts. However, these are minor disadvantages. The visitor must be thankful that so much remains intact of the setting of Ramakrishna's adult life.

Part of the land which the Rani bought for the temple grounds was once a Moslem cemetery, which was associated with the memory of a Moslem holy man. It is convex in shape; and such a formation – described as resembling the back of a tortoise – is said by the Scriptures to be particularly suitable for the worship of *Shakti*, the female principle within the Godhead. Adjoining the temple property to the north, there was a lot which the British owned and used, during Ramakrishna's time, for storing ammunition.

Seen from the river, Dakshineswar presents a symmetrical white and terra-cotta facade of domed buildings. In the foreground, on top of the riverbank, there is a row of twelve small shrines – six on either side of the stairs of the bathing-ghat, which lead up from the water to a big portico opening into the temple courtyard. If you are at water level, these shrines hide the buildings inside the courtyard, except for the towering central building, the Kali Temple, which dominates the whole.

The twelve small shrines are temples to Shiva. Each shrine has a domed roof rising to a point; the builders have simulated in masonry the domed thatch-roofs of a Bengal village. The shrines are identical inside as well as outside. They contain no image, only the small upright stone pillar which is called a *linga*; this is the usual emblem used in Shiva-worship. Lingas vary somewhat in size and shape; the ones at Dakshineswar are three and a half feet tall. They are generally worshipped very simply, with offerings of vilva leaves, rice, buttermilk, honey or yoghurt, to the accompaniment of chanting. Around the foot of the linga, a circular basin catches these offerings and carries them off through a spout.

It has been claimed by some foreign scholars that the linga and its surrounding basin are sexual symbols, representing the male and the female organs respectively. Well – anything can be regarded as a symbol of anything; that much is obvious. There are people who have chosen to see sexual symbolism in the spire and the font of a Christian church. But Christians do not recognize this symbolism; and even the most hostile critics of Christianity cannot pretend that it is a sex-cult. The same is true of the cult of Shiva.

It does not even seem probable that the linga was sexual in its origin. For we find, in the history both of Hinduism and Buddhism, that poor devotees were accustomed to dedicate to God a model of a temple or *tope* (a dome-shaped monument) in imitation of wealthy devotees who dedicated full-sized buildings. So the linga may well have begun as a monument in miniature.

On the other hand, it must be clearly understood that there is all the difference in the world between a sex-cult and a religion which recognizes the male–female principle within the Godhead. The Hindu, believing that the Godhead must by definition embody all possible functions, is logically brought to think of it as being both male and female. (One of the greatest causes of misunderstanding of Hinduism by foreign scholars is perhaps a subconsciously respected tradition that God must be one sex only, or at least only one sex at a time.) As I said above, the female principle in the Godhead is known as Shakti. Shakti is regarded as being the Power of Brahman, while the male principle is Brahman itself.

Since the multiplicity of names for divine aspects and relationships is such a difficulty in the study of Hinduism, and since Hindu theology now becomes an important feature of our story, I shall pause here to recapitulate what I have written in earlier chapters, adding some details to complete the picture.

1. The Reality or Godhead is called Brahman.

2. When Brahman is thought of as dwelling within a creature or object, it is called the Atman or Purusha.

3. Brahman-Atman does not act.

4. It is the Power of Brahman that acts. This Power is called Prakriti or Maya, or Shakti (see 8).

5. When we speak of Brahman-Prakriti – Brahman in association with its Power – we call it Ishwara. Ishwara is God with attributes, God who acts.

6. Ishwara somewhat resembles God the Father in Christian theology. He is the ruler of the universe which has been created by him. The Atman dwells within man, and man can therefore become one with the Atman by recognizing his essential nature. But man can never become Ishwara. (Here is another cause of misunderstanding. The Christian says 'God' and means, approximately, Ishwara. The Hindu says 'God' and means Brahman-Atman. To the Hindu, the statement 'I am God' is a self-evident truth. To the Christian, it is blasphemy. The blasphemous arrogance of one who attempts to usurp Ishwara's throne is described in the story of the fall of Lucifer.)

7. Ishwara may also be thought of as a trinity of personified functions. These three functions of Ishwara are: Brahma the Creator, Vishnu the Sustainer and Shiva the Dissolver. Ishwara creates the universe out of himself, sustains it for a while, dissolves it into himself and recreates it, in an eternal cycle.

8. Each of these persons of the Hindu trinity has a female principle, called a Shakti. Thus, Sarasvati is the Shakti of Brahma, Lakshmi of

Vishnu and Parvati or Devi of Shiva. There are other forms of Shakti besides these, including Kali, who will play such a large part in this story. Kali, like Durga, is one of the aspects of Devi (which means simply goddess) and can therefore be regarded as the Shakti of Shiva.

9. Vishnu is believed to have manifested himself from time to time in human form. These divine incarnations are called *avatars*. Two of the most famous are Rama and Krishna. Hindus recognize both Buddha and Jesus of Nazareth as avatars, and they anticipate the birth of more avatars from time to time in the future. The claims of Ramakrishna to be regarded as an avatar will be discussed later.

Complicated as this system of divine relationships may seem to the reader, it is in fact a simplified outline. In other books, he will find a variety of other names and epithets for the same beings. Here, I shall try always to use the same name for any given being; unless by doing so I suppress essential information.

Although the Kali Temple is such a large building, the shrine which contains the image of the goddess is relatively small and affords room only for the officiating priest and just a few worshippers. The rest have to crowd on the open terrace outside the shrine or on the marble steps which lead down from it. The reason for this apparent disproportion between the sizes of the temple and the shrine is that the Hindu regards a temple as a symbol of the human body. Within the body of the temple, the shrine symbolizes the heart, the seat of the Atman within man. Now, the Hindu scriptures teach us to regard the all-encompassing Brahman as 'greater than the greatest' and the indwelling Atman, for convenience of meditation, as being 'of the size of a thumb'. It follows, therefore, that the shrine should occupy only a tiny space within its temple.

While we are on the subject of the Hindu temple as a symbol of the body, it is worth commenting on the fact that some old temples – though not those at Dakshineswar – have erotic carvings on their outer walls. These carvings represent the outgoing sensual thoughts of man, when his senses become entangled in the maya of physical phenomena. They are set there to create a deliberately violent contrast to the mood of indrawn meditativeness which is expressed by the shrine. But here, again, is a stumbling block for the foreign observer; and many of them have exclaimed in disgust that the Hindus blend pornography with their religion.

The image of Kali at Dakshineswar is small; less than three feet in height. The goddess is represented standing upon the prostrate body of Shiva, who lies on a silver lotus of a thousand petals. The figure of Shiva is made of white marble, that of Kali of black basalt. Kali is dressed in red silk and decorated with ornaments studded with jewels. She also wears a girdle of severed arms and a necklace of skulls, all carved out of marble. She is sticking out her tongue; some explain this as a gesture of coyness once common among the countrywomen of Bengal, others say that she is licking up blood. She has four arms. One of her left hands holds a decapitated head, the other a bloody sword. One of her right hands confers blessings on her devotees, the other is raised in a gesture (similar to that which is often depicted in statues of the Buddha) signifying 'be without fear'.

The symbolism here is shockingly explicit, and it is certain to repel those who have embraced that curious Western heresy which declares that the pretty and pleasant are more 'real' than the ugly and the unpleasant. Hindu philosophy, on the other hand, declares that the unpleasant and the pleasant are equally real (or unreal) and that both these strands of our experience are woven by the same power. Kali, as we have seen, is a Shakti; and Shakti is the Power of Brahman, which both creates and destroys. So Kali is shown as the Mother and the Destroyer, giver of life and death, blessings and misfortunes, pleasures and pains. To her devotees, the fortunes and misfortunes of life are simply to be regarded as 'Mother's play'. And, surely, any other view of the human situation is mere sentimentalism. So we must learn to love Kali, whether we want to or not. When we have done so, we shall be able to accept our experience in its entirety. And thus we shall have conquered fear and aversion as well as desire.

It is sometimes ignorantly said that Kali has conquered or destroyed Shiva, because she is shown standing upon his prostrate body. But this is a misconception. Ramakrishna used to explain the real meaning of their relationship as follows. Kali stands on Shiva's chest; Shiva lies under her feet like a corpse; Kali's eyes are fixed on Shiva. This simply denotes the union of Brahman with its Power. Brahman does not act; therefore Shiva lies on the ground immobile. Kali, the Power of Brahman, keeps her eyes fixed upon Shiva since she can only act because of Brahman's presence. Only through Brahman can she create, preserve and destroy. Shiva sanctions everything that Kali does.

The Kali Temple stands between two other buildings, within the courtyard. To the south of the temple is the theatre-hall (nat-mandap), a spacious and handsome building with a double row of pillars which nevertheless belongs to the same architectural family as the simple sheltered platforms in Kamarpukur, on which Ramakrishna sat at school and went into ecstasy while performing the role of Shiva.

To the north of the Kali Temple is the Radhakanta, the temple of Krishna and Radha. Krishna was Radha's beloved, and their relationship is held to express the worship of God as the divine lover. It is taught that every one of our human relationships can be sublimated to a non-physical, non-possessive plane, on which it is directed towards God and becomes a mode of worship. Thus, God may be regarded as a Father, a Mother, a Child, a Lover, a Friend, or a Master. The approach to God as a lover or bridegroom is, of course, well known to the Christian tradition. Every Catholic nun is regarded as a bride of Christ.

In India, Krishna is worshipped in three different aspects which represent three ages in his life on earth. He is worshipped either as the baby Gopala, or as the boy shepherd who is often called Govinda, or as the mature Krishna whose teaching of Arjuna is set forth in the Bhagavad-Gita. In the Radhakanta Temple he is seen as the shepherd-boy Govinda; for it was during this part of his life that he enjoyed the pastoral idyll of his relationship with Radha, and with her friends the *gopis* (milkmaids). Govinda wears a peacock feather in his hair, and plays the flute which symbolizes his power to enchant the hearts of his devotees. The figures of Krishna and Radha in the shrine of the Radhakanta are $21\frac{1}{2}$ in. and 16 in. respectively. They are slightly inclined towards each other, to indicate mutual devotion. Krishna's complexion is traditionally represented as blue, while Radha's is fair. So, in token of the merging of their personalities, Radha wears a blue stone as a nose-drop while Krishna wears a pearl, and she is dressed in blue while he is dressed in yellow.

One side of the courtyard is formed by the row of Shiva temples with the portico in the middle. The other three sides are enclosed by blocks of rooms opening on to colonnades. These are rooms for temple officials, guestrooms, storerooms or rooms in which food is prepared for the temple worship. At the northwest corner of the courtyard, overlooking the river, is the room where Ramakrishna passed most of his adult life. This room is now, of course, the centre of interest and veneration for all who come to Dakshineswar. It is large and pleasant; certainly the best room one could have on the courtyard. And it is relatively cool, being open to the courtyard colonnade on the one side and to the river-front porch on the other. It has recently been repaved, which every devotee must regret; since one no longer has the experience of walking on the same floor that Ramakrishna trod. Otherwise, the room has been little changed. Ramakrishna's two beds still stand in their places, side by side; the one he used for sitting on during the day and the one he used for sleeping. And the views that he saw from the room can have changed very little. Beyond the courtyard to the north, near the riverbank, stands one of the two music-towers called Nahabats. It has an important place in our story. To the west, the brown river with its tides ebbs and flows strongly. Across on the opposite bank, a long, low line of palms does not quite hide signs of Calcutta's growing industrialism; here and there, the smokestack of a factory appears. But at sunset and sunrise, the Ganges becomes beautifully mysterious and timeless, with the features of the shore dimmed in a murky golden haze. High-prowed boats of the old-fashioned build, such as Ramakrishna himself must often have travelled in, slip by and are lost in the darkness. In silhouette they somewhat resemble gondolas. And indeed this magical golden half-light must remind many Westerners of sunsets on the lagoons of Venice.

The temple courtyard occupies only the southwest corner of the Dakshineswar property. The remaining area was partly planted with flower gardens and orchards, partly left as virgin jungle. There were three tanks, and a house known as the Kuthi, in which the Rani and her family used to stay when they visited Dakshineswar. Ramakrishna also spent much time there. I shall not go into further details now. Certain spots and buildings are better described later, in connection with particular events in Ramakrishna's life.

The reader may have noticed that, since the beginning of this chapter, I have begun using the name Ramakrishna instead of Gadadhar. In doing this, I follow the practice of other biographers, who have always chosen this point in the narrative to make the change-over. As a matter of fact, however, it is not clear exactly when or how Gadadhar received his new name. There are three theories about this. One is that Rama-krishna was perhaps a name bestowed on Gadadhar by his parents, who were, it will be remembered, devotees of Sri Rama. That this is so seems very doubtful; and, even if Gadadhar did possess this name throughout his boyhood, he was certainly seldom or never called by it. Another theory, favoured by Saradananda, is that Gadadhar was given the name by the monk Tota Puri at the time of his initiation; an incident which is described in Chapter 10. The third – and most generally accepted – theory is that Gadadhar was first called Ramakrishna by Mathur Mohan, the son-in-law of Rani Rasmani.

The Rani relied greatly on Mathur's judgement. He advised and helped her in all her undertakings; and the two were temperamentally well suited. When Mathur's wife, the Rani's third daughter, died, the Rani encouraged him to marry her fourth daughter, because she was eager to keep him in the family. And, indeed, she did well to value Mathur. He was a man of the world with a keen business sense; and yet it was just this extreme worldly shrewdness in judging others which made him able to recognize other-worldly, spiritual qualities when he found them in another human being. He had strong passions and prejudices; yet he was a genuine devotee, capable of great religious fervour. He could be angry and argumentative; but he was also touch-ingly humble before those whom he considered to be his spiritual superiors.

From his first meeting with Ramakrishna, Mathur showed his extraordinary powers of perception; he was instantly and strongly drawn to this youth, who was to be seen moving about the gardens with an air of radiant innocence, like a young child. Mathur wanted to keep Ramakrishna at Dakshineswar; so he decided to offer him a permanent position as assistant to Ramkumar. But when Mathur spoke of this, Ramkumar was not at all encouraging; for he had now become resigned to the idea that his young brother would never settle down anywhere or accept steady work. Mathur was an obstinate man, however, and accustomed to getting people to do what he wanted. He bided his time.

There now came to Dakshineswar another person who was destined to form a close relationship with Ramakrishna. This was Hriday Ram. Hriday was a grandson of Khudiram's sister, and therefore a cousin of

Ramakrishna's – or, according to the Hindu view of relationships, a nephew. Hriday was only four years younger than Ramakrishna, however; the two had known each other since childhood. He was tall, handsome and muscular; good-humoured and always ready for hard work. By nature he was protective and he quickly became the almost inseparable companion of Ramakrishna. Hriday was not a particularly spiritual youth, but he had a gift for devotion.

We have seen that Ramakrishna showed, from his early years, a talent for modelling. Not long after Hriday's arrival, he took some earth from the bed of the Ganges and modelled an image of Shiva, which he then proceeded to worship within the temple compound. Mathur happened to come by, and was enormously impressed when he learned that it was Ramakrishna himself who had made the image. He asked Ramakrishna to give it to him, and he later showed it to the Rani, who was equally impressed. Henceforth, Mathur was more than ever determined to prevent Ramakrishna from leaving Dakshineswar.

Ramakrishna was quite well aware of Mathur's interest in him, and he now began to avoid Mathur. He feared a meeting between them, for he held Mathur in great respect and hated the prospect of having to say No to him – and yet he was unwilling to accept the position. Ramakrishna recognized the necessity of service for those who had families to support. But he himself, being unattached, was unwilling, as he used to say, to serve anyone but God. Hriday found this attitude most unreasonable. He asked nothing better than to be employed at Dakshineswar, which he regarded as a paradise, for the rest of his life. He reasoned with Ramakrishna. Ramakrishna replied that he did not want to be committed to any permanent work; besides, if he accepted work in the Kali Temple, he would have to be responsible for the safety of the ornaments of the goddess – and this responsibility he refused to undertake. Throughout his life, Ramakrishna instinctively shrank from involvement with jewels, gold or other worldly valuables. Hriday said at once that he would gladly be responsible for the ornaments. So Ramakrishna allowed himself to be persuaded, and thus it was finally settled. Ramakrishna and Hriday became assistants to Ramkumar in the Kali Temple. Ramakrishna had to dress the image and prepare it for worship; Hriday had to look after the ornaments.

That same year, on the day after the celebration of Sri Krishna's birthday, there was an accident in the Radhakanta Temple. The priest

---

of this temple was, as we have seen, Kshetranath, the brother of Mahesh. According to custom, the images of Krishna and Radha were removed from the shrine after the worship was over and placed on beds in another room. (The idea that the Deity has to 'rest' after being worshipped is current in many parts of the world. In the cathedrals of some Catholic countries, you may see the doors of the shrine closed to protect the privacy of the Blessed Virgin after a big religious festival.) On this occasion, as Kshetranath was carrying the image of Krishna back to the bedchamber, he slipped in some water which had been spilled on the marble floor, and fell. The leg of the image was broken off.

The accident caused a commotion. It was considered unlucky and of evil omen; and Kshetranath was immediately dismissed for his carelessness. The pandits were called together to decide what should be done next. They ruled that a broken image could not be worshipped; another image must be made and the old one thrown into the Ganges.

But the Rani was unwilling to throw away an image which she had once begun to worship. At Mathur's suggestion, she consulted Ramakrishna – of whom they now both had such a high opinion that they already called him – this youth not out of his teens – 'Father'! Before replying to the question, Ramakrishna pondered over it deeply and went into an ecstatic spiritual mood. Then he said: 'If one of the Rani's sons-in-law were to break a leg, would she throw him away and put someone else in his place? Wouldn't she rather have him cured by a doctor? Let it be the same in this case. Mend the image and worship it as before.'

Some of the pandits were shocked by this demonstration of divinely-inspired common sense; but the Rani and Mathur were delighted. Ramakrishna mended the image himself – so skilfully that no one thereafter was able to see the break in the limb. Later, when Ramakrishna was asked by a somewhat stupid landowner, 'Sir, is it true that the Krishna at Dakshineswar has been broken?' he replied scornfully, 'Can He who is the indivisible Whole be broken? A fine idea!'

Ramkumar's anxieties were now put to rest. Ramakrishna appeared to be settling down in a respectable position. Ramkumar was relieved at this; for he was now in his fifties and his health was poor. He had grown old before his time.

Ramkumar began to let Ramakrishna perform the worship in the

Kali Temple while he himself performed the worship of Krishna and Radha. Perhaps he did this because he wanted to prepare Ramakrishna to take over his duties as soon as possible. Perhaps he – who had foreseen the death of others – now foresaw his own. He died the next year, quite suddenly, at a place just outside Calcutta to which he had been called on some urgent business.

This was in 1856.

6

The Vision of Kali

Thus it was that, at the age of twenty, Ramakrishna suffered a second great bereavement. Ramkumar had been even more than an elder brother to him; he had stood, especially during the past four years, in the place of Ramakrishna's father.

The young man's mind now turned altogether away from the world and its impermanence, towards the one resource which he believed to be unfailing. He became passionately resolved to obtain a vision of Kali the Divine Mother – to know the Reality within the image he worshipped daily in the shrine. Obsessed by the love he felt for Kali and by his desire to see her, he spent every moment that he could in the temple. And when its doors had to be closed, according to custom, at midday and at night, he avoided the company of others and wandered off alone into the jungle thickets which covered the northern end of the temple property.

Hriday now became concerned, for he saw that Ramakrishna was neither sleeping nor eating sufficiently. And he knew that his uncle was in the habit of going off into the jungle – a thing which nobody else at Dakshineswar would willingly do, especially at night. Since the place had formerly been a graveyard, you might expect to meet ghosts there.

One night, the devoted youth put aside his own fears and followed Ramakrishna at a distance. In order to scare him into turning back, Hriday threw some pebbles and gravel after him. They fell around Ramakrishna, who ignored them and went on into the thicket. The next day, Hriday asked his uncle outright what he had been doing in such a sinister spot, in the middle of the night. Ramakrishna then explained to him that an *amalaki* tree (which bears an astringent plum-like fruit) grew there, and that, according to the Scriptures, anyone who meditates beneath an amalaki will have his dearest wish fulfilled. Ramakrishna was meditating under the tree in order to get his vision of Kali.

Hriday became increasingly distressed by his uncle's austerities. Being himself temperamentally unable to understand this kind of devotional obsession, he felt that Ramakrishna was going beyond the bounds of propriety and even of sanity. And his feeling was shared, to some extent, by almost everybody at Dakshineswar. Their head priest was taking his religion more seriously than they thought decent.

On another occasion, Hriday went into the jungle when he knew that Ramakrishna was already there. He found his uncle seated in meditation under the amalaki. Ramakrishna had taken off his dhoti and even the sacred thread which he wore as a brahmin, and was sitting there stark naked. Hriday was so scandalized that he roused Ramakrishna from the depths of his meditation and reproached him: had he gone mad to do such a thing?

Ramakrishna replied calmly that this was the right way to meditate. Man labours from his birth under eight forms of bondage, he told Hriday: they are hatred, shame, fear, doubt, aversion, self-righteousness, pride in one's lineage and pride in one's caste-status. All these forms of bondage tie man's mind down to worldly thoughts and desires and prevent him from raising his mind to spiritual things. The sacred thread reminds a man that he belongs to the highest caste, that of the brahmins; therefore it makes him proud of his birth. And so it must be discarded, along with every other pretension, possession, desire and aversion, before one can approach the Mother in meditation.

Literalness was characteristic of Ramakrishna. He was never content with a merely mental renunciation; the thought must be accompanied by a deed. Just as he had discarded his clothes and his sacred thread, so on other occasions he performed other acts of renunciation and self-mortification which were equally drastic. For example, in order to humble his caste-pride, he cleaned out a privy with his own hands. In order to affirm his belief that the Divine is present within all beings, he ate as prasad the remains of the food which the poor had been given, outside the Kali Temple; carried the leaves they had used as plates upon his head for disposal, and himself swept and washed the eating-place clean. In order to learn to regard the so-called valuable and the so-called worthless with impartial indifference, he took in one hand some clods of earth and in the other some coins; these he threw into the Ganges, repeating to himself 'rupee is dirt, dirt is rupee', over and over again.

Ramakrishna was now entering upon that phase of life which is characterized by *sadhana*, the period of spiritual discipline. All the great religious teachers have passed through such a phase. One need only instance the wanderings and austerities of the Buddha and those years of Christ's early manhood which are passed over in the Gospel narrative; years of retirement among the Essenes, if the scholars' latest theories are correct. Except in the cases of Buddha and Chaitanya, no such sadhana has been recorded in detail. This may well be because the devotees of later times did not wish to show their Ideal in the throes of temptation, spiritual anguish and despair. They did not wish to show an incarnation of God behaving like a human being. This has never been the attitude of the truly great devotees, however. Such devotees have even felt unwilling to dwell on the power and majesty of God, lest awe should interfere with their devotion.

The orthodox Hindu view is that an incarnation is all the time fully conscious of his divinity, so that whatever he does is only a kind of play-acting (a *lila*). But Saradananda does not altogether agree with this view. According to Saradananda, the avatar's sufferings and moments of weakness are not simulated. Coming into the world with absolute knowledge of the Reality, he assumes the ignorance and the weaknesses of ordinary men, in order to be an example to others by transcending them.

Nevertheless, says Saradananda, the incarnations of God *are* aware, even from their birth, that they are other than ordinary people. And this knowledge gives them immense compassion for all who are in bondage to worldly desires. It is to help them, that the incarnation performs his sadhana.

Ramakrishna used to tell this story: 'Three men went walking in a field. In the middle of the field there was a place surrounded by a high wall. From within this wall came the sounds of music; instruments were playing and voices sang. The men were charmed by it and wanted to see what was happening. But there was no door anywhere in the wall. What were they to do? One of the men found a ladder somewhere and climbed to the top of the wall, while the other two waited below.

When the man who was on top of the wall saw what was happening inside, he was beside himself with joy. He even forgot to tell the two below what he saw; he uttered a loud laugh and jumped down inside. The other two exclaimed: "A fine friend he is! He didn't tell us what he saw. We'll have to look for ourselves." So the second man climbed the ladder. And, like the first man, he looked over the wall and burst out laughing with joy, and jumped. So what was the third man to do? He too climbed the ladder and looked over the wall and saw what was on the other side. It was like a market of happiness, given free to all comers. His first thought was to jump down and join in the rejoicing. But then he said to himself: "If I do that, no one outside will ever know that this place of joy exists. Am I to be the only one to find it?" So he forced his mind away from the sight, and he came down the ladder and began telling everyone he met: "In there is the market of happiness. Come with me – let's enjoy it together." So he took everybody with him, and they all took part in the rejoicing.'

Ramakrishna was accustomed to teach that the whole purpose of sadhana was to become able to see Brahman in all things, everywhere. Sadhana, ultimately, is the effort to know the Universal cause beyond time and space. We ordinary mortals see only the multiplicity of beings, not the one eternal substratum. We see multiplicity instead of unity because we are ignorant. We are ignorant because we are within Maya, the web of seeming which has been put forth by the Power of Brahman. This ignorance should not be thought of as an individual delusion. It is shared by all who are within Maya; that is why our perceptions are roughly identical. If I think I see a table, then so do you. Our ignorance consists in being unable to see that the table is essentially Brahman, and that nothing but Brahman exists. But, though this ignorance is shared, any one of us can individually escape from it, and thus reach freedom.

It is said that there are two main paths of sadhana: the path of discrimination and the path of devotion. Since the knowledge that life ends in death has always been common to mankind, it is probable that discrimination was practised before devotion. For discrimination consists in rejecting all that is impermanent, in order to come at last, by a process of elimination, to the permanent substratum, the Reality. The Buddha began his search in this way, after his first contact with sickness, old age and death had made him realize the impermanence of human life. It has been said, therefore, that the path of discrimination can be described by saying 'not this, not this' – meaning that nothing in the world of phenomena is permanent and that all must be rejected.

The path of devotion, on the other hand, is described by saying 'this, this' – because the devotee is constantly reminding himself that he is everywhere in the presence of Brahman. In saying this, he is not disagreeing with the man of discrimination. He does not worship phenomena *as* phenomena. He worships the Reality behind the phenomena. We find followers of these two paths in all the world's religions. The difference between them is really one of temperament. It is the nature of some people to arrive at truth by means of intellect, of others to arrive at it by means of love. Both of these paths have led countless men and women to union with the Reality. This unitive experience has been the goal of every true mystic. The Buddhists call it nirvana, the Christians the mystic union, the Hindus samadhi.

In my second chapter, I briefly mentioned samadhi – known as the fourth state of consciousness, because it is neither waking, dreaming nor dreamless sleep. But it is impossible for me to say anything very explicit about it. Like all but the merest handful of people alive in the world today, I have never come anywhere near experiencing it. And even those who have experienced it have had great difficulty in speaking of their experience. One may say, indeed, that it is by definition indescribable. For words deal with the knowledge obtained by the five senses; and samadhi goes beyond all sense-experience. It is in its highest form a state of total knowledge, in which the knower and the thing known become one. This is *nirvikalpa* samadhi. The so-called lower samadhi, *savikalpa*, is that in which the sense of duality is not yet quite lost; knower and known are still separated, but only, as it were, by a thin pane of glass. The mystic who has reached the lower samadhi is almost certain to be able to pass on to the higher, if he desires it.

Outwardly, samadhi appears to be a state of unconsciousness, since the mind of the experiencer is entirely withdrawn from the outer world. Therefore it is often referred to as a 'trance'. But, in fact, samadhi is a state of awareness unimaginably more intense than everyday consciousness. It is the very opposite of a trance, which, in its primary meaning at least, is a condition of stupor, or bewilderment.

Of the few mystics who ever reach samadhi, the majority do so towards the end of their lives or at the moment of death. Ramakrishna, as we shall see, entered samadhi not once but several times a day, over a period of many years!

The reader may now ask some such questions as these: 'You say that intense meditation can bring a man to the state of samadhi. But how does he actually get there? What is going on inside him during this process? What are the psychophysical steps which lead to complete spiritual awakening?'

According to the Hindu physiology, there is a great store of potential spiritual energy at the base of the spine. This energy is known as the *kundalini*, meaning 'that which is coiled up'; therefore it is sometimes referred to as 'the serpent power'. The Hindu physiologists tell us that most of us hardly use this energy at all. The little of it that we do arouse goes into our sex-drives and other physical appetites. But when the kundalini is fully aroused – by the practice of meditation and other spiritual disciplines – it is said to travel up the spine through six centres of consciousness, until it reaches the seventh, the centre of the brain. It is this rise of the kundalini to the higher centres which produces various degrees of enlightenment. Ramakrishna, in later life, described the process as follows:

'The Scriptures speak of seven centres of consciousness. The mind may dwell in any one of these centres. As long as the mind is attached to the things of this world, it remains in the three lower centres; at the navel, at the sex-organ and at the rectum. While there, it has no higher ambitions and no visions. It is plunged in the passions of lust and greed.

'The fourth centre is the heart. When the mind learns to dwell there, a man has his first spiritual awakening. He has the vision of light all around him. Seeing this light, he marvels and cries: "Ah, what joy!" After this, his mind does not go back to the lower centres.

'The fifth centre is at the throat. When a man's mind reaches that, it is set free from ignorance and delusion. The man does not care to hear or talk of anything but God.

'The sixth centre is at the forehead (between the eyebrows). When the mind reaches this centre, it has direct vision of God, by day and by night. But, even so, there is a little trace of egotism left. . . . It's like a light in a lantern. You feel as if you could touch the light but you can't, because the glass prevents you.

'The seventh centre is at the top of the head. When the mind reaches it, it achieves samadhi. Then one becomes a knower of Brahman. One is united with Brahman.'

Ramakrishna was, of course, speaking to people who were more or less acquainted with Hindu physiological theory. But here I must explain that the spinal column is said to contain two nerve-currents, called *ida* and *pingala*. (These have been identified, I do not know how correctly, with the sensory and motor nerves of our Western physiology.) Ida is said to be on the left of the spinal column; pingala on the right. In the middle is a passage which is called the *sushumna*. When the kundalini is aroused, it passes up the sushumna; which otherwise, in the case of normally unspiritual people, remains closed. When Rama-krishna speaks of the centres of the navel, heart, throat, etc., he is using physical organs to indicate the approximate positions of these centres; actually, they are located within the sushumna itself.

These centres are also often called 'lotuses' in Hindu writings on the subject, because they are said to appear in the form of a lotus to those whose spiritual vision enables them to see them. It is wrong to think of the centres as being gross physical organs; but it must be remembered, on the other hand, that Hindu physiology makes no sharp distinction between gross and subtle. It is all a question of degree.

It was noticed that, in the case of Ramakrishna, the ascent of the kundalini was accompanied by a constant and powerful movement of the blood towards the chest and brain. In consequence of this, the skin of his chest was always flushed.

As the months of this year, 1856, went by, Ramakrishna's spiritual efforts became more and more intense. Addressing the image of Kali in the temple, he exclaimed piteously: 'Mother, you showed yourself to Ramprasad and other devotees in the past. Why won't you show yourself to me? Why won't you grant my prayer? I've been praying to you so long!' And he wept bitterly.

'Oh, what days of suffering I went through!' Ramakrishna used to say, as he recalled this period in after-years. 'You can't imagine the agony of my separation from Mother! But that was only natural. Suppose there's a bag of gold in a room and a thief in the next room, with only a thin partition in between. Can the thief sleep in peace? Won't he try to burst through that wall and get at the gold? That was the state I was in. I knew Mother was there, quite close to me. How could I want anything else? She is infinite happiness. Beside her, all the world's wealth is nothing.'

Often, before the shrine, he became absorbed and stopped the performance of the ritual; sitting motionless for hours at a time. Because of this, some of the temple officials became impatient with him; others laughed at him for a half-crazy fool. But Mathur was impressed. And he told the Rani: 'We have got a wonderful devotee for the worship of our Goddess; very soon, he will awaken her.'

Before long, Mathur was proved right. This is how Ramakrishna describes the experience: 'There was an unbearable pain in my heart, because I couldn't get a vision of Mother. Just as a man wrings out a towel with all his strength to get the water out of it, so I felt as if my heart and mind were being wrung out. I began to think I should never see Mother. I was dying of despair. In my agony, I said to myself: "What's the use of living this life?" Suddenly my eyes fell on the sword that hangs in the temple. I decided to end my life with it, then and there. Like a madman, I ran to it and seized it. And then – I had a marvellous vision of the Mother, and fell down unconscious. . . . It was as if houses, doors, temples and everything else vanished altogether; as if there was nothing anywhere! And what I saw was an infinite shoreless sea of light; a sea that was consciousness. However far and in whatever direction I looked, I saw shining waves, one after another, coming towards me. They were raging and storming upon me with great speed. Very soon they were upon me; they made me sink down into unknown depths. I panted and struggled and lost consciousness.'

It is not quite clear from Ramakrishna's narrative whether or not he actually saw the form of Mother Kali in the midst of this vision of shining consciousness. But it would seem that he did; because the first words that he uttered on coming to himself were 'Mother, Mother!'

After this vision, Ramakrishna was so absorbed that he was often unable to perform the temple worship at all. Hriday had to do it for him. Hriday was so disturbed by the mental condition of his uncle that he called in a doctor to treat him. It would be interesting to know what form the treatment took. Needless to say, it was quite ineffectual.

On the days when Ramakrishna was able to perform the worship, a strange phenomenon would occur. 'No sooner had I sat down to meditate,' he later recalled, 'than I heard clattering sounds in the joints of my body and limbs. They began in my legs. It was as if some-one inside me had keys and was locking me up, joint by joint, turning the keys. I had no power to move my body or change my posture, even slightly. I couldn't stop meditating, or go away elsewhere, or do anything else I wanted. I was forced, as it were, to sit in the same posture until my joints began clattering again and were unlocked, beginning at the neck, this time, and ending in my legs. When I sat and meditated, I had at first the vision of particles of light like swarms of fireflies. Sometimes I saw masses of light covering everything on all sides like a mist; at other times I saw how everything was pervaded by bright waves of light like molten silver. I didn't understand what I saw, nor did I know if it was good or bad to be having such visions. So I prayed anxiously to Mother: "I don't understand what's happening to me. Please, teach me yourself how to know you. Mother, if *you* won't teach me, who will?"'

In such statements, we hear the artless accents of Ramakrishna, and they convey, more vividly than any words of his contemporaries, the personality he was more and more completely assuming; that of a child of the Divine Mother. Childlike, he now obeyed the will of the Mother in everything, no matter how trivial, and was utterly careless of what the world might think of his behaviour.

And now he had begun to see the Mother frequently. He saw her within the temple and outside it, without any longer having to make an effort of will in his meditation. He no longer saw an image in the temple but the form of Mother herself. Later, he described how 'I put the palm of my hand near her nostrils and felt that the Mother was actually breathing. I watched very closely, but I could never see her shadow on the temple wall in the light of the lamp, at night. I used to hear from my room how Mother ran upstairs, as merry as a little girl, with her anklets jingling. I wanted to be sure that she'd really done this, so I went outside. And there she was, standing on the veranda of the second floor of the temple, with her hair flying. Sometimes she looked towards Calcutta and sometimes towards the Ganges.'

Hriday has left us a description of his relations with Ramakrishna at this time, and of his uncle's astonishing behaviour. 'You felt awe-struck when you entered the Kali Temple in those days, even when Uncle wasn't there – and much more so when he was. Yet I couldn't resist the temptation of seeing how he acted at the time of the worship. As long as I was actually watching him, my heart was full of reverence and devotion; but when I came out of the temple, I began to have doubts and ask myself: "Has Uncle really gone mad? Why else should he do such terrible things during the worship?" I was afraid of what the Rani and Mathur Babu would say when they came to hear of it. But Uncle never worried. . . . I didn't venture to speak to him much, any longer; my mouth was closed by a fear I can't describe. I felt that there was some kind of barrier between us. So I just looked after him in silence, as best I could. But I was afraid he'd make a scene, some day.'

Hriday's fears were certainly justified. He continues: 'I saw how Uncle's chest and eyes were always red, like those of a drunkard. He'd get up reeling from the worshipper's seat, climb on to the altar, and caress the Divine Mother, chucking her affectionately under the chin. He'd begin singing, laughing, joking and talking with her, or some-times he'd catch hold of her hands and dance. . . . I saw how, when he was offering cooked food to the Divine Mother, he'd suddenly get up, take a morsel of rice and curry from the plate in his hand, touch the Mother's mouth with it and say: "Eat it, Mother. Do eat it!" Then maybe he'd say: "You want me to eat it – and then you'll eat some afterwards? All right, I'm eating it now." Then he'd take some of it himself and put the rest to her lips again, saying: "I've had some. Now you eat."

'One day, at the time of the food-offering, Uncle saw a cat. It had come into the temple, mewing. He fed it with the food which was to be offered to the Divine Mother. "Will you take it, Mother?" he said to the cat.'

The appalling Power that makes and unmakes the universe may also be known in the aspect of an indulgent Mother whom one can laugh with and pester for favours like a child. And that Power is everywhere present – within the air around us, within an image in a temple, within a stray cat. These are the simple and overwhelming truths which Ramakrishna was demonstrating by his seemingly insane actions. No wonder the orthodox temple officials were outraged! They sent a message of complaint to Mathur, who was away from Dakshineswar at the time. Mathur replied that he would soon return to see and judge for himself; in the meanwhile, Ramakrishna was to be allowed to continue the worship. Shortly after this, Mathur did return, unannounced. He went into the Kali Temple while Ramakrishna was making the offering. What Mathur saw convinced him that he was in the presence not of insanity but of great holiness. He gave orders that Ramakrishna was not to be interfered with on any account. 'Now the Goddess is being truly worshipped,' he said to the Rani.

But the confidence which Mathur and his mother-in-law felt in Ramakrishna was to be put to an even more severe test. One day, the Rani paid a visit to Dakshineswar, bathed in the Ganges and went into the temple for the worship. Ramakrishna was already there. The Rani asked him to sing some of the songs in praise of the Mother which he sang so beautifully and with such ecstatic devotion. Ramakrishna sang for a while. Then suddenly he stopped, turned to the Rani and exclaimed indignantly: 'Shame on you – to think such thoughts even here!' And so saying he struck the Rani with the palm of his hand.

Immediately there was a commotion. The women attendants of the Rani who were present began to scream for help. The gatekeeper and various officers of the temple came running up, ready to seize Ramakrishna and drag him out of the shrine. They only awaited the Rani's order. But the Rani herself remained calm; and Ramakrishna was now quietly smiling. 'He is not to blame,' the Rani told the officers. 'Leave him alone.'

For she already knew why Ramakrishna had struck her. Instead of listening to the song, she had actually at that moment been thinking about a lawsuit in which she was involved. She only marvelled that Ramakrishna could have known what was in her mind. Later, when her attendants exclaimed at his insolence, she replied gravely and humbly: 'You don't understand – it was the Divine Mother herself who punished me and enlightened my heart.' And she forbade them ever to refer to the incident again.

7

The Marriage of Ramakrishna

Shortly after this, Ramakrishna gave up performing the worship in the Kali Temple. It is written in the Bhagavad-Gita that, as a man progresses along the path of spiritual development, his acts will 'fall from him'; in other words, the performance of rituals and the observance of other religious duties will become less and less necessary for his spiritual welfare. Ramakrishna used to express this truth as follows: 'The mother-in-law allows her daughter-in-law to eat all kinds of food and do all kinds of work, until she conceives. But, as soon as she's with child, one must be a little careful about the kind of work and food she is given; and later, when her pregnancy is far advanced, her work is strictly limited. Just before childbirth, she doesn't have to work at all. And, when the baby is born at last, she has nothing to do but play with it.'

Ramakrishna's devotion to the Divine Mother was now so great that external acts of worship had become unnecessary. He was worshipping the Mother in spirit, wherever he happened to be and whatever else he was doing. Sometimes, it seemed to him that he had no separate existence from her at all; he would take flowers and sandalwood and decorate his own body, instead of her image. And if this sense of communion with her ceased for even a few moments, his agony would be so intense that he would throw himself down, wailing, and rub his face against the earth until it bled.

Mathur observed Ramakrishna's behaviour with mixed feelings. One half of his mind had decided that Ramakrishna was not only sane but super-sane, a being who could see the real nature of things in clearer perspective than ordinary mortals. But the other half of Mathur's mind persisted in regarding Ramakrishna as a sadly eccentric and

irresponsible young man who needed to be protected from himself
and weaned back to normal human ways.

Mathur had rebuked the temple officials who said Ramakrishna was
mad; yet now he called in a doctor, just as Hriday had done earlier, to
treat Ramakrishna for his 'nervous disorder'. Mathur was well aware of
Ramakrishna's attitude towards personal possessions and the dangers
of addiction to them. Yet he bought a beautiful shawl from Benares at
the cost of a thousand rupees and gave it to Ramakrishna. At first,
Ramakrishna was delighted. He put on the shawl and walked about the
temple grounds, admiring it and showing it to everyone he met; telling
artlessly just how much Mathur had paid for it. But then, suddenly, his
mood changed. 'What's in this thing?' he said to himself. 'Nothing
but goat's hair. Nothing but a certain blend of the five elements. Will
it keep out the cold? An ordinary blanket's just as good. Will it help
me to realize God? Not one bit! Quite the opposite – when you put it
on, you begin to think you're better than other people, and your mind
turns away from Him.' Saying this to himself, Ramakrishna flung the
shawl on the ground and spat on it and trampled it. He would even
have set fire to it, if someone had not taken it away from him. When
Mathur was told about this, he saw at once that he had been wrong to
give Ramakrishna the shawl. 'Father did the right thing,' he said.

On another occasion, Mathur and the Rani came misguidedly to
the conclusion that Ramakrishna was suffering from the effects of
unduly prolonged continence. So Mathur brought prostitutes to visit
and, if possible, seduce him; and later took him to a house of prostitu-
tion in Calcutta. But Ramakrishna saw only the Divine Mother in
these, as in all, women. Saluting Her presence, he went into samadhi.
The women themselves were profoundly moved by the experience.
They begged his pardon with tears for having tempted him in this
manner; mortally afraid that they might have incurred bad karma by
doing so. It is not recorded that Ramakrishna scolded the Rani or
Mathur; no doubt, like other great teachers before him, he judged the
intention rather than the deed.

We have already noted the literalness with which Ramakrishna suited
action to idea; here is an extraordinary instance of it. At this time, he
began to worship Sri Rama, the chosen deity of his father Khudiram.
It is related in the Ramayana – the epic poem which describes the life

of Rama – that Rama's chief devotee was Hanuman, the king of the monkeys. Hanuman is therefore revered in India as an ideal devotee, notwithstanding his animal form. So now Ramakrishna set himself to imitate Hanuman in every respect. 'I had to walk like Hanuman,' he recalled, 'I had to eat like him, and do every action as he would have done it. I didn't do this of my own accord; it happened of itself. I tied my dhoti around my waist to make it look like a tail, and I moved about in jumps. I ate nothing but fruit and roots, and I didn't like them when they were skinned or peeled. I spent a lot of my time in trees; and I kept crying "Rama!" in a deep voice. My eyes got a restless look, like the eyes of a monkey. And the most marvellous thing was – the lower end of my spine lengthened, nearly an inch! Later, when I stopped practising this kind of devotion, it gradually went back to its normal size.'

It was during the period of Ramakrishna's devotion to Rama that he had a vision of Sita, Rama's wife. This vision was experienced in daylight, with open eyes; Ramakrishna was not meditating on Sita or even thinking about her, at the time. This was how he described it: 'One day, I was sitting in the place which is now the Panchavati. I was in a state of ordinary consciousness, well aware of my surroundings. All of a sudden, a luminous female figure of exquisite grace appeared before me. She lit up everything around her with her radiance. I could see her, and at the same time I could see the trees, the Ganges, every-thing. I saw that this was a human figure, for she had no marks of a divine being upon her – such as a third eye, for instance. But such a sublime face as hers was – full of love, sorrow, compassion and fortitude – is seldom to be seen even among the goddesses! Slowly she advanced towards me, from the direction of the north, and all the while she looked at me with gracious eyes. I was amazed, and was wondering who she might be, when suddenly a monkey uttered a cry and jumped over to her side and sat by her. Then it came to me in a flash that this must be Sita; she whose whole life had been devoted to Rama, and who had suffered so greatly. Overcome by emotion, I was about to fall at her feet crying 'Mother!', when she passed into my body and became merged in it. As she did so, she told me that she was making me a gift of her smile! I fell unconscious on the ground. . . . This was the first vision I ever had with my eyes wide open, and when I wasn't meditating. Is it because my first vision was of Sita in her sorrowful aspect that I've had so much suffering in my life, since then? Who knows?'

Everyone who knew Ramakrishna agreed that he had a smile of unforgettable sweetness. Saradananda believed that his smile was literally the same as Sita's smile.

Mention has been made above of the Panchavati. A *panchavati* is a grove of five sacred trees, designed as a place of meditation. The trees which must be used are: an *aswattha*, which is a kind of fig; a *vilva*, whose leaves are used in the worship of Shiva; an *amalaki*, the wish-fulfilling tree referred to in the last chapter; an *asoka*, a flowering tree beneath which, according to tradition, Sita lived in Ceylon during the period of her abduction by the demon Ravana; and a *banyan*, the mighty tree with downward-hanging roots which occupies the central position in so many villages of southeastern Asia. The Scriptures direct that these trees must be planted according to a certain arrangement – the fig to the east, the vilva to the north, the banyan to the west, and amalaki to the south and the asoka to the southeast. An altar must be placed in the middle.

It was at this time that the Panchavati at Dakshineswar came into being. (It still partially exists and is regarded as one of the most sacred spots in the temple grounds.) The amalaki tree under which Ramakrishna had been meditating had had to be cut down, because a pond nearby was being re-excavated and the land around it cleared and levelled. So Ramakrishna, with Hriday's help, prepared this new place of meditation. He himself planted the aswattha, Hriday the other trees. When the saplings had been set in position, a hedge of vines was planted around them, to hide the Panchavati from the view of passers-by. Soon, however, the cows which wander, in the freedom of their sanctity, over the grounds of any temple in India, began to crop the hedge; and Ramakrishna saw that it would have to be protected by a fence. It is said that a particularly high tide on the Ganges washed up all the necessary articles – some mangrove posts, coir rope and even a chopper – quite close to the required spot; and Ramakrishna and one of the gardeners made a fence with them. Saradananda uses this anecdote to illustrate a statement which is made in the Upanishads, that a true knower of Brahman cannot desire anything without that desire being fulfilled.

In 1858, a certain Ramtarak came to Dakshineswar, in search of employment. Ramtarak was the son of Khudiram's youngest brother; he and Ramakrishna were therefore cousins. Ramtarak was several years the elder of the two. Ramakrishna always used to call him Haladhari, so I shall use that name here.

Haladhari was an intelligent and scholarly man, well versed in the scriptures and subtle in philosophical argument. Mathur gladly employed him – the more so because of his relationship to Ramakrishna. It was arranged that Haladhari should take over the worship in the Kali Temple, while Hriday was transferred to the temple of Krishna and Radha. But difficulties arose, even from the start.

Although Haladhari was a devotee of Vishnu, he had no antipathy to Shakti and therefore no objection to performing the worship of Kali; but he did object, as a strict brahmin, to eating cooked food from the temple. (His scruples were related to the Rani's low caste-status; they have already been discussed in Chapter 4.) Mathur agreed to provide Haladhari with raw food which he could cook himself, but at the same time pointed out to him that both Ramakrishna and Hriday always took the temple prasad. Haladhari replied, with becoming humility, 'My cousin is in an exalted spiritual state; he can do as he likes. But I have not reached that state and I must abide by my caste-rules.'

Haladhari was not as humble as he sounded, however. His was a complex nature. His considerable spiritual insight was restricted by the blinkers of caste-pride and intellectual arrogance; yet, in his half-unwilling way, he was one of Ramakrishna's sincerest early devotees. Ramakrishna himself was well aware of this, and often spoke warmly of Haladhari, despite the tensions which were continually arising between them, and which I shall presently describe.

It is customary to offer animal sacrifices to Kali at the times of the great festivals. Haladhari could not bear to see this; he found it cruel and disgusting. Here the code of the Vaishnava (devotee of Vishnu), which enjoins vegetarianism and non-violence, came into conflict with the philosophy of the devotee of Kali; she who sanctions death as well as birth. Haladhari's fault lay in this; that he had accepted the office of Kali's worshipper with reservations and a measure of disapproval. His punishment was dramatic. As he sat meditating in the temple, the Goddess appeared to him in her terrible aspect as the Destroyer.

She ordered him to leave the building at once and forever. 'Beware,' she told him, 'lest your son die because of your lack of reverence!' A few days later, Haladhari actually did receive news of his son's death. He went to Ramakrishna and told him the whole story. We must certainly admire Haladhari for his frankness in doing this, since it implied condemnation of himself. Thenceforward, it was arranged that Haladhari should perform the worship in the Radhakanta Temple and that Hriday should return to the worship of Kali.

It has already been said that the devotees of Krishna and Radha meditate upon God in the relationship of a lover. A lover – not a husband or a wife – because, it is said, one must have the reckless love and disregard for public opinion which is felt by a paramour and his mistress; married people are careful of the rules of respectability and their behaviour is more circumspect. Now the ideal to be followed in this cult of Krishna and Radha is that of absolute purity. The love of Krishna and Radha for each other is not thought of as a sexual relationship, but as one which far transcended even the thought of sex. In India, however, sects have always existed which combine the mood of worship with the act of physical love. Such sects are frowned on by the majority of devotees, and they carry on their practices in discreet retirement. These practices are known as 'left-handed Tantra'.

The Tantras are a vast body of literary works in Sanskrit, dating from the ninth to the fifteenth century A.D. They deal with various forms of ritualistic worship, magical and sacramental formulas, mystical letters and diagrams. On the upper level, the aim of Tantra is union with God, and specifically with the Divine Mother. On the lower level, it is success in love or business, avoidance of disease, revenge upon your enemies. So Tantra ranges from ritual worship to mere magic. It is two-faced, and therefore very easy to condemn. What is symbol to one participant is gross physical action to another. For example, the many tantrik pictures to be found in India and Tibet may be taken either as representations of the symbolic play of Shiva with his Shakti, Brahman with the Power of Brahman; or as illustrations to a manual on the art of sexual intercourse. In the practice of left-handed Tantra, a male and a female devotee translate the Shiva–Shakti relationship into an act of copulation.

In the classical age of the Vedas, according to Saradananda, the principle of blending worldly enjoyment with spiritual endeavour was approved of by the great teachers. They recognized that, for the ordinary man, sensual desire is too strong to be repressed. So they recommended, instead, that the devotee should remind himself that God is present, at all times, within our lowest and grossest actions as within our noblest. ('The Lord is everywhere and always perfect,' says the Bhagavad-Gita. 'What does he care for man's sin or for man's righteousness?') It is never improper to think of God, at any time. The worst act is at least the better for being associated with God. To believe otherwise is to sanction the hypocrisy of 'Sunday Religion', which will go into God's presence only in the fine clothes of respectability, never in the soiled garments of the lustful everyday self.

With the coming of Buddhism, says Saradananda, a reformation was attempted. The mass of worldly people were taught by the Buddhist reformers a way of life which was only appropriate to the wandering monk, living in the strictest abstinence. Naturally, the worldly-minded could not maintain this high standard of conduct. So they began to resort to tantrik practices in secret.

To think clearly about this matter requires some effort; because our Western minds are so steeped in puritanism. The association of the idea 'sex' with the idea 'religion' shocks us even more profoundly than we know. Yet, what is there in all this to be shocked about? You have a wife whom you love and with whom you have sexual relations. These sexual relations are motivated, as we all agree, not only by love but also by sexual desire. None of us find *this* shocking – although it might well be argued, by someone not accustomed to our ways of thinking, that love is degraded by desire and should never be associated with it. You do not accept this view. Why, then, should you be shocked when it is suggested that you associate love and desire with religious devotion, and try to regard your wife as an embodiment of the Divine Mother at all times and even when you are having sexual relations with her? True, if you fully succeed in regarding your wife as the Divine Mother, you will find that your sexual desire for her ceases. But, as long as you have not succeeded in this attempt, the mere effort is surely better than no effort at all.

That is the case for the sexual practices of Tantra, and it deserves at least to be stated fairly. Ramakrishna, whose own life and teaching were based upon strict purity, was at first inclined to condemn these practices outright. Later, when he had become acquainted with some members of the secret tantrik cults, he modified his view. He still thought such practices were dangerous and unsuitable for the majority, but he saw that some of these men and women were sincere, and that they had really progressed towards spiritual enlightenment. Therefore, when his disciples attacked the members of these cults, he used to reprove them: 'Why should you give way to hatred? I tell you, this is also one of the paths – though it's a dirty one. There are several doors leading into a house – the main door, the back door, the door by which the sweeper enters to clean out the dirt. So, this, too, is a door. No matter which door people use, they get inside the house, all right. Does that mean that you should act like them, or mix with them? No – but keep your hearts free of hatred for them.'

Now it happened that Haladhari, despite his orthodoxy, belonged secretly to one of these tantrik cults – and the secret began to leak out. The temple officials at Dakshineswar whispered and joked about it; but they did not dare say anything openly because they were afraid of Haladhari. He had a commanding personality, and was credited with psychic powers. There was a superstitious belief that his curses always came true.

As soon as Ramakrishna heard these whispers, he went straight to Haladhari and told him of them, in his usual outspoken way. Haladhari flew at once into a rage, and cried, 'You're my cousin and my junior – how dare you criticize me! Blood will come out of your mouth!' These words frightened Ramakrishna; he tried to soothe Haladhari, saying that he had only wished to warn him and save his reputation. But Haladhari would not withdraw his curse.

One evening, shortly after Haladhari had cursed him, Ramakrishna felt a tingling sensation in his palate; then blood began to come out of his mouth. As he described it: 'The colour of that blood was like the juice of kidney-bean leaves. It was so thick that only a little of it fell on the ground; the rest clotted and hung down from my lip, like the air-roots of the banyan tree. I tried to stop the bleeding by pressing one end of my wearing-cloth against my palate, but I couldn't stop it. When I saw that, I was afraid. A lot of people ran up and gathered round me. Haladhari was doing the worship in the temple, when he was told about it. He was frightened, and came out to me as fast as he could. When I saw him, I told him with tears in my eyes, "Look, Cousin, just see what you've done to me with your curse!" And, seeing the state I was in, he began to weep, too.

'Luckily, there was a *sadhu* [holy man] who had come to the Kali Temple that day, a good man. He examined the colour of my blood and the part of my mouth that it was coming from. "Don't be afraid," he told me. "It's very good that you're bleeding like this. I see you've been practising *hatha yoga*. As a result, the sushumna had opened and the blood was flowing out of your body into your head. Fortunately, this blood has made a passage for itself through the palate; otherwise you would have entered nirvikalpa samadhi and never come back to ordinary consciousness. The Divine Mother must have some special purpose she wants to accomplish through your body. I think this is why she has saved it." When I heard the words of this holy man, I was reassured and at peace.'

(One of the pandits who visited Dakshineswar had taught Ramakrishna some hatha yoga – that system of exercises which is designed to arouse the kundalini. [See Chapter 6.] In view of the popularity of hatha yoga exercises nowadays, it is worth recording that Ramakrishna did not recommend them. He said that they were unsuitable for this age, because they cause a preoccupation with the physical body and a neglect of spiritual growth.)

So Haladhari's curse was turned into a blessing. No doubt Haladhari felt repentant for a while; but still he could not learn to accept Ramakrishna unconditionally and love him for what he was. His attitude towards his cousin alternated between unwilling admiration, contempt and downright dislike. Haladhari never forgot his caste-pride; to him as a brahmin, it was inexpressibly shocking that Ramakrishna could throw off his sacred thread when meditating, and otherwise outrage the rules of orthodoxy. And yet, in spite of himself, he was sometimes deeply moved by the sweetness of Ramakrishna's devotional moods. Haladhari had enough spiritual insight to be able to catch glimpses of the tremendous Presence which had so mysteriously chosen to dwell within the body of his absurd and seemingly half-crazy cousin.

Talking about Haladhari at a later period, Ramakrishna used to recall many incidents in their comically stormy relationship, which continued to have its ups and downs throughout the years which Haladhari spent at Dakshineswar – from 1858 to 1865.

For instance: 'Many times, Haladhari would be charmed by my devotion in the temple, and he'd say to me "Ramakrishna, now I know what your real nature is!" So I'd tell him jokingly, "Then don't you get mixed up any more!" Then he'd say, "You can't deceive me again – the Lord is within you, I can see it – this time, I'm quite certain!" So I'd say, "All right – let's see how long you stay certain!" But after he'd left the temple and taken some snuff and started holding forth about the Gita or some other sacred book, he'd become full of egotism; and then he'd be quite a different person. Now and then, I'd go to see him while he was like that, and I'd tell him, "I've realized all those spiritual states you've been reading about; I can understand everything that's in the Scriptures." Then he'd get furious. "You idiot," he'd say, "you think *you* can understand the Scriptures?" "Believe me," I'd say, "the One who is inside this body of mine teaches me everything – you said He was there, yourself." Then he'd start getting frantic with rage: "Get out of here, you crazy fool! Are you claiming to be an incarnation of God? The Scriptures say there'll be only one avatar in this age, and that's Kalki. You must be out of your mind, to think such things!" So I laughed and said, "Didn't you tell me you'd never get mixed up about me again?" But of course he wouldn't listen to me, in that mood. We had the same scene, over and over again.'

Since his terrifying vision in the Kali Temple and the subsequent death of his son, Haladhari had come, not unnaturally, to look upon Kali entirely in the aspect of the Destroyer. One day he said to Ramakrishna, 'How can you spend your time worshipping a Goddess who embodies nothing but wrath and destruction?'

Ramakrishna was deeply pained by this question, which seemed to him to be a slander on his adored Mother. He hurried into the Kali Temple, and asked, with tears in his eyes, 'Mother – Haladhari, who's a great scholar and knows the Scriptures, says you're nothing but wrath and destruction! Is that really true?' At once, he received reassurance; the whole nature of Mother Kali was revealed to him. Wild with joy and relief, Ramakrishna ran across to the Radhakanta Temple, where Haladhari was seated at worship, and jumped on to his shoulders. 'Mother is everything!' he told Haladhari excitedly, again and again. 'Do you dare call her wrathful? No! She has every attribute – and yet she's nothing but pure love!'

On this – as on many other occasions later in our story – the touch of Ramakrishna communicated an instantaneous enlightenment; Haladhari's arrogant resentment and egotism vanished, and he saw the truth. He bowed down before Ramakrishna in the shrine, and offered flowers at his feet, feeling that he was in the presence of Kali herself.

Later, Hriday came to Haladhari and asked him, perhaps with a certain desire to tease, 'Didn't you say Ramakrishna was crazy and possessed by an evil spirit? Then what made you worship him?' 'I don't know,' Haladhari told him frankly, 'when he came in from the Kali Temple, he simply overwhelmed me. I could see nothing but God in him. Whenever I'm with him in the temple, he affects me like that. I don't understand it at all.'

Despite these moments of enlightenment, Haladhari continued to get 'mixed up', as Ramakrishna put it. He had seen God present within his cousin, not once but many times. And yet, when he found Ramakrishna eating some of the food which had been left over by the temple beggars, he saw nothing but a young brahmin who was breaking his caste-rules and defiling himself. 'What are you doing?' he cried in horror. 'You've touched the food of the impure! You've lost caste! What brahmin will ever marry any of your daughters now?'

This last ridiculous question was too much for Ramakrishna's patience. 'You hypocrite!' he exclaimed. 'You keep quoting from the Scriptures that the world is nothing but illusion and God is the only reality. Do you think I'm going to preach that everything's unreal, and then start begetting children? So that's all your knowledge of the Scriptures is good for!'

Meanwhile, the news of Ramakrishna's supposed insanity had reached his mother Chandra and his surviving elder brother Rameswar, in Kamarpukur. Naturally, they were both dismayed. They sent letters to Ramakrishna, begging him to visit them for a while. Like all mothers, Chandra believed in the healing power of the home environment.

So Ramakrishna returned to Kamarpukur, towards the end of 1858. His mother and brother found him greatly changed. He seemed restless and scarcely aware of his surroundings. He suffered from burning sensations in his body, probably caused by his frequent experiences of samadhi. He kept crying out for 'Mother' – and this must have been especially distressing to Chandra, for she knew that she could not comfort him; she was not the Mother he desired.

Just as the Rani and Mathur had sent for a doctor, so now Chandra sent for a local exorcist to cure her son. Ramakrishna used to tell the story with characteristic humour: 'One day, an exorcist came. He burned a lampwick which had been sanctified by special prayers, and then made me smell it. He said, "If you're possessed by a ghost, this will make it run away." But nothing happened; it was a complete failure. So then they got in a medium, who called down a spirit, and they did the worship. The spirit accepted the worship and the offerings, and was pleased. It told the medium, "He hasn't been possessed by a ghost, and he isn't suffering from any disease." Then it spoke to me, through the mouth of the medium, and it said, "Gadai, if you want to be a holy man, why do you chew so many betel nuts? Don't you know that betel nuts make people lustful?" It was true that I liked betel nuts very much, and used to chew them now and then. But, as the spirit told me to, I gave them up.'

After Ramakrishna had been a few months at Kamarpukur, he became much more outwardly normal. Chandra and Rameswar were relieved, and congratulated themselves that he had been 'cured'. Actually, it would appear that Ramakrishna had passed into an even higher state of realization, in which he felt more secure in his awareness of Mother Kali's presence. Therefore his expressions of longing for Her were now less violent.

Ramakrishna did not give up his long hours of meditation, however, and he spent much of his time in Kamarpukur's two cremation-grounds. A cremation-ground is regarded traditionally as the favourite abode of Mother Kali. It is anyhow suitable for meditation, because ordinary people shun it, even during the daytime, and because it is a perpetual reminder of life's impermanence. Ramakrishna used to take food with him, to offer to the spirits of the place and to the jackals which frequented it. If he stayed out very late, Rameswar would come looking for him, calling him by name. When Ramakrishna heard him, he would answer, 'All right, Brother, I'm coming. But don't you come any nearer – the spirits might do you harm.'

At length, Chandra and Rameswar decided that there was only one thing to be done: Ramakrishna must get married. If he could learn to love a good girl, they reasoned, he would stop being so obsessed by his visions. And he would lose his boyish irresponsibility when he had a wife and children to support.

But the problem was not so easily solved. Chandra and Rameswar were poor; and, as the family of the bridegroom, they would have to provide the marriage portion. Worse, this portion would have to be correspondingly larger because it would be for a girl on the verge of puberty. If Ramakrishna had lived the ordinary life of a Hindu boy, he would have been married at a much earlier age, during his teens, to a girl of nine or ten. (Hindu marriages, until modern times, were in fact simply ceremonies of betrothal.) By now, Ramakrishna's wife would have been coming into puberty and already a useful working member of her mother-in-law's household. But under the circumstances, Chandra felt that an older girl must be found, despite the expense, so that the marriage could be consummated with the least possible delay.

Although nothing had been said to Ramakrishna, he soon guessed what Chandra and Rameswar were planning. To their surprise, he accepted the idea without the least objection; indeed, it seemed to amuse and please him. He showed a childlike pleasure when he talked of the marriage ceremony.

But the search for a bride continued in vain. The fathers of the few available girls all demanded marriage portions which Chandra and Rameswar could not afford. At last, when the situation looked desperate, Ramakrishna – as though he had now teased them enough – went into an ecstatic state and announced, 'You must go to the family of Ram Mukhopadhyaya in the village of Jayrambati. Fate has marked my bride with a straw.'

(The expression 'marked with a straw' which Ramakrishna used, refers to a Bengal village custom. If a farmer has a particularly fine fruit or vegetable which he wishes to offer to the Lord when it is fully ripe, he twists a straw around it so that no one shall pluck it and sell it.)

When Chandra and Rameswar accordingly made inquiries in Jayrambati, they found that Ram Mukhopadhyaya did indeed have a daughter, his only girl. Her name was Saradamani, and she was barely five years old. Sarada's age seemed a great disadvantage to Chandra; but she could see no alternative. And, after all, Ramakrishna had chosen his bride in a manner which might well be divinely inspired. So the marriage was arranged, and the marriage portion – of three hundred rupees – was paid. In May 1859, Rameswar accompanied the twenty-three-year-old bridegroom to Jayrambati, and there the ceremony was performed.

Chandra's anxieties were now largely relieved; but she still had cause for embarrassment. In order to economize on the cost of the wedding, she had borrowed the necessary ornaments for the bride from her old friends, the members of the Laha family. (Dharmadas Laha, it will be remembered, was the rich landowner who took upon himself the expense of the anna-prasana ceremony for the child Gadadhar.) And now the ornaments had to be returned. Chandra could not bear to think of depriving Sarada of them, for the child had already become attached to her finery. Ramakrishna himself took the ornaments away while Sarada was sleeping, so deftly that he did not wake her; and they were sent back to the Lahas. When Sarada awoke, she asked for the ornaments. Chandra took her on her lap and consoled her; saying that Ramakrishna would later give her better ones. The child was easily comforted; but Sarada's uncle was offended by this incident and took her back with him to Jayrambati at once. Chandra was humiliated. Ramakrishna merely laughed and said, 'Whatever they say or do, they can't annul the marriage now!'

Ramakrishna remained in Kamarpukur about a year and seven months. Chandra did everything she could to persuade him to stay with her permanently; but he became more and more eager to return to Dakshineswar, especially because he now felt able to resume the worship in the Kali Temple. Also, he knew how poor his mother and brother were, and that his staying with them was a burden. As soon as he was back in Dakshineswar, he could send them money.

Ramakrishna and Sarada saw each other, during this period. Ramakrishna went to Jayrambati, and the two of them returned together for the second time to Kamarpukur; this being one of the conventions of the traditional Hindu marriage. Shortly afterwards, Ramakrishna returned to Calcutta. It was the end of 1860.

Saradananda, in his book, anticipates the reader's question: why, if Ramakrishna had dedicated himself to a monastic life, did he get married?

Certainly, says Saradananda, Ramakrishna was not bullied into marriage by his family. Anyone who has read his story even up to this point will know that nobody ever made Ramakrishna do anything against his will – or, to put it more accurately, against what he believed was the will of the Divine Mother. It is obvious that he married willingly, since it was he who chose the bride.

After dismissing some other possible reasons, Saradananda concludes that Ramakrishna married in order to show the world an ideal. The Hindu practice of marriage had become degraded at that time. The wife was a mere servant of her husband's domestic convenience and his lust. But Ramakrishna educated his wife in many ways and watched over her like a father. He did not even treat her as an equal; he worshipped her, as an embodiment of the Mother. If Ramakrishna had never married, his lay disciples might have said to themselves, 'It's very easy for him to talk about continence; he has never known the temptations of sex.' But Ramakrishna, as we shall see, preserved unbroken continence, while living with his wife in the closest intimacy at a time when she was a beautiful young woman.

It is not that Ramakrishna held up the ideal of a sexless marriage for all to follow; he was not proposing to put an end to the human race. 'Whatever I do,' he used to say, 'is done for all of you. If I do all the sixteen parts' – referring to the sixteen annas which make up the whole rupee – 'you may possibly do one.'

8

The Coming of the Bhairavi

As soon as he was back at Dakshineswar, Ramakrishna resumed the performance of worship in the Kali Temple; but he did not continue it for long. After a few days, his awareness of the Mother's presence overwhelmed him once more, and he was unable to attend to any external duties. His earlier symptoms returned; the blood flushed his chest, his body burned, he could not sleep. But now, as he said himself, he could regard these symptoms more objectively, and they did not seriously alarm him.

They alarmed Mathur, just as much as before. Again a doctor was consulted; new but equally ineffective medicines were prescribed. One day, however, when Mathur took Ramakrishna to the doctor's house in Calcutta, a colleague happened to be present. He too examined Ramakrishna and declared: 'It seems to me that the patient's condition is due to some kind of spiritual excitement – medicine won't cure him.' Ramakrishna used to say in after-years that this doctor was the first member of the medical profession to understand his condition. But the doctor's opinion was disregarded by his colleague and by Mathur.

When the news reached Kamarpukur that Ramakrishna had seemingly suffered a mental relapse, Chandra was in despair. Since all her planning and her financial sacrifices appeared to have been in vain, she decided that she must now risk the sacrifice of her own life. She must practise the fast called *prayopavesana*, in which the devotee throws himself down before the deity in the shrine and remains there until his prayer is granted or he dies of starvation. Chandra attempted to practise prayopavesana first at a Shiva shrine at Kamarpukur. But a vision directed her to approach Shiva in another temple, in the neighbouring village of Mukundapur; so there she recommenced her fast. After two

days, Shiva appeared to her in a dream and said, 'Don't be afraid –
your son is not mad; he is in this state because he is so powerfully
possessed by God.' Chandra was largely reassured. She stopped fasting
and returned home, where she devoted herself to the worship of
Rama, the family deity, praying to him that her son might find mental
peace.

Recalling this period, Ramakrishna used to say: 'No sooner had I
passed through one spiritual crisis than another took its place. It was
like being in the midst of a whirlwind – even my sacred thread was
blown away, I could seldom keep hold of my dhoti. Sometimes I'd
open my mouth, and it would be as if my jaws reached from heaven
to the underworld. "Mother!" I'd cry desperately. I felt I had to pull
her in, as a fisherman pulls in fish with his dragnet. A prostitute walking
the street would appear to me to be Sita, going to meet her victorious
husband. An English boy standing cross-legged against a tree reminded
me of the boy Krishna, and I lost consciousness. Sometimes I would
share my food with a dog. My hair became matted. Birds would perch
on my head and peck at the grains of rice which had lodged there
during the worship. Snakes would crawl over my motionless body.

'An ordinary man couldn't have borne a quarter of that tremendous
fervour; it would have burnt him up. I had no sleep at all for six long
years. My eyes lost the power of winking. I stood in front of a mirror
and tried to close my eyelids with my finger – and I couldn't! I got
frightened and said to Mother: "Mother, is this what happens to those
who call on you? I surrender myself to you, and you give me this
terrible disease!" I used to shed tears – but then, suddenly, I'd be filled
with ecstasy. I saw that my body didn't matter – it was of no importance, a mere trifle. Mother appeared to me and comforted me and freed
me from my fear.'

One day, Ramakrishna went into one of the Shiva temples and
began to recite the hymn in praise of Shiva which is known as the
Mahimna-stotra:

> *With the blue mountain for her ink,*
> *With a branch of the heaven-tree for her pen,*
> *With all earth for her writing-leaf,*
> *Let the goddess Sarada describe your greatness —*
> *She could not – though she wrote forever.*

Having reached the end of this stanza, Ramakrishna was overcome
with emotion. The tears poured down his cheeks and fell upon his
clothing. 'Oh great Lord God,' he kept exclaiming, 'how can I express
your glory?' The temple-servants gathered around him, laughing and
joking: 'He's even crazier than usual, today. Another minute, and he'll
be riding on Shiva's shoulders!' Then Mathur appeared on the scene.
One of the bystanders respectfully suggested to him that Ramakrishna
had better be removed before he misbehaved himself in some manner;
he was standing dangerously close to the linga. 'Touch him —' said
Mathur, with an exaggerated ferocity which was characteristic of him,
'if you don't value your head!' Ramakrishna, needless to say, was left
undisturbed. After a little while, he regained outward consciousness.
Seeing Mathur and the others standing around him he seemed afraid,
and asked guiltily, 'Did I do anything wrong?' 'Oh, no,' said Mathur,
'you were just reciting a hymn. I came here to see that no one interrupted you.'

Mathur's faith in Ramakrishna was finally rewarded by a vision.
One day, Ramakrishna was pacing up and down outside his room, on
the veranda which faced the music-tower. Mathur was sitting alone in
the house known as the Kuthi. Through the window, he could see
Ramakrishna, who was in profound meditation and quite unconscious
of being observed.

All at once, Mathur came running from his house, threw himself down before Ramakrishna, clasped both of his feet and began to
weep.

Ramakrishna was startled out of his meditation. Mathur's action
amazed and embarrassed him. Despite the fact that the Rani and
Mathur treated him with such reverence and often asked his advice on
spiritual matters, Ramakrishna still felt some of the respect which a
country boy would normally feel for an immensely wealthy and
powerful man who was also his patron and protector. 'What are you
doing?' he exclaimed to Mathur. 'You're a gentleman and the Rani's
son-in-law! What will people say if they see you acting like this?
Calm yourself – please – get up!' But Mathur could not stop weeping
for some time. At last, controlling himself, he explained: 'Father, I
was watching you as you walked up and down, just now – I saw it
distinctly: as you walked towards me, you were no longer yourself;
you were the Holy Mother Kali from the temple! And then, as you

86

turned to walk in the other direction, you immediately became Lord Shiva! At first I couldn't believe my eyes. I rubbed them, and looked again, and saw the same thing. As often as I looked, it happened.'

When telling this story, Ramakrishna would comment: 'I wasn't conscious at the time that anything was happening to me. I knew nothing about it. But I couldn't make Mathur understand. I was afraid someone would get to know of it and tell the Rani. Whatever would she have thought? She might perhaps have said I'd put a spell on Mathur!'

That winter, the Rani fell gravely ill with dysentery and fever. When she realized that her end was approaching, she became anxious to settle the endowment of the Dakshineswar Temple property so that the worship there might be guaranteed to continue. The deed of endowment had never been formally executed, and to do this the Rani had to get the signatures of her two surviving daughters, waiving their claims to the property. The younger daughter signed; the elder, Padmamani, refused. This refusal caused the Rani much sadness during her last days. Even a vision of the Mother Kali, which the Rani had upon her deathbed, could not altogether comfort her. Seeing that lamps had been lighted around her, she asked for them to be taken away, saying that they were useless – being dimmed by the brightness of the Mother's approach. Suddenly, 'Mother – you have come!' she exclaimed. There was a pause. Then she asked plaintively: 'Padma hasn't signed – what's going to happen, Mother?' These were the Rani's last words, and they seem to epitomize the life of this great devotee, who was nevertheless seldom free from the cares of wealth and worldly affairs. Indeed, the poor Rani's fears were quite justified, for the Dakshineswar property has frequently been the subject of litigation amongst the members of her family, from that time down to the present day.

After the Rani's death, which took place on February 20, 1861, Mathur became the sole executor of her estate. But this increase in his already great wealth and influence did not make him more worldly-minded. Since his vision of Ramakrishna in the aspects of Kali and Shiva, Mathur's faith had been strengthened; and thenceforth he devoted his life to serving Ramakrishna in every way he could.

'Everything is yours,' he used to tell Ramakrishna, 'I am only your steward.' Indeed, he would have gladly made over a fortune to Ramakrishna, if he had been allowed to do so; but, at the mere mention of such an idea, Ramakrishna scolded him severely. So he had to content himself by spending money in other ways which might please Ramakrishna. He loaded visiting pandits with gifts. He fed the poor lavishly. He bought gold ornaments for the Kali image in the temple. When Ramakrishna wanted to attend a religious festival, Mathur made all arrangements for him to do so; furthermore, he disguised himself and followed with a bodyguard, lest Ramakrishna should come to harm in the crowd. Mathur could not be grateful enough that he possessed 'Father's' affection and had daily access to him; he was well aware of his extraordinary privilege. Speaking about Ramakrishna, Mathur often used the beautiful phrase, 'He belongs to the country where there is no night.'

Mathur had a family priest named Chandra Haldar. This man became jealous of Ramakrishna's influence on Mathur and of the favours he was receiving from him. Haldar had been planning for a long time to get Mathur under his own control and enjoy his generosity. Being low-minded and cunning himself, he interpreted Ramakrishna's simplicity as a cunning pose and took it for granted that he, too, was out to squeeze as much out of Mathur as he could.

One evening, just before dusk, Ramakrishna was lying in a state of ecstatic semi-consciousness in Mathur's house at Janbazar in Calcutta. There was no one else in the room. Haldar saw his opportunity. He began to shake Ramakrishna, demanding, 'What did you do to make him obey you like this? Don't pretend! I know you understand me all right! How did you hypnotize him?' He kept repeating these questions, but Ramakrishna did not answer— for, in his ecstatic state, he had lost the power of speech. Haldar became more and more angry. 'So you won't tell me, you scoundrel?' he cried, and he kicked Ramakrishna hard before leaving him, in disgust.

Ramakrishna said nothing of this at the time to Mathur, knowing that Haldar's punishment would have been drastic. But later on, when Haldar had been dismissed for some other offence, Ramakrishna told Mathur what had passed between them. 'If I had known that,' said Mathur, 'I should have killed him.' And he probably meant it.

.   .   .   .   .

Not long after the death of the Rani, an event occurred which marked the beginning of a new phase of Ramakrishna's sadhana.

In those days, there were flower gardens on the riverbank below the Shiva temples. Although Ramakrishna no longer performed the worship in the Kali Temple, he was accustomed to collect the flowers which had to be used in the ritual. One morning, as he was doing this, a boat came up to the stairs of the ghat. In it sat a woman who wore the ochre robes of a Bhairavi – a female member of a community devoted to the worship of Shakti. The woman was in her late thirties; she was still graceful, erect and beautiful. She wore her hair hanging loosely about her shoulders. Under her arm, she carried several books; these, and a couple of wearing-cloths, were all her worldly possessions, for she was a wandering nun.

As soon as Ramakrishna saw the Bhairavi, he became excited, as though her coming were a long-expected event. He hurried back to his room and called Hriday to him. He described the Bhairavi, and said, 'Go to her and ask her to come to me.' 'But why should she come to you?' Hriday asked doubtfully. 'She doesn't know you.' 'You ask her in my name,' said Ramakrishna, 'she will come.' Hriday was surprised at his uncle's assurance.

He was even more surprised when he spoke to the Bhairavi, who by this time had disembarked and climbed the stairs to the portico of the ghat; for she accepted Ramakrishna's invitation as a matter of course and followed Hriday without any further questions. When she saw Ramakrishna, the Bhairavi's eyes filled with tears of delight: 'Ah, my child!' she exclaimed, 'here you are at last! I knew you lived somewhere along the banks of the Ganges – but that was all; and I've been searching for so long!'

'But how could you know about me, Mother?' Ramakrishna asked.

'Through the grace of the Divine Mother, I came to know that I was to meet three of you. Two I met already, in East Bengal. And today I've found you!'

The Bhairavi spoke little about herself, at that or at any future time. There was an atmosphere of mystery about her, which was heightened by her mature beauty and her air of distinction. We know only that her name was Yogeshwari and that she came of a brahmin family from the district of Jessore in Bengal. (She is sometimes referred to by

biographers as the Bhairavi Brahmani or simply as the Brahmani.)
We do not know if she was ever married; or under what circumstances she decided to renounce the life of the world and become a
wanderer.

As for the two to whom she referred – the two others whom she
was told by the Mother in a vision to seek out – their names were
Chandra and Girija. The Bhairavi had met them in the district of
Barisal, and it seems that she spent some time in giving them spiritual
guidance. Much later, the Brahmani brought Chandra and Girija to
Dakshineswar to meet Ramakrishna. Both of them were spiritual
aspirants of a high order, and both of them were suffering from the
same obstacle to ultimate enlightenment; they had developed psychic
powers of which they were foolishly vain.

Ramakrishna used to say of psychic powers, 'Shun them, like filthy
excrement. Sometimes they come of themselves when you practise
sadhana. But if you take any notice of them, you'll stick fast. You won't
be able to reach God.' Chandra had developed powers of clairvoyance
and clair-audience; he could tell what was happening in far-distant
places. But this did not prevent him from becoming entangled in a love
affair with a rich man's daughter, which ended in his humiliation. As
for Girija, he could project a beam of light from his back – a not particularly useful accomplishment. Ramakrishna liked to make fun of
such tricks by telling the following stories:

'A man had two sons. The elder left home while he was still young,
and became a monk. Meanwhile, the younger got his education and
became learned and virtuous. Then he married and settled down to
fulfil his duties as a householder. After twelve years, the monk came to
visit his brother, who was beside himself with joy. When they had
eaten together, the younger brother asked the elder, "Brother, you
have given up our worldly pleasures and wandered around as a monk,
all these years. Please tell me – what have you gained by it?" The elder
brother said, "You want to see what I've gained? Come with me!" So
he took his brother to the bank of a neighbouring river, and he said
"Watch!", and then he crossed the river, walking on the water, to the
other bank; and he called back, "Did you see that?" But the younger
brother just paid half a penny to the ferryman, crossed the river by
boat, went up to his brother and said, "Didn't you see *me* cross the
river by paying half a penny? Is that all you gained by twelve years of

austerities?'' Hearing his brother's words, the elder understood his mistake. And he now set his mind to realize God.'

'There was once a yogi who had this power: whatever he said, happened. If he said to somebody "die", that person died immediately; if he said "live", he came back to life at once. One day on a journey, the yogi met a holy man. This holy man spent his life simply repeating the name of God and meditating upon Him; he had been doing this for many years. So the vain and arrogant yogi said condescendingly to the holy man, "Well, tell me – you've been repeating the name of God all this time – what have you got from it?" The holy man answered humbly, "What should I get? I don't want to get anything. I only want to realize Him – and that's only possible through His grace. So what can I do but call upon His name and hope He will have mercy on me?" "All that effort for nothing!" said the yogi, "You ought to try to *get* something!" The holy man was silent. But after a while he asked, "And you, sir, what have you got?" "Watch this," said the yogi. And he turned to an elephant which was tied to a tree close by, and said, "Elephant, die!" The elephant dropped down dead at once. The yogi told the holy man "now watch again", and he said to the dead elephant, "Elephant, live!" And the elephant came to life at once, shook the dust off its body and stood up under the tree as before. "Well," said the yogi triumphantly, "now you've seen for yourself!" All this while, the holy man had been silent; but now he said, "I've seen an elephant die and come to life again. But what have you gained by having this power? Has it freed you from the wheel of death and rebirth? Will it save you from sickness and old age? Can it help you to realize God?" The yogi was speechless. His understanding was awakened.'

As for Chandra and Girija, their understanding was awakened, also. After they had stayed for some time at Dakshineswar and been exposed to Ramakrishna's presence, their psychic powers left them. They lost their vanity and worldly desires and began once more to progress along the path towards enlightenment.

On that first morning of the Bhairavi's visit, Ramakrishna sat down beside her in his room and began to describe, in the most intimate detail, his spiritual experiences, his physical symptoms, and the behaviour which had caused so much scandal and concern to those around him. Already, he seemed to trust her judgement implicitly. 'Mother,' he asked, 'what are these things that keep happening to me?

Am I mad, really?' And the Bhairavi reassured him: 'How can ordinary people understand your condition? I tell you – these same things happened to the Holy Radha and to Sri Chaitanya. It's all written down here, in these books I have with me. I'll read them to you —'

Hriday, watching them, was amazed to see his uncle and this stranger talking together with all the intimacy and affection of blood relatives who are reunited after a long separation.

Later that day, the Bhairavi took rice and flour from the temple stores and cooked food in the Panchavati. This she offered to a stone image of Sri Rama which she carried about with her, hanging around her neck. Having made the offering, she began to meditate, and went into samadhi.

Soon after this, as if drawn by a subconscious attraction, Ramakrishna himself entered the Panchavati in an ecstatic state. Without being aware of his action, he took the food-offering from before the image of Rama, and ate some of it. Presently, both he and the Bhairavi returned to consciousness of their surroundings. Seeing what he had done, Ramakrishna was afraid that she would regard it as sacrilege. 'Why do I do these things?' he exclaimed. 'Why do I lose control of myself like this?' But the Bhairavi told him, 'You did well. It is the One who is within you who acts in this way – that is what I saw in my meditation. And now I know that I need not perform ritual worship any more. My worship has borne fruit at last.' So saying, she reverently took as her prasad the food Ramakrishna had left over. And later she consigned her image of Rama to the waters of the Ganges. She felt that it had served its purpose, since she had now had a glimpse of the living deity within the body and mind of Ramakrishna.

In this manner, a close relationship grew up between Ramakrishna and the Bhairavi. During the next few days, they were inseparable, talking eagerly together from morning till night. After a week, however, Ramakrishna began to feel that it would be better if the Bhairavi did not continue actually to sleep within the temple compound, lest people might gossip about them. (It is to be noted that Ramakrishna was utterly indifferent to public opinion when it concerned only himself, but quite sensitive to it when there was a possibility that it might misjudge others.) He hinted at his anxieties to the Bhairavi, who agreed with him. It was arranged, therefore, that she should move to the village of Dakshineswar, which was about two miles upriver. Here she settled down in a room at the bathing-ghat. The villagers soon came to regard her with the reverence due to a holy woman and provided her with food and other necessities. She continued to visit Ramakrishna every day. She now began to establish between them the relationship of Mother and Child – seeing herself as Yashoda, the foster mother of Krishna, and him as the Baby Gopala. Thus, she could be, at one and the same time, his devotee and his mentor.

Mention has already been made of the burning sensation which Ramakrishna used to feel, all over his body. At that time, it became acute. The pain would begin at sunrise and grow until, by midday, it was almost unbearable. To ease it, Ramakrishna was obliged to immerse his body in the Ganges with a wet towel on his head, for two or three hours at a stretch. Not wanting to stay longer in the water, for fear of a chill, he would go into the Kuthi, shut all the doors and windows and roll on the marble floor, after first wetting it to make it cooler.

None of the doctors who attended Ramakrishna had been able to cure him of this malady. But the Bhairavi, consulting her books, found that it had also been suffered by Radha and Chaitanya. The Scriptures prescribed a remedy, which sounded so simple that great faith was required to take it seriously. The sufferer had only to put on a garland of fragrant flowers and anoint his body with sandal-paste. Ramakrishna did this, and was cured in three days. But the sceptics at Dakshineswar maintained that this was sheer coincidence, and that he had really been cured by the after-effects of an oil the doctor had given him.

At this time, also, Ramakrishna had one of the attacks of abnormal hunger which came upon him on several occasions during his life. To quote his own words: 'I couldn't get my fill, however much I ate. As soon as I'd eaten, I felt hungry again. I felt equally hungry when I'd taken food and when I hadn't. It was the same, day and night. . . . But the Bhairavi said, "Don't be afraid, my child. The Scriptures say that those who seek to know God may pass through such states; I'll cure you of it." So she asked Mathur to store in a room a large quantity of food of all kinds. Then she told me to stay in that room day and night, and eat whatever I liked, whenever I liked. I did so – only walking around to help myself to different things that took my fancy. After three days, the hunger stopped.'

·　　·　　·　　·

As the Bhairavi continued to observe Ramakrishna and listen to his spiritual experiences, she became convinced that she was in the presence of something greater, even, than sainthood. She came to the staggering conclusion that Ramakrishna was other than mortal; that he was actually an incarnation of God upon earth.

It is important at this point to make clear once more just what a Hindu means by the term avatar, divine incarnation; for it is something quite precise and no mere vague expression of reverence. As I have already explained in Chapter 5, it is part of the Hindu belief that Vishnu – the Sustainer of the world and second member of the Hindu Trinity – actually manifests himself from time to time in human form. Now, it may be asked, what is the difference between an avatar and a man who realizes union with the Atman in the highest form of samadhi? The man who realizes the Godhead within himself does so as the climax of many human births. His karma from past lives, growing ever better and better, has impelled him through countless births, deaths and re-births to this moment of realization; it is, as it were, the apex of a huge karmic pyramid. The Hindu will therefore entirely agree with Oscar Wilde's epigram that 'every saint has a past and every sinner has a future'. But a saint is still a human being and an avatar is not; he is other than a saint. An avatar has no 'past' in this sense, for he has no karma. He is not driven by his karma to be born; he takes human birth as an act of pure grace, for the good of humanity. Though he voluntarily enters the world of time and space, he remains eternal; he is not bound by time. He is not subject to Maya; he is the master of Maya.

We have already seen two of the avatar's peculiar powers demonstrated by Ramakrishna himself. One is his ability to remain for long periods in the state of samadhi, which would quickly destroy the physical body of an ordinary human being. The other is his power of transmitting spiritual enlightenment to another person simply by touching him – as in the case of Haladhari. This power was exercised by Ramakrishna on many different occasions throughout his life.

The Bhairavi did not keep her conclusion about Ramakrishna's true nature to herself. She spoke of it to everyone at Dakshineswar, and it is not difficult to imagine the incredulity with which it was at first received. This half-crazy young priest, who was regarded as a laughing-stock even by many who felt an affection for him, was now declared to be Incarnate God! Even Mathur was not sure what to believe. He was convinced that Ramakrishna was no ordinary man. But an avatar –!

At first, Mathur had been inclined to mistrust the Bhairavi. Could such a beautiful woman really be as pure as she seemed? One day, when she was coming out of the Kali Temple, he asked her mockingly, 'Well, Bhairavi – where is your Bhairava?' Bhairava is the masculine form of Bhairavi, and Mathur's insinuation was that the Bhairavi must have a lover somewhere in the neighbourhood. But the holy woman was not in the least put out. She looked calmly at Mathur and then pointed with her finger at the image of Shiva, lying prostrate beneath the dancing feet of Kali, within the shrine. 'But that Bhairava doesn't move,' said Mathur, still sticking to his joke. 'Why should I have become a Bhairavi,' said the holy woman with majestic simplicity, 'if I cannot move the immovable?' Her manner finally abashed Mathur, and he had the grace to feel ashamed of himself.

The Bhairavi not only maintained her conclusion that Ramakrishna was an avatar; she was determined to get it confirmed. She was ready to defend it, she said, in formal debate with any pandits Mathur cared to invite. The prospect of such a debate seemed to amuse and please Ramakrishna himself and, largely for this reason, Mathur agreed to arrange it. From Mathur's sceptical point of view, the debate could anyhow do no harm. No doubt the pandits would refute the Bhairavi, and that, thought Mathur, would be good for Ramakrishna. As long as he believed this notion of the Bhairavi's that he was an avatar, he was apt to become more and more irresponsible – since God can do anything He pleases.

The two chief guests invited to the debate were Vaishnav Charan and Gauri. Vaishnav Charan was famous both as a holy man and as a great scholar. He was the generally acknowledged leader of the sect of the Vaishnavas. Many came to him for spiritual guidance. Vaishnav Charan had met Ramakrishna about three years previously at a religious festival and formed a high opinion of him. But they had never seen each other since. Gauri was also famous, as a scholar of Tantra and a man of remarkable psychic powers.

Vaishnav Charan arrived at Dakshineswar some days in advance of Gauri, so a preliminary meeting was held without him. The Bhairavi stated her case, with many quotations from the Scriptures. Then she challenged Vaishnav Charan: 'If you disagree with me, please explain your reasons.' As Saradananda puts it, she was like a proud mother coming to the defence of her child. Ramakrishna, meanwhile, sat in the midst of the assembly, smiling and apparently unconcerned; occasionally eating a few grains of aniseed from a small bag and listening to the conversation as though it were about somebody else. From time to time, however, he would pluck Vaishnav Charan's sleeve and explain some aspect of his spiritual experience which he thought was being misunderstood.

Some say that Vaishnav Charan recognized Ramakrishna's true nature from the first moment, by virtue of his own spiritual insight. But, in any case, he also approved all of the Bhairavi's arguments from the Scriptures. The Scriptures teach, for instance, that there are nineteen kinds of spiritual mood, and that these can only be found combined in an avatar, since the body of an ordinary man, however saintly, could not sustain them and live. Ramakrishna had been shown by the Bhairavi to have combined these moods – therefore, said Vaishnav Charan, he was in agreement with her: Ramakrishna was an avatar. This quite unexpected verdict from such a great authority as Vaishnav Charan caused a sensation. But Ramakrishna took it very calmly. Turning to Mathur, he said, 'So he really thinks that! Well – anyway, I'm glad it's not a disease!'

Now the question remained: would Gauri agree with Vaishnav Charan or not?

It has been said above that Gauri had remarkable psychic powers. There is a ceremony known as the *homa* fire, in which the devotee offers up all his actions to God and is symbolically purified by the flame. Normally, of course, the homa fire is lighted on the ground. But Gauri used to stretch out his left arm and pile wood upon it; then with his right hand he would light the wood and pour the necessary offerings into the fire. Considering that the wood weighed about eighty pounds, that the heat of the fire had to be endured on the bare arm, that the homa ceremony takes three-quarters of an hour at the very least, and that the devotee must maintain his meditation throughout it, this feat can only be described as miraculous. But we have Ramakrishna's word that he actually saw Gauri perform it.

Gauri had another power which caused an absurd scene, on the day he arrived at Dakshineswar and met Ramakrishna. It was Gauri's custom, on coming to take part in a religious debate, to insure his victory by reciting the refrain of a hymn to the Divine Mother, together with certain syllables of warlike challenge, *he, re, re*; all this he uttered in a voice of superhuman power which Ramakrishna described as being like 'the rumbling of a cloud'. At the same time, he would slap his left arm with the palm of his right hand, menacingly, as Indian wrestlers do when they are about to engage their opponent. The effect seems to have been both intimidating and hypnotic. Gauri's adversaries usually lost all will to disagree with him; and he had won the dispute before he even sat down to begin it.

Ramakrishna knew nothing about this power of Gauri's. But when Gauri began, as usual, to thunder the menacing words, something prompted him to do likewise – and he found himself suddenly endowed with a voice even more tremendous! Gauri, amazed to find himself thus challenged, roared louder. Ramakrishna again out-roared him. The noise the two of them made sounded like a whole band of robbers charging to the attack; and the gatekeepers of the Kali Temple, hearing it, armed themselves with sticks and rushed to the spot. When they saw who it was that was making the commotion, they went away again, laughing. It is said that Gauri lost his superhuman voice for ever after. He was humiliated and angry at first, but soon he and Ramakrishna became friends.

The full debate with all the pandits present was to be held in the theatre-hall next to the Kali Temple. Since Vaishnav Charan, who was staying in Calcutta, had not yet arrived, Ramakrishna walked over to it with Gauri. But, before entering, he went into the temple and prostrated before the shrine of Kali. As Ramakrishna came out of the temple again, walking unsteadily in an ecstatic state, he met Vaishnav Charan, who prostrated before him and touched his feet. As so often with Ramakrishna, this act of accepting someone's prostration caused him to go into samadhi; the Atman revealing itself at the moment of worship. Ramakrishna sat on Vaishnav Charan's shoulders, communicating ecstasy to him by his touch. Vaishnav Charan immediately extemporized a hymn in praise of Ramakrishna. When Ramakrishna came out of samadhi, they all went slowly over to the theatre-hall – moved and shaken by the experience – and sat down.

And now Gauri spoke: 'Since Ramakrishna has bestowed this grace upon Pandit Vaishnav Charan, I shall not debate with him today. If I did, I should certainly be defeated. But that is not my real reason for refusing. The truth is, we have nothing to argue about; because I agree with him. His opinion of Ramakrishna is the same as my own.' And so the matter was settled.

Later, as if to test Gauri, Ramakrishna said to him, 'Listen – Vaishnav Charan calls this –' (Ramakrishna often spoke of himself as 'this', 'this place' or 'here', to avoid personal emphasis) 'an incarnation of God. Can it really be so? Please tell me what you think.'

Gauri replied, with characteristic energy: 'Does Vaishnav Charan call you an incarnation of God? I consider that an understatement! I believe that you are He by a fraction of Whose power the avatars come forth and accomplish their mission.'

Ramakrishna smiled and said, 'Ah – so you outbid him? Well – I know nothing about it.'

'That is as it should be,' Gauri told him, 'for the Scriptures have a saying: "Thou dost not know Thyself."'

Lest the reader should suspect that Vaishnav Charan and Gauri had given their verdict on Ramakrishna out of mere courtesy, or a desire to curry favour, or from any other unworthy motive, it must be added that both of them proved their sincerity by their subsequent behaviour. Vaishnav Charan continued to visit Ramakrishna at frequent intervals, and to proclaim him as an avatar to all and sundry, without fear that his own reputation as a pandit might suffer from ridicule in consequence. As for Gauri, he could not tear himself away from Dakshineswar. The more time he spent with Ramakrishna, the less taste he felt for scholarship and theology; he began to long to realize directly, in his own consciousness, the truths he had read about in the Scriptures. Gauri's wife and children kept sending letters to him, urging him to return to them. At length, it seemed probable that they would come to Dakshineswar and force him to do so. So Gauri had to make a quick decision; and he determined to renounce the world. Taking his leave of Ramakrishna, he said, 'I shall not return until I have realized God.' Ramakrishna blessed him on his search, and he set forth. Later, many people tried to find out what had become of Gauri and where he was. But none of them ever heard of him again.

5. Nahabat, Dakshineswar

6. Narendra: Swami Vivekananda

7. Rakhal: Swami Brahmananda

8. Group picture of disciples. Left to right, Swamis Trigunatitananda, Shivananda, Vivekananda, Turiyananda, Brahmananda, and below, Saradananda.
9. Swami Turiyananda and Swami Premananda

10. Swami Saradananda

11. Swami Shivananda

9

Some Visitors to Dakshineswar

Until the Bhairavi came to Ramakrishna, he had been living alone, as it were, in the midst of a crowd. Many people at the Dakshineswar Temple had learned to love him, but not one of them was sufficiently advanced in his own spiritual life to be able to understand the nature of Ramakrishna's struggle. The very object of sadhana – to obtain direct, unitive knowledge of God – can be, for most of us, only a hopeful phrase. It is not merely that we could never dare to attempt – we can scarcely even imagine – the supreme act of ego-surrender, surrender of all individual identity, through which God is known. And if we *can* dimly imagine it for a few moments at a time, it must appear to us as appalling as death itself; a leap into the utter void.

In the first phase of Ramakrishna's sadhana, he is finding out everything for himself, empirically. He has no books to instruct him. He has no one to tell him if his insights are unique or if they have been shared by others. He experiences everything as though for the first time in human history. This loneliness and the fear that went with it – that these insights were, perhaps, nothing but self-deception – was the hardest trial that Ramakrishna had to undergo.

But now he had a teacher. The Bhairavi, herself a firm believer in the Scriptures and their authority, had undertaken to show him that what he was rediscovering for himself had already been known, throughout history, to the world's great seers. The object of her training was to reassure Ramakrishna by demonstrating to him how he could obtain the vision of God by following out exactly the instructions of the Scriptures.

We may accept Ramakrishna as an avatar and nevertheless understand that he had to assume a certain measure of ignorance in order to set us the example of a great spiritual aspirant, wrestling with genuine doubts, fears and temptations. We are familiar with the similar spiritual struggles of the avatar Jesus of Nazareth in the wilderness. But perhaps some of us will ask how, if the Bhairavi really regarded Ramakrishna as an incarnation of God, can she have presumed to teach him?

The answer is, no doubt, that the Bhairavi was *not* at all times aware that Ramakrishna was an avatar. Continuous awareness of such a fact would probably be unbearable for any human being. We find the same lapses into forgetfulness in the companions of other avatars; for example, in Arjuna, the companion of Sri Krishna. It is related, in Chapter 11 of the Bhagavad-Gita, that Arjuna, wishing for an absolute confirmation of his faith, asked Krishna to reveal himself in his transcendent aspect, as Lord of the Universe. And Krishna does so. Arjuna sees Him in all the terror and glory of His power; as creator, sustainer and dissolver; father of mankind's many deities, architect of the universe, final flame into which every mortal must plunge and be annihilated. As the Gita puts it: 'Suppose a thousand suns should rise together in the sky: such is the splendour of the Shape of Infinite God.' Arjuna is overwhelmed and terrified by the vision. In his great fear, he bows down before Krishna, and says in a trembling voice: 'To think that I used to address you quite casually, as "Krishna" and "Comrade"! It was my affection that made me presume, and my ignorance of your greatness. How often I must have shown you disrespect – joking with you familiarly, as we walked, or feasted, or lay at rest together! Did I offend you? Forgive me, Eternal Lord! I bow down, I lie at your feet, I beg for pardon. Forgive me – as friend forgives friend, father forgives his son, man forgives his dear lover!'

Krishna reassures Arjuna, and returns to his ordinary form. And Arjuna cries, in his relief, 'Oh, Krishna, now that I see you in your pleasant human shape, I am myself again!' In other words, Arjuna's painful awareness has been dulled; already, he is beginning to forget Krishna's god-nature and accept his outward human appearance. We may infer a similar attitude on the part of Peter, James and John, after their vision of the transfiguration of Jesus.

Is it desirable to be continuously aware that one is in the presence of an avatar? Theoretically, yes; practically, no. But it is still most important to distinguish between the two sorts of ignorance which may blind one to an avatar's real nature. Many people meet a Jesus or a Ramakrishna and regard him as entirely ordinary, because of the ignorant grossness of their own perceptions. Or, if they do catch some hint of a mystery, they are unwilling, because of their anxiety, apathy or mental instability, to probe into it further. (In the strange interview between Jesus and Pontius Pilate, for example, we sense the momentary stirring of the Roman's interest and then his lapse into cynical indifference and anxiety for his own political future.) But there are also those, like Arjuna, who are temporarily blind to the avatar's real nature because of their love for him. Such a one, also, was the Bhairavi. As Saradananda says, love prevents you from being conscious of power in the object of your love; love makes you feel protective towards the loved one, and so your awe of him disappears. The Bhairavi, as we have seen, regarded Ramakrishna as her son. Because of this attitude, she was able to teach him. Under her guidance, he began to practise the disciplines of the Tantra.

Ramakrishna said later that at first he had had some doubts about taking up the tantrik form of sadhana, and that, before doing so, he had consulted the Divine Mother Kali and received her permission. Once he had made his mind up, however, his eagerness was extraordinary and his progress was correspondingly rapid.

The object of the tantrik disciplines is to see, behind all phenomena, the presence of God. There are two main obstacles to this insight – attraction and aversion. Even the pursuit of knowledge on the material plane cannot be carried on without overcoming these obstacles, at least to some extent. The doctor must overcome sexual desire for the bodies of his patients, aversion from a cancer-sore or a rotting limb, and fear of catching the infectious diseases he has to treat. Attraction and aversion both fasten our attention to the outward appearance and prevent us from seeing beyond it. If, however, we can get even a glimpse of God's presence beyond the appearance, then our attraction or aversion will disappear. Therefore, each of the tantrik disciplines is designed to help the aspirant overcome some particular form of attraction or aversion and realize the indwelling Godhead.

Some extraordinary psychic powers came to Ramakrishna at this time. He had not desired them, so they could do him no spiritual harm; and, after a while, they left him again. For example, it is said that he became able to understand the cries and calls of animals and birds, and to hear the great sound known as the *anahata dhvani*, which is a harmony of all the sounds in the universe, too profound to be heard by ordinary ears. Another result of his tantrik austerities, vouched for by many witnesses, was that he acquired for a time a strange and celestial kind of beauty. 'It was as if a golden light were shining forth from my body,' he recalled later. 'People used to stare at me in wonder, so I always kept my body covered with a thick wrapper. Alas, I thought to myself, they're all charmed by this outward beauty of mine, but not one of them wants to see Him who dwells within! And I prayed to the Divine Mother earnestly, "Mother, here's your outward beauty – please take it back and give me inner beauty instead!" And at last that light went in, and the body became pale again.'

Words which normally carry sensual associations suggested higher meanings to Ramakrishna in his exalted state. For example, the word *yoni*, which normally means the female sex-organ, would mean for him the divine source of all creation. Indeed, the most unconditionally obscene words were now as sacred to him as the vocabulary of the Scriptures, since all were composed of the letters of the same alphabet.

Ramakrishna continued his tantrik sadhana from 1861 throughout 1862, and completed it in 1863. By doing so, he had proved that even the severest of these disciplines could be practised in complete chastity and without the companionship of a shakti – a female sex-partner. But it should not be supposed that his self-control was an easy matter just because he was spiritually so far advanced. At a later period, Ramakrishna frankly admitted that he was once attacked by lust. Such attacks, he said, are caused by pride. If you say to yourself, 'I have conquered lust', you will at once begin to feel lust. Ramakrishna's advice was therefore to accept the existence of lust without shame or guilt. We should pray for it to pass, and meanwhile disregard it like any other disturbing behaviour of the body. If we worry about our lustful thoughts, we give them added power over us. It is better to take it for granted that they exist and will visit us from time to time. No one can be absolutely free from them in this life, without the grace of God.

At this time, Ramakrishna felt a strong desire to experience Mother Kali's power to delude — her play of seeming creation, preservation and destruction, which is called Maya. He was granted a vision which would have terrified a lesser devotee. One day, he saw a woman of exquisite beauty come up from the Ganges and approach the Panchavati. As she came nearer, she seemed to become more and more obviously pregnant. Her womb swelled visibly, until she gave birth to a beautiful child, which she suckled with the greatest tenderness. But suddenly her expression changed. She became ferocious and terrible. She began to eat the child, grinding its flesh and bones between her teeth and swallowing them. Then she turned and went back into the Ganges.

It was at this time, also, that Ramakrishna was made aware by a vision that many disciples would come to him in his later life and receive enlightenment from him. He told this to Hriday and to Mathur. Mathur replied, with a generous absence of jealousy, 'That's very good, Father. We shall all be happy together in your company.'

As a matter of fact, more than fifteen years were still to pass, and Mathur himself was to die, before the boys who were destined to become the first monks of the Ramakrishna Order began to arrive at Dakshineswar. But, in the meanwhile, the temple compound was constantly being visited by all kinds of monks and devotees. Here are a few whom Ramakrishna particularly remembered and would speak of in after-years.

'Once there came a sadhu here,' Ramakrishna would recall, 'who had a beautiful glow on his face. He just sat and smiled. Twice a day, once in the morning and once in the evening, he'd come out of his room and look around. He'd look at the trees, the bushes, the sky and the Ganges, and he'd raise his arms and dance, beside himself with joy. Or he'd roll on the ground laughing and exclaiming, "Bravo! What fun! How wonderful it is, this Maya! What an illusion God has conjured up!" That was his way of doing worship.

'Another time, there came another holy man. He was drunk with divine knowledge. He looked like a ghoul – almost naked, with dust all over his body and head, and long hair and nails. On the upper part of his body there was a tattered wrapper; it looked as if he'd got it off some corpse on a cremation-ground. He stood in front of the Kali Temple and fixed his eyes on the image and recited a hymn. He did it with such power that it seemed to me the whole temple shook and Mother looked pleased and smiled. Then he went to the place where the beggars were sitting, and got his prasad. But the beggars wouldn't let him sit near them, because of his disgusting appearance.

They drove him away. Then I saw him sitting with a dog, in a dirty corner where they'd thrown away the leaf-plates. He had put one arm around the dog, and the two of them were sharing the remains of food on one of the leaves. The dog didn't bark or try to get away, although he was a stranger. As I watched him, I felt afraid. I was afraid I might get to be like him, and have to live like that, roaming around as he did. After I'd seen him, I said to Hriday: "That's not ordinary madness; he is mad with the highest God-consciousness." When Hriday heard this, he ran out to get a look at the holy man and found him already leaving the temple gardens. Hriday followed him a long way and kept asking, "Holy sir, please teach me how I can realize God." At first, he didn't answer. But at last, when Hriday wouldn't leave him alone and kept following him, he pointed to the sewer-water around a drain in the road and said, "When that water and the water of the Ganges seem equally pure to you, then you'll realize God." Hriday said, "Sir, please make me your disciple and take me with you." But he didn't reply. He turned and went on. When he'd gone a great distance, he looked back and saw Hriday still following him. He made an angry face and picked up a brick, threatening to throw it at Hriday. When Hriday fled, he dropped the brick, left the road and disappeared. After that, he was nowhere to be found.

'This sadhu was a true knower of Brahman. Such sadhus go around in that state so people shan't bother them. They live in the world like boys, ghouls or madmen. Such a sadhu encourages boys to follow him and play around him, because he wants to learn to be like them. He wants to learn a boy's lack of attachment to things. Haven't you seen how happy a boy feels when his mother dresses him in a new dhoti? If you say, "Please give it to me", he'll answer, "I won't – Mother gave it to me"; and he'll tighten his grip on the cloth with all his might, looking at you in fear lest you should snatch it away from him. You'd think it was the treasure of his heart. But the next minute, if he sees a toy in your hand that's worth perhaps no more than half a penny, he'll most likely say, "Give me that, and I'll give you my cloth." And, maybe, a little later, he'll drop the toy and run to pick a flower. He's as little attached to the toy as he was to the cloth. And that's the way it is with the knowers of Brahman.

'There was another sadhu who had nothing with him but a waterpot and a book. The book was his treasure. Every day, he did worship before it, with offerings of flowers; and then he would read in it with intense concentration. After I got to know him, I begged him to let me have a look at it. But, when I opened the book, I found that on every page, only the same two words were written, *Om Rama*, in bold red letters. And the sadhu said to me, "What's the use of reading a whole library of books? God is the origin of all the Scriptures, and there is no difference between Him and His Name. Everything that you can read in the Scriptures is contained in His Name. I am satisfied with that.'"

It is worth pausing, at this point, to explain the significance of the word *Om* and to discuss at greater length the idea expressed to Rama-krishna by the sadhu with the book.

In the Vedas, which are the earliest Hindu Scriptures, we find it stated that: 'In the beginning was the Lord of creatures, and second to him was the Word. . . . The Word was truly the supreme Brahman (*Prajapatir vai idam agre asit, tasya vag dvitiya asit. . . . Vag vai Paramam Brahma*).' This statement is, of course, echoed by the first verse of the Gospel of St John: 'In the beginning was the Word, and the Word was with God, and the Word was God.' The belief that the Word *is* what it expresses has been entertained by mankind since the dawn of history. Certainly, words and ideas are inseparable. You cannot have the idea of God without the word which expresses God.

Of the many names for God, Om is almost certainly the oldest that has survived. It is still being used by millions of worshippers, in India and elsewhere, today. It is also the most general of the words used to express the god-idea. It refers to no one deity and implies no particular attribute. It can therefore be used by any and every sect.

How did the word Om come to be chosen for this great purpose? The Hindu explanation is simple. *God* is the most comprehensive of mankind's ideas; it must therefore be represented by the most comprehensive word that can be found. And what is the most comprehensive word? The one which combines all possible positions of the throat, mouth and tongue in word-utterance. You start with *Ah*, the root-sound, which is made in the throat without touching any part of the tongue or palate. Then comes *Ou*, which rolls through the mouth from throat to lips. Finally, *Mm* is produced by the closed lips. And so you have *Ah-ou-mm*, which is approximately how *Om* should be pronounced.

In India, when a disciple comes to his guru for initiation, he is given what is called a *mantra*. The mantra consists of one or more holy names – Om is usually included – which the disciple is to repeat to himself and meditate upon for the rest of his life. It is regarded as very private and very sacred. You must never tell your mantra to any other human being. And the act of the guru in giving the mantra to the disciple has, in itself, a double significance. The mantra is, as it were, the essence of the teacher's instruction to this particular pupil; having given this, he need give no more. Also, the mantra is a link in a spiritual chain; for, even as you are being initiated by your guru, so he himself was once initiated by *his* guru, and so on backward, perhaps, to some great holy man of the past, whose power is thus being transmitted to you.

The act of repeating your mantra is called 'making japa'. It is usually done with a rosary – thus relating thought to physical action (which is one of the great benefits of all ritual) and providing an outlet for the nervous energy of the body, which will otherwise accumulate and distract the mind. Most spiritual aspirants are instructed to make a certain fixed amount of japa every day. The rosary serves to measure this – one bead to each repetition of the mantra – so that you are not worried by having to keep count. The use of the rosary with some form of repetitive prayer is, of course, common to Hindus, Buddhists, Catholics and certain other Christian churches.

In these days of commercial and political propaganda which makes use of subliminal indoctrination and the hypnotic repetition of slogans, it should no longer be necessary to prove, even to an atheist, that japa is effective. If a television advertisement can so permeate the consciousness of a community that the little children sing it in the streets – if some demonstrable lie about a neighbouring country can, by being repeated often enough, drive a whole nation war-mad – then how dare anyone claim that the repetition of the name and idea of God will have no effect upon the individual who practises it? We are creatures of reverie, not of reason. We spend a very small proportion of our time thinking logical, consecutive thoughts. It is within the reverie that our passions and prejudices – often so terrible in their consequences – build themselves up, almost unnoticed, out of slogans, newspaper headlines, chance-heard words of fear and greed and hate, which have slipped into our consciousness through our unguarded eyes and ears.

Our reverie expresses what we are, at any given moment. The mantra, by introducing God into the reverie, must produce profound subliminal changes. These may not be apparent for some time, but, sooner or later, they will inevitably appear – first in the prevailing mood and disposition of the individual; then in a gradual change of character.

It was probably in the year 1864 that the wandering monk Jatadhari came to Dakshineswar.

This Jatadhari was a devotee of Sri Rama, and he carried with him an image of Rama when he was a boy and was known by the child-name of Ramlala. (In northwest India, to this day, boys are affectionately called lalas and the girls lalis in honour of the child Rama.) Jatadhari worshipped this image – which was made of eight different metals – with the utmost reverence. And Ramakrishna, with his spiritual insight, saw at once that Jatadhari was no common devotee; that he had had, indeed, a vision of the Boy Rama and that he now regarded the image and the Boy as identical. His devotion fascinated Ramakrishna, who would sit with Jatadhari, gazing at the image of Ramlala and sharing his vision, for whole days at a time.

This is how Ramakrishna used to tell the rest of the story:

'As the days passed, I felt that Ramlala loved me more and more. As long as I remained with Jatadhari, Ramlala would be happy and play around. But, as soon as I left and went to my own room, he followed me there at once. He wouldn't remain with the sadhu, although I ordered him not to follow me. I thought at first that this must be a fancy of mine. For how could that boy – whom the sadhu had worshipped for so long with such devotion – love me more than him? But I actually *saw* Ramlala – now dancing on ahead of me, now following me. Sometimes he insisted on being taken on my lap. But then, when I picked him up, he wouldn't want to stay there. He would run everywhere, plucking flowers in places where there were thorns, or splashing and swimming in the Ganges. I told him over and over again: "Don't do that, my child. You'll get blisters on the soles of your feet if you run in the sun; you'll catch cold and fever if you stay in the water so long." But he never listened to my words, however much I warned him. He would go right on with his pranks. Sometimes he'd look at me so sweetly with his beautiful big eyes. Or else he'd pout and make faces at me. Then I'd get really angry and scold him.

"Just you wait, you rascal," I'd tell him, "I'll give you a big thrashing today. I'll pound your bones into powder." I'd pull him out of the water or the sun, and try to tempt him with some gift to stay and play inside the room. If he went on being naughty, I'd give him a couple of slaps. But, when I'd done that, he'd pout and look at me with tears in his eyes, and I'd feel such pain. I'd take him on my lap and comfort him.

'One day, when I was going to take my bath in the Ganges, he insisted on coming with me. What could I do? I had to let him. But then he wouldn't come out of the water. I begged him to, but he wouldn't listen. At last I got angry and I ducked him, saying, "All right – stay in as long as you like!" While I was doing this, I actually saw him gasping and struggling for breath! "What am I doing?" I thought to myself in dismay. I pulled him out of the water and took him in my arms.

'Another day, he kept asking me for something to eat, and all I had to give him was some coarse parched rice which wasn't properly husked. As he was eating it, the husks scratched his delicate, tender tongue. I felt so sorry! I took him on my lap and exclaimed, "Your mother used to feed you with the greatest care on cream or butter; and I've been so thoughtless, giving you this coarse food!"'

When he retold this incident many years later, to his young disciples, Ramakrishna would burst into tears. Saradananda, who was one of them, records this, and adds that he and the other boys used to exchange glances of utter bewilderment as they listened to this story of Ramlala. It sounded to them, even in their youthful faith, absurd and impossible – and yet it was Ramakrishna who told it, and they could not think him capable of the smallest falsehood. The mature Saradananda, in his book, makes good-humoured allowances for the incredulity of the reader: 'Accept as much of this story as you can digest,' he writes. 'Omit the head and the tail, if you like.' But, at the same time, Saradananda makes it clear that he himself has come to believe every word of it.

'Some days,' Ramakrishna used to continue, 'Jatadhari would cook food to offer to Ramlala, but he couldn't find him. Then he would come running in distress to my room, and there would be Ramlala playing on the floor. Jatadhari's feelings were terribly hurt. He'd say scoldingly, "I took so much trouble to cook food for you. I look all over the place – and here you are, all the time! You don't care about me. You forget everything. And that's how you always are. You do just as you please. You have no kindness or affection. You left your father and went into the forest. Your poor father died of a broken heart, and you never even came back to show yourself to him on his deathbed!"' (This was a reference to Rama's behaviour towards his father, King Dasaratha, as it is recorded in the Ramayana. But it must be added that Jatadhari was not being quite fair in his interpretation of it; for Rama only went into the forest because his father had unjustly banished him.) 'Talking like this, Jatadhari used to drag Ramlala back to his own room and feed him. Yet the sadhu stayed on at Dakshineswar, because he didn't want to leave me and go away. Also, he couldn't bear to leave Ramlala behind, having loved him for so long.

'But then, one day, Jatadhari came to me with tears of joy and said, "Ramlala has revealed himself to me in a way I have never known before, and have always longed for; and now the desire of my life is fulfilled. Ramlala says he won't leave here; he doesn't want to leave you. But I'm not sad about that, any more. He lives happily with you and enjoys himself, and I am full of bliss when I see it. I have learned now to be happy simply in his happiness. So I can leave him with you and go away, knowing that he is with you." Then Jatadhari gave me the image of Ramlala and said Good-bye. And Ramlala has been here ever since.'

The image itself was kept in the Radhakanta Temple for many years. At the beginning of this century it was stolen, and has never been recovered.

In 1863, shortly after Ramakrishna had completed his tantrik sadhana, his mother Chandra came from Kamarpukur to Dakshineswar and settled down to spend the rest of her life there. She lived in one of the two Nahabats (music-towers); the one which stands to the north of the temple courtyard, in full view of the porch of Ramakrishna's room. So Chandra had only a few steps to walk when she wished to visit her son.

I have already described how Mathur tried vainly to get Ramakrishna to accept money from him. Now, in his eagerness to serve Ramakrishna even indirectly, he attached himself to Chandra, spending hours in her company and always addressing her as 'Grandmother'. Chandra was delighted and Mathur soon became her favourite. One day, he begged her to tell him what he might give her; she could have anything her heart desired. Chandra tried hard to make a suggestion, if only to please him, but she could think of nothing. She opened her trunk and showed him that she already had several wearing-cloths. 'And since you look after me so well,' she added, 'that I have my food and drink and a place to sleep – what more could I possibly need?' But Mathur continued to press her; and she, after racking her brains over this difficult problem, was at last able to gratify him by asking for an anna's worth of tobacco leaves. For the old lady permitted herself one small luxury; she sometimes chewed a tobacco-leaf which had been toasted with spices.

10

Tota Puri

———

I have already referred to the various attitudes which a devotee may assume in his worship of the Personal God (Ishwara). Now I must describe them in more detail, with special reference to Ramakrishna's own experience.

The simplest devotional attitude is known as *shanta*. This is the basic dualistic approach of worshipper to Worshipped, of the creature to his Creator. It does not resemble any human relationship.

Next comes *dasya*, which resembles the relationship of a child to his parent or a servant to his master. This was the attitude of Hanuman towards Rama (see Chapter 7). Hanuman regarded himself as Rama's servant; and Ramakrishna, as we have seen, identified himself for a while with Hanuman in his worship of Rama. Also, throughout most of his life, Ramakrishna regarded himself as the child of Mother Kali.

Next comes *sakhya*, in which the devotee thinks of himself as God's friend. He may identify himself, for example, with one of the shepherd-boys of Vrindavan, who were the friends of Krishna's boyhood. Ramakrishna used to say of his disciple Rakhal (who later became Swami Brahmananda) that he had been one of these shepherd-boys in a previous existence.

Next comes *vatsalya*, in which the devotee thinks of himself as God's parent. We have seen how Ramakrishna and Jatadhari assumed the attitude of parents towards Ramlala, the child Rama.

Last, there is the *madhura bhava* (the sweet mood) in which the devotee approaches God as a lover. For Hindus, the chief exemplar of this mood is Radha, the beloved of Krishna. It is said that the madhura bhava also contains within itself the other devotional attitudes. For a loving woman may be, on occasion, the servant of her lover, or his adviser and friend, or his motherly comforter and protector.

When Ramakrishna practised the madhura bhava, identifying himself with Radha in her devotion to Krishna, he actually wore women's dress and imitated feminine behaviour. The Western reader is likely to be shocked at this, finding such extremes both unnatural and unnecessary. Why, he will ask, should a male devotee try to think of himself as a woman (or vice versa)? Why, if you want to practise the madhura bhava, shouldn't you fix your devotion on a divine personality of the opposite sex?

Ramakrishna's interpretation of the madhura bhava can, however, be justified quite logically, according to the principles of Vedanta Philosophy. Vedanta teaches that there is no reality other than Brahman; name and form, as we know them in the physical world, are merely illusions which must be overcome before Brahman can be known. The world of physical forms is nothing but an expression of ideas which have taken root in the subtle mind. The idea of ego – which is the root of all illusion: *I am I, and therefore other than Brahman* – is physically expressed as *I have a body.* And from the body-idea spring two further ideas, mutually exclusive: either *I am a man* or *I am a woman.*

If the devotee can make himself seriously believe for a while that he belongs to the opposite sex, he will be well on his way to overcoming the illusion of sex-distinction altogether; for he will then know that the distinction is not absolute, as he had supposed. So the assumption of a female character by a male devotee to this end can certainly be justified; and any means which further this end – such as putting on women's dress – may certainly be necessary.

All of the devotional attitudes I have described above are sadhanas of the Vaishnava sect. The cult of Vishnu implies the cult of all his incarnations, Rama among them. Rama, as we know, was the chosen deity of Ramakrishna's family. It was, therefore, natural that Ramakrishna should have been attracted to the practice of these Vaishnavite sadhanas, after he had completed the sadhanas of the Tantra. Also, the Bhairavi, being a Vaishnava devotee, no doubt encouraged him in this undertaking.

Since childhood, Ramakrishna had shown from time to time an inclination to assume the character of a woman. Sometimes he did this simply in fun – as when he played the trick on Durgadas Pyne (see Chapter 3). Sometimes, he was expressing a devotional mood – as when he used to imagine, as a boy, that he was a child-widow devoted to the service of Krishna. There was a sweetness and gentleness in his temperament which many observers described as feminine. But the truth is that this extraordinary being had such a wide range of characteristics that he seemed to be a quite different person at different times; now predominantly masculine, now feminine. It was perhaps because the sense of sex-identity was so faint in him that he was easily able to assume the character of either sex.

As long as Ramakrishna was living the part of the Bhairavi's son, he remained predominantly masculine. Indeed, he found the attitude of the madhura bhava positively distasteful; once, when the Bhairavi started to sing a hymn to Krishna the Divine Lover, he asked her to stop. We have seen already how he always suited the outer dress to the spiritual mood, wearing the robe prescribed for each individual sadhana – red, white, or ochre as the case might be. It was therefore only logical that he should wear women's dress when approaching Krishna in the mood of a female lover. Not to have done so would have been to yield to fear of the opinion of others – which he had strongly condemned. Perfect sincerity, he had said, again and again, must express itself both outwardly and inwardly. As he put it, 'there can be no cheating in the abode of the mind'.

So, as he entered upon the sadhana of the madhura bhava, Ramakrishna asked Mathur for women's clothes. Mathur provided him with a beautiful and valuable sari from Benares, a gauze scarf, a skirt and a bodice. To complete the transformation, Mathur brought him also a wig and a set of gold ornaments. Needless to say, Ramakrishna's latest sadhana caused a whole series of scandalous rumours. But he and Mathur ignored them.

As soon as he was dressed as a woman, Ramakrishna's mind became more and more deeply merged in the mood of womanhood. Those who saw him were amazed at the physical transformation which seemed to take place; walk, speech, gestures, even the smallest actions were perfectly in character. Sometimes, Ramakrishna would go to the house in the Janbazar district which had belonged to Rani Rasmani and live there with the women of the family, as a woman. They found it almost impossible to remember that he was not really one of themselves. When the husband of any of Mathur's daughters visited the house, Ramakrishna would adorn the girl with ornaments and dress her hair with his own hands. Behaving as though he were an older and more experienced woman friend, he would show her how she should deport herself and speak in a suitably wifely fashion. Then, taking her by the hand, he would lead her in to meet her husband, make her sit down beside him, and leave them alone together.

Hriday used to describe how, 'when he remained thus surrounded by ladies it was hard for even his closest relatives to recognize him at once. One day at that time Mathur took me into the women's quarters and said, "Can you tell me which of them is your uncle?" And although I'd been living with him so long and serving him daily, I couldn't, at first. Uncle used to collect flowers every morning, with a basket. We'd watch him and we'd notice that he always stepped out left foot first, as a woman does.'

Ramakrishna was wearing women's dress during the festival of Durga that year (1864), and was taking part in the worship with the women of Mathur's family. After the first day's worship was over, he passed into a mood of spiritual absorption, losing all consciousness of his surroundings. Soon came the time for the *aratrika*; the evening service which is accompanied by the waving of lights, ringing of bells, sounding of gongs and chanting. Mathur's wife, Jagadamba Dasi, found herself in a dilemma. She was eager to go into the hall where the aratrika was being held, but she did not dare leave Ramakrishna alone; quite recently, when in a similar state, he had fallen into a pan of live charcoal and burned himself badly. So, acting on a sudden inspiration, she began decking out Ramakrishna with her most valuable ornaments and saying to him meanwhile, 'It's time to wave the lights – won't you come and fan Mother Durga?' It had often been noticed that Ramakrishna could be recalled from deep meditation to outer consciousness if some name or mantra related to the subject of his meditation was repeated in his ear several times; and Jagadamba Dasi was aware of this. After a moment, Ramakrishna responded to the name of Mother Durga, roused himself and went with Jagadamba Dasi into the hall. The aratrika began at once, and Ramakrishna started to fan the image of Durga with a *chamara*, a kind of ritual fan which is made from the tail of a yak. Presently, Mathur himself entered the hall. According to custom, the male devotees stood on one side, the female on the other. Mathur immediately noticed a strange lady standing beside his wife and fanning the image. He admired the nobility of her bearing and the richness of her dress and ornaments, and supposed her to be some wealthy matron who had been invited to take part in the ceremony. When the aratrika was over, Mathur went in to see his wife and asked who the strange lady was. Jagadamba Dasi smiled and said, 'You didn't know? That was Father.' 'No one can know Father,' said Mathur, when he had got over his surprise, 'if he doesn't allow himself to be known.'

In his character of a woman, Ramakrishna set himself to adore Krishna, feeling the wild longing for him which the gopis felt. The acute pain of separation from Krishna made him weep, reject all food, and even sweat blood from the pores of his body. He prayed to Radha, as an intermediary, and had a vision of her. Soon after, he saw Krishna himself, on several occasions. Once, while Ramakrishna was listening to a reading of the Bhagavata (which narrates, among other matters, the life of Krishna) he saw a beam of light, 'like a cord' come forth from Krishna's feet and touch the sacred book. Then the light touched Ramakrishna's heart and remained visible to him for some time as a triangle connecting Krishna, the Bhagavata and himself. 'From this I learned,' Ramakrishna used to say, 'that Bhagavata, Bhakta [the devotee] and Bhagavan [the Blessed Lord] are one and the same.'

We have just seen Ramakrishna engaged in what might be called the most extreme form of dualistic worship. Only a few months later, we find him going to the opposite extreme of non-dualism; the total identification with Brahman which is taught by non-dualistic Vedanta (so-called because it is the philosophy expounded in the early Scriptures called Vedas).

This new phase of Ramakrishna's sadhana began towards the end of 1865, with the arrival at Dakshineswar of the monk named Tota Puri. A *Puri* is a member of the Puri Sect, one of the ten monastic orders established by Shankara. It would not, however, have been suitable for Ramakrishna to use this name; for Tota Puri, as we shall see, became his guru and it was considered unorthodox for the disciple to address his guru by his real name. Ramakrishna actually called Tota Puri *Nangta*, meaning The Naked One; for Tota Puri spent most of his life absolutely naked.

To go naked was the practice of the Naga, a sub-sect within the Puri, to which Tota Puri belonged. Already as a child he had entered a Naga monastery at Ludhiana in the Punjab, which contained seven hundred monks. This was a most austere community, in which the monks were trained to a gradual renunciation of all attachment; eating and drinking sparely, cultivating endurance and hardening their bodies by discarding clothes. In due course, Tota was elected head of the monastery but he did not remain there much longer; he preferred to become a wanderer. He had been one for many years.

The Naga sect regards fire as very sacred; its monks will light a fire wherever they happen to be, and meditate and sleep beside it, never entering any house. Such a fire is called a *dhuni*. Tota's only possessions were a pair of fire tongs – which he also used, on occasion, to defend himself against wild animals – and a waterpot. He was now in early middle age, a tall powerful man. He covered his body with a cloth only when he was meditating or preparing for sleep.

When Tota came to Dakshineswar, he was on his way back towards the Punjab after visiting the shrines of Narmada and Puri. He was intending to stay three days; this being his limit in any one place. For he believed in the old saying that a wandering monk must live like a running stream, if he is to avoid attachment. There is no reason to suppose that he had any anticipation of the meeting that was to change his plans so completely. Unlike the Bhairavi, he had had no prophetic vision of Ramakrishna; probably he had never even heard of him.

Arriving at the temple compound, Tota went first to the portico of the ghat. Ramakrishna happened to be sitting there unobtrusively in a corner, amidst many other people, dressed like everybody else in a single piece of cloth. Yet Tota noticed him at once. With his keen spiritual sight, he saw that this young man was someone altogether out of the ordinary.

Tota had an imperious manner. He said to Ramakrishna with abrupt directness, 'You look as if you were fit to practise the Vedantic sadhana – do you want to?'

Ramakrishna does not seem to have been surprised at the suddenness of this proposal. 'I don't know,' he answered, 'it all depends on Mother. If she says Yes, then I'll do it.'

'All right,' said Tota, 'go and ask your Mother. But come straight back to me – I shan't be here long.'

Perhaps Tota thought at first that Ramakrishna intended to ask his human mother; but now he saw him go into the Kali Temple. A little later, Ramakrishna reappeared, semi-conscious and beaming with joy.

He told Tota that his Mother had told him, 'Go and learn – it was to teach you that the monk came here.'

Tota seems to have been charmed by the innocence of Ramakrishna's faith; but he must have regarded it also with a certain contemptuous amusement. From Tota's point of view, Bengal was given over to corrupt religious practices, such as the tantrik sadhanas and dualistic worship in general. As a non-dualist, he was convinced that the only worthwhile goal of spiritual life was to attain direct union with the impersonal Brahman in the highest form of samadhi, the nirvikalpa – as he himself had attained it many times. His proud, independent temperament inclined towards spiritual discrimination rather than devotion. Logically, he was forced to postulate the existence of Ishwara, as the Distributor of the fruits of action (karma); but he did not feel the need to approach Him with love or submission. As for the other divine personalities – gods, goddesses and avatars – Tota took little interest in them. He cared nothing for Mother Kali and her Maya, her divine play. To him, the image in the Kali Temple was just an image; and Ramakrishna was a victim of gross superstition who had somehow mysteriously managed to make great spiritual progress in spite of it. However, Tota did not risk hurting the young man's feelings by saying any of this; for he felt sure Ramakrishna would cast aside his superstitions as soon as he began to practise the non-dualistic sadhana.

In order to be qualified to practise this sadhana, Ramakrishna had first to be formally initiated by Tota Puri into monastic life; to take the vow of world-renunciation known as *sannyas* and to accept Tota as his guru. At the time of his initiation, he would have to give up his sacred thread and cut off the lock of hair which marks a member of the brahmin caste. Ramakrishna agreed to these conditions, asking only that the initiation should take place in secret because he did not want his old mother Chandra to know of it. The reader may think it strange that Chandra should object to her son's taking a formal vow of renunciation, when he had, in fact, for years already, renounced everything worldly in his search for God. But it must be remembered that, in the Bengal of those days, a monk was thought of as a wanderer. We have seen how Chandra was afraid, even when her son was a child, that the wandering monks would persuade him to go away with them. Now, if she were to hear of the initiation, she would be afraid that he would go away with Tota. Ramakrishna wanted to spare her this needless anxiety.

So Tota lighted his dhuni fire in the Panchavati and established himself there, to await a propitious hour for the initiation. This took place a few days later, about two hours before dawn, in a hut just east of the grove. (The hut still stands today and is regarded as one of the most sacred spots in the temple compound. On the map of Dakshineswar, it is marked as the Meditation Room.)

This is how Ramakrishna described what followed the initiation:

'After initiating me, the Naked One taught me many sayings expressing the philosophy of non-dualism. He told me to withdraw my mind from all creatures and objects, and plunge it into contemplation of the Atman. But when I sat down to meditate in this way, I found I couldn't make my mind go quite beyond name and form. I couldn't stop it working and make it still. My mind could stop being conscious of creatures and objects – that wasn't difficult; but whenever it did this, the Divine Mother appeared before me in that form I knew so well – that form which is made of pure consciousness. It was her own living form which stopped me from going any farther. Again and again, I listened to the instructions and sat down to meditate; and again and again it happened. I almost despaired. I opened my eyes and told the Naked One, "No – it can't be done. I can't stop my mind from working. I can't make it plunge into the Atman". The Naked One got excited. He scolded me severely. "What do you mean – can't be done?" he cried. "It must be done!" Then he looked around the hut till he found a bit of broken glass. And he stuck the point of it into my forehead, between the eyebrows. It was sharp as a needle! "Fix the mind here," he told me. So I sat down to meditate again, firmly determined. And as soon as Mother's form appeared, I took my knowledge of non-duality as if it was a sword in my hand, and I cut Mother in two pieces with that sword of knowledge. As soon as I'd done that, there was nothing relative left in the mind. It entered the place where there is no second – only the One.'

Ramakrishna had gone into nirvikalpa samadhi for the first time. In nirvikalpa, there is absolutely no distinction between the knower and the known; the Atman is Brahman, and even the faintest trace of individual identity is lost. The lower states of samadhi – into which Ramakrishna had entered many times already – lack this completeness of union. Ramakrishna *knew* that Mother Kali was not other than Brahman; yet, because of his great love for her, he was at first unable to accept this fact completely. To do so seemed as terrible as an act of murder; that is why he speaks of knowledge as a sword. Ramakrishna's love for Kali was the last-remaining trace of dualism in his mind. When he could go beyond that, he could attain union with Brahman.

Tota Puri had reached nirvikalpa samadhi as a non-dualist, by the process of strict discrimination which gradually rejects all the manifestations of name and form – saying constantly 'not this, not this', until Brahman is known as the one underlying reality. Tota, as we have seen, was cold towards any kind of dualistic devotion. He had proved, as many others had proved before him, that devotion is not essential for the attainment of the highest spiritual experience.

Discrimination is for the few, however. Devotion comes more naturally to the great majority of mankind. Ramakrishna, as an exemplar of spiritual practice, had to demonstrate, for all of us, that devotion also can lead to unitive knowledge; and that for most of us it is the easier and safer path, because discrimination demands a most powerful will and strict austerity, and its occupational risk is pride. This, we may assume, is why Ramakrishna practised the dualistic sadhanas which Tota so despised, and showed how they can lead naturally to non-dualism.

Seeing that Ramakrishna had lost outer consciousness, Tota remained for a long while seated beside him. At length, he left the building, locking the door behind him so that Ramakrishna should not be disturbed. He then took his seat in the Panchavati and remained there, waiting for a call to open the door.

But the day went on and passed into night, and another day came and passed. At the end of three days, Tota went back and opened the door. He found Ramakrishna sitting exactly as he had been left; the body showed no sign of life, except that the calm face seemed to shine. Tota was astounded. Is it possible, he said to himself, that this great soul has realized in one day what I could only accomplish after many years of sadhana? Is this truly nirvikalpa samadhi? Again and again he felt the heart, the lungs and the other organs. He then began to chant the mantra *Hari Om* in a resounding voice. At last, Ramakrishna opened his eyes and prostrated himself before his new guru. Tota embraced him with love and reverence. He was so delighted by his pupil that he decided then and there to break his own rule and remain at Dakshineswar indefinitely.

The personalities of Ramakrishna and Tota Puri present a striking and often amusing contrast. Tota had been wrong in supposing that he could change Ramakrishna's beliefs by initiating him into non-dualism. The experience of nirvikalpa samadhi did not lessen his devotion to Kali and Krishna. Since childhood, Ramakrishna had been accustomed to chant Krishna's name as the sun was setting, dancing and clapping his hands as he did so. One evening, when he was with Tota, he began acting in this manner. 'What are you doing?' Tota asked him sarcastically, 'Making *chapatis?*' (The chapati is a thin flat cake of unleavened bread which is made by clapping the dough between the palms.) Ramakrishna laughed, but he reproved Tota for his intolerance, and Tota never made fun of Ramakrishna's devotions again.

Tota used to polish his tongs and his waterpot every day, so that they glittered. And, every day, he spent long hours in meditation. 'Why do *you* need to meditate,' Ramakrishna once asked him, '– you who are a knower of Brahman?' Tota pointed to the waterpot. 'Look how bright it is,' he answered. 'But it will lose its lustre if it isn't polished every day. The mind is like that. It gets dirty if it isn't kept clean by daily meditation.' 'But,' said Ramakrishna, 'suppose the waterpot is made of gold? Then it won't get dirty, even if it isn't polished.'

Ramakrishna liked to tell a story illustrating Tota's fearlessness. Once, in the dead of night, Tota had built up the dhuni fire in the Panchavati and was about to sit down to meditate. There was a deep silence all around, except for the occasional hooting of the owls which sat on the pinnacles of the temples. There was no wind at all; but suddenly the branches of the tree under which Tota was standing began to shake and a tall male figure climbed down out of it. Looking steadfastly at him, the figure advanced to the fire and sat down. Like himself, it was naked. Tota asked the stranger who he was. 'I am an attendant of Lord Shiva,' he replied. 'I dwell in the tree to protect this holy place.' Tota was not in the least afraid. 'Good,' he said, 'you and I are the same – just two manifestations of the same Brahman. Let us meditate together.' But the apparition laughed out loud and vanished. And Tota sat down to meditate as though nothing had happened. Next morning, he described his visitor to Ramakrishna.

'Yes, it's true he lives there,' Ramakrishna answered. 'I've seen him myself, many times. Sometimes he foretells future events. Once he told me that the English were trying to buy the whole temple garden to build a powder magazine on. I was afraid I shouldn't be able to worship Mother here any more. But Mathur started a lawsuit against the English on the Rani's behalf, to stop them buying the land. And then, once again, I saw that spirit sitting under the tree. He made a sign to me that the English would lose the lawsuit; they wouldn't get the land. And that's how it actually turned out.'

On another occasion, Ramakrishna and Tota were sitting before the dhuni fire, engaged in philosophical conversation. Tota had been expounding the non-dualistic viewpoint, that Brahman was the one reality, and that, to the knower of Brahman, the world of appearance (Maya) was a trivial thing. Maya could have no power over him, he said. Ramakrishna disagreed. He knew only too well how powerful Maya could be. As they were talking, a temple servant came by. The servant wanted a light for his pipe and, seeing the fire, he came over and was about to take a piece of hot charcoal. Tota flew into a rage. To him, the servant's act was not only impertinent but sacrilegious, and Tota threatened to hit him with his tongs. The servant ran away and Ramakrishna laughed until he rolled on the ground, crying, 'Oh, for shame! You forgot already!' 'What are you laughing about?' Tota asked indignantly. 'The man was insolent!' Still laughing, Ramakrishna answered, 'Oh yes – he was insolent. But you were forgetting your knowledge of Brahman! Weren't you just telling me that there's nothing but Brahman and that a knower of Brahman can't be deceived by Maya? Yet the next moment, you forget all that and you're ready to beat one of Brahman's manifestations! You see? Maya, which you despise, is stronger than you think. Maya is omnipotent.' Tota became very serious and was silent for some moments. Then he said, 'You're quite right. I forgot Brahman under the influence of anger. Anger is a deadly thing. I shall give it up from this moment.' And it is said that Tota Puri was never seen to be angry again.

Tota's constitution had always been strong. He had had little experience of the miseries of physical life, the aches and pains which distract the mind from contemplation. But now the climate and the water of Bengal began to affect him; and he had a severe attack of blood dysentery. At the first warnings of the disease, he thought he should go away; but he found himself unwilling to leave the company of Ramakrishna, to whom he had become devoted. Several times, he made up his mind to go to Ramakrishna and bid him Good-bye; but, as soon as the two were together, they would become absorbed in talk about God and Tota would forget his purpose. So he grew steadily weaker and weaker, despite the medicines which Ramakrishna obtained for him through Mathur.

Tota had always scorned the body and believed that it should be rejected at once if it interfered with one's awareness of Brahman. One night, as he lay alone in the Panchavati, Tota found that he was in such pain that he could no longer meditate. He was filled with disgust for his body. 'I must get rid of this nuisance,' he said to himself. 'Why do I stay in it and suffer? I'll commit it to the Ganges.'

(I should make it clear, at this point, that Hinduism, like Christianity, condemns suicide. According to Hindu belief, it is a great opportunity and privilege – attainable only after many rebirths into lower forms of life – to obtain birth in a human body. For it is only during a lifetime in a human body that the goal of all life can be reached: unitive knowledge of Brahman. Therefore, to discard your body wilfully is to frustrate your own spiritual development. Such an act may have terrible consequences. It may even cause your rebirth in some lower life-form or condemn you to a long period in some kind of purgatory or limbo.

But, once Brahman *is* known, the body has served its purpose. Therefore, if a knower of Brahman like Tota Puri decides to discard it, his act will not be regarded as suicide in the culpable sense.)

Fixing his mind on Brahman, Tota waded out into the great river. But he did not drown. (Speaking about this episode many years later, Ramakrishna said that Tota must have chanced to walk along a shoal which ran out from the bank, near the bathing-ghat, a little below the surface of the water.) After a while, trees and houses began to be visible through the darkness and he realized that he had crossed almost to the other side. And now, he had a dazzling sense of enlightenment. He understood the power of Maya. 'Mother is indeed omnipotent,' he exclaimed. 'Until she wills, the body is not even able to die!' For the first time, his heart was overcome with love for the Divine Mother. He waded back the way he had come, reached the Panchavati and sat down beside the fire.

In the morning, when Ramakrishna came to visit Tota, he found him transformed. He was smiling with bliss and the sickness had entirely left him. He signed to Ramakrishna to sit down beside him, and said, 'The disease has acted like a friend to me. Ah, how ignorant I have been, all these years!' And, as the horns of the musicians sounded their morning music from the Nahabat, Tota accompanied Ramakrishna for the first time to the Kali Temple and prostrated himself before the image.

Tota felt now that the Divine Mother's double purpose in bringing him to Dakshineswar had been accomplished. A few days later, he said Good-bye to Ramakrishna and started on his homeward journey. His intended three-day visit had stretched itself to eleven months.

He never returned.

After Tota Puri had left Dakshineswar, Ramakrishna decided to remain for at least six months in nirvikalpa samadhi. 'For six months,' he used to say later, 'I was in that state from which ordinary mortals never return. Ordinarily, the body can live for twenty-one days only in that state; then it falls like a dry leaf from a tree. There's no consciousness of time; the coming of day or the passing of night. Just as flies enter the nostrils and mouth of a dead man, so they entered my mouth. But a holy man came here. He had a small stick like a ruler in his hand. He recognized my state as soon as he saw it. Therefore he would bring food from time to time. He struck my body with his stick again and again, trying to bring it back to consciousness. The moment he saw signs that I was getting conscious, he'd thrust some food into my mouth. Some days a little food found its way into the stomach. On other days none did.'

This period of nirvikalpa samadhi came to an end with a vision of the Mother, who told Ramakrishna that henceforward he must remain in the state called *bhavamukha*, because he had a mission to perform for the good of the world and must therefore not withdraw from it into nirvikalpa. Bhavamukha is defined as a state in which one is aware of the outer world and its phenomena, not in the usual way but as waves within the Cosmic Mind. One is aware not of the personal ego but of oneself as the Cosmic Ego which is the source of all creation. These are matters of profound and subtle spiritual experience, quite beyond the grasp of ordinary imagination; so perhaps it is better to oversimplify a little and say that Ramakrishna had, throughout the rest of his life, the faculty of being simultaneously aware of God and the physical universe.

One result of experiencing nirvikalpa samadhi was that Ramakrishna became even more catholic in his views and felt a keen sympathy for any and every sect which sincerely struggled to know God. At this time, a certain Govinda Roy came to Dakshineswar; he was a Hindu of the kshatriya caste by birth, but, as a seeker after truth, he had studied many religions and had finally embraced Islam. It is not known just how far he followed Moslem manners and customs, but he certainly practised the sadhanas which are taught by the Sufis.

It had always been the Rani's policy that Moslems as well as Hindus should be welcome at Dakshineswar, provided that they had renounced the world; and both kinds of devotees were supplied with appropriate food. So Govinda Roy settled down to meditate in the Panchavati. Ramakrishna happened to talk with him and was charmed by his faith and love of God. 'This also is a path to God-realization,' Ramakrishna said to himself. 'The Mother has shown herself to many people through this sadhana also. I must practise it.'

Govinda initiated him at his request. 'And then,' Ramakrishna used to relate, 'I devoutly repeated the name of Allah, wore a cloth like the Arab Moslems, said their prayers five times daily and felt disinclined even to see images of the Hindu gods and goddesses, much less worship them – for the Hindu way of thinking had disappeared altogether from my mind. I spent three days in that mood, and I had the full realization of the sadhana of their faith.' Ramakrishna also said that he had had a vision of a shining impressive personage with a long beard. This figure merged into Ishwara, and Ishwara then merged into Brahman.

Hriday told how, while Ramakrishna was practising the sadhana of Islam, he wanted to eat Moslem food. Mathur begged him not to, because this would include beef. So, as a compromise, a Moslem cook was brought to instruct a Hindu cook how to prepare food in the Moslem manner – more or less. At this time, Ramakrishna never once entered the temple courtyard. He left his own room and slept in the Kuthi.

Saradananda finds great significance in Ramakrishna's practice of Islam. He believes that Ramakrishna wished to demonstrate by it that non-dualistic Vedanta is the only valid link between the many dualistic religions. It is certainly idle to pretend, as some well-intentioned liberals do, that there is very little difference between religions, or races. There is a very big difference – on the surface. Unity can only be found by going deep, to the underlying, all-projecting Brahman.

Ramakrishna had then just recovered from acute dysentery. It was feared this might recur for lack of pure drinking water; the water of the Ganges would become salty during the approaching rainy season. So it was arranged that Ramakrishna should return to Kamarpukur for a few months. He went there sometime in May 1867, with the Bhairavi and Hriday. Chandra did not care to go too; she had resolved never to leave the bank of the Ganges again.

Ramakrishna had not been in Kamarpukur since 1860, and it will be remembered that, on that occasion, everyone had feared for his sanity. Since then, the rumours which had reached Kamarpukur from Dakshineswar had been alarming enough: Ramakrishna had been wearing women's clothes, he had become a Moslem, etc. etc. So his friends and relatives were delighted and relieved to find him very much his normal self. True, he was now surrounded by an aura of such evident spiritual power that they were shy of him at first; but his affectionate warmth quickly reassured them.

And now the ladies of Ramakrishna's family sent to Jayrambati to fetch Sarada Devi. Sarada was now a girl of thirteen. Ramakrishna began to train her in the management of a household and other wifely duties; just as he had trained Mathur's daughters. Sarada was now better able to appreciate her extraordinary husband. She delighted in his company.

Only the Bhairavi disapproved. A most unfortunate though temporary change had come over this remarkable woman. Perhaps it had started when Tota Puri arrived at Dakshineswar. Although the Bhairavi was spiritually so far advanced, she was quite incapable of understanding non-dualism. She had strongly urged Ramakrishna not to be initiated by Tota. 'My child,' she had warned him, 'don't visit him often – don't have much to do with him. His path is dry and austere. You'll lose all your devotion.' This may have been said by the Bhairavi in good faith, but she was certainly prone to jealousy and possessiveness. She could not bear that anyone but herself should instruct Ramakrishna.

And now, at Kamarpukur, she professed to believe that Rama-krishna's continence would be endangered if he spent much time with his beautiful young wife. But Ramakrishna listened to her warnings as little as he had listened when she spoke against Tota Puri. This indiffer-ence only made the Bhairavi more aggressive. To those who were about to ask Ramakrishna's opinion on some spiritual matter, she would say scornfully, 'What could *he* tell you – it was *I* who opened his eyes!' She would scold Ramakrishna's female relatives, assuming the airs of mistress of the house. Ramakrishna remained calm, however, and continued to treat her with reverence. He told Sarada to do like-wise; and the girl showed the Bhairavi the respect due to a mother-in-law.

At length, a furious quarrel arose – too trivial and too complicated to be worth describing in detail – about a matter connected with caste-rules. The Bhairavi turned upon Hriday – of whose long intimacy with Ramakrishna she was probably anyhow jealous. After uttering many threats, she repented, however, and felt ashamed of herself. She made a flower-garland and brought sandal-paste to adorn Rama-krishna, whom she then saluted as a divine incarnation, begging his forgiveness. Ramakrishna forgave her freely. The Bhairavi said Good-bye and went away to Benares, where she lived in a high state of devotion.

12. Swami Trigunatitananda

13. Swami Ramakrishnananda

14. Swami Adbhutananda and Swami Yogananda

15. Girish

16. M.

17. Mathur Nath Biswas

I I

Mathur

In the last chapter, I mentioned the Durga festival of 1864 at which Mathur failed to recognize Ramakrishna while he was dressed as a woman. I must now return to this Durga festival, to give an instance of Mathur's power of devotion. This had been growing enormously ever since his vision of Ramakrishna in the aspects of Kali and Shiva, which is described in Chapter 8.

The Durga festival lasts five days, ending on the evening of the fifth with the immersion of the image which has been used in the worship. Two kinds of image are used in Hindu ritual; permanent and temporary. The permanent image, made of marble or some other durable stone, is placed in a temple, dedicated, and worshipped every day thenceforward. The temporary image, made of clay, is used only for one particular religious festival; then it is consigned to the nearest river, lake or sea.

The temporary image is just as sacred as the permanent image; but only during the period of the festival. Before it can be worshipped, the worshipper must evoke the Divine Presence from his own heart and transfer that Presence to the image. Before the image can be removed from the shrine and immersed, the Divine Presence must be withdrawn from it again, and reinstalled within the worshipper's heart. The reason for this procedure is obvious enough. But devotion is not reasonable. And it may happen that the worshipper suffers great pain in consequence. If he can truly believe that the Presence *has* entered the image, then there is a danger that his devotion may fasten upon the image itself. Image and Presence may become completely identified in his mind. The thought that they must be separated again will then naturally fill him with dismay.

This is what happened to Mathur at the Durga festival. And when the priests came to him, at the end of the last day of worship, to tell him that it was time for the image to be immersed, Mathur was first overwhelmed with grief and then violently agitated. He cried out that the image must not be removed. It must be kept in the shrine and worshipped every day. And he uttered bloodthirsty threats against anyone who should dare to immerse it, against his will.

The priests were disconcerted. Such an extreme of devotion was unintelligible to them; and, just as in the case of Ramakrishna, they explained it to themselves by deciding that Mathur had gone mad. But, mad or not, Mathur was still master of the situation. The worship had been held in his home; and if he chose to forbid the immersion of the image the priests would have to obey him. Ironically enough, it was to Ramakrishna that they appealed for help. They begged him to go to Mathur and dissuade him from his decision.

'What are you afraid of?' Ramakrishna asked Mathur. 'Do you really think Mother will leave you, just because her image is dropped into the Ganges? Can a mother ever leave her child? For three days you've been worshipping her in the shrine. But now she's coming to be much nearer to you, within your own heart.' As Ramakrishna spoke, he rubbed Mathur's chest gently with his hand; and, as always, his touch gave power to his words. Mathur understood that his fears had been meaningless. He was happy again. And the immersion ceremony was performed.

While Ramakrishna was in an ecstatic mood, he would occasionally make some prophecy about the future of one or other of his disciples. Once he told Mathur: 'I shall stay at Dakshineswar as long as you are alive.' Mathur rejoiced to hear this; but then he remembered his wife and their son. 'Jagadamba and Dwarka are so devoted to you,' he said. 'Please don't leave them after I am dead.' 'Very well,' said Ramakrishna, 'I'll stay here as long as they both live.' And, in fact, not only Mathur himself but also Jagadamba and Dwarka were dead by 1881; more than three years before Ramakrishna left Dakshineswar.

When Rani Rasmani died, her estate was divided between Pad-mamani and Jagadamba, her daughters. One day, Jagadamba went to bathe in a pond which belonged to her sister. There she found a fine bed of watercress and, thinking no harm, plucked some to take back with her. Ramakrishna, who happened to be passing, saw her do this.

Greatly concerned, he hurried to Padmamani and reported the 'theft'. She was much amused; thinking it absurd that Ramakrishna should be shocked at the taking of anything so little valuable as watercress. However, she pretended indignation, shook her head and exclaimed, 'That was very wrong of her!' Then Jagadamba herself came by, learned what had happened, and joined in the game; reproaching Ramakrishna for betraying her crime. But, after a few moments, the sisters could no longer control themselves and began to laugh. Ramakrishna could not see that he had done anything funny. 'I don't know your worldly ways,' he told them. 'But, when property has been divided, it is not good to take anything without the owner's knowledge.' And still the sisters laughed, finding him charmingly naïve.

Mention has already been made of the strange alternations in the relationship between Ramakrishna and Mathur. Sometimes, Mathur would treat Ramakrishna as his revered spiritual father, sometimes as an innocent, irresponsible young boy. Mathur himself could behave on occasion like an irresponsible boy, but not always an innocent one. Once he even encouraged his servants to take part in a brutal gang-fight with the servants of a rival landowner. Several men were killed, and Mathur found himself in danger of prosecution. Boylike, he ran to Ramakrishna in blind panic and pleaded for his help. And Ramakrishna scolded him like a stern father, telling him that he would now have to take the consequences of his folly. But as Mathur went on pleading, Ramakrishna finally said, 'Well – it will be as Mother wishes' – greatly to Mathur's relief, because he knew from experience that this was Ramakrishna's way of agreeing to a request. Mathur never was prosecuted, after all. The case against him was dropped.

We have seen various instances of Mathur's generosity in relation to Ramakrishna. This generosity was sometimes severely tested, for Ramakrishna had no sense of money whatsoever. This he demonstrated when he went with Mathur to watch the *yatra*; the folk-plays, usually based on some sacred story, which were performed by companies of travelling players in any courtyard or open place, with the audience sitting all around them. Mathur would give Ramakrishna a hundred rupees at a time, arranged in stacks of ten, so that he could reward the various actors with a stack each. But Ramakrishna would simply push the whole hundred rupees over to the first actor who pleased him by a song or a dance. Mathur would replace the money. Ramakrishna would give it all away again. Then, wishing to reward another actor and finding no money laid out for him, he would take off the cloth he was wearing and give the actor that, even though it left him naked.

Ramakrishna went with Mathur to visit Devendra Nath Tagore. Devendra Nath was the father of the famous Bengali poet, Rabindra Nath Tagore; he was also the leader of one branch of the Brahmo Samaj, a movement which aimed at modernizing and reforming certain Hindu customs and religious beliefs. (See Chapter 13.) Mathur and Devendra Nath had been classmates at the Hindu College in Calcutta, so the visit could be made without formalities, although Devendra Nath was such a prominent public figure.

What interested Ramakrishna was to know how far Devendra Nath had advanced in spirituality; this was the only reason he ever had for wanting to meet important religious leaders. With his usual directness, he asked Devendra Nath to show him his bare chest. Devendra Nath raised his shirt and did so – perhaps with a little pardonable self-satisfaction; for his chest was flushed in the manner which indicates deep and prolonged meditation. 'This world is like a chandelier,' said Devendra Nath, 'in which every living creature is a light. God has created man to proclaim his glory. If there are no lights in the chandelier, all is darkness. One can't see the chandelier, even.' This remark greatly impressed Ramakrishna, because he himself had had a similar vision, while meditating in the Panchavati.

Devendra Nath then urged him to attend the anniversary ceremony of the Brahmo Samaj. 'That depends on the Lord,' Ramakrishna replied. 'You see the condition I'm in? There's no knowing what kind of a state he will put me into at any particular time.' Devendra Nath answered that Ramakrishna must come anyway, whatever state he was in; but added that he must please wear both an upper and a lower garment, for propriety's sake. 'That's impossible,' Ramakrishna exclaimed, 'I can't be dressed like a Mister!' Devendra Nath laughed heartily at this. But it seemed that he was not so amused, after all; for, next day, Mathur got a letter from him cancelling the invitation and explaining that he could not have Ramakrishna coming to the ceremony without proper clothes.

Mathur used to beg Ramakrishna to communicate ecstasy to him by a touch. Ramakrishna tried to dissuade him from this desire, telling him he would do much better to wait and be patient, and that, anyhow, he should keep his life balanced between devotion to God and worldly obligations; that being his dharma. But Mathur persisted, until Ramakrishna said, 'Very well, I'll ask Mother about it; she will do as she thinks best.' A few days later, Mathur went into the lower form of samadhi at his house in Calcutta.

This is how Ramakrishna would describe what happened next. 'He sent for me; and when I went there I found him altogether changed – he wasn't the same man. Whenever he spoke of God, he shed floods of tears; his eyes were red from weeping. And his heart was pounding. When he saw me, he fell down and clasped my feet. "Father," he said, "I admit it – I'm beaten! I've been in this state for the past three days. I can't apply my mind to worldly affairs, however hard I try. Everything is going wrong. Please take back the ecstasy you gave me. I don't want it." "But you begged me for ecstasy," I said. "I know I did. And it is indeed a blissful state – but what's the use of bliss, when all my worldly affairs are going to pieces? This ecstasy of yours, Father, it only suits you. The rest of us don't really want it. Please take it back!" Then I laughed and said, "That's what I told you, all along." "I know you did, Father. But what I didn't understand was that this thing like a spirit would possess me, and that I'd have to take every step and do everything exactly as it told me to, twenty-four hours a day!" So then I just rubbed Mathur's chest with my hand, and he was himself again.'

Mathur and his wife Jagadamba decided to make a pilgrimage to the chief holy places of northwestern India, and they persuaded Ramakrishna to come with them. Saradananda suggests two reasons why Ramakrishna may have agreed to do this. On the level of everyday consciousness, it is necessary for a great spiritual teacher, even an avatar, to learn, by travelling around the country, about the spiritual and physical condition of the people, and about the kind of religious ideas which are common amongst them. And, on the higher, spiritual level, there is another reason why great souls should go on pilgrimages; they visit holy places not to get but to give. They recharge, as it were, each shrine they visit, renewing the spiritual power which masses of worshippers are daily taking from it.

This pilgrimage of Mathur's was carried out on a royal scale, at huge expense. About a hundred and twenty-five people took part in it, including Mathur and Jagadamba, Ramakrishna and Hriday, with other relatives and friends of Mathur and many male and female servants. One second-class and two third-class cars were reserved for them on the railway, and these could be uncoupled at any point along the line at which it was decided to make a stop. The pilgrimage started out from Howrah station on January 27, 1868.

The first stop was made to visit the shrine of Shiva at Deoghar; and several days were spent there. Ramakrishna was overcome with compassion for the poverty of the villagers. He said to Mathur, 'You're a steward of Mother's estate. Give these people one piece of cloth and one good meal each, and some oil for their heads.' (The dry hot climate of India makes it necessary to keep the hair from becoming brittle by moistening it with oil, and it was only the very poorest who had to do without this luxury.) At first, Mathur hesitated. 'Father,' he said doubtfully, 'this pilgrimage is going to cost a great deal. And there are many people here. If I give them what you ask me to, I may find myself short of money later. What do you think I ought to do?' But Ramakrishna refused even to discuss the problem. He was shedding tears over the plight of the villagers. 'You wretch!' he cried. 'I'm not going to that Benares of yours! I'm staying here with these people. They have no one to care for them. I won't leave them.' Mathur yielded; he had cloth brought from Calcutta and did everything else for the villagers that Ramakrishna demanded. And so they went on towards Benares. Not quite without accident, however. At a wayside station near Mogulsarai, Ramakrishna and Hriday alighted from the train, and it left without them. Mathur telegraphed from the next station that they should be sent on by the next train. But, before this could be done, an official of the Railway Company happened to arrive on a tour of inspection and took them on with him in his special train.

As Ramakrishna approached Benares in a boat, crossing the Ganges, he saw in a vision that the city was made of gold; that is to say, he saw that the subtle form of the city had been made golden by the love and faith of its innumerable devotees throughout the ages. Ramakrishna had such a strong sense of the sacredness of Benares that he was even careful not to relieve himself within its limits. Nevertheless, he was disappointed. 'I had expected,' he said later, 'to find everybody in Benares merged in samadhi, contemplating Shiva twenty-four hours a day; and everybody in Vrindavan wild with joy in the company of Krishna. But, when I got to those places, I found it all different.'

Mathur rented two houses, side by side on the Kedarghat in Benares, and lived there in pomp. Whenever he went out, a servant held a silver umbrella over his head. Ramakrishna had his own palanquin, since he was unable to walk far without the danger of losing outward consciousness and falling. Mathur fed brahmin pandits and gave them presents. This caused them to squabble enviously amongst themselves. He also indulged in worldly conversation with other rich landowners. All this pained Ramakrishna; he wished himself back in Dakshineswar.

Still, not all his experiences were disappointing. He went to see the famous holy man, Trailanga Swami, and found him indeed holy. 'I saw,' said Ramakrishna, 'that the Universal Lord Himself was using the Swami's body to manifest His presence. All Benares was illumined by his stay there. He was in an exalted state of knowledge. He had no body-consciousness. The sand there gets so hot in the sun that no one can walk on it; but he lay on it comfortably. I cooked rice pudding and brought it with me and fed him with it. At that time, he couldn't speak to me because he had taken a vow of silence. So I asked him by signs whether Ishwara was one or many. He replied by signs that Ishwara is known to be one when a man enters the state of samadhi; but as long as any consciousness of "I" and "You" persists, Ishwara is perceived as many. I told Hriday, "In him you see the condition of a true Knower of Brahman."'

One day in Benares, Mathur took Ramakrishna on a boat trip to see the holy places. As they approached the chief burning-ghat near Manikarnika, the air was full of smoke; for many bodies were lying on the funeral pyres in the process of cremation. At the sight, Ramakrishna's face expressed ecstatic joy and the hairs of his body stiffened. He came out from the covered part of the boat, walked over to the bows and passed into samadhi. The boatmen ran to catch him, lest he should fall into the water. But, this time, Ramakrishna did not fall; he remained standing erect, with a wonderful smile. Hriday and Mathur stood protectively beside him but did not touch him. The boatmen gazed at this extraordinary figure in astonishment.

Later, when Ramakrishna had returned to outer consciousness, he told them that he had seen a tall white figure with matted hair approach each funeral pyre in turn, carefully raise each individual soul from its cast-off body and whisper into its ear the particular name of Brahman that liberates a soul. Meanwhile, on the opposite side of the pyre, sat Mother Kali, untying the knots of bondage created by the individual karma and thus setting the soul free. The pandits who were present confirmed the truth of this vision from their knowledge of the Scriptures. For it is written that, if the individual soul gives up its body in Benares, it will be immediately liberated from the wheel of rebirth and death, through the grace of the Lord Shiva.

After a week in Benares, the pilgrims moved on to Allahabad, where all of them bathed at the confluence of the Ganges and the river Jumna, a spot which is regarded as especially sacred. Then they went on to Vrindavan. Here, amidst the scenes of Krishna's early life, Ramakrishna was in a state of continuous ecstatic excitement. The cowherd boys returning from the pastures, the cattle crossing the river at sunset, the meadows, the little hills, the trees, the peacocks and the deer; all made him think of Krishna. 'Where is Krishna!' he cried wildly. 'Where is Krishna! Why can't I see him? Everything here has been blessed by his presence – but where is *he*?'

However, in Vrindavan, Ramakrishna met Ganga Mata, a woman in her sixties, who was a great devotee of Krishna and Radha. Ganga Mata had spent most of her life in the village of Barshana, the birthplace of Radha; and many people regarded her as a reincarnation of one of Radha's attendants. When Ganga Mata saw Ramakrishna, she recognized in him a reincarnation of Radha herself. Almost at once, the two of them assumed the roles of intimate woman friends, and Ramakrishna was ready to settle down and live with Ganga in her hut, despite the protests of Hriday. Neither Hriday nor Mathur could move him from his purpose, and it began to look as if he might stay there indefinitely. But, suddenly, Ramakrishna remembered his mother Chandra, living alone in the music-tower at Dakshineswar; and he knew that he must go back there and look after her.

After two weeks, the pilgrims returned to Benares. During their first visit to Benares, Ramakrishna had seen the Bhairavi again. She was living at one of the ghats with another woman devotee. She accompanied him to Vrindavan, and he advised her to remain there for the rest of her life. She died in Vrindavan, only a short while after Ramakrishna's return to Dakshineswar.

During his stay in Vrindavan, Ramakrishna had felt a desire to listen to the music of the stringed instrument called a *vina*. But that was not possible, for there was no competent vina-player in Vrindavan at that time. So Ramakrishna had to wait until he could visit the house of Mahesh Chandra Sarkar, an acknowledged master of the vina, in Benares. As soon as Mahesh Chandra began to play, Ramakrishna felt himself going into samadhi. 'Mother,' he pleaded, 'please let me listen to the music!' After this, he was able to remain externally conscious. He listened to the vina with delight and, from time to time, sang to accompany it. Mahesh Chandra used to visit Ramakrishna daily. Ramakrishna praised his powers of concentration, saying, 'While Mahesh plays, he loses himself completely.'

Mathur stayed in Benares until May, because he wanted to be present at a certain religious festival. When this was over, he suggested that they should visit Gaya. But Ramakrishna refused to do so. For it was at Gaya that his father Khudiram had had the vision, described in Chapter 2, in which the Lord announced that he would be reborn on earth as Khudiram's son. Ramakrishna was convinced that, if he himself were to go to Gaya, he would become merged in his own divine origin and leave the body before his mission was accomplished. For the same reason, he refused to visit places such as Puri, at which one of the avatars had given up his body.

So the party returned to Calcutta in the middle of 1868. Ramakrishna had brought back from Vrindavan some dust which he had taken from the most sacred spots of the city. This he scattered in the Panchavati, and on the floor of the hut in which Tota Puri had initiated him and he had for the first time attained nirvikalpa samadhi. 'Now,' he said, 'this place is as sacred as Vrindavan!'

Hriday's wife died shortly after his return from the pilgrimage. Up to this time, as we have seen, Hriday had not been a man of contemplative temperament; his spiritual strength lay rather in his devotion to Ramakrishna. But now sorrow made him meditative, and he began to aspire to mystical experience. Ramakrishna kept assuring him that this was unnecessary in his case. But Hriday would not listen – just as Mathur had not listened – and presently, like Mathur, he had his desire fulfilled.

Late one night, Hriday saw Ramakrishna going towards the Panchavati. Thinking that his uncle might need his waterpot and towel, Hriday took them and followed him. As he did so, his spiritual sight became opened. He saw the figure of Ramakrishna become luminous as it walked ahead of him. This was no longer the figure of a human being; it was made of light. The Panchavati was illuminated by the light which streamed from that body. Hriday now saw that the figure was not walking at all but moving through the air, just above the ground. He could not believe it. He thought he must be dreaming and rubbed his eyes. But the shining figure did not vanish; nor did the solid trees and shrubs around it. Then Hriday looked down at his own body and saw that it, too, was shining and full of light. And he became aware that this light was not other than the light which formed Ramakrishna. Light had merely detached itself from light, in order that the Master might have someone to serve him. Hriday was wild with joy at this discovery. 'Oh, Ramakrishna,' he cried, 'you and I are the same! We are no mortal beings! Why should we stay here? Come with me – let's go from land to land, setting men free from bondage!'

Ramakrishna turned to him at once, begging him to be silent. If Hriday made such a noise, he said, he would wake up everybody in the compound. People would think a murder was being committed. Placing his hand on Hriday's heart, Ramakrishna hastily begged Mother to 'make this rascal dull and stupid again!'

Hriday came down with a bump into the dull world of gross matter. He began to sob. 'Why did you do that to me, Uncle? You've taken that blissful vision away from me! Now I'll never have it again!'

'I didn't say you should never have it again,' Ramakrishna told him. 'I only wanted to calm you down. You were making such a to-do over that little vision of yours – that's why I had to ask Mother to make you dull. If you only knew how many visions I have, every day! And do *I* raise such a racket? You're not ready for visions yet. The time will come for them.'

Hriday accepted the rebuke in silence, but he felt hurt. Privately, he determined to seek further visions. And so he went secretly to the

Panchavati at dead of night, and sat down in the very spot on which Ramakrishna was accustomed to meditate. Fortunately for Hriday, Ramakrishna himself felt an impulse to meditate in the Panchavati, that night. When he reached it, Hriday cried out piteously to him, 'Uncle, save me! I'm being burned to death!' No fire was visible around Hriday, nor were his garments burned. Ramakrishna asked him what the matter was. 'No sooner had I sat down in that spot,' Hriday told him, 'than it was as if a plate of live charcoal had been thrown right over me!' Ramakrishna passed his hand over his nephew's body, cooling it at once. 'Haven't I told you again and again,' he asked, 'that you'll gain everything just by serving me?' Hriday never went back to the Panchavati after this.

Nevertheless, he was to have another vision, and without any unpleasant consequences. In 1868, he wished to celebrate the Durga Puja in his own home. Mathur gave him the money to do so; and Ramakrishna instructed him carefully in the performance of the worship. But Hriday was not satisfied. He wanted his uncle to be present; and this was physically impossible, because Mathur insisted that Ramakrishna should attend the worship in *his* house. Ramakrishna consoled Hriday by telling him that he would be present in the subtle body. On each of the three days of worship, Hriday saw the luminous figure of his uncle standing beside the image. Ramakrishna told Hriday later that he had gone into samadhi while seated before the shrine in Mathur's house, and had felt himself pass along a shining track to stand beside Hriday's shrine.

In Chapter 3, I mentioned Akshay, the motherless son of Ramkumar, Ramakrishna's eldest brother, and a favourite of Ramakrishna's since early childhood. That Akshay should return Ramakrishna's affection was all the more natural because Ramkumar, his own father, would never take him on his lap or play with him. This apparent hardheartedness was really due to Ramkumar's psychic foreknowledge of events. We have seen how Ramkumar's married life was saddened by the knowledge that his wife would die if she bore him a child. When Akshay was born, Ramkumar foreknew that his son would not live long; so he avoided showing Akshay affection lest he should become painfully attached to him, and suffer from his loss. A vain fear, after all – since Ramkumar himself was fated to die thirteen years before his son! His knowledge of the future was tragically useless; it merely made him afraid to live in the present.

Meanwhile, Akshay had grown up into a strikingly handsome and graceful youth. Everybody loved him – and, indeed, of all the family, he most resembled the young Gadadhar. Like Gadadhar, he was naturally devotional; and, like Gadadhar, he came to Dakshineswar in his teens to act as a priest. In 1865, he succeeded Haladhari and took over the worship of Vishnu.

In 1869, Akshay got married. A few months later, he fell seriously ill at the house of his father-in-law. He seemed to recover and came back to his duties at Dakshineswar. Then he fell ill again of a fever, and weakened rapidly. Ramakrishna urged the family to call in the best doctors available. 'But the boy won't recover,' he added. Hriday begged him in dismay not to utter such a gloomy prophecy. 'Do I say anything of my own accord?' Ramakrishna answered.

The end came soon afterwards. Ramakrishna was at Akshay's bedside. He told his nephew to repeat the mantra 'Ganga, Narayana, Om Rama'. Akshay repeated it three times. Then he died. Hriday burst into tears. Ramakrishna laughed aloud in ecstasy.

'I felt nothing at the time,' Ramakrishna said later. 'I stood there and watched how Man dies. It was as if there was a sword in a sheath. Then the sword was drawn out of the sheath. The sword was still the sword, as before. Nothing had happened to it. And the sheath lay there, empty. When I saw that, I felt great joy. I laughed and sang and danced. They took the body away and burned it, and came back.

'But, the next day, I was standing on the porch outside my room – and do you know what I felt? I felt as though a wet towel was being wrung inside my heart. That was how I suffered for Akshay. Oh, Mother, I thought, this body of mine has no relation even to the cloth that enfolds it; then how can it feel so much for a nephew? And if I feel so much pain, what agony must the householders suffer! Is that what you are teaching me, Mother? But, you know, those who hold on to the Lord, they do not lose themselves in grief.'

Akshay had died at the Kuthi. After his death, Ramakrishna would never consent to stay there again.

At Colootollah, in Calcutta, there was a house at which Vaishnavites used to meet and sing devotional songs or listen to readings from the religious classics. In this house, one of the sitting places for meditation was always kept vacant and decorated with flowers. It was called 'Chaitanya's Seat'.

Chaitanya, who lived in the fifteenth century, founded one of the Vaishnava sects. He is accepted as an avatar. These Vaishnavites at Colootollah regarded him as their chosen ideal, and they believed that he was actually present at their ceremonies, in the subtle body. His Seat was therefore very sacred to them.

One day, not long after Akshay's death, Ramakrishna went to this house with Hriday, at the invitation of the devotees. A recitation from the Bhagavata was in progress. Ramakrishna and Hriday entered without attracting notice. But, presently, Ramakrishna became overpowered with emotion. He ran forward and stood on Chaitanya's Seat, his hands raised, in samadhi.

At first, the devotees were more excited than shocked. Catching something of Ramakrishna's ecstasy, they chanted the name of God. But later, after he had left the house, a dispute began. Some said that his action had been sacrilegious; others excused or defended it. Unable to agree, they appealed to a famous holy man and Vaishnavite, Bhagavan Das Babaji. Bhagavan Das was angry when he heard of the occurrence, and told them to take precautions lest it should ever happen again. Ramakrishna, of course, knew nothing of all this.

In 1870, Mathur, Ramakrishna and Hriday set out by boat to visit Nadia, Chaitanya's birthplace. On the way, they stopped at Kalna, near Burdwan, where Bhagavan Das was living. While Mathur arranged for suitable lodgings, Ramakrishna and Hriday went to visit Bhagavan Das.

When they reached the place, Ramakrishna became suddenly shy. He told Hriday to go in ahead of him. As Hriday entered the room where Bhagavan Das was, he heard him say, 'It seems to me that some great soul has come here.' Having said this, Bhagavan Das looked around at his visitors. He evidently saw at a glance that Hriday was not the great soul he expected; for he went on talking about a certain sadhu who had done something wrong. Bhagavan Das exclaimed indignantly that he personally would seize the sadhu's rosary and confiscate it, and then expel him from the Vaishnava community. During this outburst, Ramakrishna entered the room. He had wrapped himself from head to foot in a cloth, so that even his face was partially hidden. He respectfully saluted Bhagavan Das and sat down among the other visitors. Hriday said, 'My uncle loses himself in the name of God. He's been doing it for a long time, now. He has come to pay a visit to you.'

Bhagavan Das then broke off his denunciation of the erring sadhu and asked politely where Ramakrishna and Hriday had come from. Hriday noticed that he told his beads from time to time; so he asked Bhagavan Das, 'Sir – why do you tell your beads, now that you have attained enlightenment? You no longer have any need to.' Bhagavan Das replied, 'It is true that I don't need to practise such disciplines for myself. But I must tell my beads to set an example to others. They always do as I do. If I don't tell my beads, I shall be leading them astray.'

It had pained Ramakrishna to hear this egotistical language from such a holy man as Bhagavan Das was reputed to be. From Ramakrishna's point of view, the pronoun 'I' should mean 'I – the servant of God', and 'I did this', 'I did this as His instrument'. So now Ramakrishna rose to his feet and exclaimed indignantly to Bhagavan Das, 'Is that how you think of yourself – even now? You think *you* teach people? You think *you'll* expel this man from your community? You think *you* can decide to give up telling your beads or not? Who made *you* a teacher? Do you think you can teach the world, unless the Lord who made it allows you to?'

By this time, Ramakrishna's words had taken on the character of an inspired utterance. There was nothing personal in his rebuke; he seemed to be addressing mankind. The cloth had fallen from his shoulders to the ground, so had the cloth from around his loins. He stood there naked, with a strange radiance shining from his face.

No one had spoken like this to Bhagavan Das for many years; he was accustomed to humility and reverence. Yet he was no ordinary man, and he was able to recognize these words as the words of truth and accept them without the resentment of injured vanity. He knew well enough that there is no doer in the world but God; and he felt grateful to Ramakrishna for reminding him of this. The two of them now talked together for some while; and their mood became ecstatic. When Bhagavan Das finally realized that it was Ramakrishna who had stood on Chaitanya's Seat, he humbly begged Ramakrishna's pardon for his anger, saying that he had misunderstood altogether the meaning of that action. And so they parted lovingly.

At Nadia, Ramakrishna displayed one more aspect of his mystical insight. In the city itself, he experienced little or no spiritual emotion. But in the boat out on the river, he had a vision of two boys, 'bright as molten gold', who rushed to meet him, smiling, and were merged into his own body. These boys were identified by Ramakrishna as Chaitanya and Nityananda, his closest friend and disciple; and Ramakrishna interpreted the vision to mean that the ancient city of Nadia, Chaitanya's actual birthplace, had been swallowed up by the river and buried under its sandbanks. That was why he had felt no emotion in the modern city.

It is said that subsequent research has confirmed this as an historical fact.

In July 1871, Mathur caught typhoid fever and died, after a short illness. Ramakrishna was not physically present at his deathbed. But Saradananda believes that, while apparently remaining in his room, he went forth in the subtle body to join Mathur and guide him through the death-experience. At five o'clock that afternoon, Ramakrishna came out of samadhi and said, 'Mathur's soul has ascended to the sphere of the Mother.' And this was, in fact, the exact hour of Mathur's death in his home in Calcutta.

Some time after this, a friend of Mathur's said to Ramakrishna, 'Sir, what became of Mathur after death? Surely, he won't have to be born again, will he?'

Ramakrishna did not answer this question positively. He said, 'Perhaps he has been born again as a king. He still had a desire for pleasure.' After which, he immediately changed the subject.

12

Sarada and Chandra

Sarada Devi had not seen her husband since his visit to Kamarpukur in 1867. After that visit, Sarada had gone back to her native village of Jayrambati and had been living there with her family ever since. Now she was growing up into a quiet, thoughtful young woman who did her household duties conscientiously and was quick to sympathize with and help people in their troubles. Those who knew her well, loved her, but perhaps rather took her for granted; a life lived without egotism is apt to appear relatively effortless and therefore somewhat uninteresting to outsiders. There can have been few, if any, of Sarada's kinsfolk and friends who realized that they were in the presence of an evolving saint.

Although Sarada had been only thirteen when she last saw Ramakrishna, the impression he had made upon her had been lasting. During these years of their separation, she had come to regard her marriage with him as a fully established relationship. She loved Ramakrishna with a spiritual love which gave her a sense of extraordinary security, because it was free from jealousy and possessiveness. Her thoughts were constantly with him in Dakshineswar and she longed to see him again; but she assured herself that he would not forget her and that he would send for her to come to him in his own good time.

Nevertheless, the years were passing; and Sarada, for all her faith in her husband, could not help being troubled by the gossip about his seemingly insane behaviour – gossip which was continually being fed with fresh rumours from Dakshineswar. The men of Jayrambati made fun of Ramakrishna; the women treated Sarada with condescending pity, as the wife of a madman. Sarada knew that Ramakrishna had certainly not been mad when he was with her in Kamarpukur; but that, after all, was a long time ago. What if he *had* changed? What if he were now really mad? That would explain why he had not sent for her; he might be needing her, just the same. If the husband is sick, physically or mentally, it is the wife's duty to be at his side. . . . Thus, Sarada came to the decision that she must somehow get to Dakshineswar as soon as possible and find out the truth for herself. By now it was 1872, and she was eighteen years old.

In the spring of the year, a religious festival is held which is called the *Dol Purnima*. During the festival, images of Krishna and Radha are swung in a swing as they are traditionally supposed to have swung on that particular day. It is also the birthday of Sri Chaitanya. On the streets, people throw handfuls of powder and squirt red water at each other to express their joy. (The colours in the powders used to be washable. Nowadays, these are fast colours, almost impossible to remove, so it is advisable to go out in your oldest clothes.) Devotees from all over Bengal come to Calcutta and other places where they can bathe in the Ganges on this auspicious day.

Some villagers who were distantly related to Sarada were planning to come up from Jayrambati to Calcutta on the occasion of the Dol Purnima that year. Sarada asked if they would take her with them; they answered that she must first get leave from her father, Ramchandra. Ramchandra guessed at once what Sarada's real reason was for wanting to go to Calcutta. Being in complete sympathy with her, he arranged to take her there himself.

At that time, there was no railway in the area and the journey from Jayrambati to Calcutta took several days. The wealthy could afford to have themselves carried in palanquins; everybody else went on foot. Sarada was unused to travelling; in her eagerness to reach her husband, she overtaxed her strength and became feverish. To her dismay, Ramchandra insisted that she must stop and rest at a wayside inn. She was put to bed, helpless and desperately impatient, with her fever mounting.

In her delirium, she was comforted by a vision. This is how she later described it: 'My fever rose until I lost consciousness. There I lay, not even able to be careful that my clothes weren't disordered. Then I saw a girl come and sit down beside me. She was black in complexion, but I never saw such beauty before. She began passing her hand over my head and body. Her hand was so soft and cool that the burning in my blood began to subside. I asked her affectionately, "May I know where you come from?" The girl said, "I come from Dakshineswar." I was astonished and said, "Dakshineswar! That's where I long to be – to see my husband and to look after him. But now I have this fever, and perhaps I shall never see him again." "Why shouldn't you see him?" said the girl. "Of course you'll get to Dakshineswar! As soon as you're better, you shall go to him. I've been taking care of him, for your sake." "How good you are!" I said. "Tell me – are you one of our relatives?" "I am your sister," she told me. I said, "Ah – so that's why you've come to me!" After this I fell asleep.'

Next morning, Sarada's fever had temporarily left her. Ramchandra decided to continue the journey, no doubt because he realized that inaction and anxiety would be worse for Sarada than fatigue. After walking only a short distance, they were lucky enough to find a palanquin for her. Presently, Sarada felt her fever returning, but it was not as high as before and she said nothing about it; this time, she did not become delirious. They arrived at Dakshineswar at nine o'clock that evening.

Ramakrishna received his wife with loving solicitude. He arranged for her to have a bed in his own room, lest she should take cold. 'Alas,' he exclaimed, 'my Mathur isn't here any more to look after you!' But he supervised her nursing capably, arranging for her medicine and diet; and, in three or four days, she was well again. She then moved from Ramakrishna's room to the music-tower in which his mother Chandra was already living. Sarada was now entirely reassured. Obviously, Ramakrishna was not mad; the sanest of husbands could not have been more thoughtful and attentive. She rejoiced that she was in Dakshineswar at last, to see him daily and to serve him.

The question may be asked: Why, if Ramakrishna was so pleased to see Sarada, had he done nothing to bring her to Dakshineswar sooner – especially since a word from him would have been sufficient? Saradananda reminds us that we must never try to judge Ramakrishna's conduct by our own standards. He had resigned himself to the will of God with a completeness which is beyond our imagination. He was therefore incapable of making any decision except from one moment to another. Planning seemed positively horrible to him. (On one occasion, it is related, he saw Hriday with a calf and asked him what he was going to do with it. 'I'm taking it home,' Hriday answered; 'in a few years it'll be full-grown and ready for the plough.' Ramakrishna was so shocked that he fell into a swoon. When he came back to his senses, he exclaimed, 'Look how worldly people hoard for the future! It's only a calf now, but it will grow and work in the fields! Always planning so far ahead! Won't they ever rely on God! Ah – that's Maya!')

Besides, says Saradananda, Ramakrishna regarded Sarada's coming as a test of purity; and it was not for him, but for God, to decide when it should take place. This test was to be, in fact, the last of his sadhanas. During the eighteen months that now followed, Ramakrishna and Sarada lived together in the closest intimacy. Often they slept together in the same bed. When Sarada spoke of this period later in her life, she would describe it as one of continuous ecstasy; a state of married bliss which was nevertheless absolutely sexless. Such a relationship is so unthinkable to most of us that we can do nothing but take it on trust.

'If she had not been so pure,' Ramakrishna used to say of Sarada, 'if she had lost her self-control and made any demand on me – who knows? Perhaps my own self-control would have given way. Perhaps I should have become sex-conscious. After I got married, I implored the Divine Mother to keep Sarada's mind absolutely free from lust. And now, after living with Sarada all that time, I know that the Mother granted my prayer.'

One day, while Sarada was massaging Ramakrishna's feet, she asked him, 'How do you think of me?' And he answered, 'The same Mother who's in the temple, and the same Mother who gave birth to me and is now living in the music-tower – that same Mother is rubbing my feet. That's the truth: I always see you as a form of the blissful Divine Mother.'

Once, at night, as he watched Sarada lying asleep beside him, Ramakrishna addressed his own mind, in a mood of discrimination: 'Oh, my Mind, this is the body of a woman. Men look on it as an object of great enjoyment; something to be highly prized. They devote their lives to enjoying it. But, if one possesses this body, one must remain confined within the flesh; one can't realize God. Oh my Mind, don't be thinking one thing in private and outwardly pretending another! Be frank! Do you want this body of a woman, or do you want God?' The mere idea of touching Sarada's body with lust made Ramakrishna's mind recoil and lose itself so deeply in samadhi that he did not regain normal consciousness all night.

Sarada became accustomed to seeing her husband in these super-conscious states, but she was always made anxious by them. And when, sometimes, she tried and failed to rouse him from them, she became terrified. Her fear would keep her awake. When Ramakrishna found this out, he told her she had better go back to sleeping in the music-tower, to spare herself anxiety.

Meanwhile, he continued the training he had begun five years ago in Kamarpukur. He taught Sarada everything he felt she ought to know, both as a wife and a devotee – how to put a wick in a lamp, how to behave when she visited someone's house, how to treat the various members of the family, how to meditate, how to worship, how to pre-pare the mind for the knowledge of Brahman. Nothing was too trivial, nothing was too sublime to be included in his instructions.

In the spring of 1872, Ramakrishna confirmed, by one of the most memorable acts of his life, the truth of the answer he had given to Sarada's question, 'How do you think of me?' It was May 25, a day of the new moon which is set aside for a special worship of the Goddess Kali. This worship was of course performed in the Kali Temple. But, on this occasion, Ramakrishna gave instructions that preparations for the worship were also to be made in his own room.

Hriday was performing the worship in the temple, so could not be present. The priest of the Radhakanta Temple had finished his worship, however, and now came to assist. Ramakrishna had sent to ask Sarada to be present. When she had arrived, he began the worship.

The first phase of the ritual is concerned with the purification of each of the objects which are to be used in the worship. They are purified by the uttering of a mantra and, in some instances, also by the making of a *mudra*, a prescribed gesture of the hands which has its special mystic significance. The worshipper sits facing north or east. Facing him, or to his left, is the seat reserved for the Goddess; a wooden seat with an ornamental design on it in liquid rice-paste.

When Ramakrishna had finished these preliminaries, he beckoned to Sarada to come forward and sit on the seat of the Goddess. Sarada, who was already in a state of spiritual exaltation and only partly con-scious of her surroundings, obeyed him without question.

He began by sprinkling Sarada with water that had been made holy by the recitation of the mantras, just as if she were an image of the Goddess in a shrine. Then he recited the prayer to the Goddess: 'Oh Lady, Oh Mother, Oh Mistress of all power, open the door to perfection. Purify the body and mind of this woman. Manifest yourself in her. Be gracious.' Then he made to Sarada the sixteen ritual offerings – including earth, ether, air, fire and water, to represent the entire universe – treating her now as the Goddess in person. When he made the food offering, he put some of the food to her mouth with his hand. At this, Sarada went into samadhi; so did Ramakrishna. They remained thus until more than half of the night had passed. Then Ramakrishna returned to semi-consciousness and made his final offering to the Goddess: himself. He offered up the fruits of all his sadhanas, together with his rosary, at her feet. And so ended the last of Ramakrishna's sadhanas.

About a year and five months later, in October or November 1873, Sarada left Dakshineswar for Kamarpukur, to live for a while with Ramakrishna's family.

During the next year, Ramakrishna got to know Shambhu Charan Mallik, a man of great generosity who came to take, to some extent, the place of Mathur as fulfiller of Ramakrishna's wishes and needs. Shambhu was a devout student of the scriptures of various religions. He was the first to read to Ramakrishna from the Bible and speak to him of Jesus of Nazareth; *Sri Isha*, as the Hindus call him. Ramakrishna's thoughts began to dwell upon the personality of Jesus. As it happened, he often took walks to a garden-house which was situated to the south of the Dakshineswar Temple grounds, and rested there; and the parlour of this garden-house was hung with pictures of holy personalities, including one of the Virgin Mary with the child Jesus sitting on her lap. Ramakrishna became especially attached to this picture. One day, while he was looking at it, he felt that the figures of the Mother and Child began to shine, and that rays of light struck forth from them and entered his heart. As this happened, he was aware of a radical change in his attitude of mind. He felt – just as he had felt during the time of his initiation into Islam by Govinda Roy – that his Hindu way of thinking had been pushed into the back of his mind and that his reverence for the Hindu gods and goddesses had weakened. Instead, he was filled with love for Jesus and for Christianity. He cried to Kali,

'Oh Mother, what are these strange changes you are making in me?' but his appeal did not alter his condition. And now he began to see visions of Christian priests burning incense and waving lights before the images of Jesus in their churches, and he felt the fervour of their prayers. Ramakrishna came back to Dakshineswar under the spell of these experiences, and for three days he did not even go into the temple to salute the Divine Mother. At length, on the evening of the third day, while he was walking in the Panchavati, he saw a tall, stately man with a fair complexion coming towards him, regarding him steadfastly as he did so. Ramakrishna knew him at once to be a foreigner. He had large eyes of uncommon brilliance and his face was beautiful, despite the fact that his nose was slightly flattened at the tip. At first, Ramakrishna wondered who this stranger could be. Then a voice from within told him, 'This is Jesus the Christ, the great yogi, the loving Son of God and one with his Father, who shed his heart's blood and suffered tortures for the salvation of mankind!' Jesus then embraced Ramakrishna and passed into his body. Ramakrishna remained convinced, from that day onward, that Jesus was truly a divine incarnation.

In October 1873, Ramakrishna's surviving brother, Rameswar, died of typhoid fever at Kamarpukur, shortly after Sarada's return there from Dakshineswar. He was forty-eight years old.

Rameswar had an easygoing and liberal nature. When wandering monks came begging to his door, he would give them anything they asked for if he had it in the house – cooking-pots, waterpots, blankets – regardless of the inconvenience he was causing himself and his family. 'We shall get more of them somehow,' he would say. 'Why worry about it?'

After the death of Akshay, Rameswar had been appointed priest in the Radhakanta Temple. However, because of his family obligations, he had often had to visit Kamarpukur, leaving some other priest to officiate for him. When he was about to leave Dakshineswar on what was to be his last journey, Ramakrishna, who was in a state of clairvoyance, had said to him, 'So you're going home? All right – but don't share your bed with your wife. If you do, you won't live much longer.' Soon after his arrival at Kamarpukur, Rameswar had fallen sick. 'So he didn't listen to the warning,' Ramakrishna said to Hriday, when they heard the news, 'now I'm afraid they won't be able to save his life.'

Rameswar himself foreknew the time of his death four or five days before it took place. He told his relatives of this, and personally made arrangements for his funeral. Seeing that a mango tree in front of the house was being cut down, he remarked, 'That's fortunate – it'll provide the wood for my pyre.' During his last hours, he continued to chant the name of Rama until he lost consciousness. He died shortly afterwards, in the middle of the night. According to his instructions, he was not cremated in the cremation-ground but on the road that ran alongside of it. When asked why he wanted this done, he had replied, 'If I am cremated on the road, the feet of many holy men will pass over the spot. I shall have the dust of their feet and be greatly blessed.' Later, Rameswar's son Ramlal brought his ashes to Calcutta and scattered them on the Ganges. Ramlal succeeded his father as priest at the Radhakanta Temple.

When the news of Rameswar's death reached Dakshineswar, Ramakrishna was afraid to break it to their mother Chandra, fearing the effects of the shock it would give her. First he entered the temple and prayed to the Divine Mother to lessen Chandra's grief; then, with his eyes full of tears, he went across to the music-tower. 'I was afraid,' he said later, 'that my mother would faint when she heard the news and that it would be hard to save her life. But, in fact, the opposite happened. Mother heard the news and expressed some grief – but then she started to console *me*. "This world is transitory," she told me, "everyone must die some day, so what's the use of grieving?" and so forth. It seemed to me that the Divine Mother had tuned Mother to a high pitch, like a stringed instrument keyed up to a very high note. That was why worldly sorrow couldn't touch her. When I saw this, I gave thanks to the Divine Mother, and I wasn't anxious about Mother any longer.'

In April 1874, Sarada returned to Dakshineswar. This time, she made the journey with a party of women pilgrims. Sarada could not walk fast enough and kept dropping behind the others. Some of them offered to stay with her, but Sarada would not agree to this, for now they were passing through an uninhabited district which was notorious as a haunt of bandits, and she did not want to endanger the lives of her companions as well as her own by delaying them there after nightfall. Thus it happened that Sarada presently found herself walking through the gathering darkness, alone and afraid. All at once, she saw approaching her a tall, dark-skinned man of sinister appearance, armed with a long stick. She knew at once that he was a bandit and stood still, since running away would have been futile. At first, the man spoke to her in a menacing tone, asking her where she was going; but then, as he came closer to her and looked into her face, his manner seemed to change and soften. 'Don't be afraid,' he told her, 'my wife is with me – she's only a little way behind.' At this, Sarada was inspired to make an extraordinary demonstration of trustfulness. 'Father,' she said, 'my friends here left me behind and I seem to have lost my way. My husband lives at the Dakshineswar Temple. If you'll take me to him he'll give you a warm welcome.' And, when the bandit's wife appeared, Sarada said to her, 'Mother, I'm your daughter Sarada. I was lost and didn't know what to do, until Father met me.' Treating her as if she were indeed their daughter, the bandits found a place for her to sleep, fed her and brought her next day to rejoin the other pilgrims. On several occasions after this, the couple visited Dakshineswar and were affectionately received by Ramakrishna.

Again, Sarada settled in the Nahabat with Chandra. Seen from the outside, these two music-towers are handsome and quite massive two-story structures with domed roofs; but most of their floor-space is taken up by arched porches designed for the musicians to play and sing in. Their interior rooms are small indeed, and the doors are too low. The visitor to Dakshineswar today must marvel that anyone could have lived there for any length of time. Yet Sarada never complained of the inconvenience. It was Shambhu Mallik who became concerned about her and decided to build a spacious thatched hut for her own use. He therefore bought a plot of land which was just outside the Dakshineswar compound, near the Temple of Kali.

Captain Vishwanath Upadhyaya, another devotee of Ramakrishna, helped Shambhu by supplying timber for the hut. Vishwanath was able to do this because he was in charge of a timberyard belonging to the State of Nepal. The timberyard was situated on the opposite bank of the Ganges, so Vishwanath had some logs of wood for the hut floated across the river to Dakshineswar. There was a strong tide that day, and one of the logs was carried away. Hriday said that this accident proved that Sarada was 'unlucky'. He often took the opportunity to disparage Sarada, of whom he was jealous; it is always hard for a

faithful attendant of Hriday's type to yield first place to a wife. However, Vishwanath replaced the lost log, the hut was built, and Sarada
moved into it. A woman was hired to help her with her household
work. Every day, Sarada cooked the food which was first offered to
the Divine Mother and then eaten by Ramakrishna. She brought it
over to the temple with her own hands, served it to her husband later
and then returned to her hut after his meal. Ramakrishna would also
visit Sarada at her hut, but he only once stayed the night there, when
caught by a downpour of rain.

After Sarada had been living for about a year in her hut, she was
attacked by dysentery. Shambhu called in a doctor, who cured her;
but when she went back to Jayrambati, to convalesce, she had a violent
relapse. Indeed, she was so seriously ill that her family did not expect
her to recover. Hearing this, Ramakrishna said to Hriday, 'Just think
– if she should die now! Her coming into the world would have been
in vain. She would have failed to achieve the only purpose of life.' This
remark seems most strange, on first hearing – for, after all – if the only
purpose of life is to know God – and Ramakrishna cannot have meant
otherwise – Sarada was in no danger of failing to achieve it; she had
already experienced samadhi. We can only assume that Ramakrishna
was referring to the great role which Sarada was destined to play in her
later life, as the spiritual Mother of the whole Ramakrishna Order.
We may also suspect that Ramarkrishna knew Sarada was not going to
die, anyway.

But Sarada herself did not have this conviction. She felt her situation
to be so grave that she determined to practise prayopavesana, the fast
to which Chandra had resorted years earlier when she believed that
her son was insane. Without telling her mother or her brothers of her
intention – Ramchandra, her father, had died some time earlier – Sarada
went to a temple in the village and began her fast. But, after only a
few hours, she was inspired by the deity to follow a certain cure, after
which she quickly recovered.

In 1876 Shambhu fell sick with diabetes. Ramakrishna went to see
him on his sickbed and came away saying, 'There is no oil left in
Shambhu's lamp.' His prediction soon proved true. Shambhu died
calmly and cheerfully. 'I have no anxiety about death,' he told his
friends. 'I've packed my baggage and I'm ready for the journey.'

.   .   .   .   .

In March of the same year, Chandra died also, at the age of ninety-four. Towards the end she had become somewhat senile and suffered from delusions. Having taken a dislike to Hriday, she even began to believe that he had killed Akshay and was trying to kill Ramakrishna and Sarada. She often warned them, 'Never do anything Hriday says.' Near the Dakshineswar garden was a jute mill. The millworkers had a midday break and were called back to work by a steam whistle. Chandra got it into her head that the sound of this whistle was celestial; that it was the blowing of conch-shell horns to announce a banquet in Vaikuntha, the paradise over which Vishnu is supposed to rule. She therefore refused to take her food until the whistle had sounded, feeling that it was impious to begin eating before the gods had begun. On holidays, when the mill was closed and the whistle silent, it was extremely difficult to get Chandra to eat at all. Ramakrishna and Hriday had to coax her in all sorts of ways.

Four days before Chandra died, Hriday was due to go home on holiday to his native village. But he felt a vague foreboding and was unwilling to leave. He told Ramakrishna, who said, 'Then you had better stay here.' Four days passed without incident. Chandra's health was normal. Ramakrishna spent the evening of the fourth day with her, talking of his childhood and telling stories which filled the old lady with delight. She was put to bed at midnight, and he returned to his room.

Next morning, Chandra did not appear, as she usually did, around eight o'clock. The woman who looked after her went upstairs to the door of her room and called her. There was no answer. The woman put her ear to the door and heard stertorous breathing. She could not go in, because the door was barred from the inside, so she ran and called Ramakrishna and Hriday. Hriday forced the door open. They round Chandra unconscious.

For three days, she remained alive, and they fed her with Ganges water and with milk, drop by drop, at frequent intervals. When she was at the point of death, they carried her to the bank of the sacred river. Ramakrishna made an offering of flowers at her feet as she passed quietly away.

The life of a sannyasin is based on the assertion that the world and all its changes and chances are unreal; therefore he cannot ordinarily take part in any religious ceremony related to birth, marriage or death.

He does not recognize their existence. Being a sannyasin, Ramakrishna could not perform his mother's funeral rites; this was done by Ramlal. But Ramakrishna felt guilty, nevertheless, that he had not honoured Chandra by any of the ritual actions proper to a son. And so, when the funeral rites were over, he wished at least to make the offering which is called *tarpana*; an offering of water to a god or the spirit of an ancestor. But the water must be offered in the cup of the hand, and this Ramakrishna was physically unable to do; every time he tried to take the water, his fingers became numb and opened of their own accord, letting it run away. He tried again and again without success. Then he begged his mother's spirit, with tears, to forgive him for his failure. ... Some time after this, Ramakrishna was told by a pandit that he had no reason to reproach himself. The Scriptures state that, when a man has reached a certain high level of spiritual development, he will be literally unable to fulfil the prescribed ritual duties, even when he earnestly wants to do so.

13

Keshab Sen

The last chapter ended in March 1876, with the death of Chandra Devi. I intentionally left out of it one most important event which took place almost exactly a year earlier; the meeting between Ramakrishna and Keshab Chandra Sen. From an historical point of view, this meeting is so full of significance that it demands a whole chapter to itself. Keshab Sen has been briefly referred to as a prominent Hindu reformer of the nineteenth century. Now I must explain in detail what it was that he wanted to reform, and how his ideas were influenced by the teaching and example of Ramakrishna.

Something has already been said, in Chapter 4, about the influence of the British upon India. One of the many evils of foreign conquest is the tendency of the conquered to imitate their conquerors. This kind of imitation is evil because it is uncritical; it does not choose certain aspects of the alien culture and reject others, but accepts everything slavishly, with a superstitious belief that if you ape your conquerors you will acquire their superior power.

The British certainly had much to offer India that was valuable: medical science and engineering, the arts of the West, a clearly-defined legal code. Unfortunately, they brought with them also two creeds – scientific atheism and missionary evangelism – diametrically opposed to each other yet equally narrow and dogmatic. These two creeds had done quite enough harm already in the West, where they were indigenous; exported to India, they had the added power of novelty and threatened to produce spiritual and cultural chaos. The young Indians who came into contact with them nearly all reacted violently. Either they lost belief in everything Hindu and got nothing from England in return but despair; or they were thrilled by the fanaticism and self-assurance of the missionaries and embraced a wretched version of

Christianity which was both abject and self-seeking. (Since the mission-aries had charge of most of the new educational facilities provided by the British, they got the opportunity to indoctrinate many of the most intelligent students of each generation.) Thus the young were growing up into cultural hybrids; laughed at and despised by the British because of their hopelessly silly efforts at imitation; condemned by orthodox Hindus of the old school as impious traitors to the religion and tradi-tions of their race.

The English missionaries attacked Hinduism as a polytheistic religion; a primitive tangle of cults and idolatry. In this they showed their utter ignorance of the Vedas, which state, again and again, that the substratum of all the many divine forms is Brahman, the one and indivisible. As for the charge of idolatry – 'the heathen in his blindness bows down to wood and stone' – it must be remembered that the great majority of missionaries, in Bengal at least, were Protestant. The Catholics could not very well condemn the cult of holy images in theory, though they showed much zeal in destroying those which belonged to other creeds.

Stupid as these accusations were, there were some Hindus who accepted them as a challenge. In spite of their own better knowledge, they had been made by their conquerors to feel that Hinduism was antiquated, and hence that it should be reformed – purged of super-stitions and obsolete customs and thus brought into line with the other world-religions. It might well have been retorted that the other world-religions needed purging, every bit as badly; but here the inferiority complex of the conquered came into play and made the criticism one-sided. We may deplore this mistaken humility, but we must realize that the urge to reform Hinduism was also motivated by a not ignoble kind of patriotism. India – said the reformers to themselves – had been conquered politically, but that was no reason why she should be conquered spiritually as well. Spirituality had always been India's greatest strength; and now India had to assert herself spiritually – as a first step (some of these reformers undoubtedly added) to regaining her political freedom.

The first important reform movement of the nineteenth century was founded by Ram Mohan Roy, who was born in Bengal in 1774. Ram Mohan belonged to an orthodox brahmin family which he offended by publishing, at the age of sixteen, a book against image worship. He then left home and travelled for some years – visiting, among other places, Tibet, where he studied Buddhist mysticism. He was also sympathetic to the teachings of Christianity and Islam. A distinguished scholar, he knew Sanskrit, Persian, Arabic, English and some European languages.

In 1828, Ram Mohan founded what he called the Brahmo Samaj, dedicated to 'the worship and adoration of the Eternal, the Unsearchable, the Immutable Being, who is the Author and Preserver of the Universe'. (The title, Brahmo Samaj, cannot be translated succinctly into English; it means the Society of believers in a personal God without form.) The God of the Brahmo Samaj was not the impersonal Brahman, but rather the Hindu Ishwara (see Chapter 5) or the Mohammedan Allah or the non-trinitarian Godhead of the Unitarians; a personal God without form but with father-attributes. Ram Mohan borrowed something from the teachings of Christianity but denied the divinity of Jesus, just as he denied the divinity of the Hindu avatars. At the same time, he quoted freely from the Hindu scriptures, choosing particularly certain passages from the Upanishads which could be interpreted according to his belief in a personal God without form. And he based his monotheistic philosophy partly on the sacred writings of Islam. The Brahmo Samaj was open to all, without regard to religion or race. Its international appeal was certainly a challenge to the critics of classical Hinduism, but perhaps, in trying to cover such a large area, it spread itself rather too thin. Its real strength was in its programme of social reform, for it demanded the abolition of those very customs to which the British most objected – child-marriage, the veto on the remarriage of widows, and the caste-system itself. The Brahmo Samaj refused to recognize any caste-differences among its own members. It also worked for the emancipation of women and their education along modern lines.

In 1830, Ram Mohan was created a raja by the Emperor of Delhi. (It must be remembered that the British did not claim the imperial title for Queen Victoria until 1877.) He was then sent to England to represent the Emperor and give evidence before a parliamentary committee on the judicial and revenue systems of India. The English politicians and scholars treated the Raja with respect and admiration; and he had the satisfaction of being present in the House of Commons when the practice of *suttee* – the Hindu widow's voluntary cremation on her husband's funeral pyre – was finally outlawed. He had worked against suttee for many years. In 1833, while still in England, he died sudddenly of a brain fever and was buried at Bristol.

Ramakrishna therefore never had the opportunity of meeting Ram Mohan. He did, however, meet Ram Mohan's successor, Devendra Nath Tagore, as we have seen in Chapter 11. Devendra Nath took over the leadership of the Brahmo Samaj eight years after the Raja's death. During this interval, the movement had greatly weakened, but Devendra Nath reorganized it and soon made it stronger than ever before. He agreed with Ram Mohan in condemning image worship, but he was not much concerned with other world-religions. A monotheist, he drew his inspiration entirely from the Hindu scriptures and fought to prevent Christian ideas from infiltrating the Samaj. On this point he was altogether at variance with his successor, Keshab Chandra Sen.

Keshab was two years younger than Ramakrishna and a whole generation younger than Devendra Nath. He was born in a Bengali family of moderate means and educated at an English school. He did not know Sanskrit. He had little natural sympathy with the popular traditions of Hinduism. He was, indeed, very powerfully influenced by the personality of Jesus, and, if he differed from the Christians, it was only because of their claim to possess the one truth faith. Keshab held that Jesus, Moses, Buddha and Mohammed should be equally honoured.

Some of Keshab's followers carried his neo-Christian ideas even farther. They wanted a new, Indian kind of Christianity which should embrace all religions in the name of Jesus Christ. Here is part of an article which appeared in one of the last issues of the *New Dispensation*, a magazine which was founded by Keshab and continued after his death:

'Who rules India? What power is that which sways the destinies of India at the present moment? It is not the glittering bayonet nor the fiery cannon of the British Army that can make our people loyal. . . . No. If you wish to secure the attachment and allegiance of India, it must be through spiritual influence and moral suasion. And such indeed has been the case in India. You cannot deny that your hearts have been touched, conquered and subjugated by a superior power. That power need I tell you – is Christ. It is Christ who rules British India, and not the British Government. England has sent out a tremendous moral force in the life and character of that mighty prophet, to conquer and hold this vast empire. None but Jesus ever deserved this bright, this precious diadem, India, and Jesus shall have it.' It is amusing to think that this, and other expressions of a similar opinion, must have dismayed the Christian missionaries almost as much as the orthodox Hindus. And, in fact, Keshab's activities had the effect of much reducing missionary influence in Bengal. At the same time, Keshab was compelled by his own views to break with Devendra Nath Tagore. In 1868, he founded The Brahmo Samaj of India. Devendra Nath retained leadership of the other half of the movement, which was now called the Adi Samaj, or First Brahmo Samaj.

In 1870, Keshab went to England. He was warmly welcomed there, especially by the Unitarians. Queen Victoria herself received him in audience. While at Oxford he visited Edward Pusey the theologian, in the company of Max Müller, who describes one of their discussions as follows: 'At the end of their conversation the question turned up whether those who were born and bred as members of a non-Christian religion could be saved. Keshab Chandra Sen and myself pleaded for it, Pusey held his ground against us. Much of course depended on what was meant by salvation, and Keshab defined it as an uninterrupted union with God. "My thoughts," he said, "are never away from God;" and he added, "my life is a constant prayer, and there are but few moments in the day when I am not praying to God." This, uttered with great warmth and sincerity, softened Pusey's heart. "Then you are all right," he said, and they parted as friends, both deeply moved.' This anecdote alone is enough proof that Keshab's nature was capable of great humility and tolerance in the face of provocation; of compassion too, no doubt, for the naturally good-hearted but dogma-bound old man.

In 1875 another Samaj, called the Arya, was founded by Swami Dayananda, a famous Sanskrit scholar. Dayananda worked for the same reforms as Devendra Nath and Keshab, but he was unconditionally opposed to all non-Hindu religious influences in India; Moslem, Christian and Buddhist alike. He was a pugnacious man and the Arya Samaj was a fighting movement. Although he reinterpreted the Vedas to suit his own kind of monotheism, his ideas were sufficiently orthodox to appeal to the masses and not merely the intellectuals. The influence of the Arya Samaj was strongest in the Punjab, where the struggle between Hindus and Moslems was most embittered.

Ramakrishna met Dayananda during one of his visits to Bengal. Mahendra Nath Gupta once heard him refer to this meeting and has recorded what Ramakrishna said. (*Gospel of Sri Ramakrishna*; October 11, 1884.) 'Yes, I went to see him [Dayananda]. At that time he was living in a garden-house across the Ganges. Keshab was expected there that day. He was longing to see Keshab as the chatak bird longs for rain.' (According to legend, the chatak bird will only drink rain-water; it declines all other water, no matter how frantic with thirst it may become. Ramakrishna was fond of using this bird as a metaphor for intense spiritual thirst.) 'He was a great scholar. He believed in the existence of the various deities. Keshab didn't. Dayananda used to say, "God has created so many things – why couldn't he have created the deities?" Dayananda believed that the Ultimate Reality has no form. Captain (Vishwanath Upadhyaya) was chanting the name of Rama. Dayananda said to him sarcastically, "You'd do better to keep saying 'sandesh'!"' (Sandesh is a kind of sweetmeat made of cheese and sugar. In other words, Dayananda did not approve of making japa, or of any similar devotional practice.)

One day in March 1875, while Ramakrishna was in samadhi, he felt a prompting to go and visit Keshab. It so happened that he had seen Keshab once, many years before this, when they were both young men. Ramakrishna had seen Keshab meditating at the Brahmo Samaj, which was then still under the undisputed control of Devendra Nath Tagore. With his spiritual insight, he had realized that Keshab was the only one among the devotees present who had achieved a state of true meditation. Now, in samadhi, he had a vision of Keshab in the form of a peacock, with its tail outspread and a ruby adorning its head. The peacock's tail, he later explained, symbolized Keshab's followers and the ruby Keshab's own nature; his qualities of leadership and proselytizing zeal.

Keshab was engaged in sadhana with his disciples at a garden-house in Belgharia, a few miles to the north of Calcutta. Ramakrishna went to visit him there with Hriday, in a carriage belonging to Captain Vishwanath. On this occasion, Ramakrishna was dressed simply but quite adequately, in a dhoti with a red border, one end of which was thrown over his shoulder. They arrived about an hour after noon. Getting out of the carriage, Hriday saw Keshab and his disciples seated on a brick-built ghat at the edge of the garden pond. Hriday went first alone to speak to Keshab, just as he had gone into the house of Bhagavan Das, in order to introduce his uncle. 'My uncle is a great lover of God,' he said. 'He loves to hear talk and songs about the Lord. When he hears them, he goes into samadhi. He has heard that you are a great devotee, and he has come to listen to you talking about God and his glories. With your kind permission, I'll bring him to you.' Keshab of course agreed, and Hriday helped Ramakrishna out of the carriage and led him over to them. Keshab and the others had been awaiting him with keen curiosity, but now they felt disappointed. On first inspection, Ramakrishna did not seem to them to be anyone out of the ordinary.

'Is it true, gentlemen,' Ramakrishna asked humbly, 'that you have the vision of God? I want so much to know what it's like. That's why I've come to see you.' Presently he sang to them – it was a well-known song of Ramprasad's: 'Who knows what Kali is? The six philosophies cannot explain her.' Immediately after singing, he went into samadhi. Even this did not greatly impress the onlookers. They took Ramakrishna's loss of outer consciousness to be some kind of mental illness, or, worse still, a trick played to impress them. But when Hriday recalled his uncle to his senses by chanting the name of Om in his ears, and when they saw a smile of dazzling innocence and sweetness overspread Ramakrishna's face, they began to be charmed out of their scepticism. And then Ramakrishna spoke to them, using his favourite parables, comparing the many aspects of God to the different parts of the elephant that the blind men touched, or to the different colours of the chameleon seen at different times by different men – and taken always by their ignorance to be the *only* aspect, the *only* colour. . . . Soon, his hearers were listening and gazing at him enthralled – not so much by his teaching as by the manner of it. Indeed, they felt themselves to be in the presence of an enlightenment which was altogether beyond their understanding. They were unaware that the time for the next meal had long since gone by, and that they were even in danger of omitting the next period of prayer. It amused Ramakrishna to see this change in their attitude. He said to them, smiling, 'If any other kind of animal comes to a herd of cattle, they'll turn on it and gore it with their horns. But, if a cow joins the herd, they'll lick its body and welcome it as one of themselves. . . . That's what has happened to us here today.' Then, addressing Keshab, he added, 'Your tail has dropped off.' This odd-sounding remark startled and displeased Keshab's disciples; they took it at first for some kind of insult. But Ramakrishna went on to explain, 'As long as the tadpole has its tail, it can only live in the water, it can't come on land; but, when the tail drops off, it can live on land as well as in the water. As long as a man wears the tail of ignorance, he can only live in the world; but, when the tail drops off, he can live either in the knowledge of God or in the world, whichever he pleases. Your mind, Keshab, has reached that state now. You can live in the world and still be aware of God.'

From that day onward to the end of his life, Keshab remained under the influence of Ramakrishna. True, he did not yield to this influence immediately or unconditionally. At first he mistrusted his own judgement and sent some of his followers over to Dakshineswar to observe Ramakrishna and report their impressions of him. And even much later, when Keshab had become absolutely convinced of Ramakrishna's spiritual greatness, he was still tormented by the conflict between his own previous ideas and prejudices and Ramakrishna's teachings. Nevertheless, the influence grew in strength, until Keshab found that he could hardly endure to stay away from Ramakrishna for more than a few days at a time. Sometimes he would come to Dakshineswar; sometimes he would invite Ramakrishna to visit him at his house in Calcutta, which was called the Kamal Kutir, the Lily Cottage. Sometimes Keshab and a party of Brahmo devotees would take Ramakrishna for a steamer trip on the Ganges, so that they could enjoy his society without fear of any intrusion.

Although Keshab was now one of the most famous men in India, and was himself looked up to as a teacher, he always treated Ramakrishna with the utmost humility and respect. Whenever they met, Keshab brought the offering of fruits which is traditional when the pupil visits his guru. And, like a devoted pupil, Keshab would seat himself at Ramakrishna's feet. Once, Ramakrishna said to him playfully, 'Keshab, you delight so many people with your lectures – please expound something to me, too!' To which Keshab replied, 'Sir, am I to sell needles in a blacksmith's shop?' (The Indian proverbial equivalent of 'carrying coals to Newcastle'.) 'Please talk and let me listen. People are delighted whenever I tell them anything you have told me.'

One day, Ramakrishna said to Keshab that, if one admits the

existence of Brahman, one must also necessarily admit the existence of Brahman's Power, through which the universe is created – since Brahman and its Power are eternally one and the same. To this Keshab agreed. Ramakrishna then told him that the Scriptures, the Devotee and God are also one and the same. To this also Keshab agreed. Ramakrishna next told him that the Teacher, God and the Devotee are also one. But Keshab became disturbed and perplexed. At length, he said respectfully, 'Sir – just now I can't accept anything more. Please, let us not speak of this for the present.' 'Very well,' Ramakrishna told him. 'Then we'll stop there.'

In 1878, a scandal split the Brahmo Samaj. The Maharaja of Cooch-Behar had asked for the hand of Keshab's daughter. The marriage was one of the most brilliant that a Hindu girl could possibly have made, and Keshab agreed to it. There is no reason to suppose that he did this from motives of self-interest, because of the Maharaja's rank and huge wealth; no doubt he was thinking only of his daughter's future. Unfortunately, however, the girl was not yet quite fourteen years old, and so Keshab was acting against one of his own publicly declared objectives: the abolition of child-marriage. Immediately a conflict broke out and two parties were formed – one defending Keshab, the other condemning him as the worst of traitors and hypocrites. The opposition party then left The Brahmo Samaj of India and founded a movement of its own, called the General Brahmo Samaj.

When Ramakrishna heard of this schism, he was much distressed. He had never approved of Keshab's campaign against child-marriage. 'Birth, death and marriage are all subject to the will of God,' Ramakrishna had said. 'They can't be made to obey hard-and-fast rules. Why does Keshab try to make such rules?' Nevertheless, if anybody spoke of the Cooch-Behar marriage in Ramakrishna's presence and blamed Keshab, Ramakrishna would defend him: 'How is Keshab to blame? He's a family man. Why shouldn't he do what he thinks best for his sons and daughters? He wasn't acting against religion or morality. He has only done his duty as a father.' Ramakrishna refused to take sides in the quarrel, and remained on friendly terms with members of both movements.

One of the most prominent of these was Vijay Krishna Goswami. After the Cooch-Behar schism he had become a leader of the newly-formed General Samaj. He visited Ramakrishna often and would tell everyone he met that Ramakrishna was the greatest soul in India, bewailing the blindness of those who could not recognize this fact. He used to say to Ramakrishna, 'Dakshineswar is so near to Calcutta – we can visit you whenever we like; there are plenty of boats and carriages. If we don't understand you and value you highly enough, it's only because you're so near home and so easily available. If you were sitting on a mountain-top, and we had to walk miles without food and climb precipices to reach you, clinging on to the roots of trees – then we would know what a treasure you are. As it is, we imagine there must be better teachers living far away from here; and so we run seeking them this way and that way, and put ourselves to endless trouble for nothing.'

Ramakrishna thought very highly of Vijay's spiritual attainments. 'Vijay has reached the room just next to the innermost chamber,' he would say, 'and now he's knocking at its door.'

Before the schism, Keshab and Vijay had been good friends; after it, they stopped seeing each other. However, as both continued to visit Ramakrishna regularly, a meeting between them was sooner or later inevitable. Mahendra Nath Gupta tells us that Vijay was sitting with Ramakrishna in his room at Dakshineswar, on the afternoon of October 27, 1882, when some of Keshab's followers arrived with an invitation. Keshab had chartered a steamer which had just dropped anchor opposite the temple compound; would Ramakrishna go out with them in a rowboat to the steamer and join him? Ramakrishna agreed, and Vijay went along with him – we are not told how willingly or unwillingly.

The encounter could hardly have begun more embarrassingly. No sooner was Ramakrishna in the rowboat than he went into samadhi. They had difficulty in getting him on board the steamer. Partially conscious of his surroundings but still moving stiffly and mechanically, he was helped downstairs into a cabin. Keshab and the others bowed to him. He did not seem to recognize them. He was placed in a chair. Keshab and Vijay sat down on two others. As many devotees as could squeeze into the cabin squatted on the floor; the rest peered in through the door and the windows, which had to be opened because the cabin had already become terribly stuffy. Meanwhile, Ramakrishna went back into samadhi. Keshab and Vijay were thus left virtually alone together, awkwardly enthroned in the midst of this audience which was, no doubt, eagerly curious to see if they would show any signs of their hostility. They appear to have behaved with formal politeness.

Gradually, Ramakrishna returned to external consciousness. He whispered to himself, 'Mother, why have you brought me here? They're shut in. They're not free. Can I free them?' A Brahmo devotee spoke to him of a holy man whom some of them had visited, and added, 'He keeps a photograph of you in his room, sir.' This seemed to amuse Ramakrishna. Pointing to his body and smiling, he said, 'It's just like a pillowcase.' A train of ideas had thus been started, bringing him back to the plane of consciousness on which he was able to speak as a teacher. And now he began to talk to them about the heart of the devotee which is the 'favourite parlour' of God, about the dream which we call our life, about the dance of Mother Kali. He compared the Divine Mother just before the recreation of the universe to a housewife who keeps a pot of seeds ready for the next sowing. He mimicked the sound of the English language: *Foot fut it mit.* He sang hymns to Kali and Durga. His hearers were so delighted that they did not want the voyage to end, and Keshab asked the captain to steam a little farther down the river. Puffed rice and grated coconut were served.

Yet there was still a constraint between Keshab and Vijay. Ramakrishna noticed it and said to Keshab, 'Look – here is Vijay. Your quarrel reminds me of the fight between Shiva and Rama. Shiva was Rama's guru. They fought each other but they soon made it up again. It was their followers, Shiva's ghosts and Rama's monkeys, who went on making faces and chattering at each other; they wouldn't stop! You have a religious society, so Vijay thinks he has to have one too. That's quite natural. While Sri Krishna, who was incarnate God himself, was happy in the company of the gopis at Vrindavan – even then, those two troublemakers, Jatila and Kutila, had to appear on the scene. Why? Because the plot can't thicken without troublemakers. Without Jatila and Kutila there's no fun.' Ramakrishna's affectionate teasing of Keshab and Vijay had been greeted by loud laughter, and now the two leaders were forced to become reconciled with each other. But Keshab's 'ghosts' and Vijay's 'monkeys' continued to carry on the feud, just as Ramakrishna had hinted that they would.

The public recriminations caused by the Cooch-Behar marriage had had one good result: Keshab now began to feel a distaste for all the vanities of public life and a longing for spiritual experience. Under

Ramakrishna's influence, he now accepted many Hindu rituals and symbolic acts which he had previously rejected as meaningless: the offering of oblations, bathing in consecrated water, shaving the head, wearing the ochre-dyed cloth. Within two years, he had formulated and began to preach a new creed which he called 'The New Dispensation'. 'The New Dispensation' was, fundamentally, a presentation of Ramakrishna's teachings – as far as Keshab was able to understand them. What chiefly appealed to Keshab in Ramakrishna was his universality, and particularly the fact that he had had the vision of Jesus of Nazareth. But, over and above this, he regarded Ramakrishna as a living embodiment of his creed. When he came to Dakshineswar he would bow down before Ramakrishna and symbolically take the dust of his feet, exclaiming, 'Victory to the Dispensation! Victory to the Dispensation!' It was through Keshab that Ramakrishna first became known to the general public of Calcutta.

Ramakrishna delighted in Keshab's spiritual growth. He now began to appear frequently, unannounced, at meetings of the Brahmo Samaj, joining with the Brahmo devotees in their *kirtan* (singing of religious songs). Not unnaturally, the Brahmos were encouraged by his visits to regard him as their exclusive property and to imagine that he shared their particular beliefs and theirs only. They could not understand that Ramakrishna's absorption in God made him eager to take part in religious observances of any kind.

Ramakrishna tried to wean the Brahmos away from their excessive preoccupation with social reform and turn their minds towards meditation and the realization of God. But he knew human nature and did not expect too much of them. 'I have said whatever came into my head,' he used to tell them. 'Take as much of it as you want. You can leave out the head and the tail.' Later in his life, he would describe the Brahmo meetings to his own disciples: 'I went to Keshab's house and watched them praying. After the speaker had talked a long time about the glories of God, he said, "Let us now meditate on him." I wondered how long they'd meditate. But, oh dear, they'd scarcely had their eyes shut for two minutes before it was all over! How can one know God by meditating like that? While they were meditating, I was watching their faces. Afterwards, I said to Keshab: "I've seen a lot of you meditate, and do you know what it reminded me of? Troops of monkeys sometimes sit quietly under the trees at Dakshineswar, just as if they were perfect gentlemen, quite innocent. But they aren't. They're sitting thinking about all those gourds and pumpkins that householders train to grow over their roofs, and about all the gardens full of plantains and eggplants. After a little while, they'll jump up with a yell and rush away to the gardens to stuff their stomachs. I saw many of you meditating like that." And when they heard that, they laughed.'

Ramakrishna would also try to correct the Brahmos' ideas about worship. 'Why,' he would ask them, 'are you always talking so much about the various powers of God? Does a child who's sitting beside his father keep thinking how many horses, cows, houses and estates his father has? Isn't he simply happy to feel how much he loves his father and how much his father loves him? The father feeds and clothes the child – and why shouldn't God? After all, we are his children. If he looks after us, is that so extraordinary? So, instead of dwelling on that, a real devotee makes God his very own, through love. He begs – no, he *demands* that his prayers shall be answered and that God shall reveal Himself to him. If you dwell so much on God's powers, you can't think of him as your nearest and dearest – and so you can't feel free to demand things of him. Thinking about his greatness makes him seem distant from his devotee. Think of him as your very own. That's the only way to realize him.'

Ramakrishna did succeed to a large extent in curing the Brahmos of their unreasonable fear of image worship, which was based on the conviction that God is without form. Some of them, at least, began to understand what Ramakrishna meant when he said, 'You should never set limits to God's nature' – that God is both with form and formless.

Ramakrishna himself was no reformer, and he did not worry at all about the effects of Western culture upon India – believing, as he did, that nothing could have happened or would happen without the sanction of the Divine Mother. But the Brahmo Samaj and its kindred movements were destined, as we shall presently see, to exert an important influence, both direct and indirect, upon Ramakrishna's disciples and hence upon the Mission which bears his name.

18. Keshab Sen and Brahmo followers

19. Death picture of Ramakrishna

1. M. (Mahendra Nath Gupta)
*2. Kali (Swami Abhedananda)
3. Manilal Mallick
4. Navagopal Ghosh
5. Gangadhar
   (Swami Akhandananda)
*6. Gopal Sur
   (Swami Advaitananda)
*7. Manomohan Mitra
8. Harish
9. Tarak (Swami Shivananda)
10. Vaikuntha Nath Sannyal
11. Nitya Niranjan
   (Swami Niranjanananda)
12. Narayan

*Identification not certain

13. Bhavanath Chatterjee
14. Baburam (Swami Premananda)
15. Narendra
   (Swami Vivekananda)
16. Ram Chandra Datta
17. Sarat (Swami Saradananda)
18. Balaram Bose
19. Sashi
   (Swami Ramakrishnananda)
20. Latu (Swami Adbhutananda)
21. Rakhal (Swami Brahmananda)
22. Nityagopal
23. Jogindra (Swami Yogananda)
24. Devendra Nath Mazumdar

20. Kamarpukur

21. Street scene, Kamarpukur

14

The Coming of the Disciples

We have seen that Ramakrishna did not expect too much of the Brahmos; their previous conditioning had left them incapable of any radical change of life and mind. Contact with them made Ramakrishna long all the more earnestly for some really dedicated disciples – young ones preferably – who would be ready to renounce every worldly desire and follow his teaching without any reservations. The others, he was accustomed to say, could no more be taught true spirituality than a parrot can be taught to speak after the ring of coloured feathers has appeared around its neck.

'In those days there was no limit to my yearning,' he would recall. 'During the daytime, I could just manage to keep it under control, though the talk of worldly-minded people tormented me. I would yearn for the time when my beloved companions would come to me; I kept thinking what a relief it would be to talk freely and openly to them about my experiences. Everything that happened made me think of them; I couldn't keep my mind on anything else. I kept planning what I should say to this one and what I should give to that one, and so forth. When evening came, I couldn't master my feelings any longer. I was tortured by the thought that another day had passed and that they hadn't arrived! When the evening worship started and the temples resounded with the ringing of bells and the blowing of conch-shell horns, I would climb up on to the roof of the Kuthi and cry out at the top of my voice in the anguish of my heart, "Come to me, my boys! Where are you? I can't bear to live without you!" A mother never longed so for the sight of her child, or a friend for his friend or a lover for his sweetheart, as I did for them! Oh, it was beyond all describing! And, soon after this, they did at last begin to come.'

The Brahmo Samaj was actually the means of bringing several of these monastic disciples, as well as many householder devotees, to Ramakrishna. Its influence in this direction worked both positively and negatively; there were those who came to Ramakrishna because they had heard his greatness constantly proclaimed by the lectures and writings of Keshab, and there were those who came because they were disappointed in the Samaj and hoped to get from Ramakrishna the spiritual reassurance which it had been unable to give them.

Ram Chandra Datta and his cousin Manomohan Mitra had read about Ramakrishna in Keshab's newspaper, *Sulabh Samachar*. Ram Chandra was a doctor who had a post at the Calcutta Medical College. Manomohan was a businessman. Both of them were agnostics with a leaning towards outright atheism; but their lack of faith made them restless, not merely complacent, and they had the saving virtue of intellectual curiosity. They decided to go to Dakshineswar and see for themselves what Keshab's saint was like. This was towards the end of 1879.

The cousins arrived at Dakshineswar expecting to meet a freak and probably a fake. The door was opened to them by a plainly-dressed person who looked disappointingly ordinary. His hair was not matted, his body was not smeared with ashes; he was not at all their idea of a holy man. Yet this was Ramakrishna himself. He welcomed them as though he had been awaiting them, and at once began to ply them with questions. Hearing what Ram Chandra's profession was, he called to Hriday, who was suffering from a fever, 'Hriday, come – here's a doctor! Let him feel your pulse!' Ram Chandra and Manomohan were both charmed by his unaffected cordiality. They felt completely at ease with him, and stayed the whole afternoon. Before they left, Ramakrishna fed them with sweetmeats and asked them to visit him again.

Ram Chandra and Manomohan were men of considerable intuition, and they became aware, even after that first encounter, that they had been in the presence of spiritual greatness. A profound though gradual change began to work in them, and their thoughts turned away from worldly matters. Soon their relatives noticed this and became alarmed. One day, when Manomohan was about to visit Ramakrishna, his aunt tried to persuade him not to go. He refused to listen to her and set out, with Ram Chandra. They found Ramakrishna sitting on his bed, looking sad. When they asked him what was wrong, he answered, 'There's a devotee who likes coming here, but his aunt doesn't approve; she tries to stop him. It makes me sad to think that he may listen to her and give up coming.' Manomohan and Ram Chandra were astonished at Ramakrishna's clairvoyance. Not long after this, Manomohan's wife also objected to his visiting Dakshineswar and Ramakrishna behaved and spoke in the same manner.

'Does God really exist?' Ram Chandra asked. 'Of course he exists,' Ramakrishna told him. 'You don't see the stars in the daytime, but that doesn't mean that the stars don't exist. There's butter in milk, but how could anyone guess that by looking at it? To get the butter you must churn the milk in a cool place. To get the vision of God you must practise mental disciplines – you can't see him just by wishing.'

Ram Chandra came of a family of Vaishnavas and was therefore familiar with the life of Sri Chaitanya. One evening, he was at Dakshineswar and alone with Ramakrishna in his room. 'What are you looking at?' Ramakrishna asked him, suddenly. 'I am looking at you,' Ram Chandra told him. 'And what do you think of me?' 'I think you are Chaitanya.' There was a silence. Then Ramakrishna said quietly, 'Well – the Bhairavi used to say the same thing.'

At such times, Ram Chandra was full of faith. But then again doubts crept in upon him. Was Ramakrishna truly a knower of God or merely endowed with extraordinary psychic powers? He could not decide.

One night he dreamed that Ramakrishna gave him a mantra and told him to repeat it several times a day. Next morning, he hurried to Dakshineswar with this news and Ramakrishna assured him that this was indeed a blessed experience. No sooner had Ram Chandra left his presence, however, than he began to say to himself that a dream was only a dream after all; it proved nothing.

A few days later, he was talking to a friend in the College Square, in the middle of Calcutta. They had been speaking of Ram Chandra's doubts. All at once they were aware of a very dark-skinned man who was standing beside them. 'Why are you so anxious?' he asked. 'Have patience.' The next moment, he had vanished – and yet they had both seen him. When Ramakrishna was told of this, he said, 'Yes – you'll be seeing many more things like that!'

But Ram Chandra remained obstinately doubtful; and, the more he doubted, the more he loathed his life and the world around him. When he came back to Dakshineswar for help, Ramakrishna amazed and dismayed him by exclaiming impatiently, 'What can *I* do? It all depends on God's will.' 'But, sir,' cried Ram Chandra, 'I've been relying on you. If you won't help me, what shall I do?' 'I don't owe you anything,' Ramakrishna told him with seeming indifference, 'you can keep on coming here if you want to – please yourself.' This kind of shock-treatment was no doubt exactly what Ram Chandra needed. He rushed out of the room determined to drown himself in the Ganges, but a little reflection brought him to his senses; he decided to make a serious effort on his own account, instead of expecting Ramakrishna to save him in spite of himself. Accordingly, Ram Chandra lay down on the northern veranda outside Ramakrishna's room and began to repeat the mantra Ramakrishna had given him in the dream. Hours passed. In the middle of the night, Ramakrishna opened the door and told him, 'Serve the devotees of the Lord and you will find peace.' Having said this, Ramakrishna went back into his room.

Now it happened that Ram Chandra was miserly by nature, and so Ramakrishna's advice was distasteful to him; if he followed it, he would have to spend a lot of money. At first he did nothing. But Ramakrishna returned to the subject a short while later and set a day on which he and the devotees would visit Ram Chandra's house. Ram Chandra was therefore obliged to arrange for their entertainment, and, as he did so, he began to understand that Ramakrishna had accorded him a great privilege in allowing him to be of service.

The evening after Ramakrishna's visit, Ram Chandra went to Dakshineswar. Ramakrishna received him affectionately and they talked until ten o'clock. The night was very dark. Ram Chandra had already taken his leave and was standing on the veranda when he saw Ramakrishna coming towards him. 'Tell me what you want,' Ramakrishna said. Ram Chandra at once felt himself to be in the presence of something more than human, a power which was really able to grant him anything he might wish for. His voice shook with emotion as he answered, 'Lord, I don't know what to ask for. You decide.' Ramakrishna held out his hand. 'Give me back the mantra I gave you in your dream,' he said, and as he spoke he passed into samadhi. Ram Chandra prostrated himself and repeated the mantra. Ramakrishna touched him on the head with the toe of his right foot. They remained thus for a long time. Then Ramakrishna took his foot away and Ram Chandra stood up. 'If there is anything you want to see,' Ramakrishna told him, 'look at me.' Ram Chandra looked, and he saw that Ramakrishna was the embodiment of his Chosen Ideal, the form of God that was dearest to his heart. 'You needn't practise any more spiritual disciplines,' Ramakrishna told him. 'Just come here and see me now and then. And you should bring some little offering with you, any little thing.'

From that time on, Ram Chandra became not only a steadfast devotee but a lavishly generous provider for the needs of Ramakrishna and his disciples.

Manomohan, Ram Chandra's cousin, was naturally generous and his devotion came to him more easily. He had a different defect; envy arising out of spiritual pride. One day, in Manomohan's presence, Ramakrishna praised a devotee named Surendra Nath Mitra, saying that his devotion was 'unequalled'. Manomohan was proud of his own devotion and took this praise to mean that Ramakrishna valued Surendra more highly than himself. Bitterly hurt, he left the room, resolving never to return to Dakshineswar. Since he was a regular Sunday visitor, his absence was noticed at once by Ramakrishna, who asked Ram Chandra to find out what was the matter. But Manomohan would not, of course, admit to his motive for staying away; and Ram Chandra could only report that his cousin was well and that there seemed to be no explanation of his behaviour. Manomohan, meanwhile, was saying mentally to Ramakrishna, 'Enjoy yourself with your devotees – you don't need me – to you, I'm nobody.' By now, he had cultivated his resentment to the point of insanity. It was Ramakrishna, he told himself, who had driven him away from Dakshineswar. And, when Ramakrishna continued to send messengers urging him to come back, he actually moved to Konnagar, a few miles outside Calcutta, even though he had to take a train into the city every day, to be at his office. Thus Manomohan became increasingly miserable. He could not stop thinking about Ramakrishna and attend to business. At last he had to admit to himself that he did not hate Ramakrishna but loved him dearly.

One day, he went to bathe in the Ganges. He remembered how Ramakrishna had often spoken of its great sanctity, and the memory brought with it a vision of Ramakrishna, so vivid that he could not get it out of his mind. And now, as Manomohan stood beside the water, he became aware of a boat with two figures in it. One of them was Ramakrishna himself. The other was Niranjan, one of Rama-krishna's boy disciples. (See Chapter 17.) Manomohan was amazed to see them. This was like a materialization of his vision. 'Why don't you come to Dakshineswar?' Niranjan asked him. 'Sri Ramakrishna has been so anxious about you.' It was a very hot day and Ramakrishna was fanning himself. He passed into samadhi as the boat drew nearer to Manomohan. 'And he has taken all this trouble for my sake!' Manomo-han thought. 'How I have wronged him!' He burst into tears and was about to fall, when Niranjan jumped out of the boat and caught him. Ramakrishna returned to outer consciousness and told Niranjan to help Manomohan on board. 'I was so worried about you,' he said tenderly to Manomohan, 'that I had to come for you.' Manomohan threw himself at Ramakrishna's feet, sobbing, 'Sir – it was all because of my vanity!' Niranjan turned the boat towards Dakshineswar.

Surendra Nath Mitra, the innocent object of Manomohan's envy, had a good job with an English firm in Calcutta and was a relatively wealthy man. Before he met Ramakrishna, he was not much interested in religion. He drank a great deal and was sexually promiscuous. At the same time, however, he was well known for his generosity to the poor.

Surendra was friendly with Ram Chandra Datta, and Ram Chandra was always suggesting that they should go to Dakshineswar together. At first, Surendra refused. But at length he said, 'All right – but if that holy man of yours is a fake, I shall pull his ears!' When the two of them arrived in Ramakrishna's room, it was full of devotees. Surendra was determined to preserve an attitude of critical independence, so he sat down without offering Ramakrishna any mark of respect. Ramakrishna was saying, 'Why does a man behave like a young monkey and not like a kitten? The monkey has to cling to its mother by its own effort as she moves around. But the kitten just stands there and mews until its mother comes and picks it up by the scruff of its neck. The monkey sometimes loses its hold on its mother; then it falls and hurts itself badly. But the kitten is in no such danger, because the mother herself carries it from place to place. That's the difference between trying to do things for yourself and giving yourself up to the will of God.' This parable made a tremendous impression on Surendra; it seemed to reveal to him just what was wrong with his own life. 'I behave like the young monkey,' he thought, 'and that's the cause of all my troubles. From now on, I'll be satisfied with any condition the Divine Mother puts me into.' And he felt great happiness and inner strength. When he was about to leave, Ramakrishna said to him, 'Be sure to come again.' Surendra now willingly prostrated himself at Ramakrishna's feet. And, on the way home, he exclaimed enthusiastically, 'Ah – how he turned the tables on me! It was he who pulled *my* ears! How could I have dreamed that there could be such a man? He read my innermost thoughts. Now at last I feel that my life has some meaning.'

Surendra's warm generous nature was easily turned towards spiritual devotion. Even after this first meeting with Ramakrishna, he was visibly changed. But this did not mean that he immediately gave up his old habits. He would still visit prostitutes from time to time and then be so ashamed that he would stay away from Dakshineswar, pretending that he was kept in Calcutta by business. However somebody – such people are never lacking in the company of the holy – reported to Ramakrishna what Surendra had really been doing. Ramakrishna did not seem at all worried or shocked. 'Oh yes,' he said, 'Surendra still has some desires. Let him enjoy them for a while longer. He'll become pure soon enough.' Surendra was told that Ramakrishna had said this about him, so he was emboldened to return to Dakshineswar the next Sunday. But he did not presume to approach Ramakrishna. He took his place in a corner of the room. Ramakrishna saw him, however, and invited him affectionately to come nearer. Then, in a semi-conscious state, Ramakrishna said, 'When a man goes to a bad place, why doesn't he take the Divine Mother with him? She would protect him from many evil actions.' Surendra was guiltily embarrassed by this remark, fearing that Ramakrishna was about to expose him before the whole company. But Ramakrishna said no more. And Surendra found this advice very helpful in the future, when he was struggling against his sexual inclinations.

Surendra was even less inclined to give up his drinking, though Ram Chandra tried to dissuade him from it – not so much because he feared it would harm Surendra's health as because he felt Ramakrishna's reputation would suffer when it became known that one of his prominent devotees was a drunkard. But Surendra told his friend to stop lecturing him. 'The Master would certainly warn me,' he said, 'if he thought this was really bad for me. He knows all about it.' 'Very well,' said Ram Chandra, 'then let's go and visit him. I'm certain he'll tell you you ought to give it up.' Surendra agreed to this, but he cautioned Ram Chandra not to bring up the subject. 'If the Master refers to it of his own accord and tells me to stop, then I promise I will stop.'

On this understanding, they went to Dakshineswar where they found Ramakrishna sitting under a tree in a high state of spiritual exaltation. As soon as they had greeted him, he began talking to them as though he were continuing a conversation which had been briefly interrupted: 'But, Surendra, why, when you're drinking wine, do you have to think of it just as ordinary wine? You should offer it first to Mother Kali and then drink it as her prasad. Only you must be careful not to get drunk. Don't let your footsteps stumble or your mind wander. At first, you'll feel only the kind of excitement you usually feel; but that will soon lead to spiritual joy.' Surendra followed Ramakrishna's instructions from that day onward. He would always offer a little wine to the Goddess before he drank any himself, and this action filled him with devotion. He began to cry plaintively for the Divine Mother, like a child, and wanted to talk of her only. Often he would become absorbed in deep meditation. He never became intoxicated again.

There were many other devotees – of varying quality – who came to Ramakrishna about this time. There was Kedarnath Chatterjee, who had a great talent for philosophical argument. Ramakrishna sometimes asked him to give preliminary instruction to the newcomers – for there were now more of them than he could possibly teach himself. There was the wealthy and charitable Maharaja Jatindra Mohan. There was Kristodas Pal, editor of a newspaper called *The Hindu Patriot*, who used to declare that all Ramakrishna's talk of renunciation was escapism, and that one should spend one's life working for the betterment of social conditions. Ramakrishna reproved him for this attitude, drawing a distinction between the secret sense of superiority which thinks in terms of egotistically *helping* the world and the true lack of egotism which is expressed in the idea of *serving* the world. 'How dare you talk of helping the world? God alone can do that. First you must be made free from all sense of self; then the Divine Mother will give you a task to do.'

Mahima Charan Chakravarty had been a visitor to Dakshineswar for several years already. He was a man of some spiritual growth, but a great show-off – boasting of his initiation by Tota Puri, who, he claimed, had told him to remain in the world as a householder. He had a liking for names which were elaborate to the point of absurdity. Thus, he opened a free school which he called, 'The Educational Section of the Institute of the Oriental Aryans' and named his only son, 'Holy-mouthed One with the Moon upon his Head'. Mahima had a library of Sanskrit and English books in his house. Once, when a group of Ramakrishna's young disciples were visiting him, they asked Mahima if he had read everything in his library. Mahima answered 'Yes', with the becoming modesty of a great scholar. 'Then why, sir, are the pages of some of these books uncut?' 'Well, you see,' Mahima blandly explained, 'these are books which people borrowed and did not return. I had already read them but I replaced them with new copies. Now I don't lend my books any more.' The boys were not impressed by this explanation – and rightly; for they later discovered that all the books in Mahima's house were uncut.

Pratap Chandra Hazra was one of those troublemakers who, according to Ramakrishna, are necessary to make the plot thicken. He had a spiteful, mercenary nature, but Ramakrishna tolerated his presence and some of the disciples found his sharp tongue amusing. There will be more to write about him later.

Now it is time to speak of the coming of the monastic disciples for whom Ramakrishna had longed. The first three of these to be mentioned are Latu, Gopal Ghosh and Rakhal.

Rakhturam – more usually known by Ramakrishna's name for him, Latu – was the first to come to Ramakrishna. He had been born of very poor parents in a village of Bihar, the state immediately northwest of Bengal. His parents died when he was a child and an uncle looked after him. This uncle was later obliged to leave the village and seek work in Calcutta. Latu went along with him and found employment as a houseboy. His employer – out of all the possible employers in Calcutta – was Ram Chandra Datta! We shall have several other occasions to remark how tightly woven was the web of circumstances which gathered in Ramakrishna's disciples-to-be.

Latu proved himself a faithful and willing servant. But he was proud, plain-spoken to the point of rudeness, and no respecter of persons.

Once, a friend of Ram Chandra's hinted a suspicion that Latu might pocket some of the money he had been given for marketing. Latu did not take the accusation meekly. 'Understand this, sir,' he exclaimed, in his broken Bengali, 'I am a servant, not a thief!' There was a natural dignity in him which silenced his accuser; but the man felt offended that the boy had dared to speak to him in such a tone of rebuke and he complained to Ram Chandra. But Ram Chandra refused to mistrust Latu.

At the time of Latu's arrival, Ram Chandra had already become a devotee of Ramakrishna, so there was frequent talk of God in the household. Latu heard Ram Chandra say, 'Anyone who is earnest in seeking God will realize him without fail', and 'one should go into solitude and pray and weep for him – only then will he reveal himself'; remarks which he was of course quoting from Ramakrishna. Latu took them to heart and began acting upon them; thereafter he was often to be found lying covered with his blanket, wiping tears from his eyes with his hand. The ladies of the family were touched by this, and supposed that the boy must be grieving for his native village or the company of his uncle. Latu never enlightened them. Indeed, throughout his life, he remained extremely reticent about himself.

Having heard Ram Chandra talk of Ramakrishna, Latu was impatient to visit him. He soon found an opportunity to go to Dakshineswar. In Ramakrishna's company he felt immediate joy. The second time he went there, Ramakrishna was just about to begin eating. He offered Latu food. But Latu, like most of the orthodox people of Bihar, had been trained not to eat food cooked by strangers or by people not of his own caste; so he refused. Ignoring this, Ramakrishna brought him a cup of Ganges water and a plantain leaf for a plate. Again, Latu refused. 'Why won't you eat?' Ramakrishna asked him. 'This food has been cooked in Ganges water and, besides, it's the prasad of Mother Kali.' 'Please excuse me,' said Latu in great embarrassment, 'I can't take it.' But Ramakrishna went on pressing him to eat and, suddenly, he found himself giving way – he scarcely knew why. 'All right,' he told Ramakrishna, 'I'll take the food if it's *your* prasad.'

Latu soon became so devoted to Ramakrishna that he could no longer work for Ram Chandra with his former zest; his only happiness was to be sent by Ram Chandra to Dakshineswar with gifts of sweetmeats for Ramakrishna. Ram Chandra's family noticed this lack of enthusiasm, but they understood its cause and, being fond of Latu, did not scold him for it.

In 1880, Ramakrishna was away from Dakshineswar on what was to be his last visit to Kamarpukur. Latu was miserable. During Ramakrishna's absence, he would sometimes go to Dakshineswar, but these visits only made him miss Ramakrishna more. In later years, he used to say, 'You can't imagine how I suffered at that time. I used to go into Sri Ramakrishna's room or wander around the gardens, but everything seemed tasteless. I would weep to unburden my heart. Only Ram Babu [Ram Chandra] could partly understand what I was feeling. He gave me a photograph of the Master.'

When Ramakrishna returned from Kamarpukur, he felt the need of a personal attendant and asked Ram Chandra if he could have Latu. Ram Chandra agreed. So Latu became Ramakrishna's servant, and this, in itself, was his whole spiritual life. To serve the guru, to obey him literally and implicitly, was Latu's way of finding God. Because Ramakrishna had once mildly reproved him for sleeping during the evening, saying, 'If you sleep then, when will you meditate?' Latu gave up sleeping at night altogether. Instead, he meditated, and took short naps only in the daytime. He was quite unsophisticated and without education. Ramakrishna, who was very little of a scholar himself, tried to teach Latu to read, but Latu could never master the letters. His funny Hindi accent made Ramakrishna laugh, and then Latu would begin laughing at himself. Finally, the lessons were given up as hopeless.

When the monks assumed monastic names, after Ramakrishna's death, Latu became Swami Adbhutananda. He lived till 1920 and kept his Hindi accent and his childlike disposition throughout his life. Ramakrishna used to say that frankness is a virtue which enables one to realize God very easily; and Latu was certainly frank. When, in later years, disciples came to him for instruction, he told them simply to repeat the name of God. 'How can we surrender ourselves to a God we have never seen?' one of them asked. And Latu answered, 'It doesn't matter that you've never seen him. You know his name. What do you do when you go to an office? You send in your application to an official you've never seen; you only know his name, but that's enough. So apply to God by name, and you'll get his grace.' When asked how he had had time for worship and meditation while he spent such long hours looking after Ramakrishna, he would reply, 'Service to the Master was our highest worship and meditation.'

All of the monastic disciples loved Latu. Naren (Swami Vivekananda) was particularly devoted to him and called him Latu-bhai (Brother Latu). Latu called Naren 'Loren', not being able to pronounce his name correctly. Naren used to say of him, 'Latu is Ramakrishna's greatest miracle. Without any education at all, he acquired the deepest wisdom, just by virtue of Ramakrishna's touch.'

Gopal Ghosh was by far the eldest of this group of future monks. He was a few years older than Ramakrishna himself. He was a paper merchant and a widower. The shock of losing his wife had turned his mind towards religion. A friend advised him to go to see Ramakrishna. This he did, and his grief for his wife began gradually to disappear. Gopal was neat and clean and by temperament methodical and orderly. Ramakrishna would address him as 'Old Gopal' or 'Overseer'. The other monastic disciples called him Gopalda or Gopal the Elder Brother. He later became Swami Advaitananda.

Rakhal Chandra Ghosh, like Latu, came to Ramakrishna while still in his teens. He was born in 1863 at Sikra, a village near Calcutta. His father was a very wealthy landowner. His mother was a devotee of Sri Krishna and she had therefore named her only son Rakhal (Cowherd of Vrindavan) in honour of the cowherds who were the companions of the youthful Krishna.

When Rakhal was twelve, he was sent by his family to Calcutta to study at an English secondary school. The boys of this school used to exercise at a gymnasium, and it was there that Rakhal met Naren. Rakhal's gentle, affectionate nature was at once drawn to Naren's aggressive boldness, and Naren felt equally drawn to Rakhal. Thus it happened that the two who were destined to become the leaders of the future Ramakrishna Order were already close friends before either of them met Ramakrishna.

Naren joined the Brahmo Samaj and persuaded Rakhal to do likewise. Both of them signed the Brahmo pledge to worship and meditate upon God without form. Rakhal was naturally contemplative and he now became so preoccupied with the mystery of life and death that he neglected his schoolwork and lost all other worldly interests. His father was concerned about this and hit upon the usual remedy, marriage. Rakhal accepted his father's decision with his customary submissiveness. At the age of sixteen he was married to a young girl named Visweswari. No doubt Rakhal's father imagined that he had thus protected his son from other-worldly influences; as a matter of fact he had done the opposite. For Visweswari's brother was Manomohan Mitra, and it was Manomohan who took Rakhal to visit Ramakrishna, early in 1880.

Some time before the coming of Rakhal, Ramakrishna had prayed to the Divine Mother for a companion: 'Bring me a boy who is like myself, and is pure-hearted and devoted to you.' A few days later, he saw in a vision a boy standing under a banyan tree in the temple grounds. Later, in a second vision, the Divine Mother placed a boy, recognizably the same but much younger, on his lap and told him, 'This is your son.' Ramakrishna was dismayed at first, supposing that he would have to beget this son by an act of sex, but the Mother reassured him; this would be his spiritual, not his physical child. Then, on the very day that Rakhal and Manomohan were coming to visit him at Dakshineswar, Ramakrishna had a third vision. He saw a lotus blooming on the surface of the Ganges and two boys dancing upon it. One of them was Krishna, the other was this same boy.

And then the boat arrived, carrying Manomohan and Rakhal, and Ramakrishna recognized in Rakhal the boy of his visions. For some time he stared at Rakhal in silent amazement. Then he turned to Manomohan and said with a smile, 'There are wonderful possibilities in him.' Thereafter, he talked to Rakhal as if they were already old friends.

The love which Ramakrishna now began to feel for Rakhal seems to have been motherly rather than fatherly. He identified himself with Yashoda, the foster mother of Krishna. Such a relationship is mysterious beyond our comprehension. It was more than a re-enactment, it was – one must suppose – a recreation of a relationship which existed in the past and continues to exist eternally. What is most strange is that Rakhal, a teen-age schoolboy, was able to accept this relationship and enter into it as completely as Ramakrishna himself did. It is hard to explain Rakhal's behaviour without admitting that he and Ramakrishna actually did 'recognize' each other; that they recommenced an association which had begun in another life and time.

This is what Ramakrishna said of it: 'In those days, Rakhal had the nature of a child of three or four. He treated me just like a mother. He would keep running to me and sitting on my lap. He wouldn't move a step from this place. He never thought of going home. I forced him to, from time to time, lest his father should forbid his coming here altogether. His father was a landowner, immensely rich, but a miser. At first he tried to stop his son from coming here, in various ways. But then he came here once and saw how many rich and famous people visit this place, and so he didn't object any more. After that, he came now and then, to visit Rakhal. I was most respectful and attentive to him. He liked that.'

'As for the family of Rakhal's wife, they raised no objection – because the ladies all used to come here very often. Soon after Rakhal first came here, his mother-in-law brought Visweswari, his wife. I wanted to see if she would stand in the way of Rakhal's devotion to God. I examined her physical features minutely and saw that there was no cause for fear. She represented an auspicious aspect of the divine Shakti. I sent word to the Nahabat [i.e. to Sarada] to give Visweswari a rupee and unveil her face.' (This was the traditional ceremony by which a mother-in-law welcomed her daughter-in-law. The daughter-in-law arrived wearing a veil. The mother-in-law gave her a present, removed the veil and kissed her. Since Rakhal was to be the spiritual son of Ramakrishna and Sarada, Visweswari became their daughter-in-law.)

'What a wonderfully childlike nature Rakhal had! Sometimes I fed him and played with him to keep him happy. Often I'd carry him around on my shoulders. When he did anything wrong, I scolded him. One day, he took butter from the temple prasad and ate it, without waiting for me. "How greedy you are," I said. "You ought to have learnt, from being here, to control yourself!" He shrank into himself with fear and never did that again. . . . And he was jealous too, like a child. He simply couldn't bear it if I loved anyone but him. I was afraid he would do himself harm by being jealous of the people the Divine Mother brought to this place.'

Three years after Rakhal first came to Dakshineswar, he went to visit Vrindavan. Ramakrishna was anxious about this visit, because he was convinced that Rakhal had actually been one of the cowherd companions of Krishna and he feared that Rakhal would remember his divine identity and leave his present body. So Ramakrishna prayed, and Rakhal returned safely.

'Mother has revealed many things to me about Rakhal,' Ramakrishna used to say. 'And some of them I am forbidden to tell.'

Hriday, as we have seen, became Ramakrishna's personal attendant in 1855. He had devoted the whole of his adult life to serving his uncle and had certainly proved the strength of his affection and loyalty. As a young man, he had had his faults; but these were the endearing faults of youth, silliness and impulsiveness. However, as Hriday grew older, his character had hardened. By the age of forty, Hriday had changed from a willing helper and protective friend into a despotic, jealous and unkind guard, who behaved at times like a jailer. Anyone who wanted to see Ramakrishna had to go first to Hriday and give him money; otherwise he would not permit the meeting to take place. Ramakrishna found out that Hriday was extorting these bribes and reproved him strongly. But Hriday paid no attention and would not change his ways. In his arrogance, he used every opportunity to show the world that his uncle was completely dependent on him. He would speak rudely to Ramakrishna in public and bully him into submission over trifles. Hriday even dared to put on the airs of great sanctity, imitating the gestures Ramakrishna made when he was in his ecstatic moods and singing and dancing as Ramakrishna did. No doubt he was often laughed at behind his back; but he was a person of too much power and influence to be insulted to his face.

Once, when Ramakrishna was in bed with fever, some devotees came to visit him in Hriday's temporary absence, bringing with them a cauliflower as a gift. Ramakrishna was very pleased, but he said hastily, 'Please hide it and don't tell Hriday, or he'll be angry with me.' He went on to defend Hriday, however, praising his past services and adding, 'Mother has rewarded him richly for his faithfulness. He has been able to buy land for himself. He can afford to lend out money to people. And he's a very important personage in this Temple, highly honoured.' No sooner had Ramakrishna finished saying this than Hriday entered the room and saw the cauliflower. Ramakrishna seemed dismayed; he said pleadingly to his nephew, 'I never asked them to bring me this. They brought it of their own accord. Believe me – I never asked them to!' But Hriday flew into a rage and scolded

Ramakrishna severely, saying that the doctor had forbidden him to eat cauliflower, because it disagreed with him. (No doubt the real reason for Hriday's anger was that he had not been consulted, and saw this visit and this gift as a challenge to his authority.) Meanwhile, Ramakrishna weepingly addressed the Divine Mother, 'Oh Mother, you freed me from all worldly ties and yet you let Hriday humiliate me like this!' But then, with one of those sudden changes of mood which often made his apparent grief or fear seem like a game he was playing, he smiled and added, 'Mother, he only scolds me because he loves me dearly. He's only a boy still – he doesn't know what he's doing. You mustn't be angry with him, Mother.' After this, he passed into samadhi.

Hriday was steadily making enemies for himself among the temple officials at Dakshineswar; there were many who hoped and waited for his downfall. Ramakrishna was well aware of this, and kept warning him to be less aggressive. In February 1881, Sarada Devi came up from the country, where she had been staying for some time, to see her husband. Hriday insolently told her that she was not wanted, and she started back to Jayrambati that same day. Ramakrishna had often said to Hriday, 'If you insult the Being that dwells in this body,' referring to himself, 'Mother may save you. But if you insult Mother,' meaning the Divine Mother within Sarada, 'then you cannot be saved, even by Brahma, Vishnu and Shiva.'

Hriday's downfall, which soon followed this incident, did not come about in any of the ways which might have been expected.

Towards the end of that May, Trailokya Nath, one of Mathur's sons, arrived at Dakshineswar with his wife and children to take part in the annual festival which commemorated the founding of the Temple. Trailokya's eight-year-old daughter – unaccompanied by her parents – was present in the Temple of Kali while Hriday was conducting the worship. Suddenly, Hriday felt moved to worship the Goddess in the person of the little girl. This was not unorthodox. Girls who have not yet reached the age of puberty are often worshipped in this manner during the puja of the Divine Mother. (What had made Ramakrishna's worship of Sarada, in 1872, so unorthodox was the fact that she was already a grown woman and his wife.) The little girl submitted without complaint; and Hriday, according to prescribed ritual, laid flowers before her and decorated her feet with touches of sandal-paste.

It was the sandal-paste which betrayed Hriday. Trailokya's wife noticed it as soon as her daughter returned from the ceremony. When she was told what Hriday had done, she was horrified; for there was a superstition that if a brahmin worshipped a girl of lower caste, she would be widowed soon after marriage. (Hriday and Ramakrishna belonged, as we have seen, to a brahmin family; the Rani and Mathur to a family of sudras, the lowest of the four castes.) It is hard to believe that Hriday was not aware of these facts; and, indeed, with his arrogant temperament, he may well have decided to flout the superstition and show that he did not care what Trailokya and his wife might think. In any case, he went too far. Trailokya was as superstitious as his wife, and therefore just as horrified and just as furious. He ordered Hriday to leave the temple precincts instantly.

Hriday went to Ramakrishna, told him what had happened and said, 'You'd better come with me – if you stay here any longer, they'll insult you, too.' 'Why should I go?' said Ramakrishna. 'I shall stay.' But it appeared that Trailokya, in the first wildness of his rage, had made some remark against Ramakrishna, implying that it would be well to get rid of him, too. Accordingly one of the temple officials came to Ramakrishna and ordered him to leave at once. Without the least sign of resentment or dismay, Ramakrishna picked up his towel, slung it over his shoulder, and walked unprotestingly out of the room which had been his home for the past twenty-six years. He had almost reached the gate of the compound when Trailokya came running after him, crying, 'Sir, where are you going?' 'But didn't you want me to go away?' Ramakrishna asked him innocently. 'No – they misunderstood – I never meant that,' Trailokya assured him, 'I beg you to stay!' At this, Ramakrishna smiled; turned without saying a word, went back to his room, sat down, and continued a conversation he had been having with some devotees, as if nothing unusual had taken place.

Hriday did not go far away. He settled down in the garden-house of Jadu Mallick, just outside the temple grounds. Still, he was permanently debarred from re-entering them; so now Ramakrishna was delivered from his tyranny and interference. If Hriday had not been expelled, it would have been impossible for Ramakrishna to receive and instruct the young disciples who were now beginning to arrive.

For a while, Hriday kept trying to persuade Ramakrishna to leave Dakshineswar and go off with him in search of some other Kali temple, where they could be together again. But Ramakrishna refused, and Hriday finally went away to farm some property which he owned in the country. Ramakrishna only saw him on the rare occasions when he returned to Calcutta.

M. records one such meeting, at which he himself was present. It took place on October 26, 1884. Ramakrishna was sitting in his room, that afternoon, surrounded by devotees, when someone came to tell him that Hriday was out at the garden-house. Ramakrishna did not hesitate. 'I shall have to see him,' he told the others, 'but please don't leave.' He put on his slippers and went out with M. to meet Hriday. They walked down the road to Jadu Mallick's garden and there was Hriday, waiting by the gate with folded hands. As soon as he saw Ramakrishna, he prostrated himself before him. When Ramakrishna told him to get up, Hriday burst into tears and cried like a child. Ramakrishna also shed tears. M. marvelled at this, remembering all the bad treatment he had received from Hriday.

Ramakrishna then asked Hriday why he had come.

HRIDAY (*still weeping*): I have come to see you. Who else is there I can tell my troubles to?

RAMAKRISHNA (*smiling*): You can't avoid suffering. Pleasure and pain are part of the life of the world. (*Pointing to M.*) That's why ne and the others come here now and again. They hear about God and they get some peace of mind. . . . What is troubling you?

HRIDAY (*weeping*): I suffer because I'm not allowed to be with you.

RAMAKRISHNA: But wasn't it you who told me: You go your way and I'll go mine?

HRIDAY: Yes – I said that. But I spoke like a fool.

RAMAKRISHNA: I'll say good-bye to you now. Come another day and we'll have a talk. Today is Sunday and a lot of people have come to visit me. They're in my room, waiting. . . . Have you had a good crop, out in the country?

HRIDAY: Not bad.

On the way back to the temple, Ramakrishna said to M.: 'He tormented me quite as much as he served me. When I had that stomach

trouble, and my body had shrunk to the bones and I couldn't eat anything, he said to me, one day, "Look at me – how much I eat. It's
just your imagination that you can't eat." Another time, he said to
me, "You're a fool. If I weren't living with you, who'd ever believe
you were a holy man?" One day he made me so miserable that I went
and stood on the river embankment, ready to escape from this body by
jumping into the Ganges – it was a flood-tide. . . . But, in spite of all
that, he did serve me well, and for such a long time! How could he
ever have fallen into the state he's in now? He used to take care of me
like a parent bringing up a child. And I would be quite unconscious of
the world for days and nights on end. I was sick for a long time, too. I
was completely in his hands.'

15

Naren

―――――――

Narendra Nath Datta – Naren, as he was called for short – was born in Calcutta on January 12, 1863. His family belonged to the second highest caste, the kshatriyas. The kshatriyas were, it will be remembered, traditionally the caste of the warriors, administrators, leaders of men; a most fitting ancestry for Naren himself. But the Dattas were distinguished rather as scholars and philanthropists; they were very wealthy.

Naren's grandfather, Durgacharan, had longed since childhood for the monastic life; and when he had done his duty to society, as the Scriptures enjoin, by marrying and begetting a son, he left his family and his fortune behind him and disappeared. A few years later, his wife came to Benares, no doubt because she hoped to find him there. One day, on her way to visit a temple, she fell down in the road, which was slippery after a rainstorm. A monk helped her to her feet; then made her sit down on the temple steps and examined her carefully to be sure that she was not injured. Their eyes met. It was her husband. The moment they recognized each other, he turned and hurried away without even a backward glance.

It is customary for a monk to revisit his birthplace twelve years after he has taken the monastic vow. So, in due course, Durgacharan came back to Calcutta. He asked leave to stay at the house of an old friend, begging him not to tell the family. But the friend well-meaningly betrayed Durgacharan and the family came and took him back home with them, practically by force. For three days and nights the captive monk sat in a corner of the room, in miserable silence, not moving, his eyes shut. The family at last became afraid that he was going to fast till death, so they left the door open, and next day he was gone forever.

Vishwanath, Durgacharan's son and Naren's father, was, by contrast, a man of the world; an agnostic who was inclined to make fun of religion, though in a gentle, civilized manner. He was an attorney of the High Court of Calcutta and he earned a great deal of money. He loved travel, sophisticated cooking, English and Persian literature, and music, for which he had a talent. But, unlike the ordinary man of the world, Vishwanath had almost no anxiety about his possessions. He spent money lavishly, helped people whether they deserved it or not, and never worried about what would happen on the morrow. When Naren grew older, he reproached his father for helping relatives who only spent his money on drink. Vishwanath answered that Naren would one day realize how full of sorrow human life is, and that then he would not blame people who tried to ease it by getting drunk. He never got angry and shouted at his children, but found semi-comic ways of reproving them which they remembered for a long time afterwards. Once, when Naren had spoken rudely to his mother, Vishwanath wrote with charcoal on one of the doors, 'Narendra spoke to his mother as follows —' It so happened that Naren was just bringing some friends home with him, and they all read this inscription, to his bitter humiliation.

When Naren asked his father in a moment of unkind frankness, 'What have *you* ever done for me?' Vishwanath did not take offence. 'Go and look in the mirror,' he said, 'and you'll see.' But, in general, Naren was very fond of his father and respected his opinion. Once he asked Vishwanath, 'How ought I to behave, when I'm out in the world?' and was told, 'Never show surprise at anything' – a reply which any nineteenth-century English gentleman might equally well have given his son. Naren followed this advice in later life, though not quite in the spirit in which it was given. For the calm with which he was to encounter all kinds of hardships and mishaps was the calm of the discriminating monk, not the good-humoured indifference of a Vishwanath.

Naren's mother, Bhuvaneswari, was a beautiful and stately Hindu lady of the old school; deeply devout, with little formal education but an astonishingly good memory. This enabled her to retain much information which she had heard only once in the course of a conversation. She ran her large household with efficiency and seeming ease.

She had three sons – Naren was the eldest of them – and four daughters; two of these, however, died in childhood.

Physically, Naren resembled his grandfather rather than his father; and it was noticed that, even at a very early age, he was fascinated by wandering monks, just as Durgacharan had been. Indeed, Naren had to be locked up whenever one of them came to the door; otherwise he would give the monk anything in the house he could lay hands on, including his mother's clothes. When he was only four or five, he would buy images of gods and goddesses in the market, bring them home and sit down before them in the posture of meditation, with his eyes closed. This was because he had heard tales of the ancient sages and how they meditated until their hair grew downward and struck roots in the earth, like the banyan tree. Naren hoped that the same thing would happen to him.

From his childhood, Naren was possessed of a supernormal faculty. This is how he described it in his later life:

'From the earliest times that I can remember, I used to see a marvellous point of light between my eyebrows as soon as I shut my eyes to go to sleep, and I used to watch its various changes with great attention. In order to watch it better, I'd kneel on the bed in the attitude a devotee takes when he prostrates before a shrine, his forehead touching the ground. That marvellous point of light would change colours and get bigger and bigger until it took the form of a ball; finally it would burst and cover my body from head to foot with white liquid light. As soon as that happened, I would lose outer consciousness and fall asleep. I used to believe that that was the way everybody went to sleep. Then, when I grew older and began to practise meditation, that point of light would appear to me as soon as I closed my eyes, and I'd concentrate upon it. At that time, I was practising meditation with a few friends, following the instructions of Devendra Nath Tagore. We told each other about the visions and experiences we had had. And that was how I found out that none of them had ever seen that point of light or gone to sleep in that way.'

The boy was subject to attacks of rage, during which he would smash furniture to bits. But his mother found she could calm him by pouring water over his head and repeating the name of Shiva. Once, when he was playing with some other boys, he fell down a staircase and cut his forehead; this left him with a scar over his left eye for the rest of his life. When Ramakrishna was told of this in later years, he commented, 'It was probably a good thing; if Naren hadn't lost some of his blood, his energy would have been too great. He'd have turned the world upside down.' Naren used to say that it was through the grace of Ramakrishna that he finally became able to control his anger.

Naren was always a natural leader among boys of his own age. He was temperamentally energetic, restless and aggressively independent; but cheerful, never sullen. He had strong passions but an even stronger self-discipline which held him back from sensuality of any kind. He enjoyed sports – swimming, wrestling, boxing and riding horseback. He loved music, and could sing, dance and play several musical instruments with outstanding skill. He organized a theatrical troupe, made models of gasworks and factories, learned to cook, taking up each new occupation or hobby with characteristic enthusiasm. He had a powerful body which became somewhat heavy in later life but always remained agile. His features were large and well proportioned, but his beauty, on which so many people remarked, came essentially from within; it was the projection of his personality.

His memory was even more phenomenal than his mother's; he could absorb the contents of a school textbook at a single cursory reading. His teachers all found him exceptionally intelligent. As he matured, this intelligence became predominantly analytical and critical. Naren was a doubter – in no mean-spirited way but as a man must be whose drive to understand Life is really urgent. He *had* to doubt in order to know. He dared not take anything that was told him on trust. As a small boy, he climbed a tree whose owner pretended it was guarded by a ghost, just to prove to his playmates that the man was lying. To Naren, the truth was too sacred to be trifled with; and it was for this reason that he poured such bitter scorn on those whom he discovered to have been merely exaggerating or quibbling.

In the last chapter I mentioned the gymnasium at which Naren met Rakhal. One day, Naren and some fellow gymnasts were struggling to set up a heavy wooden frame for a trapeze. A crowd gathered to watch them but no one offered to help. Naren noticed a muscular British sailor in the crowd and appealed to him. The sailor was willing and began trying to fit the legs of the frame into the sockets of its stand, while the boys hauled on the tackle by which the frame could be lifted. Suddenly the rope broke, the frame fell, and the sailor was knocked unconscious by one of its legs. Blood gushed from the wound in his head. The crowd ran away, fearing that the police would come and accuse them of attacking an Englishman. The boys ran away too – all except for Naren and two or three of his close friends. Naren tore a piece off his wearing-cloth, soaked it in water, bandaged the wound and then sprinkled water in the sailor's face and fanned him until he came to his senses. Then the boys helped him into a near-by school building, and sent word to a neighbour to come with a doctor. The doctor told them that the wound was not serious but that the sailor would need a week's nursing before he could recover completely. Naren arranged for this, providing the necessary medical supplies; and, when the sailor was well again, he even raised a small subscription for him.

Few people indeed are born equally fitted for the life of action and the life of contemplation, as Naren was. 'Every night when I went to bed,' he used to recall, 'two ideals of life appeared before me. One of them was to be a man of great wealth, surrounded by servants and dependants and enjoying high rank and immense power. I saw myself as foremost among the great men of the world; and I certainly had the necessary ability in me to fulfil that ambition. But then, the very next moment, I would picture myself as having renounced everything in the world. I was wearing nothing but a loincloth, eating without anxiety whatever food came my way, sleeping under a tree and living in complete reliance on God's will. I knew it was within me to lead this life of the sages and ascetics, if I should choose to do so. These two pictures of the two directions in which I could bend my life kept appearing before me; but I always ended by choosing the latter. I knew that this was the only path by which a man could achieve true happiness, and I resolved to follow it and not the other. As I dwelt on the happiness of such a life, my mind would become absorbed in God and I would fall asleep.'

When Naren was fifteen years old, his father had to go to Raipur in the Central Provinces. Finding that his business would keep him there for some time, Vishwanath decided to have his family join him. In those days, there was no railway connection between the Central Provinces and Bengal, so they had to make part of the journey in bullock carts. For more than two weeks, they traversed dense forests full of wild animals, and this made a lasting impression upon Naren. To quote his own words, 'What I saw and felt as we passed through that forest has always remained printed in my memory. And one day more than all the others. . . . It was the day we skirted the lofty range of the Vindhya hills. The peaks on either side of the road rose very high into the sky. On the slopes, the trees and creepers were wonderfully beautiful; heavy with fruit and flowers. Birds of all colours were flying from grove to grove or swooping to the ground in search of food, and filling the gorge with sweet cries. Seeing all this, I felt an extraordinary peace of mind. The slowly moving chain of bullock carts reached a place where two great rocks had come together in an embrace like lovers over the narrow forest trail. Looking round me attentively at the point where they met, I saw that there was a very deep cleft from the top to the bottom of the rock on one side of the trail and that, inside the cleft, there hung an enormous honeycomb; the result of the bees' labour throughout many years. Filled with wonder, I thought about the kingdom of the bees – how it had begun and how it had ended – and my mind became so deeply absorbed in the thought of the infinite power of God, ruler of the three worlds, that I lost all consciousness of my surroundings for some time. I don't know how long I lay in the bullock cart in that condition. When I regained external consciousness, I found that we had passed that place and were already far away. As I was alone in the cart, no one ever knew that this had happened to me.'

In the following year, 1879, Naren and his family returned to Calcutta. Shortly after this, he graduated from high school and entered the Presidency College of Calcutta. A year later, he joined the General Assembly's Institution. His favourite subject was History. By this time, he was very widely read. He studied Western logic, Western philosophy and the ancient and modern history of various European nations.

A fellow student, Brajendra Nath Seal, later a famous scholar and educator, wrote about Naren as follows: 'He was undeniably a gifted youth, sociable, free and unconventional in his manners – an excellent singer – the soul of social circles – a brilliant conversationalist, though somewhat bitter and caustic, piercing with shafts of wit the shows and mummeries of the world – sitting in the scorner's chair but hiding the tenderest of hearts under that mask of cynicism – altogether, an inspired bohemian but possessing what bohemians lack, an iron will —'

At this time, Naren had become a temporary disciple of John Stuart Mill and Herbert Spencer and was beginning to call himself an agnostic. He was a strict vegetarian, slept often on the bare floor and never used more than one blanket. He had resolved to remain celibate. When his parents urged him to marry, he flatly refused – even when the father of one of his proposed brides offered to pay for his schooling in England so that he might qualify for the Indian Civil Service. Probably Naren himself could not have explained exactly why he was practising these austerities. Instinctively, he was preparing himself to play a great and dedicated part in life, without quite knowing, yet, what that part would be.

His doubt was his passion. He longed to believe but could find no foundation for faith. Books could not satisfy him, or experiences got at second hand. He had met Devendra Nath, now leader of the Adi Brahmo Samaj, and had asked him, 'Sir, have you seen God?' Devendra Nath was too honest to give the boy an insincere reassurance; and Naren was disappointed. But Devendra Nath told him, 'You have the eyes of a yogi. You should practise meditation.' As we saw in the previous chapter, Naren joined the Brahmo Samaj and persuaded his friend Rakhal to do likewise. Naren felt uplifted by the congregational prayers and the devotional singing of the Samaj, but he soon realized that he was not getting the only thing he wanted; direct spiritual experience.

The principal of the General Assembly's Institution was then Professor W. W. Hastie, an Englishman who regarded the culture of India with unusual reverence and understanding, and who had made himself loved by many Indians who came in contact with him. Hastie at once recognized Naren's quality; indeed, he spoke of him as 'a genius'. 'I have never come across a lad of his talents and possibilities,' he said; adding rather quaintly, 'even among the philosophical students in the German Universities.' Hastie also had the distinction of being one of the very few non-Indians who had met Ramakrishna. One day, in a literature class, Naren heard him lecturing on Wordsworth's *The Excursion* and the poet's nature-mysticism. This led the Professor to speak of those states of deep meditation in which outer consciousness is lost. He told his students that such states were only possible as the result of purity and concentration and that they had anyway become extremely rare in modern times. 'I have known only one person,' he added, 'who has achieved such meditation, and that is Ramakrishna of Dakshineswar. You will understand it better if you visit this saint.'

But neither Professor Hastie nor Rakhal was the means of bringing Naren to Ramakrishna. Perhaps Naren feared another disappointment and therefore hesitated to follow their advice. And, as it finally turned out, he was not required to make the decision. According to Saradananda, in November 1881, Naren went to the house of Surendra Nath Mitra, who had asked him to play and sing to entertain his guests at a party. One of these guests was Ramakrishna.

Ramakrishna showed an eager interest in Naren from the first moment he saw him. He called Surendra Nath and Ram Chandra Datta and questioned them minutely about the boy. Then, when Naren had finished singing, Ramakrishna spoke a few words to him, studying his face intently as he did so. Evidently he was looking for certain physical signs which would confirm his belief that this was indeed one of his destined disciples. Then he invited Naren to visit him at Dakshineswar. Naren agreed to do so.

For the next few weeks, however, he had to study for his examination at the University of Calcutta. And then there was some conflict with his family. Once again, Vishwanath was trying to get Naren to marry. The father of the bride was offering an exceptionally handsome dowry, because his daughter had a dark complexion, which was regarded as a social disadvantage. Naren refused, as before. Ram Chandra Datta, who was a cousin of Naren's, had been strongly urging him to agree to the match. When he saw that Naren was really not to be moved, he said to him, 'All right then – if you seriously want to live a spiritual life you ought to talk to Ramakrishna. You won't find anything at the Brahmo Samaj.' And he offered to take Naren to Dakshineswar himself. They went there a few days later, in a hired carriage with two or three friends.

When, at a later date, Ramakrishna was asked about Naren's first visit to Dakshineswar, he said, 'Naren entered the room by the western door, the one that faces the Ganges. I noticed that he had no concern about his bodily appearance; his hair and his clothes weren't tidy at all. He seemed altogether unattached, as if nothing external appealed to him. His eyes showed that the greater part of his mind was turned inward, all of the time. When I saw this, I marvelled to myself, "How is it possible that such a great spiritual aspirant can live in Calcutta, the home of the worldly-minded?"

'There was a mat spread out on the floor. I asked him to sit, and he sat down near the jar of Ganges water. A few of his friends were also with him that day. I saw that their nature was that of ordinary worldly people, just the opposite of his. They were thinking only of their pleasure.

'I asked him about his singing, and I found that he knew only two or three songs in Bengali. I asked him to sing them. He began singing the Brahmo song:

> *Oh mind, let us go home –*
> *Why do you roam the world, that foreign land,*
> *And wear its alien garb?*

'He sang that song with his whole soul, as though he were deep in meditation. When I heard it, I couldn't control myself. I went into ecstasy.'

That was all Ramakrishna himself would tell; and, as we shall see, he showed unusual reticence. Perhaps the emotions connected with that meeting were so powerful that he did not wish to recall them. However, Naren has described for us the amazing scene which immediately followed:

'As soon as I had finished that song, the Master stood up, took me by the hand and led me on to the northern veranda. It was winter, so the open spaces between the pillars were covered with screens of matting to keep out the north wind; and this meant that, when the door of the room was closed, anyone standing on the veranda was hidden from both inside and outside. As soon as we were on the veranda, the Master closed the door. I thought he must be going to give me some instruction in private. But what he said and did next was something I could never have believed possible. He suddenly caught hold of my hand and began shedding tears of joy. He said to me, affectionately as if to a familiar friend, "You've come so late! Was that right? Couldn't you have guessed how I've been waiting for you? My ears are nearly burned off, listening to the talk of these worldly people. I thought I should burst, not having anyone to tell how I really felt!" He went on like that – raving and weeping. And then suddenly he folded his palms together and began addressing me as if I was some divine being, "I know who you are, My Lord. You are Nara, the ancient sage, the incarnation of Narayana. You have come back to earth to take away the sufferings and sorrows of mankind." I was absolutely dumbfounded. I said to myself, "What kind of a man is this? He must be raving mad! How can he talk like this to me, who am nobody – the son of Vishwanath Datta?" But I didn't answer him, and I let this wonderful madman go on talking as he chose. Presently he asked me to stay there on the veranda, and he went back into the room and came out again bringing butter, rock candy and a few pieces of sandesh; and then he began feeding me with his own hands. I kept asking him to give me the sweetmeats, so I could share them with my friends, but he wouldn't. "They'll get some later," he said, "you take these for yourself." And he wouldn't be satisfied until I'd eaten all of them. Then he took my hand and said, "Promise me – you'll come back here soon, alone." I couldn't refuse his request; it was made so earnestly. So I had to say, "I will." Then I went back into the room with him and sat down beside my friends.'

This was certainly a searching experience for an eighteen-year-old college intellectual; and it is a proof of Naren's maturity of judgement that he did not leave Dakshineswar at the first opportunity and break his promise to return. Instead, he sat watching Ramakrishna and trying to relate what had just happened on the veranda to his present behaviour. For now, in the presence of the others, Ramakrishna seemed perfectly sane. He spoke lucidly and beautifully about renunciation.

Naren's story continues: '"Here is a true man of renunciation," I said to myself; "he practises what he preaches; he has given up everything for God." "God can be seen and spoken to," he told us, "just as I'm seeing you and speaking to you. But who wants to see and speak to God? People grieve and shed enough tears to fill many pots, because their wives or their sons are dead, or because they've lost their money and their estates. But who weeps because he can't see God? And yet – if anyone really wants to see God, and if he calls upon him – God will reveal himself, that's certain."

'When I heard these words, I became more and more convinced that he wasn't like any of the other teachers of religion I had met – full of poetic talk and fine figures of speech – but that he was talking of what he directly knew, of what he himself had actually obtained, by giving up everything and by calling on God with his whole heart and strength. I thought, "Well, he may be mad – but this is indeed a rare soul who can undertake such renunciation. Yes, he *is* mad – but how pure! And what renunciation! He is truly worthy of reverence." Thinking this, I bowed down before his feet, took my leave of him and returned to Calcutta that day.'

Nevertheless, Naren stayed away from Dakshineswar for a whole month. Saradananda points out in his book that this is hardly surprising. Naren hesitated to visit Ramakrishna again because he feared the possible power of his influence, and felt instinctively that Ramakrishna represented a challenge to his way of thinking. Even though Naren was dissatisfied with the spiritual life of the Brahmo Samaj, he was enthusiastic for its reformist ideals. He was critical of the traditional Hinduism for which Ramakrishna stood. He believed – or thought he believed – in reason rather than in intuition, in discrimination rather than devotion. Ramakrishna's ecstasies embarrassed him. He could not imagine himself shut up inside a temple compound, spending his days in meditation and worship. His restlessness demanded a wandering life; his reformist conscience made him eager for social service.

The meeting with Ramakrishna had disturbed him profoundly. Naren kept repeating to himself that this was a madman, a monomaniac. Yet Naren knew that he loved him and, in spite of himself, was almost ready to follow him. Almost – but no, it was impossible. One can't become the disciple of a madman. And Ramakrishna *must* be mad. He *had* to be mad. Because if – terrible thought! – he was sane, then John Stuart Mill and Herbert Spencer were mad, the Brahmo reformers were mad, the whole of the rest of the world was mad. If Ramakrishna was sane, then everything that the world believed in and taught must be turned inside out and upside down. And Naren would have to turn himself inside out, too.

The violence of Naren's struggle not to believe in Ramakrishna is a measure of his greatness. He could not accept anything partially. For him, the alternative to doubt was absolute self-dedication. Years later, when Naren had become Vivekananda, he said to one of his Western disciples who had been teased by a friend because of her doubts, scruples and hesitations to believe, 'Let none regret that they were difficult to convince! I fought my Master for six long years, with the result that I know every inch of the way.'

Here is Naren's description of his second visit to Dakshineswar. This time, he had to go the whole way there on foot.

'I had no idea that the Dakshineswar Temple was so far from Calcutta, because I had been there only once before and that was in a carriage. This time, it seemed as if the journey would never end, however far I walked. But, after asking many people the way, I arrived at Dakshineswar at last and went straight to the Master's room. I found him sitting, deep in his own meditations, on the smaller bed which stands beside the bigger one. There was no one with him. As soon as he saw me, he called me joyfully to him and made me sit down on one end of the bed. He was in a strange mood. He muttered something to himself which I couldn't understand, looked hard at me, then rose and approached me. I thought we were about to have another crazy scene. Scarcely had that thought passed through my mind before he placed his right foot on my body. Immediately, I had a wonderful experience. My eyes were wide open, and I saw that everything in the room, including the walls themselves, was whirling rapidly around and receding, and at the same time, it seemed to me that my consciousness of self, together with the entire universe, was about to vanish into a vast, all-devouring void. This destruction of my consciousness of self seemed to me to be the same thing as death. I felt that death was right before me, very close. Unable to control myself, I cried out loudly, "Ah, what are you doing to me? Don't you know I have my parents at home?" When the Master heard this, he gave a loud laugh. Then, touching my chest with his hand, he said, "All right – let it stop now. It needn't be done all at once. It will happen in its own good time." To my amazement, this extraordinary vision of mine vanished as suddenly as it had come. I returned to my normal state and saw things inside and outside the room standing stationary, as before.

'Although it has taken so much time to describe all this, it actually happened in only a few moments. And yet it changed my whole way of thinking. I was bewildered and kept trying to analyse what had happened. I had seen how this experience had begun and ended in obedience to the will of this extraordinary man. I had read about hypnotism in books and I wondered if this was something of the same kind. But my heart refused to believe that it was. For even people of great will-power can only create such conditions when they are working on weak minds. And my mind was by no means weak. Up to then, in fact, I had been proud of my intelligence and will-power. This man did not bewitch me or reduce me to his puppet. On the contrary, when I first met him, I had decided that he was mad. Why then should I have suddenly found myself in this state? It seemed an utter mystery to me. But I determined to be on my guard, lest he should get further influence over me in the future.'

After Naren had recovered from his vision, Ramakrishna joked with him and gave him food, behaving with such frank affection that Naren felt embarrassed. When evening came, he told Ramakrishna that he must return home. Ramakrishna seemed pained and disappointed. He made Naren promise to return as soon as he possibly could.

When Naren did return, about a week later, he was very much on his guard; determined not to be hypnotized. Ramakrishna proposed that they should walk together in a near-by garden just south of the Dakshineswar compound, because the compound itself happened to be crowded with devotees. They went into the garden-house – the same in which Ramakrishna had first seen the picture of the Virgin with the child Jesus – and sat down. After a short while, Ramakrishna passed into samadhi. Naren watched him. Suddenly, Ramakrishna touched him, just as on the previous occasion. Despite Naren's strong will to resist, he was unable to cling to his consciousness. This time he became completely unconscious. When he came to himself, he found that Ramakrishna was passing his hand over his chest and smiling at him, sweetly and gently. He had no idea what had happened in the meanwhile.

On a later occasion, Ramakrishna told some of his other disciples, 'That day, after Naren had lost consciousness of his present individuality, I asked him many questions – such as who he really was, where he had come from, how long he would stay in this world, and so forth. I made him able to enter into his innermost being and find the answers to my questions there. These answers confirmed what I'd already learned about him in visions. It is forbidden to tell all those things. But I can tell you that, on the day when he knows who he really is, he will no longer remain in this world. With a strong effort of will he will immediately give up his body through the power of yoga. Naren is a great soul, perfect in meditation.'

Ramakrishna also described a vision – one of those which, as he said, were confirmed by the answers Naren had given him. His mind, while in samadhi, had ascended through the world of gross matter into the subtle world of ideas, and thence to what he described as 'the fence made of light' which separates the divisible from the indivisible. Beyond this fence, even the gods and goddesses could not penetrate, because all Form ceased there. Nevertheless, within the realm of the indivisible, Ramakrishna saw seven sages, whose bodies were made only of the light of pure consciousness. These sages sat in samadhi and their greatness exceeded the greatness of the gods. As Ramakrishna watched, he saw a something shape itself out of the undifferentiated light, and this something took the form of a child. The child came down to one of the sages, threw its arms around his neck and tried to rouse him from his samadhi. The sage awoke at last. Seeing the child, his face became bright with delight, and Ramakrishna knew that they were eternal companions. 'I am going down there,' the child said to the sage, 'and you must come with me.' The sage did not answer, but his eyes expressed his joyful agreement. He went into samadhi again, and then Ramakrishna saw a part of him come down to earth in the form of a bright light. 'And,' Ramakrishna added, after telling this to his disciples, 'hardly had I set eyes on Naren for the first time when I knew he was that sage.' When they questioned Ramakrishna further, he admitted that the child in the vision had been himself.

I have already explained, in Chapter 8, the Hindu concept of the avatar. To this must be added the concept of the 'eternal companion'. It is the Hindu belief that every divine incarnation has such companions and that he brings them with him when he comes to earth in human form. (A Hindu would of course be ready to believe that the apostles of Jesus of Nazareth were also 'eternal companions'.) Therefore, for Naren to realize 'who he really was' was to remember his eternal relationship with Ramakrishna, in which their few years together on earth in India was a tiny episode. Rakhal was another such companion; but his relationship with Ramakrishna was even closer, being that of spiritual parent and son.

The second experience of Ramakrishna's power convinced Naren that he was in the presence of a being whose will was altogether superior to his own. Yet it was still hard for him to submit. Naren had always been opposed to the traditional Hindu idea that the disciple must follow his guru in blind obedience. He still felt it was wrong to surrender one's freedom of judgement to another. He was now ready to admit that Ramakrishna was more than an ordinary human being, and therefore a teacher he should follow and learn from. But he was determined to test for himself everything that Ramakrishna taught him. And we cannot be too grateful for this attitude of Naren's. His scepticism makes him one of the most reliable of all the witnesses to Ramakrishna's greatness.

DAKSHINESWAR TEMPLE

Main gate   Calcutta, 4 miles →   N

Orchard

Tank

Orchard

Kitchens, stores, dining rooms, offices, guestrooms

Tank

Plate-washing ghat

Natmandir

Kali temple

Nahabat

Flower gardens

Main ghat

Shiva temples

Courtyard

Chandni

Sri Ramakrishna's room

Semicircular porch

N.─┐
N.E.─ veranda
S.E.─┘

Gate to courtyard

Nahabat of Holy Mother

Bakultala ghat

Banyan

Panchavati

Meditation room (hut)

Radhakanta temple

Kuthi

Goose tank

Orchard

Bel tree (vilwa)

Back gate

Pine grove (Jhautala)

G A N G E S

0   100'   200'   300'   400'

22. Map of Dakshineswar Temple

23. Ramakrishna's room, exterior

24. Ramakrishna's room, interior

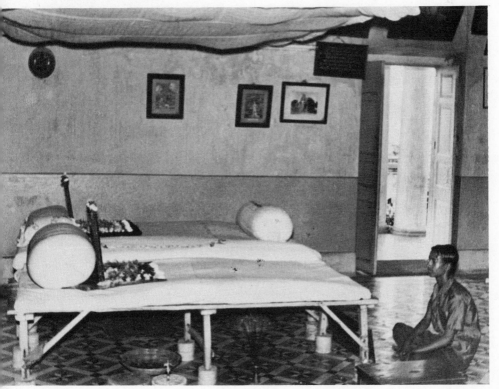

25. Landing ghat, Dakshineswar

16

The Training of Naren

———————

In the last chapter we saw how Ramakrishna became convinced that this young college student, Narendra Nath Datta, was actually an incarnation of one of his 'eternal companions'. It may well be asked how Ramakrishna, once he had arrived at this conviction, could have continued to feel even the smallest anxiety about Naren's future. For how could such a being ever come to any spiritual harm? In answer to this question, Saradananda points out that even an avatar, when he assumes a body and enters the sphere of Maya, must suffer some blurring of his spiritual insight. Ramakrishna was prone to occasional doubts about the truth of his own visions; perhaps he had been mistaken, he would say to himself. And so he continued to be anxious and to subject Naren to various tests.

Ramakrishna used to say that there are eighteen qualities or manifestations of power which can possibly be found in a human being. Even two or three of these qualities are sufficient to enable an individual to gain great fame and influence in the world – and Ramakrishna saw that Naren had all eighteen of them. In moods of anxiety, Ramakrishna feared that Naren might misuse these powers as he grew older; that he might be satisfied with a partial realization of God, and that, on the basis of this partial realization, he might merely found a new religious sect and make himself famous and powerful in the usual worldly way. Ramakrishna's own life was, as we have already seen, both a protest against sectarian exclusiveness and a demonstration that every sect can show the way to knowledge of God. He need not have worried about Naren, who was to prove, in the writings and lectures of his later life as Vivekananda, how well he had learnt this lesson: 'I accept all the religions of the past and I worship God with every one of them. Can

God's book be finished? Must it not be a continuing revelation? Difference is the first sign of thought. I pray that the sects may multiply until at last there will be as many sects as human beings.'

Ramakrishna's devotion to Naren astonished everybody. Often, when Naren arrived at Dakshineswar, Ramakrishna would exclaim, 'There's Na—' and be unable to complete the name because he passed into samadhi. If Naren stayed away from Dakshineswar even for a few days, Ramakrishna would shed tears. 'I can't bear it when I don't see him,' he told the other young disciples. 'I wept so much and still Narendra didn't come! He doesn't understand at all what I feel for him. . . . What will people think, seeing a man of my age weeping and pining for a boy like him! With you, I don't feel ashamed of it – you are my very own. But what must the others think? And yet I can't stop myself —'

It was not to be expected that Naren would charm everybody. Lacking Ramakrishna's spiritual insight, many devotees saw only that their beloved and revered Master was being treated in this inconsiderate fashion by a mere youth, and a seemingly self-satisfied and arrogant one. Saradananda recalls how he talked with a neighbour of Naren's before becoming personally acquainted with him, and was told, 'There's a boy who lives in that house – I've never known anyone so hopelessly spoilt. Since he got his B.A. degree he's so vain, he thinks nothing in the whole world matters but him. When his father and other older people are present he'll start singing and beating time on a kettle-drum, quite rudely, without any respect. He'll smoke cigars, too, right in front of them!'

No outside observer could possibly have understood the subtlety and comedy of the relationship between these two infinitely strange beings. Beneath the surface of behaviour, they were communicating and exchanging signals and probing each other. One day, Keshab Sen and Vijay Krishna Goswami visited Dakshineswar with a number of Brahmo devotees. Naren was also present. After Keshab and Vijay had left, Ramakrishna said to some of the Brahmos who had remained, 'I could see the light of knowledge burning in Keshab and Vijay; it was like the flame of a candle. But in Naren it was like a blazing sun.' Naren later protested violently to Ramakrishna against this remark: 'People will think you're mad if you talk like that! Keshab is famous all over the world. Vijay is a saint. And I'm nobody. How can you speak of us in the same breath? Please, I beg of you, never say such things again!'

'But, my child,' said Ramakrishna, with his innocent smile, 'what can *I* do about it? You don't suppose I'd say such things of my own accord? It was Mother who showed me the truth about you, and so I had to tell it. Mother has never told me a lie.'

'How do you *know* it was Mother who told you?' Naren objected. 'All this may be a fiction of your own brain. Science and philosophy prove that our senses often deceive us, especially when there's a desire in our minds to believe something. You are fond of me and you want to believe that I'm a great man – that may be why you have these visions.'

When Ramakrishna was in a high state of spiritual insight, Naren's scepticism merely amused him. But sometimes he would become worried, appeal to the Divine Mother for guidance, and be told, 'Why do you listen to Naren? He will accept the truth before long.'

Once, when Naren had stayed away from Dakshineswar longer than usual, Ramakrishna grew so anxious that he decided to go into Calcutta and look for him. The day happened to be a Sunday, so Ramakrishna went to the headquarters of the Brahmo Samaj, knowing that Naren was usually there on Sundays to sing devotional songs during the evening service. Ramakrishna felt confident of a warm welcome, because of his affectionate relations with Keshab and some other Brahmo leaders; what he did not realize was that there were other prominent Brahmos who resented the change he had brought about in Keshab and Vijay, and who had stopped coming to Dakshineswar for that very reason.

Ramakrishna got to the Brahmo headquarters in the middle of the service. His arrival caused a disturbance; many people stood up on benches to get a look at him, and there was noise and disorder. This naturally annoyed the prominent Brahmos who were present and particularly the preacher, who was obliged to end his sermon abruptly. But Ramakrishna was quite unaware of this. Without glancing to left or to right, he advanced to the altar, where he went into samadhi. This excited the congregation more than ever. The ushers, finding that they could not restore order, turned out all the gaslights to make people leave the building; a stupid move which resulted in a stampede for the doors in the dark.

Naren himself was among the members of the choir and saw all this. He managed to elbow his way to Ramakrishna's side, led him out through a back door, got him into a carriage and rode with him to Dakshineswar.

Later, Naren used to say, 'What pain I felt that day, when I saw the Master being humiliated like that, and all on my account! How I scolded him for what he had done! But he didn't care one bit about my scolding or his humiliation; he was just happy to have me with him again. So then I spoke to him very severely: "It's written in the Puranas that King Bharata thought so much about his favourite deer that he himself became a deer after his death. If that's true, you should beware of thinking too much about me!" The Master was simple as a young boy. He took what I said literally, and asked me in great distress, "You are right — so what's going to happen to me, since I can't bear not seeing you?" Then he went off anxiously to consult the Divine Mother. After a while he came back beaming with delight, and exclaimed, "Leave me in peace, you rascal! I'll never listen to anything you tell me again! Mother said to me: 'You love him so much because you regard him as Narayana [Vishnu] himself. If the day ever comes when you don't see Narayana in him, then you won't spare him a single glance!'"'

When Naren started coming to Dakshineswar, he was, of course, delighted to find his old friend Rakhal already among Ramakrishna's disciples. But Naren soon discovered that Rakhal was breaking the Brahmo pledge. Under Ramakrishna's influence, Rakhal, with his naturally devotional temperament, had turned back to the worship of God with form. He went daily into the temples and bowed down before the images of the various deities. Naren still despised all image worship and he rebuked Rakhal with his usual bluntness. Rakhal was too gentle-natured to argue with his friend but he was much hurt and began to avoid Naren when he came to Dakshineswar. However, Ramakrishna heard about this and made peace between them, telling Naren that he must respect Rakhal's way of worship even though it was not his own.

In the meantime, Ramakrishna was trying to teach Naren the doctrine of pure Vedanta, which declares the absolute identity of Brahman and Atman. He made Naren read books expounding non-dualism. Naren found them worse than Rakhal's image worship; indeed, positively blasphemous. 'What's the difference,' he exclaimed, 'between this and atheism? How can a created soul think of itself as the Creator? What could be a greater sin? What's this nonsense about *I am God, you are God, everything that is born and dies is God?* The authors of these books must have been mad – how else could they have written such stuff?' And Ramakrishna would smile at Naren's indignation and answer mildly, 'You may not be able to accept these truths at present, but is that a reason to condemn the great sages who taught them? Why do you try to limit God's nature? Keep calling on him. He is truth itself. Whatever he reveals to you, believe that to be his true nature.'

But Naren refused, for the moment, to be convinced. How very surprised he would have been if he could have heard himself, less than fifteen years later, horrifying his Christian audiences in the United States by such non-dualistic declarations as, 'See no difference between ant and angel – every worm is the brother of the Nazarene!'

In Chapter 14, mention was made of Pratap Chandra Hazra. Hazra was a subject of disagreement between Ramakrishna and Naren. Here is part of a typical conversation they had about him, recorded by M. (April 24, 1885):

NAREN: Hazra has become a different man, nowadays.

RAMAKRISHNA: You can't be sure of that. There are people whose mouths are full of Rama's name, yet they carry stones hidden under their arms to throw at others.

NAREN: I don't agree with you, sir. I questioned him about all the things people say against him. He says they're untrue.

RAMAKRISHNA: I once prayed to the Divine Mother, 'Oh Mother, if Hazra's a hypocrite, then please take him away from here.' Later, I told him what I'd prayed. A few days afterwards, he came to me and said, 'I'm still here, you see. . . .' You don't understand him. You think you understand people – that's why I'm telling you this. Do you know how I regard a man like Hazra? I know that God assumes the form of holy men – well, then, he must also assume the form of swindlers and rogues.

Hazra's mouth was full of the highest philosophy and the most exalted sentiments. He made japa with a rosary and let himself be seen doing it by everyone. He treated Ramakrishna with a respect which was too exaggerated to be quite genuine. On one occasion, when he was about to take the dust of Ramakrishna's feet, Ramakrishna recoiled from his touch, avoiding instinctively a physical contact with what was insincere and untruthful. (Taking the dust of the feet of a holy man is a symbolic gesture of reverence and humility, still widely practised in India today.)

But Naren was amused by Hazra's sharp and witty tongue, and Hazra listened to everything Naren said with flattering respect. One day, Naren was telling Hazra about Vedantic non-dualism and his unwillingness to accept it. 'Can it be,' he said, 'that the waterpot is God, that the drinking-vessel is God, that everything we see and all of us are God?' Naren laughed scornfully at the idea and Hazra joined in, like the sycophant he was. While they were laughing, Ramakrishna came up to them. 'What are you two talking about?' he asked Naren affectionately; then, without waiting for an answer, he touched Naren and himself went into samadhi.

'And then,' Naren would relate, 'at the marvellous touch of the Master, my mind underwent a complete revolution. I was aghast to realize that there really was nothing whatever in the entire universe but God. I remained silent, wondering how long this state of mind would continue. It didn't pass off all day. I got back home, and I felt just the same there; everything I saw was God. I sat down to eat, and I saw that everything – the plate, the food, my mother who was serving it and I myself – everything was God and nothing else but God. I swallowed a couple of mouthfuls and then sat still without speaking. My mother asked me lovingly, "Why are you so quiet? Why don't you eat?" That brought me back to everyday consciousness, and I began eating again. But, from then on, I kept having the same experience, no matter what I was doing – eating, drinking, sitting, lying down, going to college, strolling along the street. It was a kind of intoxication; I can't describe it. If I was crossing a street and saw a carriage coming towards me I didn't have the urge, as I would ordinarily, to get out of its way for fear of being run over. For I said to myself, "I am that carriage. There's no difference between it and me." During that time, I had no sensation in my hands or my feet. When I ate food, I felt no satisfaction from it; it was as if someone else was eating. Sometimes I would lie down in the middle of a meal, and then get up again after a few minutes and go on eating; thus it happened that on those days I would eat far more than usual, but this never upset me. My mother became alarmed; she thought I was suffering from some terrible disease. "He won't live long," she'd say.

'When that first intoxication lost part of its power, I began to see the world as though it were in a dream. When I went for a walk around Cornwallis Square, I used to knock my head against the iron railings to find out if they were only dream-railings or real ones. The loss of feeling in my hands and feet made me afraid that I was going to be paralyzed. When I did at last return to normal consciousness I felt convinced that the state I had been in was a revelation of non-dualistic experience. So then I knew that what is written in the Scriptures about this experience is all true.'

Suddenly, one day, Ramakrishna's whole attitude to Naren – the humble joy he had shown in his presence, the tears he had shed when Naren was absent – seemingly changed. When Naren arrived that morning, Ramakrishna looked at him without the least sign of pleasure and remained silent, instead of asking his usual solicitous questions about Naren's health and welfare. Naren supposed that he must be in some high spiritual mood, and therefore unwilling to speak. So, after waiting for a while, he went outside and began talking to Hazra. Then he heard Ramakrishna's voice, in conversation with some other visitors, and came back into the room. But Ramakrishna continued to ignore Naren. He lay on his bed with his face turned away from him. At last, when evening came, Naren prostrated himself reverently before Ramakrishna and returned to Calcutta.

On his next visit to Dakshineswar, less than a week later, Ramakrishna received him with the same apparent indifference. Yet Naren did not stop coming on this account. Ignored by Ramakrishna, he spent the days talking to Hazra and the disciples. Ramakrishna was privately sending one or other of the boys to report to him on Naren's life and behaviour in Calcutta. Naren could not have known this, but he never showed the least resentment at Ramakrishna's seeming loss of interest in him.

Saradananda tells how, finally, after more than a month, Ramakrishna suddenly asked Naren, 'Why do you keep coming here, when

I don't speak a single word to you?' 'Do you think I come here just to have you speak to me?' Naren answered. 'I love you. I want to see you. That's why I come.' Ramakrishna was delighted. 'I was testing you,' he told Naren, 'to see if you'd stop coming when you didn't get love and attention. Only a spiritual aspirant of your quality could put up with so much neglect and indifference. Anyone else would have left me long ago.'

On another occasion, Ramakrishna put Naren to a different kind of test. He called him into the Panchavati and said, 'As the result of the austerities I've practised, I have long since become possessed of all the supernatural powers. But what would a person like me do with such powers? Why, I can't even keep a wearing-cloth tied around my own waist! So I'm thinking of asking Mother to transfer them all to you. She's told me that you'll be able to use them when necessary. What do you say?'

'Will they help me to realize God?' Naren asked. 'No,' said Ramakrishna, 'they won't help you to do that. But they might be very useful after you have realized God and start doing his work.' 'Then let me realize God first,' said Naren, 'after that, it will be time enough to decide if I need them or not. If I get these marvellous powers now, perhaps they'll make me egotistic. I might forget the whole purpose of my life and use them to gratify some worldly desire. Then they would only have been my ruin.'

Sometimes Naren would remain at Dakshineswar and spend the night in meditation. While he meditated, he would be annoyed, during the early morning hours, by that same steam whistle from the jute mill which the aged Chandra had thought was a celestial trumpet. Ramakrishna advised him to meditate upon the sound of the whistle itself; when Naren did this, he found that it no longer distracted him. Naren told Ramakrishna how difficult it was for him to forget the existence of his body, so Ramakrishna did what Tota Puri had done, many years earlier; he dug his fingernail into the skin between Naren's eyebrows and told him to concentrate on the pain. In this way, Naren became able to lose consciousness of the rest of his body for long periods of time.

Above all, Ramakrishna insisted on the importance of continence.

He told Naren that, if a man maintains absolute continence for twelve years, his mind becomes purified and opened to the knowledge of God. Meanwhile, Naren's father Vishwanath and the other members of his family continued to urge him to marry. Once, when Ramakrishna was visiting the house, the grandmother overheard him preaching chastity to Naren. Henceforward, the family was opposed to Ramakrishna, despite their admiration for his saintliness. But Naren had always done as he liked, and they were quite unable to dissuade him from visiting Dakshineswar.

Ramakrishna used to say to Naren, 'You must test me as the money-changers test their coins. You mustn't accept me until you've tested me thoroughly.' One day, Naren came out to Dakshineswar and found that Ramakrishna had gone into Calcutta. Naren was alone in the room, and suddenly he felt a desire to test the genuineness of Ramakrishna's often-expressed contempt for money. So he hid a rupee under Ramakrishna's mattress. Then he went to the Panchavati and began meditating. Presently, Ramakrishna returned and entered his room. No sooner had he touched the bed than he started back; he had felt actual physical pain. As he was looking around him in bewilderment, unable to understand what it was that had happened to him, Naren came in and stood watching him without saying a word. Ramakrishna called one of the temple attendants and asked him to examine the bed. The rupee was discovered, and Naren then explained what he had done. Ramakrishna fully approved.

Early in 1884, Naren's father Vishwanath died of a heart attack; he had been ailing for some time. When Vishwanath died, Naren was away from home at the house of some friends, and one of them had to break the news to him. Naren returned home at once and performed the customary rites. When the time came to look into Vishwanath's financial affairs, it was found that he had been spending more than he earned and had left nothing but debts. Some relatives even tried to get a share in the family home by means of a lawsuit. They lost the suit, but Naren was still faced by his duty, as the oldest male member of the family, of supporting his mother and brothers. He had never known adversity of any kind, before.

'Even before the prescribed period of mourning was over,' he used to relate, 'I was running hither and thither in search of a job. Dizzy

from lack of food, I had to go from office to office barefoot in the blazing
sun, carrying my application papers. Everywhere I met with a refusal.
From that first experience I learned that unselfish sympathy is very
rare in this world; there is no place here for the poor and the weak.
Even those who, only a few weeks previously, would have regarded
it as a piece of luck if they could do me a favour, now made wry
reluctant faces, though they could easily have helped me if they had
wished. One day, during that time, when I was walking around in the
sun, the soles of my feet became blistered. I was completely exhausted
and had to sit down in the shade of the Ochterloney Monument on
the Maidan. A friend who happened to be with me wanted to console
me, so he sang:

> *Here blows the wind, the breath of Brahman —*
> *It is his grace we feel —*

But when I heard that song, I felt as if he was beating me violently
on the head. Thinking of the helplessness of my mother and my
brothers, I was filled with resentment and despair. "Be quiet!" I told
him. "That fanciful nonsense is all right for people living in the lap of
luxury – people who have no idea what hunger is – people whose
nearest and dearest aren't going in rags and starving. No doubt it
sounds true and beautiful to them – as it did to me, in the old days.
But now I've seen what life is really like. That song is just a pack of
lies."

'I dare say my friend was terribly hurt by my words. How could
he understand the grinding poverty which had made me utter them?
Some mornings, when I got up, I would find that there wasn't enough
food for all of us, so I'd tell Mother, "a friend has invited me to
lunch." On such days I had nothing to eat, for I had no money in my
pocket. I was too proud to say anything about this to anyone outside
our family. Sometimes, rich men would invite me into their houses
to sing and play at their parties, and I went, just as I had always done.
Most of them never concerned themselves about how I was getting
along. A very few used to ask, "Why do you look so pale and sad today?" But only one of them ever found out – and that wasn't through
me – how things really were. He used to send money to my mother
from time to time, anonymously. I am under an eternal debt to him.'

Despite what he had said to his friend on the Maidan, Naren still kept trying to reassure himself that God is good. He used to repeat the Lord's name as he got out of bed in the morning. One day his mother overheard him and said bitterly, 'What's the use of that? You've been repeating the name of the Lord since childhood, and what has he done for you?' Naren had always known his mother as the most pious of devotees. That despair could move her to speak like this shocked him deeply; and now he began seriously to doubt. How could God exist, he asked himself, if the most piteous prayers remained unanswered? How could he be benign, when his creation was so full of evil?

'It was against my nature,' Naren's narrative continues, 'to do anything and conceal it from others. Even as a child, I had never been able to conceal my least thought or action, either from fear or any other motive. So it wasn't surprising that I now began to tell people aggressively that God did not exist; and that, even if he did exist, it was no use calling on him because it produced no results. Of course, the rumour soon spread around that I had become an atheist, and furthermore that I was mixing with people of bad character and visiting houses of ill repute. Those lies only made me all the more aggressive. I now began telling everyone, even those who didn't ask my opinion, that I had no objection to anybody's drinking wine or going to a brothel if only this would help him to forget his hard lot in this world of pain. And I added that I would do these things myself, without the least regard for public opinion, if I could ever be convinced that they would make me happy, even for a single moment.'

(Naren was being unfair to himself in saying this. As a matter of fact, his determination to preserve his sexual purity never wavered, even in the most trying days of his poverty and religious doubts. At this time, there were at least two women who offered him money to become their lover. He refused them with contempt.)

'Such news travels fast. It didn't take long for these words of mine, in a completely distorted version, to reach the ears of the Master, not to mention those of his devotees in Calcutta. Some of them came to visit me, to find out the truth, and they made it obvious that they believed at least part of what they had heard, if not all. I was bitterly wounded to realize that they could think so little of me. I told them that it was cowardice to believe in God merely from fear of hell. Quoting Hume, Mill, Bain, Comte and other Western philosophers, I argued fiercely that there is no evidence of the existence of God. And so they went away, more than ever convinced, as I afterwards learned, of my downfall. In my defiant mood, this actually made me happy. Then the thought came to me that perhaps the Master now believed the same thing. As soon as I thought that, I felt terrible pain. But then I said to myself, "Let him believe it, then. If he does, I can't help it. People's good or bad opinions are worth nothing, anyhow." Later, I discovered that the Master *had* heard all of these lies about me. At first he had made no comment. Then, when one of the devotees wept and said, "Sir, we never dreamed Naren would sink so low!" he cried out excitedly, "Silence, you scoundrels! Mother has told me that he could never do such things. If you talk about this any more, I won't have you in the room!"

'But what was this atheism of mine? Nothing but egotism and pride. The experiences I had had from childhood and, most of all, since meeting the Master, rose vividly into my mind in the brightest colours and I said to myself, "God certainly does exist – otherwise, what is life for, what is it worth? The path to God has to be found, no matter how great the struggle."

'Summer had passed and the rainy season had begun. I went on looking for work, as before. One night, when I was drenched with rain and hadn't eaten all day, I was returning home with tired legs and a mind even more tired than my body. At length I was so exhausted that I couldn't go one single step farther. I lay down like a log on the open veranda of a neighbouring house. Perhaps my external consciousness left me for a while. All kinds of thoughts and pictures went through my mind and I had no power to ignore any of them or concentrate upon certain ones. Then suddenly I felt as if screen after screen had been raised in my mind by the power of providence, and now all the problems which had been tormenting me – where is the harmony between God's justice and his mercy, why does evil exist within a benign creation – all were solved. I was beside myself with joy. Afterwards, when I continued my walk home, I found that there wasn't one iota of fatigue in my body and that my mind was filled with infinite peace and strength. The day was just breaking.

'I now became absolutely indifferent to the praise or blame of the world. I was firmly convinced that I wasn't born to earn money, support a family or seek worldly enjoyments. Secretly, I was preparing to renounce the world, as my grandfather had done. The day arrived on which I had decided to start life as a wandering monk – and then I heard that, on that very day, the Master was coming to the house of a devotee in Calcutta. I thought this was very fortunate: I should see my guru before I left home forever. But, as soon as I met the Master, he told me imperiously, "You must come with me to Dakshineswar today." I offered various excuses, but he wouldn't take No for an answer. I had to drive back with him. In the carriage we didn't speak much. When we got to Dakshineswar, I sat in his room for some time. Others were present. Then the Master went into a state of ecstasy. He came over to me suddenly, took my hand in his and sang, with tears pouring down his face:

> *I am afraid to speak,*
> *I am afraid not to speak,*
> *For the fear rises in my mind*
> *That I shall lose you —*

All this time, I had fought back the strong emotion I was feeling; now I couldn't do so any longer, and my tears poured down like his. I felt sure that the Master knew all about my plans. The others were astonished to see us behave in this way. After the Master had returned to normal consciousness, one of them asked him what was the matter. He smiled and answered, "It's just something between the two of us." That night he sent the others away and called me to him and said, "I know you have come to the world to do Mother's work; you can never lead a worldly life. But, for my sake, stay with your family as long as I'm alive."'

So Naren promised to do this. And now he set himself to find employment with renewed energy. He got a post in an attorney's office. He translated some books. But these were temporary jobs; they brought no real security to his mother and brothers. So now Naren decided to ask Ramakrishna to pray on his behalf that the family's money-troubles might be overcome. Ramakrishna answered that it was for Naren himself to pray. He must forget his earlier scruples, accept the existence of the Divine Mother and pray to her for help. 'Today is Tuesday,' Ramakrishna added, 'a day specially sacred to Mother. Go to the temple tonight and pray. Mother will grant you whatever you ask for. I promise you that.'

Naren was now almost free of the prejudices he had acquired from the Brahmo Samaj. Experience had taught him to have faith in Ramakrishna's words, and he was eager to do as he had been told. He waited impatiently for the night. At nine o'clock, Ramakrishna sent him to the temple. As Naren was on his way there, a kind of drunkenness possessed him; he was reeling. And when he entered the temple, he saw at once that the Divine Mother was actually alive. Naren was overwhelmed and prostrated himself again and again before her shrine, exclaiming, 'Mother – grant me discrimination, grant me detachment, grant me divine knowledge and devotion, grant me that I may see you without obstruction, always!' His heart was filled with peace. The universe completely disappeared from his consciousness and Mother alone remained.

When Naren came back from the temple, Ramakrishna asked him if he had prayed for the relief of his family's wants. Naren was taken aback; he had forgotten to do so. Ramakrishna told him to return quickly and make the prayer. Naren obeyed, but again he became drunk with bliss, forgot his intention and prayed only for detachment, devotion and knowledge as before. 'Silly boy!' said Ramakrishna, when he returned and confessed this. 'Couldn't you control yourself a little, and remember that prayer? Go back again and tell Mother what you want – be quick!' This time, Naren's experience was different. He did not forget the prayer. But when he came for the third time before the shrine he felt a sense of deep shame; what he had been about to ask seemed miserably trivial and unworthy. 'It was,' he said later, 'like being graciously received by a king and then asking him for gourds and pumpkins.' So, once more, he asked only for detachment, devotion and knowledge. However, as he came out of the temple, he felt suddenly convinced that all this was a trick Ramakrishna had played on him. 'It was certainly you,' he told Ramakrishna, 'who made me intoxicated. Now you must at least say a prayer for me that my mother and brothers will never lack food and clothing.' 'My child,' Ramakrishna told him affectionately, 'you know I could never offer a prayer like that for anyone; the words wouldn't come out of my mouth. I told you that you'd get whatever you asked Mother for; but you couldn't ask that, either. It is not in you to ask for worldly benefits. What am I to do about it?' But Naren answered firmly, 'You must say the prayer, for my sake. I'm certain they'll be freed from want if only you'll say they will.' At length, Ramakrishna yielded to Naren's urging and said, 'All right – they will never lack plain food and clothing.' And this statement was proved true.

This acceptance by Naren of the worship of God with form, was, of course, a most important event in his life. During his later years he was accustomed to say, 'Ramakrishna was a *jnani* [a man of intellectual discrimination] within and a *bhakta* [a man of devotion] without; but I am a *bhakta* within and a *jnani* without.' In general, Naren's teaching as Vivekananda laid emphasis on discrimination rather than on devotion. He once wrote to an American lady, in that serio-comic style which was so characteristic of his mature personality, 'Kali worship is my especial *fad*.' But he was experienced enough to know that the concept of Mother Kali is one which the majority of potential devotees in the West will always find hard to accept; and he seldom mentioned her in his American and British lectures.

There was a young man named Vaikuntha Nath Sannyal who knew Naren slightly, through having once worked with him in the same office. This Vaikuntha Nath happened to visit Dakshineswar on the morning after the events which have been related above. He found Ramakrishna standing in his room and Naren still asleep outside on the veranda. Ramakrishna's face was beaming with delight. Here is Vaikuntha Nath's description of what he witnessed that day:

'No sooner had I approached and made my prostration than the Master pointed to Naren and said, "Look at that boy – that boy is very good – his name is Narendra. He wouldn't accept the Divine Mother before. It was only last night that he did. He was in need of money. So I advised him to ask Mother for it. But he couldn't. He said he felt ashamed. When he came back from the temple, he asked me to teach him a song in praise of Mother. So I taught him, 'Mother, thou art the Saviour', and he sang it all night. That's why he's sleeping now." And then the Master smiled with joy and said, "Narendra has accepted Kali. That's very good, isn't it?" Seeing that he was as happy as a child about this, I answered, "Yes, sir, it is very good." A little later he smiled and said again, "Narendra has accepted the Mother. It's very good. What do you say?" And he kept smiling and saying that, over and over.

'When Naren awoke, he came and sat beside the Master. This was at about four o'clock in the afternoon. It seemed that Naren would now take leave of him and return to Calcutta. But the Master went into ecstasy, and moved up close to Naren. "What I see is that I am this body," he said, "and that I'm also that body. It's true – I see no difference. If you lay a stick on the surface of the Ganges, the water seems to be divided into two parts; but it's really all one, there's no division. The same thing here. Can you understand that? What else exists but Mother? Isn't that true?" Then he suddenly said, "I'll smoke." I hastily prepared the water-pipe and gave it to him. After taking a few puffs, he said, "No – I'll smoke straight from the bowl," and he took the tobacco-bowl in both his hands. He puffed again, then held it to Naren's mouth and said, "Take a puff or two, between my hands." Naren hesitated. The Master said, "What ignorance! Are you and I different? This is I and that's also I." Saying this, he put his hands to Naren's mouth and forced him to smoke. Naren took a couple of puffs and then stopped. Seeing that he had stopped, the Master was about to start smoking again when Naren said quickly, "Sir, wash your hands before you smoke!" But the Master wouldn't do so. "You wretch," he told Naren, "you're awfully conscious of differences!" Then he continued to smoke through his hands, although Naren's lips had touched them, and uttered many spiritual truths in that state of ecstasy. In general, the Master could not partake of anything which had been shared by another person – to him it was like leavings. Therefore, when I saw him behave in this way to Naren, I marvelled and realized the closeness between them.'

Throughout the rest of his life, Naren would say frequently, 'Ever since our first meeting, it was the Master alone who always had faith in me – no one else, not even my own mother and brothers. That faith and that love of his have bound me to him forever. The Master was the only one who knew how to love and who really loved. Worldly people only feign love to gratify their own self-interest.'

17

The Young Monks

In telling this part of the story, it seems better not to keep strictly to the chronological order of events. I have already followed the course of Naren's spiritual training through to the year 1885, without stopping to record many contemporary happenings. And now, having written about Naren, Rakhal, Latu, and Gopal Ghosh, it seems more logical to complete the list of those who eventually became monks of the Ramakrishna Order than to introduce them by twos and threes, according to the dates of their arrival at Dakshineswar, amidst a lot of unrelated people and events. I shall briefly sketch the life of each individual to its end, although that will take us far into the future. By so doing, I hope to make the various personalities stand out in sharper contrast and impress themselves more deeply on the reader's memory. If I were to show them only as a group of young men and youths during the very short period of their association with Ramakrishna, they might appear confusingly alike.

For the sake of completeness, I shall begin by naming all sixteen of Ramakrishna's disciples, including the ones who have already been described. I shall first give the pre-monastic name of the disciple and then the name he assumed as a monk, followed by a translation of it. (The invariable suffix *ananda* means bliss; in this connection, 'he who has the bliss of . . .' For example, *viveka* means spiritual discrimination. So Vivekananda means 'he who has the bliss of spiritual discrimination'. But there is no need to keep repeating 'he who has the bliss of' on the list that follows.) Nearly all of these monastic names were chosen by Naren, often on the basis of something Ramakrishna had said about that person. Naren gave them to his brother disciples at the time when they took their monastic vows, soon after Ramakrishna's death, in 1886.

Naren gave himself various names (which need not concern us) in order to hide his identity during his life as a wandering monk. He did not assume the name of Vivekananda until 1893, under circumstances which I shall describe in the last chapter.

Narendra Nath Datta	VIVEKANANDA 'spiritual discrimination'
Rakhal Chandra Ghosh	BRAHMANANDA 'Brahman'
Latu	ADBHUTANANDA 'that which is wonderful'
Gopal Ghosh	ADVAITANANDA 'non-dualism'
Baburam Ghosh	PREMANANDA 'ecstatic love'
Nitya Niranjan Sen	NIRANJANANANDA 'one who has no spot of guilt'
Jogindra Nath Choudhury	YOGANANDA 'yoga'
Sarat Chandra Chakravarty	SARADANANDA 'Sarada Devi, the Holy Mother'
Shashi Bhushan Chakravarty	RAMAKRISHNANANDA 'Ramakrishna'
Tarak Nath Ghoshal	SHIVANANDA 'Shiva'
Hari Nath Chatterjee	TURIYANANDA 'the fourth state of consciousness – i.e. samadhi'
Sarada Prasanna Mitra	TRIGUNATITANANDA 'that which is beyond the three gunas'
Subodh Chandra Ghosh	SUBODHANANDA 'spiritual intelligence; jnana'
Gangadhar Ghatak	AKHANDANANDA 'the undivided, the infinite'
Hari Prasanna Chatterjee	VIJNANANANDA 'supreme wisdom'

Kali Prasad Chandra   ABHEDANANDA
                                   'that which has no differ-
                                   entiation; non-dualism'

BABURAM GHOSH (PREMANANDA) was born in 1861 in the village
of Antpur, in the Hoogli district of Bengal. His parents were pious,
and the boy showed a strong religious vocation from childhood. I
have already spoken of the extraordinary interrelation of circumstances
which brought so many disciples to Ramakrishna. Baburam's sister
was married to Balaram Bose, a wealthy man who became one of
Ramakrishna's most prominent devotees during the last years of his
life. (See Chapter 18.) When Baburam started his secondary education
in Calcutta, the principal of his school was Mahendra Nath Gupta and
one of the students in his class was Rakhal. Rakhal took Baburam to
visit Dakshineswar in the autumn of 1882.

During this first visit, Ramakrishna subjected Baburam to certain
physical tests. Ramakrishna often did this, saying that an examination
of a man's physical characteristics revealed his spiritual character – at
least, to the insight of an initiated person. For example, Ramakrishna
would say that eyes shaped like lotus petals betokened good thoughts;
that eyes like those of a bull betokened a predominance of lust; that
the eyes of a yogi were reddish and had an upward cast. Those who are
in the habit of looking out of the corners of their eyes from time to
time, during a conversation, are more intelligent than the common run.
Again, a man of devotional nature has a soft body with easily flexible
joints; even if he is thin, his joints do not seem angular. Ramakrishna
would weigh your forearm, asking you to hold it loose; if it was lighter
than ordinary he would say that this showed a 'beneficent intelligence'.
He weighed Baburam's forearm in this manner, and also gazed into his
face and examined his limbs. The verdict was evidently satisfactory,
for Ramakrishna urged Baburam to visit him again. He particularly
praised the young man's purity, saying that, when he was in a high
spiritual mood, Baburam was one of the very few he could bear to have
touch him. Two years later, he asked Baburam to become his attendant,
and he told M.: 'When I ask Baburam, "Why don't you come here?"
he answers, "Why don't you make me come?" Then he looks at Rakhal
and weeps. "Rakhal is so happy here," he says.' Baburam's hesitation
to accept Ramakrishna's invitation was due to his fear of making his

mother unhappy. But, soon after this, Baburam's mother, who had also become a devotee of Ramakrishna, came to Dakshineswar. Ramakrishna asked her to give her son the necessary permission and she did so gladly, only asking him in return that she might become perfect in devotion to God and not live to witness the death of her children.

Baburam begged Ramakrishna to give him the lower form of samadhi, bhava samadhi or ecstasy. Ramakrishna appealed to the Divine Mother and was told that Baburam could not have ecstasy but that he would have non-dualistic knowledge of Brahman instead.

Baburam impressed all who met him by his sweetness. Ramakrishna would say of him that he had the nature of a woman; adding that he was like a clean new pot in which milk could safely be kept without fear of its turning sour. Yet this self-effacing young man matured into a marvellous teacher and trainer of the young, during the period when, as Swami Premananda, he virtually presided over the Ramakrishna Math (monastery) at Belur, from 1902 to 1916, two years before his death. He looked after the young monks and novices in his charge devotedly. His love seemed inexhaustible; it forgave and often overcame even their worst failings. Nevertheless, he would say to them, 'Do I love you? No – for if I really did, I should have bound you to me forever. Oh, how dearly the Master loved us! We don't have even a hundredth part of that love towards you.'

NITYA NIRANJAN SEN (NIRANJANANANDA) first came to Ramakrishna at the age of eighteen. At that time he was living in Calcutta with an uncle. He was a big youth, with a fine physique, and extremely handsome. In his boyhood, he had clairvoyant powers and was used as a medium by a group of spiritualists. He was also a psychic healer. A rich man who was suffering from insomnia once came to him for help. Niranjan used to say later that he did not know if he had been able to cure the man, but that the sight of this suffering in the midst of wealth made him realize the worthlessness of all earthly possessions.

It is said in one account of Niranjan's first visit to Dakshineswar that he was accompanied by his spiritualist friends who had heard of Ramakrishna and wanted to use him as a medium. Ramakrishna is said to have submitted to this experiment with his usual innocent trustfulness, but later to have sensed something evil in it, and to have refused to continue. At all events, we know that Ramakrishna did, at this meeting, reprove Niranjan for taking part in spiritualistic practices. 'My boy,' he told him, 'if you let your mind dwell on ghosts, you'll become a ghost yourself. If you fix your mind on God your life will be filled with God. Now – which are you going to choose?'

M. tells us that Ramakrishna often praised Niranjan for his guileless-ness and frankness. 'Niranjan has no spot of guilt on him,' he would say. When Niranjan took a job in an office, Ramakrishna was at first distressed. He told the youth, 'I feel as if there were a dark shadow over your face.' Then, however, he learned that Niranjan had only done this to support his mother, and he agreed that he was justified. But, in general, Ramakrishna felt that his young disciples should serve no master but God.

Niranjan was habitually good-natured. But he had a violent temper. One day, when he was coming to Dakshineswar on the public ferry-boat, he overheard some of the other passengers speaking sneeringly of Ramakrishna, saying that he was not a true man of renunciation but a hypocrite who enjoyed good food and every comfort, and whose disciples were gullible schoolboys. Niranjan protested strongly, but the speakers ignored him. At this, Niranjan became enraged, jumped to his feet and began to rock the boat, threatening to capsize it in midstream. Niranjan was a powerful swimmer; he could easily have swum ashore after carrying out his threat. The passengers were frightened and they begged to be forgiven.

When Ramakrishna heard about this incident, he rebuked Niranjan severely. 'Anger is a deadly sin,' he said, 'you ought never to let it carry you away. The seeming anger of a good man is something different. It's no more than a mark made on water. It vanishes as soon as it's made. As for those mean-minded people who talked against me, they weren't worth getting into a quarrel with – you could waste your whole life in such quarrelling. Think of them as being no more than insects. Be indifferent to what they say. See what a great crime you were about to commit, under the influence of this anger! Think of the poor helmsman and the oarsmen in that boat – you were ready to drown them too, and they had done nothing!'

After the death of Ramakrishna, Niranjan was one of those who showed special devotion to the worship of his ashes and other relics.

He was devoted also to Sarada Devi, whom the disciples then called the Holy Mother. He died of cholera in 1904.

It is amusing and instructive to contrast Ramakrishna's rebuke to Niranjan with the quite different kind of rebuke he gave to another of his young disciples, JOGINDRA NATH CHOUDHURY (YOGANANDA), on a similar occasion. Jogindra, also, was once in a ferryboat on the Ganges when he heard some passengers talking about Ramakrishna in the same sneering way. At first, Jogindra was indignant; but he had a mild nature and soon reflected that the speakers were not to be blamed. After all they were only speaking in ignorance; they did not know Ramakrishna personally. What business is this of mine, Jogindra said to himself. So he remained silent.

Later, Jogindra told Ramakrishna about the incident, expecting that he would laugh at it. But Ramakrishna dismayed him by exclaiming indignantly: 'They spoke ill of me without any reason, and you sat in silence and did nothing! Do you know what the Scriptures say? A disciple should cut off the head of anyone who speaks ill of his guru!'

On another occasion, Ramakrishna discovered cockroaches in a chest which he used for his clothes. He told Jogindra to take the clothes outside, shake out the cockroaches and kill them. The softhearted Jogindra did not want to kill the cockroaches, so he merely shook them out of the clothes and let them run away in the garden. He did not expect that Ramakrishna would give the matter a second thought, since the clothes were now clean. But he was wrong. Ramakrishna asked him if he had done as he had been told, and Jogindra was obliged to confess that he had not. 'Always do exactly as I tell you,' said Ramakrishna. 'Otherwise, sooner or later, you'll follow your own whim about something that really is important; and then you'll be sorry.'

Once, Jogindra went to the bazaar to buy an iron pot. The shopkeeper greatly impressed him by his pious talk. When Jogindra got back, he found that the shopkeeper had cheated him – he had been sold a pot that was cracked. Ramakrishna reproved him: 'What – you bought a pot and didn't examine it first? The shopkeeper was there to do business, not to practise religion. Why did you believe him and get cheated? Just because you're a devotee, that's no reason to be a fool.'

Jogindra had first come to Ramakrishna at the age of about twenty. His family had known of Ramakrishna for a long while and did not approve of him: they thought him eccentric if not downright crazy. So Jogindra paid his visits to the temple secretly. Soon his family found out what he was doing. But they could not stop him. With all his gentleness, Jogindra had another side to his nature that was strongly independent.

This independence showed itself in Jogindra's sometimes critical attitude, even towards Ramakrishna. One night, for example, he was sleeping in Ramakrishna's room. In the middle of the night, he woke to find the door open and Ramakrishna gone. He got up and looked out, but Ramakrishna was nowhere to be seen. Then the terrible suspicion came to Jogindra: perhaps the Master has gone to the Nahabat, to be with his wife! Can it be that all his purity is a pretence? Determined to find out the truth without delay, Jogindra went out of doors and stationed himself near the Nahabat, so that Ramakrishna would not be able to leave it unseen by him. But while he lurked there and watched, Ramakrishna suddenly appeared, walking from the direction of the Panchavati, where he had been meditating. Jogindra was bitterly ashamed at his own lack of faith. But Ramakrishna told him 'You are quite right – before you accept anyone as your guru, you should watch him by day and by night.'

Similarly, after the death of Ramakrishna and the founding of the Order, Jogindra, now Yogananda, often criticized the opinions and policy of Vivekananda, although the two loved each other dearly. He became the attendant of Sarada the Holy Mother and remained with her until he died, in 1899.

Ramakrishna said on several occasions that six of his disciples differed from all the rest in being *ishwarakotis*: that is to say, beings who are eternally free from the bondage of karma and who allow themselves to be reborn simply in order to do good to mankind. Thus, an ishwarakoti has some of the characteristics of an avatar.

The six who were named by Ramakrishna as ishwarakotis were Naren, Rakhal, Baburam, Niranjan, Jogindra, and Purna Chandra Ghosh.

Purna is not on the list at the beginning of this chapter because he never took the monastic vow. He came to Ramakrishna in 1885 as a boy of thirteen, and his visits, like those of Jogindra, had to be secret, because of the disapproval of his guardians. At their second meeting, Ramakrishna asked him, 'What do you think of me?' Purna replied without hesitation, 'You are God himself, come to earth in flesh and blood.' Ramakrishna was amazed and delighted by the boy's faith. He said that it could only be founded on the spiritual knowledge he had gained in previous births. When Purna grew up, he was obliged by family circumstances to marry. But he remained in close touch with his fellow disciples, who were now monks of the Ramakrishna Order; and they all honoured him for his spiritual greatness.

SARAT CHANDRA CHAKRAVARTY (SARADANANDA) first came to Dakshineswar with his cousin, Shashi Bhushan Chakravarty (Ramakrishnananda) in October 1883, when they were eighteen and twenty years old respectively. Both were highly intelligent. Sarat's father owned a pharmacy and therefore wanted his son to become a doctor. Sarat was willing to do this, especially when Naren approved of the plan, and he entered the Calcutta Medical College. But when Ramakrishna became fatally ill, Sarat at once abandoned his medical studies in order to nurse his Master. He never returned to them; for he became a monk. Throughout the rest of his life, however, he showed a vocation for nursing the sick. This he did fearlessly, even in cases of the most infectious diseases.

Sarat was noted for his courage and imperturbable calm, the calm of the true yogi, which he displayed in the midst of various dangers. On one occasion, when he was travelling by carriage in the mountains of Kashmir, the horse took fright and bolted down a steep slope; it was only saved from disaster because the carriage was stopped by a tree. Saradananda got out just a moment before the horse was killed by a great rock which fell from above. When he was asked later how he had felt at the time of the accident, he said that his mind had remained detached throughout, observing what took place with objective interest. On another occasion, Saradananda was coming up the Ganges by boat with one of the devotees when a violent windstorm arose. The boat seemed likely to sink, but the Swami never stopped puffing away at his hookah. His aplomb irritated the nervous devotee so much that he finally seized the pipe and threw it into the water.

In 1893, Vivekananda went for the first time to the United States and spent more than three years there and in Europe lecturing. (I shall describe this visit in detail in the last chapter.) In 1896, he wrote asking Saradananda to come to the West and carry on his work. The two met in London, where Saradananda had been giving some lectures. Then Vivekananda left for India and Saradananda sailed for New York, where he remained, as the head of the Vedanta Society, until his return to India in 1898. He later became the first secretary of the Ramakrishna Math and Mission and held this office until his death in 1927.

Among Saradananda's many duties was the direction of a magazine called the *Udbodhan* (Awakening), which had been founded by Vivekananda. In 1908, he decided to build a house which would serve both as an office for the magazine and a home for the Holy Mother. It was to pay off the debts incurred in building this house that Saradananda began to write the articles which formed his *Ramakrishna the Great Master* (called in Bengali *Sri Sri Ramakrishna Lilaprasanga*). It was typical of him that he demanded no special privacy for himself while he was engaged in this enormous task. Sitting cross-legged at a low desk in a tiny room, with the chatter of visitors all around him, he worked away with perfect concentration, breaking off, whenever necessary, to attend to some administrative detail.

In 1909, two nationalist revolutionaries, both accused of terrorist activities against the British rule, asked to be admitted into the Order as monks, declaring that they were ready to give up their former way of life. Saradananda accepted them at once, although his action was criticized; there were many who feared that he might thus have involved the Order in trouble with the British. Saradananda, however, went to the Chief of Police and other high officials in Calcutta and personally guaranteed the good faith of the two young men. He was not mistaken in them. They kept their pledge and did valuable work for the Order.

Saradananda continued his work on the Ramakrishna biography until the death of the Holy Mother in 1920. After that, he seemed to lose all desire to finish it; and this is why an account of the last days of Ramakrishna is missing from the book. Instead, the Swami busied himself in arrangements for the building of a temple to the Holy Mother at her native village of Jayrambati. It was consecrated in 1923.

SHASHI BHUSHAN CHAKRAVARTY (RAMAKRISHNANANDA) was known, like Niranjanananda, as a great devotee. It was he who gathered the relics of Ramakrishna after the body had been cremated at the burning-ghat and made a shrine for them. He would never leave this shrine unattended, even to visit places of pilgrimage, for he regarded it as holier than any of them. In the early days of the Order, he looked after his brother monks like a mother, and was even ready to support them by begging. When Naren chose their monastic names he wanted at first to take the name Ramakrishnananda for himself, because it was the one he most desired; but he decided that Shashi's devotion gave him the better claim to it.

In 1897, Ramakrishnananda became the founder of the Ramakrishna Mission in Madras and remained in charge of it until his death in 1911. Since boyhood he had had a brilliant intellect; and, though he had gladly sacrificed his studies to devote his life to his Master, he retained a love of astronomy and mathematics and would often solve mathematical problems for his own amusement. The Madras devotees marvelled at the amount of work he could accomplish. He would reply that the body is really a passive instrument, like a pen. Does a pen complain that it has written too many letters? If we can realize that our bodies are instruments of a Higher Power and if we can surrender ourselves to being used by that Power, then, said Ramakrishnananda, we shall feel no fatigue. The Swami himself had this sense of being an instrument at all times. Though he had to hold classes and give lectures, he never posed as a teacher. He would pray earnestly to his Master that this work might not arouse a sense of ego in him. He was not a superficially entertaining speaker and it once happened that not one single student attended his class. Ramakrishnananda held the class anyway, speaking to an empty room. 'I have not come here to teach others,' he would say, 'to me, this work is worship. I must fulfil my duty, no matter if people come to hear me or not.'

He was very careful in his choice of novices for the Madras monastery; and he could be strict with them and with the householder devotees. Visitors who brought a newspaper with them were told, 'Put it away. You can read that anywhere. When you come here, you should think of God.' A member of a maharaja's staff once began entertaining one of the devotees with court gossip. Meanwhile, the Swami shifted uneasily in his chair, until they asked him if he was feeling unwell. 'I am all right,' he answered, 'but I don't like your conversation.' A pandit came to see him and boasted of his many acts of public benevolence and schemes for social reform. Ramakrishnananda listened to him for some time in silence. Then he said quietly, 'I wonder what God did before you were born.'

The father of TARAK NATH GHOSHAL (SHIVANANDA) had been a legal adviser to the Rani Rasmani, and had met Ramakrishna at Dakshineswar a number of times during the late 1850's. Tarak met Ramakrishna in 1880, when he was twenty-six, at the home of Ram Chandra Datta. There he saw Ramakrishna pass into samadhi. Shortly after this, Tarak went to Dakshineswar. He had been a member of the Brahmo Samaj and therefore a devotee of God without form. But, when evening came, Ramakrishna told Tarak to accompany him to the Kali Temple. Ramakrishna prostrated himself before the image of the Mother, and Tarak, after a moment's hesitation, did likewise. For Tarak had said to himself: 'Why should I have such prejudices? Even if this image is only an image, God must still be present in it, since he is everywhere.' Ramakrishna was greatly pleased by Tarak's response to this test, and accepted him as a disciple. He said to the young man, 'I don't usually ask anyone who comes here about his home and family, but I knew, as soon as I saw you, that you belonged to this place. So, please tell me about them.' Ramakrishna was astonished when he heard who Tarak's father was, saying that he remembered him well and wished to see him again. So Tarak's father came to Ramakrishna, and bowed down at his feet, weeping with joy. Ramakrishna placed his foot on the head of Tarak's father and passed into samadhi.

Tarak felt obliged to get married, for family reasons; but the marriage was never consummated, and his wife died a short while later. This confirmed Tarak in his resolution to renounce the world; and he did so with his father's blessing.

After Ramakrishna's death, Tarak, now Swami Shivananda, spent some years as a wandering monk. His natural inclination was towards solitude and meditation. But he was always ready to accept his share of the duties which were imposed by the foundation of the Math and Mission. In 1902, Shivananda opened a monastery of the Order at Benares. In 1922, after the death of Brahmananda, he became the second president of the Order. Like many other great contemplatives, he showed himself able, when the need arose, to change his manner of life, assume responsibility and deal with executive problems. Despite chronically poor health, he amazed everyone by his cheerfulness. He would sometimes point to his pet dog and then to himself, saying, 'Here is that fellow's master'; then again he would point to himself and to the picture of Ramakrishna on the shrine, adding, 'and *this* fellow is *his* dog.'

One of his devotees records the memory of an evening at the Belur Math, when Shivananda, up in his room, could hear the laughter of the young novices coming from the veranda below. He smiled to himself and murmured, 'The boys are laughing so much – they do seem to be happy. They have left their homes and families in search of bliss. Oh Master, make them blissful!'

He died in February 1934.

HARI NATH CHATTERJEE (TURIYANANDA) was born in north Calcutta in 1863. His family belonged to the brahmin caste; and Hari, from an early age, was drawn to the brahmin ideal of orthodoxy and asceticism. He would bathe three times a day, recite the whole of the Gita before dawn, sleep on the floor, spending most of the night in meditation, and eat only the simplest food. He took so much physical exercise that his elders would warn him not to overstrain himself; he was determined to harden his body to endure the severest austerities. Although he was so orthodox in most respects, he was quite without sectarian narrowness, however; when he went to a school run by Christian missionaries he would always attend the classes on the Bible, which the other Hindu boys avoided. Any kind of religious book fascinated him.

When Hari was only fourteen years old, he had his first glimpse of Ramakrishna. Hearing that Ramakrishna was to visit a house in the neighbourhood, Hari went with several other boys to see this already famous *paramahamsa* (a title of honour given to a monk who is regarded as a great knower of Brahman). A carriage drove up, with Ramakrishna and his nephew Hriday in it. Hriday got out first. This is how Hari later described him; 'He was well built. There was a big vermilion mark on his forehead. A golden amulet was tied on his right arm. Looking at him one felt that he was a strong person and a very shrewd one.' Hriday then helped Ramakrishna to alight, and the boy watching in the crowd noted that he was 'very thin. He had a shirt on his body and his wearing-cloth was securely tied over his waist. . . . He was completely unconscious, and it seemed as if someone quite drunk was being taken out of the carriage. But when he got down, what a wonderful sight! There was an indescribable radiance in his face. I thought, "I have heard from the Scriptures about the great sage Sukadeva. Is he the same Sukadeva?" By that time, many others joined them and took them to the second floor of the house. I followed them. When the Paramahamsa became a little conscious of the outer world, he opened his eyes and saw a large picture of Mother Kali on the wall. He immediately saluted her and started to sing in a soul-bewitching manner. . . . It is impossible to describe the extraordinary feeling this song aroused in everybody. After that, the Paramahamsa spoke on many spiritual matters.'

Hari's second encounter with Ramakrishna did not take place until two or three years later, probably in 1880. He went to Dakshineswar with some friends. Ramakrishna singled him out at once as a future disciple, and asked him to visit him on weekdays, when fewer people were around.

One day, Hari asked Ramakrishna, 'Sir, how can we free ourselves completely from lust?' and was told that his attitude was wrong. Lust is only one manifestation of the vital force. To try to destroy this force is futile. To condemn it as evil is absurd. It should be redirected towards God. On another occasion, Hari told Ramakrishna that he had a horror of women, and that he could not bear to have them near him. 'You talk like a fool,' said Ramakrishna. 'You must never look down on women. They are manifestations of the Divine Mother. Bow down before them with reverence. That's the only way to avoid becoming sensually ensnared by them. If you hate them, you will fall into the snare.'

After Hari had become Turiyananda, he spent the greater part of the next thirteen years wandering from place to place or meditating in seclusion, sometimes in the company of Brahmananda, Saradananda or Vivekananda, sometimes alone. There was a time when Turiyananda was troubled by doubts about the life he was leading. He said to himself that everyone else in the world was doing something useful, and that he was merely a useless vagrant. Then he fell asleep under a tree and had a dream. He saw himself lying asleep on the ground, and then he saw his body begin to expand in all directions. It went on expanding until it seemed to fill the entire world. And then he thought: why do you call yourself useless? One grain of truth will cover a whole world of delusion. Get up and realize the truth. To do that is the greatest of all ways of life.

In 1899, when Vivekananda was planning to visit America for the second time, he asked Turiyananda to come with him, saying that he wanted to show the West an example of an ideal Indian sannyasin. At first, Turiyananda refused; he preferred to go on leading his austere, orthodox life amidst familiar surroundings. But his brother swamis pressed him to agree, and when Vivekananda threw his arms around his neck, wept, and begged touchingly for his help, he gave way.

Wishing to prepare himself for this journey, Turiyananda asked an Irishwoman who was a disciple of Vivekananda and had been given the name of Sister Nivedita, how he should behave when in America. Nivedita picked up a knife by its blade and offered it, handle first, to the Swami, saying, 'Sir, whenever you give something to someone else, always take the inconvenient and unpleasant part yourself and give the convenient and pleasant part to the other.' With this single piece of advice for his guidance, Turiyananda set forth, in June of that year, to face the New World.

Vivekananda's instinct was proved right; Turiyananda was exactly the kind of Swami the American devotees needed. One of them, shortly before the arrival of Vivekananda and Turiyananda in New York, had written, 'We do not want a Westernized Swami; business and lecturing we have enough of in America. We want a simple, meditative man.' Turiyananda did not care to lecture much; he preferred to work with a few chosen individuals. In 1900, a devotee offered Vivekananda a property in the San Antonio Valley, Santa Clara County, California, to be used as an *ashrama* (a monastery or retreat). He accepted the gift and persuaded Turiyananda to take charge of the retreat, which was to be named the Shanti Ashrama. (*Shanti* means peace, and is a word of benediction at the end of a grace or prayer.)

In August 1900, Turiyananda, with a dozen men and women devotees made the complicated journey from San Francisco – by ferryboat across the Bay, by train to San Jose, by stagecoach around Mount Hamilton and down to a point at which the party had to split up and cover the last twenty-two miles to the site of the Ashrama on horseback, by bicycle, or in a small spring wagon, as the case might be. It was the hottest time of the year in this mountainous and largely barren area. One lady fainted from the heat. A small cabin and a shed were the only buildings on the property, so most of them had to sleep out-of-doors. The nearest source of water was six miles away. They had not brought enough food. Even Turiyananda, with his long experience of such hardships, was momentarily depressed.

But, as the weeks passed, their life became better organized. Tents and supplies arrived from San Francisco. A cabin was built for meditation. The Gita was studied. The devotees worked joyfully at their allotted household chores. To be with the Swami, to hear him talk of Ramakrishna, to watch him react to and comment on the various daily problems and happenings, to meditate in his presence and listen to his chanting, this was, in itself, a spiritual education. They kept to a vegetarian diet and tried to practise non-violence. One day, a rattlesnake got under the wooden floor of the Swami's tent. They agreed that it must not be killed, so they caught it in a noose of rope, carried it far away from the camp and set it free, cutting the rope off short, close to its neck. Next day, however, the snake appeared again, still wearing the noose. They nicknamed it 'the snake with the necktie'.

Turiyananda spent the greater part of his two years in California at the Ashrama, returning to San Francisco now and then to lecture and hold classes. In 1902, his health began to break down and he kept expressing a desire to see Vivekananda, who had already returned to India. The devotees presented him with a steamship ticket, hoping that he would recover in his native land and, one day, come back to them. But he never did. When Turiyananda's ship docked at Rangoon, early in July, he heard the news that Vivekananda had died, only a few days previously. He was heartbroken and retired into solitude in various holy places, where he practised meditation and spiritual austerities for about eight years. Then he returned to the life of the Order and remained in one or other of its monasteries, training the young monks, until he died in 1922, after a long series of illnesses.

SARADA PRASANNA MITRA (TRIGUNATITANANDA) was born in 1865. He belonged to a rich landowning family and was over-indulged as a child, so that he became accustomed to being waited on. Like Rakhal and Baburam, he attended Mahendra Nath Gupta's school. When he went to take the entrance examination at the Calcutta University, it was expected that he would do brilliantly, for he was one of the school's best pupils. But, on the second day of the examination, Sarada Prasanna lost a gold watch which was his most treasured possession; this upset him so much that he failed to do himself justice and passed in the second division only. For weeks, Sarada was in despair. M. loved the boy, and instead of laughing at him as a cry-baby, took him to see Ramakrishna. Sarada began to visit Dakshines-war regularly.

One hot day, Ramakrishna asked Sarada to bring water and wash his feet. Sarada, regarding all kinds of work as menial, flushed with humiliation, especially as several of his friends were present. But Ramakrishna repeated the request and he had to obey. He used to say later that this incident was the beginning of his education in the spirit of service.

He started going to college, but often missed classes in order to be with Ramakrishna. His parents wanted him to marry. He refused, ran away from home and was brought back. Yet he passed his examination, although he had hardly studied for nearly a year. His elder brother feared so greatly that Sarada would become a monk that he paid a huge sum of money for the performance of a six-weeks-long sacrificial ceremony which was supposed to change Sarada's mind by supernatural means and incline him towards a worldly life. It failed to do so.

After Sarada had become Trigunatitananda, he made several pil-grimages but spent most of his time in Calcutta. During the famine of 1897 in the Dinajpur district, he organized relief work. He himself had strange eating capacities. He could live for a long time on a few pieces of fruit a day; then again he could eat enough for four or five people at a sitting. Once, when Trigunatitananda was on a pilgrimage, he went into an inn accompanied by a young boy. The Swami asked the innkeeper if he would charge less for the boy's food, since he would certainly not eat as much as an adult. But the innkeeper replied curtly that everyone must pay the same price. So Trigunatitananda, to teach him a lesson, began to eat and eat and eat. At last the innkeeper appeared and told him humbly, 'Holy Sir – I won't charge you anything for what you have eaten, but now you must stop, because we have no more food in the house.'

After Vivekananda's death in 1902, Brahmananda, knowing that Turiyananda would not now return to America, asked Trigunatitan-anda to go and take the Swami's place at the San Francisco Centre. So Trigunatitananda sailed for the United States towards the end of that year. He was determined to remain a vegetarian at all costs, and, believing in his simplicity that there might not be any vegetables in America, he went fully prepared to live on bread and water.

Under Trigunatita's direction, the first Hindu Temple in America was built in San Francisco and dedicated in 1906, shortly before the earthquake and fire. It survived these disasters and stands to this day, a charmingly quaint old building with small oriental domes on its roof.

Every year, the Swami would take a selected group of devotees to the Shanti Ashrama and teach and meditate with them there. He was fond of teaching by means of maxims and mottoes, and had these framed and hung on the walls. 'Eternal vigilance is the price of liberty', 'Live like a hermit but work like a horse', 'Do it now', 'Watch and pray', 'Do or die – but you will not die'. He believed in singing as a devotional exercise and led his young male disciples in hymns and chants up on the roof of the temple or down by the shore of the Bay in the early morning, astonishing the fishermen and sailors passing on boats.

In December 1914, Trigunatitananda, although unwell, was holding a Sunday service in the temple when a young man, a former student who had become mentally unbalanced, threw a bomb at him. The young man was killed instantly by his own bomb and the Swami was badly hurt. On the way to the hospital, Trigunatitananda spoke of his attacker with deep compassion. He died of his injuries early in January 1915.

SUBODH CHANDRA GHOSH (SUBODHANANDA) was born in Calcutta in 1867. His father and mother were both devout people. When Subodh was eighteen, his father gave him a book in which some of Ramakrishna's teachings had been recorded. This made Subodh eager to know Ramakrishna himself, and he visited Dakshineswar at the first opportunity. Ramakrishna had already met Subodh's parents and he welcomed Subodh warmly. Holding the boy's hand, he meditated for a few minutes and then told him, 'You will attain the goal; Mother says so.'

During their second meeting, Ramakrishna wrote something with his finger on Subodh's tongue, saying, 'Awake, Mother, awake!' Then he told Subodh to meditate. Subodh felt his whole body trembling and a current rushing up his spinal column to the brain. Ramakrishna was surprised at the boy's power of concentration. Subodh explained that he had meditated regularly at home on the gods and goddesses his mother had described to him.

After this meeting with Ramakrishna, Subodh began to see a strange light between his own eyebrows. His mother cautioned him never to speak about this to anyone else, for fear of some supernatural consequences. But Subodh answered, 'What harm could it do me, Mother? It's not the light I want, but That from which it comes.'

Subodh, like Latu, was outspoken. Once, Ramakrishna asked him, 'What do you think of me?' and was answered, 'People say many different things about you. I won't believe any of them until I find clear proofs.' But he soon became convinced of Ramakrishna's greatness – so much so, indeed, that he no longer wanted to meditate, feeling it to be unnecessary, now that his spiritual life was in his Master's care.

When Ramakrishna told him to go and visit Mahendra Nath Gupta, he replied, 'He hasn't been able to renounce his family – what could I learn about God from *him*?' Ramakrishna was pleased to find Subodh so stern in his renunciation, but he said, 'He won't talk about himself; he'll only tell you what he has learned from me.' So Subodh went to see M. and, in his blunt way, related this conversation to him. M. said humbly, 'I am nobody, but I live beside the ocean of knowledge and bliss and I keep a few pitchers of that water. When a guest comes, I offer him that. What else am I to talk about?' And thus the two became friends and Subodh learned to respect M. greatly.

Although Subodh took the name of Subodhananda officially, he was known to Vivekananda and the rest of his brother monks by the nickname of Khoka (Child) because he was so young. And even at the end of his life everybody in the Order called him Khoka Maharaj.

He was one of the most beloved of all the swamis, because of his childlike and sympathetic nature and his ability to cheer people up. If he was questioned about spiritual matters, he was apt to reply, 'What do *I* know? I am a Child,' and he would refer the questioner to one of the senior swamis. Nevertheless, he initiated a large number of devotees and even some children, saying, 'They will feel the power of it when they grow up.' Many of these devotees were untouchables.

In 1897, Vivekananda, back in India from his first visit to the West and full of zeal for the development of the Ramakrishna Mission, which he had just founded, decided that his brother monks ought all to be accustomed to speak in public. So he persuaded them to give weekly lectures in turn. When Subodhananda's turn came, he tried his best to be excused, but Vivekananda was firm. The other monks thought this very funny, and gathered eagerly in the hall to watch Khoka make a fool of himself. Poor Khoka mounted the platform, miserable and unwilling, and opened his mouth to speak. But before he could say a word, the building began to vibrate and rock, and trees crashed down outside – this was a major earthquake. Vivekananda said later, when the confusion was over, 'Well, Khoka, you made an earth-shaking speech!'

Once, when Subodhananda was lying sick at Rishikesh, Ramakrishna appeared to him in a vision, stroking his forehead to soothe his fever. Ramakrishna asked, 'Shall I send you a rich man who will give you everything you need?' 'No,' said Subodhananda, 'just keep me sick, so you'll have to go on looking after me.'

Since boyhood, Subodhananda had loved to drink tea. One evening, Vivekananda, Brahmananda and Subodhananda were sharing a room. Vivekananda had been meditating, while the other two were asleep. When he had finished, he woke up Subodhananda and asked him if he would mind bringing him a pipe to smoke. Subodhananda did so, and Vivekananda was so pleased that he exclaimed impulsively, 'Any boon you ask for shall be granted!' 'What could I possibly ask for?' said Subodhananda: 'The Master gave us everything we need.' But Brahmananda said, 'No, Khoka, ask for something . . .' So Subodhananda considered carefully and then said, 'Grant me this – that I may never, for the rest of my life, miss my daily cup of tea.' The Swami was asked, many years afterwards, if this boon had really been granted. He answered that it had, and that the tea had sometimes arrived against all expectations, just as he was about to go to sleep at night.

He died in December 1932.

It was Hari (Turiyananda) who brought his friend GANGADHAR GHATAK (AKHANDANANDA) to Dakshineswar in 1884. Ramakrishna told Gangadhar that he ought to associate with Naren and learn from his example. Gangadhar followed this advice and, as a result, became devoted to Naren. In later life, as Swami Akhandananda, he was one of the most ardent exponents of Vivekananda's philosophy of social service: 'The poor, the illiterate, the ignorant, the afflicted – let these be your God.' He led the first famine relief project of the Ramakrishna

Mission in 1897; then, collecting the children of those who had died in the famine, he started an orphanage and industrial school. The rest of his life was devoted to such work: collecting money and food for famine relief, agitating for the improvement of the educational system, teaching his orphans, nursing patients during a cholera epidemic. The sight of hunger moved him so painfully that he himself would refuse to eat, until doctors warned him that he would collapse and have to be waited on. This was the only argument which could make any impression on him, for he dreaded the thought of ceasing to be useful to others.

After taking the monastic vow, in 1886, Akhandananda had wandered all over the Himalayas and had spent three years in Tibet. He wrote articles about this period in his life for the *Udbodhan*.

In 1934, after the death of Shivananda, he became the third President of the Order. He died in 1937.

HARI PRASANNA CHATTERJEE (VIJNANANANDA) was born in 1868. Like Hari (Turiyananda), Hari Prasanna got a glimpse of Ramakrishna during his early teens, when Ramakrishna was visiting a house in Calcutta. But it was not until Hari Prasanna was seventeen or eighteen that Sarat (Saradananda), who was a college friend of his, took him to Dakshineswar. This is how Swami Vijnanananda would describe the meeting in later years:

'I felt in Sri Ramakrishna's room a tangible atmosphere of peace. The devotees present seemed to be listening in blissful absorption to the words which poured from the Master's lips. I don't recall what he said, but I still remember the transport of delight I experienced then as if it was yesterday. For a long time I sat there, beside myself with joy, and my whole attention was concentrated on Sri Ramakrishna. He did not say anything to me, nor did I ask him anything. One by one the devotees took their leave, and suddenly I found myself alone with him. Sri Ramakrishna was looking at me intently. I thought it was time for me to depart, so I prostrated before him. As I stood up to go, he asked, "Can you wrestle? Come, let me see how well you wrestle!" With these words he stood up ready to grapple with me. I was very much surprised at this kind of challenge. I thought to myself, "What kind of holy man is this?" Anyhow, I replied, "Yes, of course I can wrestle."

'Sri Ramakrishna came closer, with a smile on his lips. He caught hold of my arms and began to shove me. But I was a muscular young man, and pushed him back to the wall. He was still smiling and holding me with a strong grip. Gradually I felt a sort of electric current coming out of his hands and entering into me. That touch made me completely helpless; I lost all my physical strength. I went into ecstasy, and the hair of my body stood on end. Then Sri Ramakrishna let me go. He said, smiling, "Well, you are the victor." With these words he sat down on his cot again. I was speechless. Wave after wave of bliss was engulfing my whole being. After a while, Sri Ramakrishna got up from his seat. Patting me gently on the back, he said, "Come here often." Then he offered me some sweets as prasad, and I returned to Calcutta. For days the spell of the intoxicating joy lingered, and I realized that he had transmitted spiritual power to me.'

On another visit, Hari Prasanna complained that he could not meditate properly. Ramakrishna touched his tongue and then told him to go to meditate in the Panchavati, where he lost all outward consciousness. 'From now on,' Ramakrishna told him afterwards, 'you will always have deep meditations.'

Hari Prasanna was not able to see Ramakrishna many more times, because he had to move with his family to Bankipore, Bihar, and then go to Poona to study civil engineering. While he was there, he had a vision of Ramakrishna standing before him; and, the next day, he got the news that Ramakrishna had died. Later, he worked for the Government, and in due course became a District Engineer. But he always wished for the monastic life, and in 1896 – having now earned enough money to provide for his widowed mother – he joined the Order. His training as an engineer continued to prove very useful, however. As Swami Vijnanananda, he supervised the building and maintenance of the Belur Math and of the embankment along the Ganges in front of it. In collaboration with Vivekananda, he designed the Belur Math Temple, and lived to lay its cornerstone in 1935, and to dedicate it in 1938. He wrote two books in Bengali, one on astrology and the other on engineering, as well as making many translations from the Sanskrit. He was the last of Ramakrishna's direct disciples to become President of the Order, succeeding Akhandananda. He died in the following year, 1938.

·   ·   ·   ·   ·

KALI PRASAD CHANDRA (ABHEDANANDA) was a precocious scholar. At a very early age he learned Sanskrit and studied Western philosophy. He was naturally open-minded and felt no prejudice in favour of any one religion. Having become fascinated by the Yoga Sutras of Patanjali, he was eager to find someone who could teach him to follow the methods of meditation they prescribe. One of his classmates told him about Ramakrishna, so he went to visit him.

As soon as Ramakrishna set eyes on the boy, he told him, 'You were a great yogi in your previous birth. This is your last birth. I am going to initiate you into the practice of yoga.' Thenceforward, Kali came to Dakshineswar as often as he possibly could. When Ramakrishna fell sick, he was among those who nursed him most devotedly. After Ramakrishna's death, he entered the Order and became known as Abhedananda.

In 1896, while Vivekananda was in London, he sent for Abhedananda to join him. When Abhedananda arrived, he found, to his dismay, that Vivekananda had already arranged a lecture for him and announced it to the Press. Abhedananda had never spoken in public before in his life; but, such was his faith in Vivekananda's decisions, that he appeared in front of an audience which filled the hall to its capacity and gave a brilliant lecture. Vivekananda was delighted, and left for India with perfect confidence that his work would be carried on as well as could be wished. Abhedananda remained in England for a year.

In 1897, Vivekananda asked him to take charge of the Vedanta Society in New York. There, too, Abhedananda was most successful. He appears to have felt more at home in America than any of his brother swamis. With the exception of one short visit to India in 1906, he stayed on there, teaching and lecturing, until 1921.

Abhedananda was always an individualist. When he returned to Calcutta, he founded his own Vedanta Society, which gradually dissociated itself from the Belur Math, though there were no unfriendly feelings between the members of the two institutions. By 1939, the year of his death, Abhedananda was the last survivor of the direct disciples and one of the very few people still alive who had ever met Ramakrishna.

There were, needless to say, other young men who were regular visitors to Dakshineswar. Of some of these, Ramakrishna had a high opinion, praising their purity and their zeal for renunciation. The fact that, for one reason or another, they did not subsequently join the Order certainly does not prove that they were backsliders or that this contact with Ramakrishna failed to influence their later lives. If I do not mention them individually, it is only because I am trying to simplify this story. During these final years, the stage becomes so crowded with newcomers that Ramakrishna himself is apt to be hidden in their midst. And I think the reader has already been given sufficient illustration of Ramakrishna's methods of training monastic disciples.

18

Some Great Devotees

Balaram Bose came of a rich family which had estates in Orissa and was noted for its piety and good works. From his youth, Balaram had lived chiefly in holy places, spending most of his time in meditation and privacy. He left the management of the family estates to a cousin and drew from them only a small income just sufficient for his needs. He belonged to the sect of the Vaishnavas. Balaram had married, as we saw in the last chapter, the sister of Baburam Ghosh, the future Swami Premananda. They had three children.

Balaram first heard about Ramakrishna through Keshab Sen's newspaper. In 1882, when Balaram was in his late thirties, he had to go to Calcutta to be present at the wedding of his eldest daughter; so he took this opportunity of visiting Dakshineswar. He arrived there on foot – this was typical of his unassuming way of life – to find Ramakrishna's room crowded with people; Keshab and a number of his Brahmo followers were there. Balaram did not introduce himself but sat down quietly in a corner of Ramakrishna's room, remaining there until it was time for the others to go out and eat. Then Ramakrishna turned to Balaram and said, 'Is there anything you want to ask me?' 'Yes, sir. Does God really exist?' 'Certainly he does,' said Ramakrishna; but he added that God only reveals himself to the devotee who regards him as his nearest and dearest. Balaram asked, 'Then why can't *I* see him, when I pray to him so much?' Ramakrishna smiled. 'Is he really as dear to you as your own children?' Balaram had to admit that he had never felt as strongly about God as all that. The next morning, Balaram returned to Dakshineswar. As before, he came on foot. Ramakrishna noticed this and was pleased.

During the rest of their association, Ramakrishna worked on Balaram to make him less strict and sectarian in his attitude towards conduct and ritual observances. As a Vaishnava, Balaram had been fanatically scrupulous in his practice of non-injury; he had even thought it wrong to kill the mosquitoes which disturbed his meditation. But when he had been for two or three years under Ramakrishna's influence, Balaram began to question his former scruples; surely, he said to himself, all that matters when you are meditating is to keep the mind fixed upon God. And how can you do that while you are being bitten? He decided to go to Ramakrishna and lay the problem before him.

On the way to Dakshineswar, Balaram continued his debate with himself. He now found that he could not remember ever having seen Ramakrishna kill mosquitoes; on the contrary, Ramakrishna had always seemed far more acutely sensitive to the suffering of others than anyone else he had known. Balaram remembered how once, when he and Ramakrishna were watching a man walking across a field of newly grown grass, Ramakrishna had actually winced with pain and exclaimed that he could feel the man's footsteps like thumps on his own chest. So my question is answered, Balaram thought; I need not even ask it. Of course he will tell me to practise absolute non-violence. Balaram decided to visit Ramakrishna, nevertheless.

When he arrived at Ramakrishna's room, he saw to his amazement that Ramakrishna was busy killing bedbugs. As Balaram approached and prostrated, Ramakrishna said in a matter-of-fact voice, 'They've been breeding in the pillow. They bite me day and night, and keep me from sleeping. So I'm killing them.' Thus was Balaram's question answered for him. Balaram remained convinced, however, that Ramakrishna had killed the bedbugs expressly for his benefit. For if, Balaram reasoned, the Master were in the habit of killing insects, I should certainly have surprised him at it before this, since I've been coming here unannounced at all hours of the day. The Master must have waited to teach me this lesson until he knew that I had sufficient faith in him to be able to learn it.

Shortly after Balaram's first meeting with Ramakrishna, Balaram's cousin had bought a house for him in the district of Baghbazar in Calcutta. The buying of this house was the outcome of a family plot to prevent Balaram from returning to live in Puri, where he had been staying for a while. To Balaram's father and cousin, Puri seemed dangerous because it was a sacred city; if Balaram were to stay there much longer, they feared that he might renounce the world and his wife and children. Balaram agreed to the move to Calcutta, although, at first, he felt unhappy there and longed to return to Puri. But later, as his devotion to Ramakrishna grew, he rejoiced in his new home. Not only could he visit Dakshineswar as often as he wished but he could have the privilege of entertaining Ramakrishna as his guest. During the next years, Ramakrishna and his followers would eat their midday meal at Balaram's house whenever they came into Calcutta; and they went there also for religious festivals and evening parties. Balaram thus joined the fortunate company of the suppliers of Ramakrishna's wants, which had included Mathur, Shambhu Mallik and Surendra Nath Mitra. Ramakrishna used to say, 'The food Balaram serves is pure; it has been offered to the Lord who has been worshipped by the family for generations. I can eat the food Balaram gives me with pleasure; it goes down my throat of its own accord, as it were.'

Ramakrishna would poke affectionate fun at Balaram's chief fault, which was – despite all his hospitality – a certain miserliness. M. quotes Ramakrishna as saying that, at Balaram's house, there were no proper instruments to accompany the singing. 'Do you know how Balaram manages a festival? He's like a miserly brahmin raising a cow. The cow must eat very little, but it's expected to give milk in torrents. Sing your own songs and beat your own drums – that's Balaram's idea of a festival!' And again: 'One day, Balaram hired a carriage for me from Calcutta to Dakshineswar. He said the carriage fare would be twelve annas. I said, "Surely the driver won't take me all the way to Dakshineswar for only twelve annas?" "Oh, that'll be plenty," he said. Before we'd got to Dakshineswar, one side of the carriage fell out. And, besides, the horse kept stopping. It simply refused to go. The driver would whip the horse and then it'd trot, but only a few steps.'

Nevertheless, Ramakrishna would continually exclaim, 'What a nice nature Balaram has! What devotion to God!' And M. describes how Balaram, while the devotees sat eating in his home, would stand watching them humbly, like a servant. No one would have dreamed that he was the master of the house.

Towards the end of 1883, Keshab Sen became gravely ill. His recovery was already almost despaired of when Ramakrishna paid him what was to be the last visit, on November 28.

M. relates how Ramakrishna arrived at the Lily Cottage, Keshab's home, with Rakhal, Latu and other devotees. He was received by Keshab's relatives, who took him upstairs to a veranda which opened out of the drawing-room. Here they waited for Keshab to appear. Ramakrishna, knowing the seriousness of Keshab's condition, kept asking to be allowed to go in and see him. He wanted to spare Keshab unnecessary fatigue. But Keshab's disciples, acting no doubt in accordance with a misguided idea of politeness, insisted that Keshab would soon come out to receive his guest. One of them told Ramakrishna, 'Keshab is now an altogether changed person. He talks to the Divine Mother just as you do, sir.' On hearing this, Ramakrishna went into samadhi.

They waited and waited. It grew dark outside. Lamps were lighted, and the party was requested to move into the drawing-room. Ramakrishna was helped inside; only then did he begin to return to the plane of normal consciousness. Seeing the handsome furniture of the room all around him, he muttered to himself, 'These things were necessary once – but what use are they now?' He recognized Rakhal, with seeming surprise, 'Oh – are *you* here?' Then, as he sat down on a couch, his mood became ecstatic again. He talked to the Divine Mother, just as he had talked to Rakhal, 'Mother – so you're here too! Why are you showing off in that gorgeous sari? Please sit down.' Then, in an ecstatic soliloquy, he compared the body and soul to the shell and meat of a coconut. When the coconut is green, the two can hardly be separated; once it is ripe, separation becomes easy. The realization of God is like the moment when the nut becomes fully ripe. After this, body and soul are known to be separate.

Then, at last, Keshab entered the room. He was shockingly changed; a mere skeleton covered with skin. He could scarcely stand and had to keep holding on to the wall for support. Meanwhile, Ramakrishna had left the couch and was sitting on the floor. With great difficulty, Keshab also sat down; he bowed and touched Ramakrishna's feet with his forehead. Then he took Ramakrishna's hand and stroked it gently. 'I am here, sir,' he said.

After a while Ramakrishna became conscious of his surroundings. He began to talk to Keshab. M. notes that at first Ramakrishna spoke only of God; he did not even inquire after Keshab's health. But at length he said, 'Why are you sick? There's a reason. Many spiritual emotions have passed through your body. . . . I've seen big steamers going by, along the Ganges. While they're passing, you hardly notice anything. But, oh my goodness, what a tremendous noise there is, when the waves they make start to splash against the banks!'

Ramakrishna compared the process of acquiring the knowledge of God to a conflagration. He said, 'The fire of knowledge first destroys the passions, then egotism; lastly it attacks the physical body.' Then, changing the metaphor, he likened this process of acquiring knowledge to the treatment of a patient in a hospital – saying that Keshab's physical illness was actually a sign of his spiritual transformation. 'But,' said Ramakrishna, 'God won't release you as long as the least trace of your illness is left. As long as your illness isn't entirely cured, the doctor won't give you a permit to leave. Why did you register your name at the hospital at all?' Keshab thought this very funny and laughed again and again.

Later, Ramakrishna compared Keshab to the Basra rose, from which the gardener must clear away the soil down to its roots, in order that they may get as much moisture as possible from the dew. 'Perhaps,' he said, 'that's why you too are being exposed to the very roots. It may mean that you will do something great in the near future.'

Ramakrishna then told Keshab how anxious he had been on a previous occasion when Keshab was sick; adding that, this time, he had been anxious only for two or three days and not to the same degree. This sounded reassuring; but, when Keshab's mother asked Ramakrishna to bless Keshab, he answered gravely, 'What can *I* do? It is only God who can bless us all.' He continued, 'There are two things which make God laugh. He laughs when two brothers divide a piece of land between them. They draw a cord across the land and tell each other, "This side's mine and that side's yours." God laughs and says to himself, "This whole universe is mine, and they take this little clod of it and say, this side's mine and that's yours!" God also laughs when a doctor says to a mother who's weeping because her child is mortally sick, "Don't be afraid, Mother – I shall cure your child." The doctor does not understand that nobody can save that child if God wills it shall die.'

When Ramakrishna had finished speaking, everyone fell silent. The aptness of his words was painfully obvious. Keshab was seized by a terrible fit of coughing. He coughed for a long time, while the others watched him, sad and powerless to help. The coughing left

Keshab so exhausted that he could not talk any more. He bowed low before Ramakrishna and made his way slowly out of the room, supporting himself against the wall, as before.

In January 1884, Keshab died. When Ramakrishna heard the news, he was overwhelmed; he would not speak to anyone and remained in bed for three days. Later, he said, 'When I heard of Keshab's death, I felt as if one of my limbs were paralyzed.' And again, 'Oh, how happy we used to be together! How we used to sing and dance!'

Throughout the rest of his life, Ramakrishna would speak often of Keshab – sometimes critically or humorously, but always with profound affection.

Very shortly after Keshab's death, Ramakrishna was walking in the garden at Dakshineswar when he passed into an ecstatic mood, fell and dislocated a bone in his left arm. M., who visited him a few days later, on February 2nd, tells how Ramakrishna addressed the Divine Mother like a reproachful child, 'Why did you do this to me, Mother? Just look at my arm – how badly it's hurt!' Turning to the devotees, he asked anxiously, 'Am I going to get all right again?' They reassured him as one reassures a child. . . . But, a few moments later, he was talking and laughing as if nothing had happened. And then he began teaching the devotees how to pray. Was he really suffering? Nobody could be sure. Even while the doctor was bandaging his arm, he laughed and joked.

One of Ramakrishna's most remarkable devotees was Nag Mahashay, a homoeopathic physician. Nag Mahashay had made a reputation as a doctor in Calcutta before he met Ramakrishna, and he might easily have become wealthy if his code of ethics had not been so strict. From his poorer patients he would accept no fee at all; he would even help them with gifts of food and clothing. From the rich he would accept only his regular fee and the actual cost of the medicines. And in no case would he ask for money; the patient himself had to offer it.

But Nag Mahashay was not content with humanitarianism; he longed to realize God, and spent much time in meditation and religious discussion. A friend and fellow-devotee heard from the Brahmo Samaj of a great saint who was living at the Dakshineswar Temple. He told Nag Mahashay and the two of them went to visit Ramakrishna.

This visit led to others, and soon Nag Mahashay became convinced that Ramakrishna was not merely a great saint but incarnate God. Once, when they were alone, Ramakrishna said to him, 'You're a doctor – please examine my feet and see what's the matter with them.' Nag Mahashay examined his feet and could find nothing wrong with them. 'Look again,' Ramakrishna told him, 'look more carefully.' Nag Mahashay then realized that Ramakrishna was simply granting his unspoken wish, that he might touch these feet which he now regarded as holy. 'There was no need to ask him for anything,' Nag Mahashay said later. 'He could read the minds of his devotees, and he gave them whatever they truly wanted.'

Everything that Ramakrishna said, even in joke, Nag Mahashay took to be unqualified truth. On one visit, he heard Ramakrishna say to some devotees, 'It's difficult for doctors, lawyers or brokers to make much progress towards God. . . . If the mind clings to tiny drops of medicine, how can it conceive of the Infinite?' That same evening, Nag Mahashay threw his medicine-chest and medical books into the Ganges, resolving to devote himself entirely to the spiritual life. He went to Ramakrishna and asked permission to become a monk. But Ramakrishna told him to remain a householder and keep his mind fixed on God. 'Your life will become an example to all householders,' Ramakrishna added.

Henceforward, Nag Mahashay and his wife lived lives of the most austere devotion. Ramakrishna had told them to stay at home and associate with holy men. When asked, 'How shall I recognize a holy man?' he had answered, 'They will come to you.'

After Ramakrishna's death, Nag Mahashay and his wife moved back to Deobhog, his native village in East Bengal, not far from Dacca. And here they made Ramakrishna's prophecy come true in the fullest possible sense, for they received *every* visitor to their home as a holy being, an embodiment of God. No service, no sacrifice was too great to ensure the comfort of their guests. They had hardly any money. Nag himself ate barely enough to keep himself alive, and he was a chronic sufferer from colic. Nevertheless, he would never allow anyone to wait on him and he would never fail to provide food and hospitality. Once, when there was no fuel to cook for a guest, he cut down one of the wooden supports of his house. His humility was positively terrifying. Two young monks who came to see him were so embarrassed by the reverence with which Nag Mahashay treated them that they left as soon as possible. He insisted on going with them to the station. The train was crowded, and the other passengers were at first unwilling to let the monks board it. Seeing this, Nag Mahashay was so distressed that he uttered cries of agony and beat his forehead, until the passengers were ashamed and relented. On another occasion, when the house badly needed repair, Nag Mahashay's wife hired a carpenter; but Nag Mahashay refused to let the man work for them. He made him sit down, fanned him and prepared a pipe for him to smoke. When Nag Mahashay had to make a journey by boat, he would insist on doing the rowing himself. For this reason, people would avoid being in a boat with him.

Like Ramakrishna, Nag Mahashay was above all religious prejudice. He made no fundamental distinction between Hindus, Moslems and Christians. He would bow down in front of a mosque and utter the name of Jesus whenever he passed a church. After Ramakrishna's death, he returned to Dakshineswar several times, but he visited the Master's room only once; the experience was so painful for him that he could not repeat it. Thereafter, he would salute the room from a distance and then withdraw. He would visit Sarada the Holy Mother and the monastery at Alambazar; but he would never consent to spend a night at the monastery. For Ramakrishna had told him to remain in the world, and he obeyed all the Master's directions to the letter.

When Nag Mahashay died, in December, 1899, he was already revered as a saint throughout Bengal.

Girish Chandra Ghosh was born in 1844, in the district of Baghbazar, Calcutta. His parents both died when he was still very young. He got married soon afterwards, but the marriage did not stabilize his life. Girish had within himself powerful forces which were often in conflict: great talent as a dramatist, a songwriter and an actor, a devotional nature, a sceptical intelligence inspired by Western ideas, and the sensuality of an unusually strong constitution. He had to earn his living by doing a succession of boring office jobs. His spare time became divided between writing, amateur acting, playing practical jokes, and various kinds of debauchery, violently indulged in for a while, abstained from with bitter pangs of conscience, and then returned to with equal violence. He was, in fact, a bohemian artist; a type already quite familiar to the big cities of nineteenth-century Europe but comparatively rare and therefore scandalous in Calcutta where the strict standards of the old Hindu society were still, despite foreign influences, honoured in theory if not in practice.

In Girish's case, talent and debauchery gradually achieved a state of more or less workable coexistence; he continued to indulge his appetites but he also continued to write and act. In his thirties, he had already begun to be recognized as Bengal's modern pioneer of the drama. For centuries, Bengali drama had been practically extinct. Now here was Girish, producing a vast body of dramatic work in the Bengali language; religious and historical verse-plays on the Shakespearean model and contemporary social plays in the current idiom. At the same time, Girish was training actors and actresses (who all adored him) to perform these plays and was taking part in them himself. Such was his versatility that he often played two or three different roles in the same drama. In 1883, the Star Theatre was opened in Calcutta, with his money and under his direction. It became the pioneer theatre of modern Bengal.

Meanwhile, the conflict between two other forces in Girish's nature – his scepticism and his urge towards devotional religion – continued and could not be resolved. In an article written during his later life, Girish describes his state of mind before he met Ramakrishna:

At such a crisis, I thought, 'Does God exist? Does he listen to the prayers of man? Does he show the way from darkness to light?' My mind said, 'Yes.' Immediately I closed my eyes and prayed, 'Oh God, if thou art, carry me across. Give me refuge. I have none!' ... But I had nurtured doubt all these years. I had argued long, saying, 'There is no God.' ... Again I fell victim to doubt. But I had not the courage to say boldly, 'God does not exist.'

Everybody with whom I discussed my problem said unanimously that without instruction from a guru doubt would not go and nothing could be achieved in spiritual life. But my intellect refused to accept a human being as a guru.

The date of Girish's first encounter with Ramakrishna is uncertain. In any case, it was unsatisfactory. Girish had read in a newspaper that there was a paramahamsa who was living at Dakshineswar and that Keshab Sen was visiting him frequently, with his disciples. Girish was sceptical of the enthusiasms of the Brahmo Samaj and he decided that this paramahamsa of theirs was probably a fake. However, when he was told that Ramakrishna was to visit the house of an attorney who lived in his neighbourhood, he went there to see for himself. It was dusk, and lamps were being brought into the room. Yet Ramakrishna kept asking, 'Is it evening?' Girish had never before observed anyone in the superconscious state which so often made Ramakrishna unaware of his external surroundings. All Girish saw was this odd-looking man who asked, 'Is it evening?' while the lamps burned right in front of him. Not unnaturally, he was sceptical and contemptuous. What pretentious play-acting this is, he said to himself, and he left the house.

Some years after this, in early September, 1884, Girish saw Rama-krishna again, at the house of Balaram Bose. This time, Girish was much more favourably impressed. He had expected that Ramakrishna would behave as a holy man was conventionally supposed to behave; that he would sit aloof in majestic silence. But now he saw Ramakrishna saluting the other guests with the utmost respect and humility, bowing his head to the ground. A dancing girl named Bidhu was seated at his side, singing devotional songs for him. One of Girish's old friends came up to him and whispered sneeringly that Ramakrishna and Bidhu must be lovers; that was why he was laughing and joking with her. Even at the time, this insinuation shocked Girish; he did not believe it could be true. But he had not yet become convinced that this was a real paramahamsa. When another of his friends, who was not much impressed by Ramakrishna, said to him, 'I've had enough of this – come on, let's go,' Girish went with him. He had half-wanted to stay but was embarrassed to admit this, even to himself.

Only a few days after this, on September 21, 1884, Ramakrishna and some of the devotees visited the Star Theatre, to see a play by Girish about the life of Chaitanya. Girish himself was strolling in the outer compound of the theatre when a member of Ramakrishna's party came to him and said, 'The Master has come to see your play. If you'll give him a free pass, that will be very kind; otherwise we'll buy him a ticket.' Girish answered that Ramakrishna need not pay for his seat, but that the others would have to. He then went to greet Ramakrishna in person. But, before he could bow to Ramakrishna, Ramakrishna bowed to him. Every time Girish bowed, Ramakrishna bowed; until Girish, fearing that this might continue all evening, bowed mentally instead of physically, and led them all upstairs to a box. He then went home, as he was not feeling well. Thus Girish missed hearing Ramakrishna's delighted comments on the play and witnessing his frequent periods of ecstasy. When Ramakrishna was asked later how he had liked it, he answered, 'I found the representation the same as the reality.'

Three days later, Girish was sitting on the veranda of a friend's house when he saw Ramakrishna approaching along the street. They exchanged greetings. Girish felt a strong urge to join him, but did not. Then someone came to him with a message that Ramakrishna was asking for him. So Girish followed him into the house of Balaram, whom he was visiting. Ramakrishna was in a semi-conscious state. As if in answer to Girish's previous scepticism, he murmured, 'No – this is not pretence; this is not pretence.' Presently he returned to normal consciousness. Girish was always longing to find a guru, although, as we have seen, he obstinately refused to believe that any human being could stand in that relation to another. 'What is a guru?' he now asked Ramakrishna. And Ramakrishna answered, 'He is like a procurer. A procurer arranges for the union of the lover with his mistress. In the same way, a guru arranges the meeting between the individual soul and his beloved, the Divine Spirit.' Then he added, 'You need not worry. Your guru has already been chosen.'

The conversation turned to the theatre. Ramakrishna told Girish, 'I liked your play very much. The sun of knowledge has begun to shine on you. All the blemishes will be burned away from your heart. Very soon, devotion will come to sweeten your life with joy and peace.' Girish could not bear what he regarded as such utterly unmerited praise. He told Ramakrishna bluntly that he had no good qualities, and that, anyhow, he had only written the play to make money. Ramakrishna passed over this reply in silence. 'Could you take me to the theatre and show me another of your plays?' he asked. 'Any day you like,' said Girish. 'You must charge me something, though.' 'All right, you can pay eight annas.' 'That's the price of a wretched seat in the balcony. It's so noisy up there.' 'Oh, but you won't have to sit there. You'll sit where you sat last time.' 'Then you must accept one rupee.' 'Very well – if you want me to.' After this playful exchange, Girish took his leave. A friend who accompanied him asked what he thought of Ramakrishna. 'He is a great devotee,' Girish answered. His heart was now full of joy. All his doubts and objections seemed to be dissolving; and he kept remembering how Ramakrishna had said, 'Your guru has already been chosen.'

But Girish was a complicated person; a mixture of shyness, aggression, humility and arrogance. Although he had now begun to believe that Ramakrishna might really be the guru he was looking for, a part of his nature passionately resisted this idea. On December 14th, Girish was in his dressing-room at the Star Theatre when a devotee came to tell him that Ramakrishna had arrived in a carriage. 'All right,' Girish said, rather haughtily, 'take him to the box and give him a seat.' 'But won't you come and receive him personally?' the devotee asked. 'What does he need me for?' said Girish, with some annoyance. Nevertheless, he followed the devotee downstairs. At the sight of Ramakrishna's radiant face, Girish's mood changed; he was filled with shame for his rudeness. He not only escorted Ramakrishna upstairs but bowed down before him, touched his feet, and offered him a rose. Ramakrishna accepted it for a moment; then he handed it back to Girish saying lightly, 'Only a god or a dandy should have flowers. What am I to do with this?'

That day, the play was about the life of the Child Prahlada, a great devotee, who remained faithful to Vishnu, his chosen ideal, even though he was tortured for his devotion by his father, the demon Hiranyakashipu, who hated God. When Ramakrishna complimented Girish on his art as a dramatist, Girish answered modestly that he wrote without real authority, since he could never assimilate the truths that he taught in his plays. Ramakrishna disagreed, saying that no writer could create a godlike character, as Girish had, without having the love of God in his heart. Later, when Girish confessed that he felt inclined to give up the theatre altogether, Ramakrishna told him that he must not do so, because his plays would teach people a great deal.

One night, while Girish was in a brothel with two of his friends, he felt a sudden desire to visit Ramakrishna. Despite the lateness of the hour they took a carriage out to Dakshineswar. They were very drunk. Everyone at the temple was asleep. But, when Girish and his friends came staggering into Ramakrishna's room, Ramakrishna received them joyfully. Going into ecstasy, he grasped both of Girish's hands and began to dance with him and sing. (This was only one of several occasions on which Ramakrishna behaved in this way. The reeling of drunkards made him think of the state of ecstatic bliss, in which he himself would reel. Ramakrishna had been known to get down from a carriage to dance with drunken strangers on the roadside.)

Girish was not always so pleasant when drunk. Once, at the theatre, he publicly abused Ramakrishna, using the coarsest and most brutal words. This turned nearly all the devotees against him. Only Ram Chandra Datta tried to defend Girish by saying to Ramakrishna, 'Sir, he has worshipped you with his abuse, according to his nature. The serpent Kaliya asked Lord Krishna, "Since you have given me poison, how can I offer you nectar?"' Ramakrishna seemed pleased by Ram Chandra's argument, and said to the others, 'You hear what Ram Chandra says?' He then told them to get a carriage, because he wanted to go and visit Girish right away.

In actual fact, it seems unjust and a little absurd to compare Girish to a venomous snake. His wickedness has been much overrated. With the devotees who met him in later life, as an almost saintly old man, Girish liked to dwell on his previous sins in order to emphasize the transforming effect of Ramakrishna's grace. He would say melo-dramatically, 'I have drunk so many bottles of wine, that if you were to place one bottle on top of another they would reach the height of Mount Everest.' He certainly did drink a great deal and was apt to be violent and quarrelsome when drunk. He frequently visited brothels. He smoked opium for fifteen years before he met Ramakrishna. But there is no evidence to show that he was a seducer, or a cheat, or a hypocrite, or a spiteful slanderer, or capable of cold-blooded cruelty.

Meanwhile, Ramakrishna's influence was steadily gaining its hold upon Girish. One night, Girish drank himself into unconsciousness at the house of a prostitute. In the morning, he hastened to visit Rama-krishna. He was full of remorse, but had not neglected to bring a bottle of wine with him in the carriage. On arriving at Dakshineswar, he wept repentantly and embraced Ramakrishna's feet. Then, suddenly, he felt an urgent need of a drink, and discovered, to his dismay, that the carriage had already driven off. But now Ramakrishna smilingly pro-duced not only the bottle, but Girish's shoes and scarf as well; he had privately told a devotee to bring them from the carriage, before it left. Girish could not control himself; he drank shamelessly before them all – and, having done so, was again repentant. 'Drink to your heart's content,' Ramakrishna told him, 'it won't be for much longer.' Girish said later that this was the beginning of his abstention from intoxicating drinks. But the abstention was gradual; and this was certainly not the last time that Girish was drunk in Ramakrishna's presence.

Girish had a writer's scepticism about the authority of the written word; he knew only too well how easy it was for him to compose fine phrases. 'I don't want advice,' he once told Ramakrishna, 'I have written cartloads of advice to others. It doesn't help me. Do something to transform my life.' Ramakrishna was greatly pleased by this proof of Girish's faith in him. He told his nephew Ramlal to recite a verse from the Scriptures, 'Go into solitude and shut yourself in a cave – peace is not there. Peace is where faith is. Faith is at the root of all things.' Girish asked again if he should give up his work in the theatre. Ramakrishna told him to continue it. He now treated Girish with fatherly affection, as though he were a little child, and often fed him sweets with his own hands.

Then, one day, Ramakrishna told Girish that he must remember God at least twice a day; once in the morning and once in the evening, no matter how much work he had to do. Girish agreed that this sounded simple enough. But then he reflected that his life was so disorganized, so busy, so much at the mercy of impulses and emergencies, that he did not even have fixed hours for eating or sleeping; how could he promise to remember God? He couldn't conscientiously do so. 'Very well,' said Ramakrishna, 'then remember God just before you eat or sleep, no matter what time that is.' But Girish would not make even such a promise. The truth was that any kind of self-discipline was repugnant to him. 'In that case,' said Ramakrishna, 'you must give me your power of attorney. From this moment on, I'll take full responsibility for you. You won't have to do anything at all.'

Girish was delighted. This was what he had been wanting all the time; to be rid of responsibility and guilt forever. He agreed to Ramakrishna's suggestion and thought to himself, now I shall be as free as air.

But Girish was quite wrong – as he soon found out. He had made himself Ramakrishna's slave. One day, when Girish happened to remark, about some unimportant matter, 'I shall do this,' Ramakrishna corrected him, saying, 'You mustn't talk in that dogmatic way; say – I shall do this if God wills.' Henceforward, Girish tried to surrender his will altogether to Ramakrishna. In later years, he used to tell young devotees that the way of complete self-surrender in the religious life was actually much harder than the way of self-reliance and effort. 'Look at me,' he would add, 'I'm not even free to breathe!' meaning that he felt that he could not perform any action of his will, without the help of the Lord.

Girish died in 1912, after many ups and downs of fortune; a nobly battered figure, steadfast to the end in his devotion to Ramakrishna. One curious result of their association is that, today, Ramakrishna's picture is to be found hanging backstage in nearly every theatre in Calcutta. The actors bow to it before they make their entrances. By giving his approval to Girish's art and encouraging him to continue practising it, Ramakrishna became, as it were, the patron saint of the drama in Bengal.

Aghoremani Devi was a brahmin. She had been widowed when still a young girl, and had settled down in the precincts of a Krishna Temple at Kamarhati about three miles along the Ganges north of Dakshineswar. She had been initiated by a guru who was a Vaishnava, and had devoted herself to the worship of Gopala, the baby Krishna. For this reason, she was usually known as Gopaler Ma, Gopala's Mother. She had been living this solitary pious life for thirty years.

Aghoremani probably visited Ramakrishna for the first time in 1884, with another woman devotee. A few days later, she returned alone, bringing some sandesh with her. She had been unable to get any fresh sandesh at the market, and this was stale; she had brought it only because she had nothing else, and custom demanded a formal offering when you visited a holy man. To her dismay, Ramakrishna actually wanted to eat the sandesh, and to her astonishment, he seemed to relish it. 'I feel a great desire to eat food that has been cooked by you,' he told her, and proceeded to name all the dishes he wished her to prepare for him. Aghoremani had practically no money and did not think she could possibly afford even these ordinary dishes. Besides, it shocked her deeply that Ramakrishna had said nothing about God and had talked only of food. She decided not to visit him again. But something drew her back to Dakshineswar, and this time she brought food she had cooked herself. It was nothing out of the ordinary, but Ramakrishna praised it extravagantly, exclaiming that it was 'nectar'. As we have seen on other occasions, it was the cook that mattered to him, not the cooking; food prepared by the right hands could actually give him spiritual sustenance.

One morning, while Aghoremani was sitting meditating in her room at Kamarhati, she had a vision of Ramakrishna, with his right fist half clenched, in the traditional attitude of Gopala. She caught him by the hand. As she did so, Ramakrishna vanished and the figure of the ten-month-old Gopala appeared in his place and demanded to be fed. This baby figure seemed physically real to her. It climbed on her lap and on to her shoulders. Wild with joy, Aghoremani carried it all the way to Dakshineswar in her arms.

She entered the Dakshineswar compound looking like a madwoman, her hair dishevelled, her wearing-cloth trailing on the ground; 'Gopala! Gopala!' she cried. She fed Ramakrishna with the food she had brought, and kept declaring that the baby was passing between them, now entering into his body, now returning to her lap. During the next few days, she had a continuous vision of Gopala, accompanying her as she went about her household duties, and sleeping with her at night. When next she saw Ramakrishna, he told her that she need not make japa any more, because she had attained 'everything'. But she continued to make japa for Gopala's sake; and Gopala became more and more closely identified with Ramakrishna in her mind. These visions continued to come to her for the next two months; then they became rarer. Ramakrishna said that, if she had gone on experiencing them, she could not have lived long. But Aghoremani was very sad because of Gopala's absence.

One day, Naren and Aghoremani happened to visit Dakshineswar at the same time. Ramakrishna always enjoyed confrontations of this kind. He urged Aghoremani to describe her visions to Naren. She hesitated – for Ramakrishna had only recently warned her that one should never talk of spiritual experiences to others. But he smiled and told her to begin. So Aghoremani, in a voice choked with tears, began to describe how she first saw the baby Gopala. From time to time, she would break off and appeal to Naren, 'My child, you are so learned and intelligent – and I'm poor and know nothing – please tell me truly, did these things happen, or did I only imagine them?' And Naren, despite his natural scepticism, was moved to tears. 'No, Mother,' he assured her, 'what you have seen is all true.'

After Ramakrishna's death, Aghoremani lived in retirement. Fifteen years later, three of Vivekananda's Western disciples went to visit her at Kamarhati. One of these disciples was Nivedita. She wrote about the visit as follows:

A few of us went, one full-moon night, to visit her. How beautiful was the Ganges, as the little boat crept on and on! And how beautiful seemed the long flight of steps rising out of the water and leading up, through its lofty bathing ghat, to where in a little room – built probably in the first place for some servant of the great house at its side – Gopala Ma had lived and told her beads for many a year. . . . Her bed was of stone, and her floor of stone, and the piece of matting she offered her guests to sit on, had to be taken down from a shelf and unrolled. The handful of parched rice and sugar candy that formed her only store and were all that she could give in hospitality were taken from an earthen pot that hung from the roof by a few cords. . . . On those beads, Gopala Ma had become a saint!

When Vivekananda was told of their visit, he said, 'Ah, that was the old India you saw – the India of prayers and tears, of vigils and fasts, that is passing away, never to return!'

In 1904 Aghoremani became seriously ill. They brought her into Calcutta, to the house of Balaram. Nivedita, who was fascinated by the old woman, begged her permission to nurse her. So Aghoremani moved in to live with Nivedita and remained there until July 1906. Then, when death was seen to be approaching, she was prepared for it according to the ancient custom, decked with flowers and garlands, and taken to lie beside the Ganges. She died two days later, aged about eighty-five.

 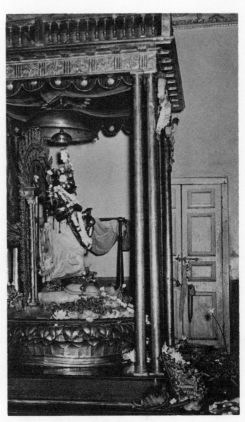

26. Image of Kali, front view   27. Image of Kali, side view

28. Old hackney carriage

19

The Gospel of Sri Ramakrishna

I have already often referred to M. (Mahendra Nath Gupta) and quoted from his *Gospel of Sri Ramakrishna,* called in Bengali *Sri Sri Ramakrishna Kathamrita.* Now I must write in detail about M's life, his book, and the account it gives us of Ramakrishna's personality and teachings.

Mahendra Nath was born in Calcutta in 1854. When he was still a small child, he was taken by his mother to see the Dakshineswar Temple, which at that time had only recently been built. In the crowded temple courtyard, Mahendra Nath became separated from his mother and started to cry for her. Then a young man came out of one of the buildings, saw the little boy in tears and remained with him, comforting him, until his mother reappeared. In later life, Mahendra Nath liked to believe that this young man had been Ramakrishna himself.

Mahendra Nath grew up to be a brilliant student. He graduated third in his class from the University of Calcutta, in 1875. While still in college, he married a girl who was related to Keshab Sen; and thus became one of Keshab's most devoted followers. Having graduated, he started his career as a teacher. He was teaching at the Metropolitan Institution at the time when he first went to Dakshineswar and met Ramakrishna, in 1882. (Throughout the *Gospel,* M. is nearly always precise about dates, and it seems odd that he does not tell us in so many words exactly when this first meeting took place. He does give us two clues, however, which fix the date; it was a few days after February 23rd and it was on a Sunday in February. In the year 1882, the only Sunday between February 23rd and the end of the month fell on the 26th.)

The *Gospel* opens with an artless abruptness and incoherence which

give an immediate impression of its authenticity. It is as if M. has been
so moved by his experiences that he has not even paused to rehearse the
sequence of events in his mind before starting to write:

The temple of Mother Kali is on the bank of the Ganges at
Dakshineswar. It was here, in spring, in February 1882, a few days
after the birthday celebration of Sri Ramakrishna, that M. met him.
On February 23rd, Sri Ramakrishna had taken a boat trip with
Keshab Sen and Joseph Cook. A few days later, at dusk, M. entered
Sri Ramakrishna's room. This was his first visit.

He found Sri Ramakrishna seated on the wooden couch, facing
east. With a smile on his face, he was talking of God. The devotees
were sitting on the floor. The room was crowded. In silence, they
were drinking the nectar of his words.

M. stood there speechless. It seemed to him as if Sukadeva himself
were teaching the wisdom of God; as if all the holy places had come
together, as it were, in this very room. Or as if Sri Chaitanya himself,
with his devotees Ramananda, Swarup and the rest, were singing the
praises of the Lord as they sat in Puri, the sacred city.

Sri Ramakrishna was saying: 'When a man sheds tears and when
his hair stands on end if he utters the name of Hari or Rama even
once, then you may know for certain that he no longer needs to
perform any rituals. Then only does he have the right to renounce
them – or rather, they themselves will drop away from him. Then
it will be enough merely to chant the name of Rama or Hari, or just
the Word Om.' Continuing, he said: 'Ritualistic worship becomes
merged in the sacred Gayatri mantra; and the Gayatri likewise
becomes merged in Om.'

While out visiting several other gardens, M. and his friend Sidhu
happened to arrive at the temple garden of Dakshineswar. It was
Sunday. A few minutes previously, while they were walking in the
garden of Prasanna Bannerji, Sidhu had said, 'There is a beautiful
garden on the bank of the Ganges. Would you care to visit it? A
holy man, a paramahamsa, lives there.'

Entering through the main gateway of the temple, both M. and
Sidhu went straight to Sri Ramakrishna's room. As M. looked on in
wonder, he thought to himself, 'Ah, what a fascinating place! And
what a fascinating man! I don't want to leave this place.' But then,

after a while, he thought, 'I'll take a look around first and find out exactly where I am. Then I'll come back and sit here.'

When M. and Sidhu left the room, they could hear the sweet music of the vesper service, made by gong, bell, drum, and cymbals, combined. Sweet music also issued from the nahabat at the south end of the garden. The sounds of music seemed to roll away over the bosom of the Ganges and become lost in the distance. A soft spring wind was whispering, laden with the fragrance of flowers. The moon had just risen. It was as if Nature in all her aspects were preparing for the evening worship. M. took part in the vespers which were held in the twelve Shiva temples, the Radhakanta Temple and the Temple of Mother Kali, and his heart was filled with great joy. Sidhu remarked, 'This temple garden was founded by Rani Rasmani. Regular services are held in all the temples here. Many holy men and beggars are fed here every day.'

Talking thus, M. and Sidhu walked across the temple courtyard from the Temple of Mother Kali, and reached the door of Sri Ramakrishna's room. This time, they found the door shut.

M. had been trained in the manners of the English; he would not enter a room unannounced. Brinda, a maidservant, was standing by the door. M. addressed her, 'Hello! Is the Holy Man in there now?' Brinda answered, 'Yes, he's in there.'

M: How long has he been living here?

BRINDA: Oh – many years.

M: Does he study a great number of books?

BRINDA: Books? Oh dear, no! They're all on his tongue.

M. was fresh from the university. He was amazed to learn that Sri Ramakrishna was not a scholar.

M: Perhaps he is now engaged in his evening worship? Is it possible for us to go in? Will you please get his permission for us to see him?

BRINDA: Go right in, children. Just go in and sit down.

When they entered the room, they found Sri Ramakrishna sitting alone on the wooden couch. Incense was burning and all the doors were shut. As he came in, M. saluted the Master with folded hands. The Master asked them to be seated. M. and Sidhu sat down on the floor. Sri Ramakrishna asked them, 'Where do you live? What's your occupation? Why have you come to Baranagore?' and similar questions. M. introduced himself by answering all these questions, but he noticed that the Master became absent-minded from time to time. Later he learned that this mood is called bhava (ecstasy). This attitude of mind is like that of a fisherman who sits rod in hand, fishing. The float bobs up and down, for a fish has swallowed the bait. He watches the float with eagerness and concentration. At this time, he will speak to no one. Such was Sri Ramakrishna's state of mind. Later, M. not only heard but observed for himself how Sri Ramakrishna would enter into this mood after dusk. Then, again, he would sometimes lose outer consciousness altogether.

M: Would you like to perform your evening worship, now? Should we take leave of you?

SRI RAMAKRISHNA (*still in ecstasy*): No. Evening worship? No, it is not that.

After some further conversation, M. saluted the Master and took leave of him. Sri Ramakrishna said, 'Come again.'

On his way home, M. began to think, 'Who is this serene-looking man? How I wish I could go back to him! Is it possible for a man to be great without being a scholar? How amazing! I want to see him again. And he himself asked me to come again. I shall go to him either tomorrow morning, or the day after.'

It is a pity that M. does not write more about his first impressions of Ramakrishna's physical appearance. However, we find a contemporary description in Nagendra Nath Gupta's book, *Reflections and Reminiscences*. Here the author relates how he saw Ramakrishna come on board a river-steamer to meet Keshab Sen, sometime in the year 1881:

The Paramahamsa boarded the steamer to meet Keshab and his party. He was wearing a red-bordered dhoti and shirt, unbuttoned. He was dark-complexioned, with a beard, and his eyes, never wide open, were introspective. He was of medium height, slender almost to leanness and very frail-looking. . . . He spoke with a very slight but charming stammer in very uncultured Bengali, mixing the two 'you's' frequently.

M., as we shall see in a moment, refers to Ramakrishna's stammer also, in his account of his second visit to Dakshineswar. There is no mention of this stammering in accounts of Ramakrishna's earlier life, and we have no way of knowing if it was habitual or only occasional, under the influence of excitement.

Ramakrishna's Bengali was the dialect of his native village, Kamarpukur; ungrammatical and uncultured by the standards of an educated man. In that rural community, it was natural to speak without shame about the parts and functions of the body and the mating-habits of animals. Throughout his life Ramakrishna continued to use words and similes which struck his more sensitive hearers as shockingly crude. But even those who were shocked had to admit that, in Ramakrishna's mouth, the words lost much of their offensiveness; for he used them with such innocence.

And now to continue M's narrative:

M's second visit was at eight o'clock in the morning. The Master was about to be shaved. It was still cold, and his body was wrapped in a moleskin shawl, the edge of which was bound with a fine red cloth. When Sri Ramakrishna saw M., he said, 'So you're back. Good. Sit down here.'

This conversation took place on the southeast veranda. The barber was present. The Master sat on that veranda and conversed occasionally with M. while being shaved. He had the shawl wrapped around his body, slippers on his feet, and a sweet smile on his face. He stammered a little as he spoke.

SRI RAMAKRISHNA (*to* M.): Tell me, where is your home?

M: In Calcutta, sir.

SRI RAMAKRISHNA: Where are you staying here?

M: I am staying with my elder sister at her house at Baranagore. It's the house of Ishan Kaviraj.

SRI RAMAKRISHNA: Oh, at Ishan's house! Do you know how Keshab is? He was very sick.

M: I hear that too. But I think he is well now.

SRI RAMAKRISHNA: I prayed to Mother and vowed to offer her green coconut and sugar for Keshab's recovery. I used to wake up early in the morning and weep before Mother, saying, 'Mother, please cure Keshab's illness. If Keshab doesn't go on living, who shall I talk to when I go to Calcutta?' That was why I vowed to Mother to offer her green coconut and sugar. Tell me, do you know a Mr Cook who has come to Calcutta? Keshab took me on a steamer, and Mr Cook was there too. I understand he is giving lectures.

M: Yes, sir, I also heard something like that. But I haven't attended his lectures. I don't know much about him.

SRI RAMAKRISHNA: Pratap's brother was here for a few days. He was out of work and he said he wanted to live here. I learnt that he has a whole brood of children. He left them and his wife in his father-in-law's house. I said to him, 'Look here! You have children to support. Do you think the neighbours are going to feed them and bring them up? Aren't you ashamed that you left them at your father-in-law's, so he'll have to take care of them?' I scolded him hard and told him to find a job. It was only then that he wanted to leave. (*to* M.) Are you married?

M: Yes, sir.

SRI RAMAKRISHNA (*shuddering*): Oh, Ramlal, what a shame! He is married!

Ramlal was a nephew of Sri Ramakrishna and was employed as a priest in the Kali Temple. M. was confused and sat hanging his head in silence, like one who is guilty of a grave crime. He thought to himself, 'What is wrong in getting married?'

Then the Master asked, 'Have you any children?'

M's heart was beating fast. He said nervously, 'Yes, sir, I have children.'

The Master became very sad on hearing this and exclaimed, 'What a shame! He even has children!'

Thus rebuked, M. remained speechless. His pride began to be humbled. After a few moments, Sri Ramakrishna looked at him graciously and said to him in a kind tone, 'You see, you have certain auspicious signs which I recognize by looking at your forehead, eyes, and so forth. . . . Tell me, what kind of a woman is your wife? Does she possess power for good or power for evil?'

M: She is a good woman, sir, but she's ignorant.

SRI RAMAKRISHNA (*cuttingly*): And you're a wise man, are you?

M. did not yet know what constitutes knowledge and what constitutes ignorance. He supposed that a person who is educated and who studies books acquires knowledge. Later on, this misconception was corrected. For he learned that knowledge is to know God and that ignorance is not to know God. When the Master asked, 'And you're a wise man, are you?' M's ego received a severe blow.

SRI RAMAKRISHNA: Tell me, do you believe in God with form or without form?

M. was surprised and said to himself, 'If one believes that God has form, how can one believe that God is without form? Or again, if a man believes in a formless God, how can he believe in a God with form? Can two contradictory ideas both be true? Can milk be white and black at the same time?'

M: Sir, I like to believe in God without form.

SRI RAMAKRISHNA: That's good. It's enough to have faith in one aspect of God. You have faith in God without form. That is very good. But never get it into your head that your faith alone is true and that every other is false. Know for certain that God without form is real and that God with form is also real. Then hold fast to whichever faith appeals to you.

M. was amazed to hear that both these ideas could be true. This was something beyond his book-learning. His ego had received a third blow. But, since it was not yet completely crushed, he was ready to continue the argument with the Master.

M: But, sir, assuming it is true that God has form, he is surely not identical with the clay image of him?

SRI RAMAKRISHNA: Why say that the image is clay? The image is composed of spirit.

263

M. could not understand what was meant by an 'image composed of spirit'. He said, 'But those who worship the clay image should be made to understand that the clay image is not God, and that while they are bowing down before the image they must remember that they are worshipping God. They must not worship the clay.'

SRI RAMAKRISHNA (*sharply*): Making others understand – giving them lectures – that's all you Calcutta people think about! You never ask yourselves how *you* can find the truth. Who are *you* to teach others? It is the Lord of the Universe who teaches mankind. Will he who has done so much for us fail to bring us to the light? If we need to be taught, he will teach. He knows our inmost thoughts.

Supposing it *is* a mistake to worship God in the image – doesn't he know he alone is being worshipped? He will certainly be pleased by that worship. Why should *you* get a headache over that? It would be better if you struggled to get knowledge and devotion, yourself.

This time, M. felt that his pride was completely crushed. M. said to himself, 'What he says is very true. Who am I to teach others? Have I known God? Do I even have any devotion to him? I am like a man who has no bed to lie on, and yet invites a stranger to share it with him. I do not know God, nor have I heard much about him. How shameful, how utterly foolish of me to think that I can teach others about God! This is not like mathematics, or history, or literature – those one can teach to others. This is the truth of God – the only Reality. . . . I like what the Master says.' This was his first argument with the Master and also his last.

SRI RAMAKRISHNA: You were talking of worshipping a clay image. Even if it is made of clay, there is a need for that sort of worship. God himself has arranged for many ways of worship to suit the varied temperaments of his worshippers in their different stages of growth.

A mother has five children. There is fish to be cooked. She prepares different kinds of fish dishes, to agree with every kind of stomach. For one child, she cooks fish pilau, for another pickled fish, for another baked fish, fried fish and so forth. She has cooked all kinds of dishes to appeal to their different tastes and digestions. Do you follow me?

M: Yes, sir. (*humbly*): How can we devote our minds to God?

SRI RAMAKRISHNA: Chant the name of God and sing his glories unceasingly; and keep holy company. Now and then one should visit holy men and devotees of God. If a man lives in the world and busies himself day and night with worldly duties and responsibilities, he cannot give his mind to God. So it's important to go into solitude from time to time, and think about God. When the plant is young, it should be fenced on all sides. Unless there's a fence around it, goats and cattle may eat it up.

When you meditate, go into the solitude of a forest, or a quiet corner, and enter into the chamber of your heart. And always keep your power of discrimination awake. God alone is real, that is to say, eternal; everything else is unreal, because it will pass away. As you discriminate in this manner, let your mind give up its attachment to the fleeting objects of this world.

M (*humbly*): How is one to live in the world and lead a family life?

SRI RAMAKRISHNA: Attend to all your duties but keep your mind fixed on God. Wife, son, father, mother – live with all of them and serve them, as if they were your very own. But know in your heart of hearts that they are not your own.

The maid in the house of a rich man attends to her work, but her mind dwells in her home in her native village. Furthermore, she brings up her master's children as though they were her own. She speaks of them as 'my Rama' or 'my Hari', but she knows in her own mind that they do not belong to her. The tortoise moves about in the water of a lake. But do you know where her mind is? On the bank, where her eggs are laid. Do all your duties in the world, but let your mind dwell on thoughts of God. If you enter into family life before you have cultivated love for God, you will get more and more entangled. You will not be able to face and withstand the attack of dangers, griefs, and sorrows. And the more you think of the objects of the world, the more you will become attached to them.

Before you break open a jack fruit you must rub your hands with oil, otherwise the gummy juice of the fruit will stick to them. Anoint yourself with love for God, and then you can attend to the duties of the world.

But to develop this love of God, one must live in solitude. To make butter, the milk must first be curdled in a secluded spot. If you stir up the milk, it does not curdle. You must stop all your other tasks, and sit down quietly and churn the curd. Then only will you get butter.

If you apply your mind to meditation on the Lord in solitude and silence, you will acquire dispassion, knowledge and devotion to the Lord. But if you give up your mind to worldly thoughts, it becomes degraded. In the world, the only thoughts are of lust and greed.

The world may be likened to water and the mind to milk. If you pour milk into water, they mingle, and the pure milk can no longer be found. But if you first curdle the milk and churn the curd into butter, you can put it into water and it will float. So you must first practise spiritual disciplines and obtain the butter of knowledge and devotion. This cannot be contaminated by the water of the world. It will float, as it were.

At the same time, keep your power of discrimination active. One enjoys lust and gold for a while only. God alone is eternal. Money – what can it give you? Food, clothes and a place to live in, that's all. It cannot help you to realize God. So money can't be the goal of life. . . . This is what's known as practising discrimination. Do you follow me?

M: Yes, sir. I have just read a drama called Prabodha Chandrodaya. It deals with the search for the Eternal Reality through the practice of discrimination.

SRI RAMAKRISHNA: Yes, that's it – to find the Reality through discrimination. You have to consider what the things are that money can buy, or what the value is in a beautiful body. If you discriminate, you'll find that the body of even the most beautiful woman consists of bone, flesh, fat and other nasty things. Why should a man give up God on their account? How can a man live in forgetfulness of God?

M: Sir, can one *see* God?

SRI RAMAKRISHNA: Most certainly you can! And this is what you must do in order to see him: Live in solitude from time to time. Chant the name of the Lord and his glories. And discriminate between the eternal and non-eternal.

M: What state of mind makes a man able to see God?

SRI RAMAKRISHNA: Cry to him with a yearning heart, and you will see him. Men weep a jugful of tears for their wives and children. And for money they shed enough tears to flood a river. But who weeps for God? Seek him with a loving heart.

Having said this, the Master sang:

> Seek Mother Shyama, O my mind,
> With a longing heart,
> With a yearning heart,
> She will not withhold herself.
> For how can the Mother withhold herself?
> How can Kali the Mother withhold her presence?
>
> Seek her, O my mind, seek her only.
> Gather the vilwa leaves,
> Gather hibiscus flowers,
> Then anoint them with sandal-paste,
> The sandal-paste of devotion,
> And lay them, as your offering, before her feet.

Sri Ramakrishna continued: 'Yearning for God is like the coming of dawn. Dawn comes before the sun itself rises. When yearning for God comes, the vision of God himself must follow.

'The worldly man loves his wealth; the mother loves her child; the chaste wife loves her husband. If your love for God is as intense as all these three attachments put together, then you will see God.

'Call on God with a longing heart. The kitten simply calls its mother, crying "mew, mew". It stays wherever the mother cat puts it. It doesn't know what else to do. And when the mother cat hears its cry, no matter where she may be, she runs to the kitten.'

It was Sunday, March 5th. M. arrived at the temple garden of Dakshineswar at 4 p.m., from Baranagore, with Nepal. They found Sri Ramakrishna seated on the small couch in his room. The room was crowded with people. As this was Sunday, very many devotees had found time and leisure to visit the Master. M. had not as yet become acquainted with any of them. He took his seat in a corner. Sri Ramakrishna was talking to the devotees with a smiling face.

He addressed his words particularly to a young man of nineteen. When the Master looked at him, he seemed very happy. The young man's name was Narendra. He was a student and attended the religious services at the Brahmo Samaj. When he spoke, his words were spirited. He had bright eyes and the look of a devotee.

SRI RAMAKRISHNA (*to* NARENDRA): 'Narendra, what do you say? Worldly people speak all kinds of evil against men of God. But you know, when the elephant walks, many beasts howl after it; and the elephant never looks back. How would you feel if people spoke ill of you?'

NARENDRA: I should think to myself: Let the dogs bark.

SRI RAMAKRISHNA (*smiling*): Oh no, you mustn't go that far! (*Everybody laughs.*)

God dwells in all beings. But be intimate only with good people. Avoid the company of the wicked. God is also in the tiger, but that's no reason to hug the tiger. (*All laugh.*) If you argue 'Why should I run away from the tiger, which is also a form of God?' the answer is, 'Why shouldn't you listen to those who say "run away"? They are forms of God, too.' Listen to a story. In a forest, there once lived a holy man who had a number of disciples. He taught them that they must bow down before all living creatures, recognizing that God dwells in all. One day, a disciple went into the forest to gather fuel for the sacrificial fire. As he did so, a loud cry was heard, 'Out of the way, whoever you are! A mad elephant is coming!' Everybody else ran away, but the disciple remained. For he said to himself that the elephant is also a form of God. So why should he run away? He remained there and, after bowing down, he began to sing the praises of the Lord. The mahut kept shouting 'Get away! get away!' but the disciple still didn't move. At last the elephant seized him with its trunk, threw him aside and went on. The disciple was severely bruised and hurt; he lay unconscious on the ground. Hearing of this, the guru and the other disciples lifted him up and carried him to the ashrama, where they nursed him. After a while, when he regained consciousness, someone asked him, 'When you heard that mad elephant coming, why didn't you run away?' He answered, 'Our Master has taught us that it is God alone who has assumed the forms of men, beasts and all living creatures.

Therefore I didn't run away when I saw the elephant God coming.' Then the guru said, 'It's true, my son, that the elephant God was coming, but the mahut God warned you to go. If all are forms of God, why didn't you listen to the mahut God? One should heed the words of the mahut God also.' (*All laugh.*)

A DEVOTEE: Sir, if a wicked person harms us or tries to harm us, should we keep quiet?

SRI RAMAKRISHNA: When you live in the world and meet all sorts of people, you need to make a show of resistance, in self-defence. But don't resist evil by doing evil in return. Listen to a story:

In a meadow, where some cowherds looked after their cattle, there lived a poisonous snake. Everyone feared it and kept on the watch for it. One day, a holy man was seen, walking along the path through the meadow. The cowherd boys ran to him and said, 'Holy sir, please don't go that way! A poisonous snake lives over there.'

The holy man answered, 'My sons, let it be there if it must – I am not afraid of it, for I know a secret spell which will subdue it.' So saying, the holy man continued on his way; but none of the cowherd boys dared to follow him. And now the snake appeared, moving towards him with its hood spread. But, as it drew near, the holy man uttered his spell and it fell at his feet as helpless as an earthworm.

Then the holy man said to it, 'Why do you go about doing harm to others? I am going to give you a mantra. As you repeat God's holy name, you will be set free from all desire to harm others; you will learn devotion to God and you will end by seeing him.' Having said this, the holy man whispered the holy name to the snake. And the snake, having been thus initiated, bowed down before its guru and asked, 'What disciplines shall I practise, holy sir?' The guru replied, 'Repeat the holy name and do no harm to anyone.' Then, as he was about to leave, he said, 'I shall come back here again.'

As the days passed, the cowherd boys discovered that the snake would no longer bite anyone. So they pelted it with stones, but the snake didn't get angry; it behaved like an earthworm. One day, one of the boys grabbed it by the tail, whirled it around and dashed it against the ground. The snake vomited blood and lay on the ground unconscious. It showed no sign of life and the boys left it, thinking it was dead.

But, in the middle of the night, the snake revived and slowly dragged itself with the greatest difficulty to its hole. Its body was crushed. It could hardly move. Many days passed. The snake was a mere skeleton. It used to come out once every night, in search of food. During the day, it did not come out, for fear of the boys. Since it had received its initiation and the holy name of God, it had never hurt anyone. It kept alive by eating leaves and fruit that had fallen on the ground.

About a year later, the holy man came along that path again and at once asked about the snake. The cowherd boys told him it was dead. But the holy man could not believe this; for he knew that the snake could not die until the holy word he had given it at its initiation had borne fruit in the vision of God. So he looked for it, calling it by the name he had conferred on it. Hearing the voice of its guru, the snake came out of its hole and bowed down with deep devotion. 'How are you?' the holy man asked. 'I am well, sir,' the snake answered. 'Then why do you look so thin?' asked the holy man. And the snake answered, 'Master, you ordered me not to hurt any living creature, so I have been living on leaves and fruit only. Perhaps that's why I look thin.' For the snake had developed such purity of heart that it could not harbour any malice; and so it had almost forgotten how the cowherd boys had half killed it. 'You couldn't be in such a state just because of your diet,' said the holy man. 'There must be some other reason. Try to remember what it is.' Then the snake remembered that the cowherd boys had dashed it against the ground; and it said, 'Yes, Master, I remember now. One day, these cowherd boys dashed me against the ground. It was only their ignorance, for how could they know that my heart had been changed? How could they know that I wouldn't bite any more or harm anyone?' 'For shame!' said the holy man. 'Are you such a fool that you don't know how to protect yourself? I told you not to bite. I didn't tell you not to hiss. Why couldn't you have scared them away by hissing?'

You have to hiss at wicked people. You have to scare them, or they'll harm you. But you must never shoot venom into them. You must never harm them.

There are four classes of men: the bound, who are caught up in worldliness, the seekers for liberation, the freed souls, and the ever-free.

The ever-free – such as Narada and others like him – live in the world for the good of mankind, that they may teach others.

The bound souls are those who remain obsessed by the objects of the world; they forget God and never think of him.

Then there are the seekers for liberation. Some of them attain it, others do not.

The freed souls are those who are not attached to lust and greed – the sadhus and mahatmas. There is no taint of worldliness in them. Their minds remain fixed on the lotus feet of God.

When a net is cast into the waters of a lake, there are some fish so clever that they don't get caught in it. These are like ever-free souls. However, most fish do get caught in the net. Some of these struggle to escape – they are like seekers for liberation – but not all of them get free. A very few escape from the net with great splashes, and then the fishermen say, 'There goes a big one!' Most of the fish can't escape and don't even try to; with the net in their mouths, they bury themselves in the mud and lie there quietly, thinking they are safe and that there's nothing more to fear. They don't realize that the fishermen are going to drag them out of the water on to the land. These are like the bound souls.

The bound souls are entangled in the net of lust and greed; they are bound hand and foot. They even believe that in the mud of lust and greed they can find happiness and safety. They don't realize that they are about to meet their death in a state of bondage. When the bound soul is about to die, his wife says, 'You are going – but what are you leaving behind for me?' And his attachment to worldly possessions is so great that if, even at that moment, he sees the lamp burning brightly he will say, 'Dim that lamp – it's burning too much oil.' And yet he's lying on his deathbed!

The bound souls do not think of God. If they have any leisure, they waste it in idle gossip or useless activity. If you ask one of them what he's doing, he'll answer, 'I can't sit still, so I'm putting up a fence.' Or, perhaps, when time hangs heavy on them, they'll start playing cards. (*All remain gravely silent.*)

A DEVOTEE: Sir, is there then no help for such worldly-minded people?

SRI RAMAKRISHNA: Of course there is – if only they will go to see holy men occasionally and meditate upon God in solitude, from time to time. Also they must practise discrimination and pray for devotion and faith.

(*Addressing* KEDAR): You must have heard about the tremendous power of faith? It is written in a Purana that Rama, who was the embodiment of the absolute Brahman, had to build a bridge to travel to Ceylon. But Hanuman, relying on the power of Rama's holy name, jumped across the sea to Ceylon. He didn't need the bridge. (*All laugh.*)

(*Pointing to* NARENDRA): Look at this young man sitting quietly here! A naughty boy, when he's sitting by his father, seems so well behaved; but when he's playing in the market place he's a different person entirely. Boys like Narendra belong to the class of the ever-free. They never become bound by worldliness. As they grow older, their spiritual consciousness becomes awakened and they go straight towards God.

(*Addressing* M.): Is there any book in English on the art of reasoning?

M: Yes, sir. It is called *Logic*.

SRI RAMAKRISHNA: Tell me how it reasons.

M. felt a little embarrassed. He said: 'There is one kind of reasoning, the deductive process, which leads from the general proposition to the particulars. As for example – all men are mortal, scholars are men, therefore scholars are mortal.

'There is another kind of reasoning, the inductive process, which leads from the particulars to the general proposition. As – for example – this crow is black, that crow is black, all the crows we have seen are black; therefore all crows are black.

'But this kind of reasoning may lead to a false conclusion. For, if one makes many inquiries, one may find that there are white crows in some other country.

'There is another example given: whenever it rains there are clouds, so the conclusion is to be drawn that clouds bring rain.'

Sri Ramakrishna was hardly paying any attention. As he listened, he became absent-minded. So the conversation stopped.

The meeting ends. The devotees go out to walk in the gardens. M. walks by the Panchavati. It is about five o'clock in the afternoon. After a while, he starts to walk back towards Sri Ramakrishna's room. On the small north veranda, he comes upon a strange sight.

Sri Ramakrishna is standing there motionless. Narendra is singing. A few devotees stand around. M. listens to the song and it charms him. He has never heard any sweeter music, except the singing of the Master himself. As M. looks at the Master, he is struck with wonder. The Master stands without moving, his eyes fixed; it seems that he is scarcely breathing. On inquiry, M. learns from a devotee that this state is known as samadhi. M. has never seen or heard of anything like it. He is amazed. He thinks to himself: 'Can a man completely lose his outer consciousness by thinking of God? How strong one's faith and devotion must be, in order to reach such a state!'

As the last line of the song was sung, the Master began to shudder. The hairs of his body stood on end. Tears of joy flowed from his eyes. Now and then he appeared to be seeing some vision, and there was a smile on his lips. Was this what is known as the vision of God in his spiritual form? How many spiritual disciplines, how many austerities, how much faith and devotion must be necessary in order to have such a vision of God?

M. returned home with an impression in his mind that could not be wiped out: this first glimpse of samadhi and the bliss of divine love.

The next day was also a holiday. M. arrived at Dakshineswar at about three in the afternoon. Sri Ramakrishna was seated in his room. There was a mat spread on the floor. Narendra, Bhavanath and one or two other devotees were sitting on it; they were all young men of nineteen or twenty years old. Sri Ramakrishna sat on the small couch with a smile on his face. He was talking happily with the young men.

As the Master saw M. come into the room, he laughed aloud and said to the young men, 'Look, here he comes again.' And so saying he laughed once more. All joined in his laughter. M. prostrated himself before him and sat down. Previously, he had saluted the Master with folded hands, as people do who have been educated by the English. But that day he had learnt to prostrate at the feet. As M. sat down, Sri Ramakrishna explained to Narendra and the other devotees why he had laughed.

'You know,' he said, 'there was once a peacock that was given a dose of opium at four in the afternoon. Next day, at four o'clock exactly, the peacock returned. It had felt the intoxication of the opium and so it came back at exactly that same hour.' (*All laugh.*)

M. thought: 'How right he was! I go home, but my mind dwells on him night and day. I keep thinking, when shall I see him next? Someone is pulling me to this place, as it were. Even if I wished to, I couldn't go anywhere else. I have to come here.' While M. was thinking this, the Master was having fun with the young men and was teasing them, as though he was of their own age. Peals of laughter filled the room – it seemed to be the very home of joy.

M. looked with wonder at this strange man and said to himself, 'Only yesterday I saw him absorbed in samadhi and the bliss of God – a sight I never saw before! And today, this same being is behaving like an ordinary man. Wasn't it he who scolded me when I came here before, saying, "And you're a wise man, are you?" Didn't he tell me that God with form and God without form are both real? Didn't he say to me that God alone is real and that everything else is unreal? Didn't he teach me to live in the world like a maidservant in a rich man's house?'

Sri Ramakrishna was having fun with the boys. He glanced at M. now and then, and watched him sitting in silence. Then the Master said to Ramlal, 'You see, he's getting on in years, that's why he looks serious. The youngsters are having such fun, but he sits there quiet.' M. was at that time twenty-seven years old.

The Master addressed M. and Narendra and said, 'I would like to hear you two argue about something in English.'

M. and Narendra both laughed. They talked together, but in Bengali. It was impossible for M. to enter into an argument with another person while the Master was present. He urged them once more to speak English; but they could not.

It was five o'clock in the afternoon. All the devotees went home, except M. and Narendra. M. wandered about in the temple garden. As he approached the goose-pond, he saw Ramakrishna standing on the steps of the pond, talking to Narendra and saying to him, 'Listen, you must come here more often. You're a newcomer. When people are first acquainted, they should visit each other often, like two lovers –' (*Narendra and M. laugh*) 'Isn't that so? Then come, won't you?'

Narendra, being a member of the Brahmo Samaj, was scrupulous about making positive promises, so he laughed and said, 'Yes, I shall try.'

As they were returning to the Master's room, Sri Ramakrishna said to M., 'You see, when peasants go to market to buy bullocks, they know how to test them, to distinguish between the good and the bad. They touch the tail; if the bullock lies down when it is touched, they don't buy it. They select ones that jump and become restless when they're touched. Narendra is like a bullock of that class. There's spirit in him.' Sri Ramakrishna laughed as he said this, then he continued, 'On the other hand, there are people who have no mettle in them; they are like flattened rice soaked in curd – soft, mushy, no spirit in them.'

It was evening. The Master was meditating on God. He said to M., 'Go and get acquainted with Narendra; then tell me how you like him.' The vesper services were over in the temples. M. met Narendra and conversed with him. Narendra told him that he was a member of the Brahmo Samaj, a student in a college, and so forth.

It was now late in the evening and M. had to leave, but he felt reluctant to. After parting from Narendra, M. went looking for the Master. His heart and mind had been captivated by the Master's singing, and he wanted very badly to hear him sing again. At last he found the Master pacing back and forth alone in the theatre-hall in front of the temple of Mother Kali. There were lighted lamps on either side of Mother's image in the temple. A single light was burning in the spacious open theatre-hall; this light was dim.

M. felt that the Master's sweet singing had enchanted him, as a snake is charmed by a spell. He approached the Master and asked, with some hesitation, 'Will there be any more singing, this evening?' The Master reflected a little and then said, 'No, not tonight.' Then, as if remembering something, he added, 'This is what you can do –

I shall be going to Balaram Bose's house in Calcutta – you come there. There'll be singing there.'

M: Yes, sir.

SRI RAMAKRISHNA: Do you know Balaram Bose?

M: No, sir.

SRI RAMAKRISHNA: He lives in Bosepara.

M: Very well, sir. I shall find his house.

SRI RAMAKRISHNA (*as he and* M. *walk up and down the hall together*): Let me ask you something. How do you feel about me?

M. remained silent. Sri Ramakrishna asked again, 'How do you feel about me? How many annas of knowledge of God do I have?'

M: Sir, I don't know what you mean by 'annas'. But this much I can say: Never before have I seen anywhere such wisdom, such ecstatic love, such faith and such dispassion and such broad-mindedness.

Sri Ramakrishna began to laugh.

After this conversation, M. bowed down before the Master and took his leave. He had gone as far as the main gate of the temple when he thought of something he wanted to ask the Master, so he returned. He approached the Master in the theatre-hall. Sri Ramakrishna was still pacing the hall, alone – rejoicing in the Atman and needing nothing else – like a lion who loves to roam alone in the forest. M. regarded this great soul in silent wonder.

SRI RAMAKRISHNA (*to* M.): Why did you come back again?

M: Sir, perhaps it is a rich man's house. They may not let me in. I'll come here and meet you here.

SRI RAMAKRISHNA: Oh no – why do that? Just mention my name and tell them you've come to see me. Then someone will bring you to me.

M: Yes, sir.

Again he bowed down before the Master, and then took his leave.

So ends M's narrative of his first four meetings with Ramakrishna.

In its complete version – I have made a few cuts here, to avoid repetitions – it forms the opening chapter of the *Gospel*; the first of fifty-two chapters. (This will give the reader some idea of the size of the book.) The narrative runs more or less continuously from February 1882 to April 1886. M. records how, on April 24, 1886, he came to visit Ramakrishna with his wife and one of his sons. M's wife was desperately unhappy because of the death of another of her sons, and this was why Ramakrishna had asked M. to bring her to him. By this time, Ramakrishna was already lying mortally sick, and Sarada Devi was in attendance on him. Nevertheless, he showed compassionate interest in M's wife, and invited her to come and spend a few days with Sarada, and bring her baby daughter. M. realized that his wife would find comfort and strength in this association, and he was deeply grateful. He records how, at nine o'clock that evening, he was fanning Ramakrishna, who wore a garland which some devotees had placed around his neck. Ramakrishna took off the garland and murmured something to himself. Then he put the garland on M. M. writes that the Master's mood was 'most benign'. This is our parting glimpse of Ramakrishna, for M. has left us no record of the last three and a half months of his life. During this period, Ramakrishna was devoting most of his remaining energy to the training of his young monastic disciples; he may therefore have had less time for his householder devotees; besides, his physical condition gradually became worse. However, M. almost certainly saw him now and then. It is said that M. left this gap in his narrative because he could not bear to write about the final stages of the cancer which caused his Master's death. He appears, with characteristic modesty, in the extreme background of a photograph of disciples and devotees standing beside Ramakrishna's body, just before it was taken away to be cremated, on the afternoon of August 16, 1886.

In the *Gospel*'s fifty-second and final chapter, M. describes some visits he paid to the monastery which the young monks had founded at Baranagore. The first of these is dated February 21, 1887; the last, May 10th of the same year. There will be more to say about this part of the narrative, later.

One of M's great virtues as a biographer is his candour. We have seen how he describes his humiliation during his second visit to Ramakrishna. Elsewhere in the *Gospel*, he tells how Ramakrishna praised him and treated him with affection. A self-consciously humble man might have omitted the praise. But there is a more genuine lack of egotism in M's simple relation of fact.

M. is equally candid about Ramakrishna himself. His firm belief in the divinity of Ramakrishna's nature was just what stopped him from presenting his Master as the glorified figure of a holy man. Anything that Ramakrishna says or does is sacred to him; therefore he omits nothing, alters nothing. In his pages, we encounter Ramakrishna as an authentic spiritual phenomenon; by turns godlike and childlike, sublime and absurd, now expounding the highest philosophy, now telling funny animal-stories as parables, now singing and dancing, now staggering in ecstasy like a drunkard, now admonishing his devotees with the mature wisdom of a father, now dropping his wearing-cloth and walking naked like a baby.

He is eager to meet anyone who seeks knowledge of God. If some of these seekers betray a weakness for human fame, an excessive respect for philosophy-books, or a secret attachment to the worldly pleasures they pretend to have renounced, Ramakrishna deals with them gently and laughs unmaliciously at them later. He is at his strictest with young aspirants, because their faults can still be corrected. He is most at his ease with men of enlightenment; hemp-smokers, he says, love each other's company. He regards children with humour and, at the same time, reverence. In one of the *Gospel*'s most charming passages (July 3, 1884) M. tells how a little girl, six or seven years old, bowed down before Ramakrishna, and then reproached him because he did not notice. She bowed down to him again. And he, in turn, bowed down to her, touching the ground with his forehead. He then asked her to sing. 'I don't sing,' she told him, adding a Bengali expression which means 'cross my heart!' Again he pressed her to sing, and she retorted, 'I said "cross my heart" – doesn't that settle it?' So Ramakrishna sang folk songs, to amuse the little girl and her friends. One of them began:

> *Come – let me braid your hair.*
> *You must do all you can*
> *To please your man!*

Then, turning to the adult devotees who were present, he said that the young child is like a knower of Brahman, for he sees consciousness everywhere. 'Once I was staying at Kamarpukur,' he continued, 'when my nephew Shivaram was four or five years old. One day he was by the pond, trying to catch grasshoppers. The leaves were rustling, so he told them, "Ssh, be quiet! I want to catch a grasshopper." Another day, there was a storm and the rain poured down. Shivaram was with me in the house. The lightning kept flashing. He wanted to open the door and go out but I scolded him and wouldn't let him. Still, he peeped out, now and then. When he saw the lightning, he cried, "Look, uncle! They're striking matches again!"'

If I had to use one single word to describe the atmosphere of the *Gospel* narrative, it would be the word *Now*. The majority of us spend the greater part of our lives in the future or the past – fearing or desiring what is to come, regretting what is over. M. shows us a being who lives in continuous contact with that which is eternally present. God's existence has no relation to past or future; it is always as of *now*. To be with Ramakrishna was to be in the presence of that Now. Not everybody who visited Dakshineswar was aware of this. M. was aware, from the first; and he never ceased to be thankful for the privilege he was enjoying. He describes every scene of his narrative with a thankful wonder that he – the ordinary unworthy schoolmaster – should have been permitted to take part in it. M's sense of the greatness of each and every such occasion gives even his simplest descriptive passages a quality of excitement and magic:

> The carriage passed through the European quarter of the city. The Master enjoyed looking at the beautiful mansions on either side of the brightly lighted streets. Then, suddenly, he said, 'I'm thirsty. What shall we do?' Nandalal the nephew of Keshab stopped the carriage in front of the India Club and went inside to get some water. The Master asked if the glass had been well washed. When they assured him that it had been, he drank the water.
>
> As the carriage drove on, the Master put his head out of the window and watched everything that went by – the people, the vehicles, the horses and the streets, all bathed in the light of the moon. Now and again, he could hear the European ladies singing to the music of the piano. He was in a very happy mood.

M. shows us Ramakrishna by day and by night, chiefly at Dakshineswar but also at the houses of Balaram and other devotees, on riverboats with Keshab Sen, or driving in a carriage through the streets.

Usually, there are quite a lot of people present: disciples, householder devotees and casual visitors. Naturally, they tend to ask Ramakrishna the same questions and so Ramakrishna's answers often repeat or paraphrase themselves. M. records these repetitions, as well as the words of all the songs Ramakrishna sings. A newcomer to the *Gospel* may find this tiresome at first. But, if he reads the book straight through from beginning to end, instead of merely dipping into it, he will probably agree that it is these very repetitions which give the narrative its continuity and its sense of life actually being lived from day to day. In any case, a teacher who never repeats himself is a creation of art and editorship rather than a live being!

Already, in this opening chapter, we find the methods of Ramakrishna's teaching illustrated and its main precepts stated. Ramakrishna sometimes teaches by making direct statements, based on the authority of his spiritual experience; sometimes by means of comparisons and parables. The latter are nearly always taken from the circumstances of country life in Bengal, and they are often comic, combining worldly and spiritual wisdom, as in the story of the snake which did not hiss. It must be remembered that M. was a householder and that he could not be present when Ramakrishna was giving special instruction to his monastic disciples. Therefore, the *Gospel* deals mainly with instructions to householders.

But the most important function of Ramakrishna as a teacher was available to householder devotee and monastic disciple alike. Both had the opportunity of watching him in the silence of samadhi, in the incoherent mutterings of ecstasy, in the radiant joy of devotional dancing and song. And it was in these manifestations that even some casual visitors to Dakshineswar caught a glimpse of Ramakrishna's true nature. To those who were not utterly insensitive, this was a demonstration, more convincing than the Master's most eloquent words, of the reality of God's presence.

M. appears to have taken copious notes immediately after each of his meetings with Ramakrishna. It is said that he was often busy for three days writing down the sayings and events of a single visit. Nevertheless, when the time came for publication, he worked over all of his material, during the last thirty-five years of his life.

At first, M. was unwilling to publish at all; he had made these notes, he said, simply as a basis for his own study and meditation. But many influences combined to make him change his attitude. Soon after Ramakrishna's death, when the young monks founded their first monastery at Baranagore, M. became one of their most faithful friends and helpers. Indeed, he took employment at two schools simultaneously, in order that he could support his family with the salary from the one and give the rest of his earnings to the monks. Needless to say, they kept urging M. to publish his notes, but he could not be persuaded. In 1889, however, M. made himself responsible for part of the support of Sarada, the Holy Mother. She asked him to read the notes to her and was greatly pleased with them. She told him that he must publish them. M. accepted this as a command.

So, in 1897, he published two pamphlets containing a small part of his material, expanded and translated into English. This version reads quaintly, because M. believed that his subject demanded a special sort of archaic, evangelical language. Here, for example, is the last sentence of his account of the first meeting:

A short while after, M. saluteth the Master. He biddeth M. good-bye, and saith 'come again'.

Vivekananda praised the pamphlets enthusiastically, in a characteristic letter: 'C'est bon, mon ami – now you are doing just the thing. Come out, man. No sleeping all life; time is flying. Bravo! That is the way.' Nevertheless it was generally agreed that Ramakrishna should be described and heard to speak in his native language; and now M. began to expand and publish the notes in their original Bengali. They appeared in three or four different magazines, in serial form. In 1902, everything already printed was collected by Trigunatitananda and published in one volume.

Four more volumes, making up the whole of what is now the *Gospel*, were published in due course; the last of them posthumously in 1932, the year of M's death. M. worked slowly. This was partly because of his other duties – in 1905 he bought a school of his own, called The Morton Institution; partly because he approached this work as a form of worship – whenever he sat down to write, he would pass much of the time in meditation and eat only one meal that day.

In 1907, Swami Abhedananda, at M's request, edited M's English version, modernizing the language, and adding sections directly translated from the Bengali. But this book, was, of course, not complete; M's full text not being available until twenty-five years later. M. put together his five Bengali volumes in the form of selections, skipping back and forth in time to choose the parts he considered most significant. And it was not until Swami Nikhilananda published his English translation in 1942 that the whole of the *Gospel* material was presented in strictly chronological sequence.

M. would have been overwhelmed, no doubt, if he could have known that Aldous Huxley would one day compare him to Boswell and call his *Gospel* 'unique in the literature of hagiography'. Yet Huxley's praise is no more than a statement of fact. The service M. has rendered us and future generations can hardly be exaggerated. Even the vainest of authors might well have been humbled, finding himself entrusted with such a task. M. was the least vain.

M. embodies Ramakrishna's ideal of the householder devotee. He was a distinguished teacher and scholar, vested with authority and held in honour. Yet he thought of himself always as a servant and the least of men. The world could never win him, even with its love; and everyone who met him loved him. It is said that he would often take his bedroll at night and lie down to sleep in the open porch of a public building, among the homeless boys of the city – to remind himself that, like the maid in Ramakrishna's parable, his real home was elsewhere.

He died on June 4, 1932. His last words were, 'Holy Mother – Master – take me on your laps!'

29. Sword of Kali

30. Courtyard, Nat-mandap, and Kali temple

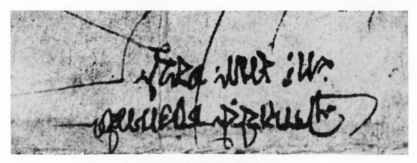

31. Ramakrishna's signature

32. Panchavati

20

The Last Year

<hr />

The early part of 1885 was unusually hot. Since Ramakrishna suffered from the heat, the devotees suggested that he should suck pieces of ice and put ice in his sugared drinks. He became very fond of ice. However, when, towards the end of April, he began to complain of a pain in his throat, the devotees blamed the ice, and themselves.

The pain was caused by a sore, which did not yield to treatment but grew gradually worse. The doctor advised Ramakrishna not to talk more than was absolutely necessary and to avoid, if he possibly could, going into samadhi. In samadhi, the blood rushes to the throat, and the doctor feared that this would aggravate Ramakrishna's condition.

In May, the Vaishnavas held an annual festival at the village of Panihati, on the bank of the Ganges, a few miles upriver from Dakshineswar. The festival commemorated an occasion on which Sri Nityananda, the chief disciple of Sri Chaitanya, was entertained at a feast in this same village by Raghunath, a householder devotee. Nityananda encouraged Raghunath to persevere in begging Chaitanya's permission to renounce the world and become a monk.

Ramakrishna had attended the Panihati festival many times already; but this year he wanted to take his young disciples, who had never seen it. When objections were made to this expedition because of his illness, he brushed them aside, saying that he would only stay an hour or two and that he would be careful not to go into samadhi. It was agreed that he must not take part in the kirtan, the singing of holy songs, as this invariably threw him into ecstasy.

After visiting the home of a wealthy landowner and resting there for a little while, Ramakrishna and his party went to watch the dancing and singing in the courtyard of the Radhakanta Temple. As they stood there, a man dressed as a Vaishnava began to dance and shout in an apparently ecstatic state. Ramakrishna knew him at once for an impostor. Smiling indulgently, he whispered to Naren, 'What a fake!' He seemed to be observing the scene objectively, with perfectly controlled emotions; and the young disciples felt reassured. But the very next moment, before any of them could stop him, he bounded down into the midst of the dancers and went into samadhi. The disciples could do nothing but crowd around and watch. Sarat (Saradananda), who was present, describes how Ramakrishna then regained partial outer consciousness and started dancing with a power and beauty such as the boys had never seen before. Sometimes, says Saradananda, he strode like a lion; sometimes he moved like a fish swimming in a sea of ecstasy. His body was so flexible that one could not believe it contained hard bones; the music seemed to pass through it in visible waves.

In about half an hour, Ramakrishna began to come to himself, and the disciples urged him to leave the kirtan party and start for home, after first paying homage to some sacred images which were lodged in a near-by shrine. Ramakrishna agreed; but, as they left the temple, the kirtan players, who had no idea that he was ailing, followed them, still singing their songs. Ramakrishna therefore kept stopping and going into samadhi, and their progress was very slow. All of them witnessed, that day, the phenomenon which has already been referred to in this story. Saradananda says that Ramakrishna's figure appeared to grow taller and become luminous, 'like a body seen in a dream'. His skin was much lighter than usual and actually shone; it seemed to blend with the bright ochre colour of his silk wearing-cloth so that he looked as if enclosed in flames. The kirtan players were amazed and enraptured. They started to sing a hymn to Nitai (Nityananda), making the words refer to Ramakrishna himself.

> *It seems that our Nitai, the love-giver is here!*
> *Here comes our Nitai, bringing divine love!*
> *Without him, how could our heart's longing be appeased?*
> *Here is our Nitai, the love-giver!*

Again and again, pointing their fingers at Ramakrishna, they sang, 'Here is our love-giver!' Other kirtan parties joined in the singing, and soon nearly all of the devotees who had come to the festival surrounded Ramakrishna in a vast excited throng.

An ugly twisted man in the garb of a wandering monk snatched a

plate of prasad from a woman devotee and with his own hand put some
of the food into Ramakrishna's mouth. Ramakrishna did not resist,
being in samadhi; but, as soon as he was touched, he winced and
returned to outer consciousness, spitting out the food and then washing
his mouth. The onlookers concluded that the man must be somehow
unclean and a hypocrite; they regarded him scornfully and he slunk
away, humiliated. Ramakrishna confirmed their suspicions by willingly
taking prasad from another of the devotees.

The immense crowd further retarded Ramakrishna's progress, and
it was nearly four hours later that he and his disciples finally reached
the boat that was to take them back to Dakshineswar. A devotee
named Navachaitanya Mitra came running in wild haste and threw
himself at Ramakrishna's feet, weeping and begging for his grace.
Ramakrishna touched him and he became ecstatic, dancing and singing
the Master's praises until he was calmed by a second touch. Navachaitanya had met Ramakrishna several times previously, but this
experience changed his life. He put his son in charge of the family and
retired to live in solitude on the bank of the Ganges.

After the visit to Panihati, Ramakrishna's throat grew worse. It had
rained on and off during that day, so the doctors blamed the weather.
Ramakrishna himself, with typical mischievousness, blamed Ram
Chandra and some of the other older devotees, saying that he would
never have gone to the festival if they had forbidden him more ener-
getically. The doctors gave him an internal salve and a plaster to put
on the outside of the throat, without causing any improvement. They
also told him not to talk, but he disobeyed them.

By now, July was half over. Ramakrishna was in considerable pain
and his throat was so much swollen that he could swallow no solid food
and had to live on milk with cream of wheat boiled in it. The doctors
decided that he was suffering from what was called in those days
'clergyman's sore throat', a form of laryngitis brought on by overstrain-
ing the voice. They prescribed medicine and diet but Ramakrishna
continued to break their two principal rules: he went into samadhi
and he talked. Devotees were coming to visit him in ever-increasing
numbers and he never refused to instruct them. However, he would
keep complaining to the Divine Mother, 'Why do you bring so many
people here? There's such a crowd I don't have time to wash or eat.

This body's nothing but a drum with holes in it – how long can it last if it's played day and night?'

During the month of September, a lady invited some of the young disciples and householder devotees to have supper at her house. She knew that Ramakrishna was sick but, with the ruthlessness of a hostess, she nevertheless sent him a message pressing him to come, even if only for a few minutes. The messenger returned to report that this was out of the question; Ramakrishna's throat had started to bleed. All the guests were dismayed, and Naren became silent and very grave. Later, he told them, 'He who has made us all so happy may be going to leave us. I've been reading medical books and questioning friends who are doctors. They say that this kind of throat ailment can develop into cancer. And now this bleeding makes me even more afraid that that's what it is. If so, there is no known cure for it.'

It was therefore agreed that Ramakrishna must be put under a more systematic and efficient treatment without delay. Next day, some of the older householder devotees went to Dakshineswar and persuaded him that he could be better cared for if he moved into Calcutta. A few days later, they were able to rent a small house in the Baghbazar district. From its roof the Ganges could be seen, and this was regarded as a great asset, since Ramakrishna loved the river so dearly. Nevertheless, when they brought him there, he declared at once that he could not stay a single night; the place seemed unbearably shut in after the spaciousness of the Dakshineswar gardens. He actually walked to the house of Balaram Bose, who received him lovingly and begged him to remain there until a more suitable lodging could be found.

Meanwhile, the devotees called in several well-known Calcutta physicians to examine Ramakrishna. They all diagnosed cancer, and their attitude was pessimistic; but they were prepared to treat him to the best of their ability. The devotees chose Dr Mahendralal Sarkar, chiefly because he was a homoeopathist. Homoeopathy – which was being much discussed at that period – is a method of treating a patient by drugs which would produce, in a healthy person, symptoms like those of the patient's disease. These drugs are usually administered in minute quantities. The devotees therefore knew that Dr Sarkar would not overdose Ramakrishna; too much medicine had always seemed to disagree with him. Under the circumstances, this was probably as good a reason for choosing a doctor as any other.

The news of Ramakrishna's move to Calcutta spread by word of mouth all over the city. Crowds of people, both friends and strangers, invaded Balaram's house from early morning till night, and Ramakrishna was available to them all day long, with a break of only two hours for his midday meal and rest. It was as if he had come to Calcutta for their greater convenience, to spare them the journey to Dakshineswar, rather than for his own medical care. Very few of those who saw him can have dreamed that he was mortally ill. He spoke of God with his customary fervour and went frequently into samadhi.

In a few days, another house was found – 55 Shyampukur Street – and Ramakrishna moved into it after having stayed at Balaram's about a week. The rooms which could be occupied by him and his devotees were all on the upper floor of the house, and there were not enough of them for comfort. There was no one able to cook food in the way that Ramakrishna needed; so Sarada Devi, who was still at Dakshineswar, had to be asked if she would do this. Sarada's shyness was well known; it was a real ordeal for her to live in a house full of men. But she came to Shyampukur Street nevertheless, and managed to do her cooking on a tiny covered terrace near the door which led to the roof. When the food had to be served, it would either be fetched by one of the devotees or brought to Ramakrishna by Sarada herself, after everyone else had been asked to leave his room. She would not come down to her own room to sleep until the others had retired for the night; and, since there was only one bathroom, she would get up at three in the morning so as to be able to use it in complete privacy.

It was found that Dr Sarkar had met Ramakrishna already, many years previously, while visiting Dakshineswar to attend Mathur and his family. When he came to examine Ramakrishna, he recognized him at once. The doctor charged a fee for his first visit. But when he had learned that the entire cost of Ramakrishna's lodging, food and nursing was to be borne by the devotees – even though this could mean rationing the food for themselves and their children, pawning family ornaments and mortgaging their homes – he announced that in future he would attend Ramakrishna free of charge. At first, Dr Sarkar did not give up all hope of his patient's recovery. He believed that the disease might possibly be curable, though admittedly the cure would be difficult and lengthy.

The devotees were united in their readiness to make drastic material sacrifices for their Master. But, as the weeks passed, they became divided into three groups, each with a different interpretation of the meaning of his illness.

The first group, which was headed by Girish Ghosh, reasoned as follows: The Master is a divine incarnation. Therefore he is not subject to karma, in the form of illness or mishap. If he is sick, then he is sick for some purpose of his own; and, in this sense, it is a kind of play-acting. As soon as his purpose has been fulfilled, he will cast off the appearance of sickness and return at once to normal health.

The second group stressed the fact that Ramakrishna had always declared himself to be the child and instrument of the Divine Mother, with no will other than her will. Therefore, they reasoned, it is the Mother who has made the Master sick. No doubt she is doing this, in some way, for the good of humanity. We cannot know what her purpose is. Indeed, it is possible that the Master himself does not know. We can only be sure that, when the Mother's purpose has been fulfilled, the Master will recover.

The third group disagreed radically with this (from a practical viewpoint) fatalistic attitude. They believed just as firmly as the others in the divinity of the Master's nature; but they drew a clear distinction between that divine nature and the physical nature of the body in which he was now living on earth. This body, they said, was mortal like any other and subject to disease from natural causes. Therefore it could be healed by human science; and it was the duty of the Master's devotees to use the help of this science, instead of passively waiting for God's will to be revealed. This group was headed by Naren and it contained most if not all of the young monastic disciples.

Dr Sarkar soon became fascinated by Ramakrishna. He would visit him daily at different hours, so as to watch him in various conditions. In order to do this, the Doctor neglected his paying patients. 'I have made you talk too much,' he would say. 'That was unwise. But don't talk to anyone else for the rest of the day. Then no harm will be done.'

When Sarkar learned that many of the devotees regarded Ramakrishna as a divine incarnation, his scientific scepticism was affronted. 'Divine incarnation,' he exclaimed scornfully, 'what kind of a thing is that? To grovel before a human being who excretes filth – how ridiculous!' He would declare that he himself admired Ramakrishna simply for his love of truth.

However, the Doctor had another side to his character. M. tells how he admitted that, 'That fellow the intellect is extremely narrow-minded; if he meets any difficulty, he cries "impossible!" But the heart doesn't believe in impossibilities – and that's how all real discoveries are made and will be made in the future.' No doubt Sarkar enjoyed playing the down-to-earth scientist in order to shock the more sentimental among the devotees. At the same time, he maintained an admirable open-mindedness. When two of the young disciples went into ecstasy after singing religious songs, Sarkar took their pulses and agreed that they had genuinely lost consciousness of external objects, as though they had fainted. Then Ramakrishna passed his hand over their chests and uttered the name of God, making them conscious again. Sarkar said, 'This seems to be all your play.' Ramakrishna answered smiling, 'Not my play but God's.' During the Durga Puja, Sarkar took the opportunity of examining Ramakrishna with a stethoscope while he was in samadhi. No heartbeat could be detected. He also touched Ramakrishna's eyeball with his finger. There was no reaction. The Doctor recorded these facts and said he was unable to explain them.

Ramakrishna showed much affection for Sarkar and enjoyment of their talks. One day, he impulsively put his foot in the Doctor's lap, and then told him, 'You are certainly very pure. Otherwise, I couldn't have put my foot in your lap.' He described how the Divine Mother had made it known to him in a vision that Sarkar would accumulate a great deal of knowledge but that it would be 'dry knowledge'. Then he added, smiling, 'But you will soften.'

Dr Sarkar was exceedingly strict about Ramakrishna's diet. One day, when Ramakrishna's condition had taken a turn for the worse, he traced the cause to the presence of cauliflower juice in the soup. And yet, with all his strictness, he seems to have made up his mind quite soon that the case was hopeless. On October 25th, M. was alone with Sarkar and told him that one of the devotees believed Ramakrishna had created the disease merely to 'pamper the Doctor's ego' and that he could cure himself whenever he wished. Sarkar exclaimed impatiently that this was nonsense. 'The disease is incurable,' he added. 'There's no doubt about that.'

.   .   .   .

Early in November came the day for the celebration of the Kali Puja. On Ramakrishna's instructions, a small ceremony was arranged to be held in his room. About thirty people gathered there. Everything was ready. But Ramakrishna himself made no move to take part in the worship. Then Girish Ghosh had an inspiration: the Master must be giving them this opportunity of worshipping the Divine Mother within his own body. So he took flowers and sandal-paste and offered them at Ramakrishna's feet, exclaiming, 'Glory to the Divine Mother!' A thrill passed through Ramakrishna's body and he went into samadhi. Girish's action was then imitated by M., Rakhal and all the other devotees in turn. M. writes that, as they looked at Ramakrishna, his face was transformed and began to shine with an unearthly light, and his hands assumed the traditional gesture of the Divine Mother, one of them conferring blessings, the other bidding the devotees to be without fear.

Genuine and deep as Girish's devotion to Ramakrishna was, it set an example which could be unwholesome for smaller natures. Such people were apt to infer from Girish's life and behaviour that religion was a mere matter of emotion, tear-shedding, ecstatic singing and dancing. Even Girish's famous granting of 'the power of attorney' to Ramakrishna sounded delightfully easy to many who had absolutely no notion what true self-surrender means.

It may be imagined how vigorously Naren attacked this attitude. He pointed out that Ramakrishna had been through long years of the strictest self-discipline and that his ecstasy was the fruit of that discipline, not a superficial emotionalism. 'When people try to practise religion,' said Naren, 'eighty per cent of them turn into cheats, and about fifteen per cent go mad. It's only the remaining five per cent who get some direct knowledge of the Truth and so become blessed. Therefore, beware!'

At first, even the young disciples were unwilling to agree with Naren; they felt he was being too severe. But then it was discovered that several devotees were actually trying to induce the outer physical symptoms of samadhi and imitate the movements of one who is dancing in a state of ecstasy. Naren reasoned with these devotees and persuaded them to stop starving themselves and eat wholesome food, and to try to control their emotions instead of cultivating hysteria. The result was an increase in spirituality and a decrease in outward show. For the few who would not be persuaded, Naren had a more drastic form of treatment; he made such fun of their posturings that the other devotees laughed at them, shaming them into common sense.

While he was at Shyampukur, Ramakrishna had a vision in which he saw his subtle body emerge from his gross physical body while he was walking about the room. He observed that the back of the subtle body was covered with sores, especially where the trunk joined the throat. He wondered why this was so. The Divine Mother explained to him that many people who had committed evil deeds had touched him and thus become pure. Their bad karma had been transferred to him and had produced the sores on his body. Ramakrishna did not seem at all disturbed by this discovery. Indeed, he said repeatedly that he was ready to be reborn many thousands of times more, if his incarnations could be of service to others. However, Naren and the young disciples, when they were told of the vision, determined that no newcomer should be allowed to touch Ramakrishna as long as he was sick. They also tried to cut down the ever-growing number of visitors by ruling that no one could be admitted who was not known to at least one of the regular devotees.

Girish Ghosh said of these restrictions, 'There's no harm in trying, but it isn't possible to stop people from seeing the Master, for that's the whole purpose of his coming to earth.' As for Ramakrishna, he continued to talk about God to anyone and everyone who could get into his room. One day, he was teaching a young man the best postures for meditation on God with form and without form. 'But I can't show you any more,' he added. 'As soon as I sit in that posture, the mind becomes absorbed in samadhi and the vital force of the body rises. That hurts the sore in my throat. So the doctor has told me particularly that there mustn't be any samadhi.' 'Then why have you been showing me all these things?' the young man exclaimed, in dismay, 'You shouldn't have done that!' 'I know,' said Ramakrishna, 'but I had to show you something.'

During one of Ramakrishna's visits to the Star Theatre in 1884, he had greatly praised an actress who played the part of the young Chaitanya. At the end of the play, Ramakrishna had passed into samadhi, and this actress had taken the opportunity to bow down and touch his feet. Since then, she had become his devotee, regarding him as a divine incarnation. When she heard of his illness, she determined to see him once again.

In those days, actresses in the Bengali theatre were regarded as no better than prostitutes – a prejudice which also persisted in England until at least the beginning of the nineteenth century. It was therefore unthinkable that the strict young disciples would allow her inside the house. So the actress went to a devotee named Kalipada Ghosh and asked for his help. Kalipada was a close friend of Girish Ghosh and, like him, believed that Ramakrishna was an avatar and his illness a play, and that therefore he could not possibly be harmed by anybody's touch, even if it were impure. He dressed the actress up in male European clothes – such as were fashionable at that time among the young men of Bengal – and brought her thus disguised to Shyampukur. They were able to enter Ramakrishna's room at a time when no other visitors were present. Kalipada immediately told Ramakrishna who the supposed young man really was, and Ramakrishna laughed heartily, praising the actress's courage and devotion. He gave her some spiritual instruction and allowed her to touch his feet with her forehead. When she and Kalipada had left, he told the disciples of the trick which had been played on them, with so much enjoyment that they could not be angry.

Meanwhile, Ramakrishna's condition grew steadily worse. Dr Sarkar became convinced that the polluted air of Calcutta was harming him. The Doctor therefore advised a second move – to a house outside the city. A garden-house was found in the northwestern suburbs, on the way to Dakshineswar: 90 Cossipore Road. The rent was eighty rupees a month; somewhat higher than the rent at Shyampukur. When Ramakrishna heard this, he called Surendra Nath Mitra to him and asked him to undertake to pay the whole amount, saying that the financial strain on the other, poorer devotees would be too great. Surendra gladly agreed to this. The move was made on December 11, 1885, shortly before the end of the Hindu month of Agrahayan. Some haste was necessary, because custom forbids a change of dwelling during Paush, the month that follows it.

The Cossipore house stood in a pleasant garden of about four and a half acres which contained a small pool and a much larger pond and was planted with fruit trees – mango, jack fruit and lichee – as well as vegetables for use in the kitchen. The house was a two-story building, more spacious than the house at Shyampukur. (Vivekananda had always wished that the property could belong to the Ramakrishna Order. It was finally purchased by the Order in 1946, but, by then, the house was much dilapidated. It has since been torn down and replaced by a new building made to look as nearly as possible like the original at the time of Ramakrishna's occupancy.)

Since the Cossipore house was far from those parts of Calcutta in which most of the boys had their homes, Naren decided that they would have to live on the premises; otherwise they would not be able to take their turns at the night-nursing. The boys all agreed to this arrangement, although many of their parents or guardians were strongly against it. So now, for the first time, they found themselves making a deliberate choice between home-life and life with their Master; a first step, in fact, towards renouncing the world. Naren himself was not even as free as the rest of them because he had the responsibility to his family which had fallen on him after his father's death. At that time, he still planned to support his mother and brothers by becoming an attorney – a project which he soon afterwards abandoned – and was studying for his bar examinations. However, he resolved somehow to find time at Cossipore for his studying.

His presence there was certainly needed. The boys were relying on him more and more for leadership and inspiration. Naturally enough, some of them were troubled by doubts. What was this way of life to which they were committing themselves? Did they really want to become monks? Could they dare to say that they knew better than their own fathers, who kept telling them that this was all madness? And now their Master, whom they had learned to look upon as a superhuman being, was wasting away before their eyes. . . . One day, a rumour somehow spread among them that his horrible disease was infectious. When the time came to attend him, some of them hung back. Naren found out the reason of their fear and forced them all into Ramakrishna's room. In a corner was a cup with the remains of some gruel which he had been unable to finish; it was mixed with his saliva. Naren picked up the cup without hesitation and swallowed its contents.

One night, Naren could not sleep. Finding that Sarat and a few of the others were awake, he said to them, 'Come, let's stroll in the garden and have a smoke.' While they were walking there, Naren said, 'The Master's disease is very bad – who knows, he may have made up his mind to abandon the body? So let us now make as much spiritual progress as we possibly can – by service to him and by meditation and devotion. Otherwise, when he leaves us, how shall we ever forgive ourselves? Are we going to put off calling on the Lord until all our worldly desires are satisfied? See how we're letting the days slip by! We're getting more and more tied up in this net of desires – they'll be the death and destruction of us! Let's give them up! Yes, let's give them all up!' Naren sat down under a tree. The others did likewise. Then, seeing a heap of dead grass and broken branches lying near by, Naren said, 'Let's set fire to them. Holy men light dhuni fires at this hour of the night, to burn up their desires. Let's do the same.' So they made a fire. As the flames rose, they felt an extraordinary bliss; as if their desires were indeed being consumed. 'Why did we never do this before?' someone said; and they resolved to light dhuni fires whenever they got the opportunity. By the time they had run out of fuel, it was four o'clock in the morning.

Shortly after his arrival at Cossipore, Ramakrishna was able to walk for a little while in the garden. The devotees were glad, thinking that the exercise would build up his strength; but instead it seemed to exhaust him. So the Doctor recommended a broth of kid's meat. This produced a slight improvement. As at Shyampukur, Sarada Devi had charge of the cooking, but now she was helped by Ramakrishna's niece Lakshmi Devi, the daughter of his brother Rameswar.

The pioneer exponent of homoeopathic medicine in Calcutta was Rajendra Nath Datta. It was he who had originally converted Dr Sarkar to this method of treatment. Rajendra Nath knew that if he could cure Ramakrishna he would win a spectacular victory for the cause of homoeopathy; so he now asked Dr Sarkar for permission to examine his patient. Dr Sarkar did not object; although he was one of the most famous doctors in the city, he was admirably free from professional vanity. After careful consideration, Rajendra Nath treated Ramakrishna with the drug he had selected, lycopodium (200). Ramakrishna appeared to respond to this treatment for a few weeks, and the hopes of the devotees rose accordingly.

Meanwhile, he showed an ever-increasing love for his disciples and devotees. M. describes how, on the morning of December 23rd, he said to Niranjan, 'You're my father – I'll sit on your lap!' Touching the chest of Kalipada Ghosh, he said, 'May your spirit be awakened!' He blessed two women devotees, and they shed tears of joy.

In the evening, he asked M. how long it would take him to recover. M. answered evasively that it would perhaps take five or six months. Ramakrishna behaved as if surprised and impatient. 'As long as that?' he exclaimed. And he added, 'How is it that I am so ill – in spite of all these visions, and this ecstasy and samadhi?' As on similar occasions, one seems to detect a teasing and testing of his companions.

'It was revealed to me in a vision,' he continued, 'that during my last days, I should have to live on pudding. One day – since I've had this disease – my wife brought me pudding to eat. I burst into tears and I said to her, "Is this what it meant about my last days – living on pudding, and so painfully, too?"'

It was in December, also, that a pandit named Sasadhar came to Cossipore. He said to Ramakrishna: 'The Scriptures tell us that a paramahamsa like yourself can cure his physical sickness by his own will power. Why don't you try it, sir?'

'You call yourself a pandit,' exclaimed Ramakrishna, 'and you can make such a suggestion! This mind has been given up to God, once and for all. How can I withdraw it from him and make it dwell on this worthless body?'

Sasadhar was silenced. But, after he had left, Naren and the others who had been present begged Ramakrishna to cure himself – for their sake if not for his own. 'Do you think I'm suffering like this because I want to?' Ramakrishna retorted. 'Of course I want to get better! But it all depends on Mother.' 'Then please pray to her,' said Naren. 'She can't refuse to listen.' Ramakrishna protested that he could never utter such words. But they continued to plead with him and at last he agreed that he would do what he could. A few hours later, Naren asked him, 'Well, did you pray to her?' And Ramakrishna told him, 'I said to Mother, "I can't eat anything because of this pain – please let me eat a little!" But she pointed to all of you and said, "Why, you're eating through so many mouths already!" So then I felt ashamed and couldn't utter another word.'

At Dakshineswar, even as much as five years before the onset of this disease, Ramakrishna had spoken from time to time about the circum-stances which would indicate his approaching death. 'When you see me staying nights in Calcutta, and taking food from anyone and everyone, without distinction, and even eating part of the food which has been given to someone else – then you'll know that my end is coming.' Again, he had said, 'Before I go, I'll cast my whole secret to the winds. When many people have discovered who I really am, and start to whisper about it, then this body will cease to exist, by the Mother's will. At that time, it will be shown which of the devotees belong to the inner circle and which to the outer.' And now, at Cossipore, Ramakrishna repeated and clarified this last statement. 'The devotees are being sifted by this illness,' he said; 'it is showing who belongs to the inner circle and who to the outer. Those who are living here, renouncing the world, belong to the inner circle; and those who pay occasional visits and ask, "How are you, sir?" – they belong to the outer.'

Ramakrishna's prediction that 'I'll cast my whole secret to the winds' – in other words, that he would publicly declare and demon-strate his divine nature – must certainly have referred to the events of January 1, 1886. On the afternoon of that day, Ramakrishna, who was still maintaining the slight improvement apparently caused by Rajendra Nath's treatment, said he felt strong enough to take a walk in the garden. This was at about three o'clock. As the day was a holiday, householder devotees had been arriving since noon to visit the Master; by the time he came downstairs from his room more than thirty of them were gathered in groups in the garden or inside the hall of the house. Seeing him, they all rose and bowed reverently. Ramakrishna began walking slowly through the garden towards the gate, with the devotees following him at a respectful distance.

Girish Ghosh was sitting under a tree in conversation with some friends. As Ramakrishna approached, they rose and came to meet him. 'Well, Girish,' said Ramakrishna, without any preliminary salutation, 'I hear you're saying all these things about me to everyone, wherever you go. What is it you see in me, that you can say such things?'

Falling to his knees on the ground and folding his palms, Girish answered in a voice choking with emotion, 'Who am *I* to speak of him? The sages Vyasa and Valmiki could have found no words to measure his glory!'

Ramakrishna seemed delighted. He blessed Girish and the assembled devotees, exclaiming, 'What more need I tell you? Be illumined!' Then he went into samadhi. At this, an overwhelming fervour possessed the devotees; forgetting that they were not to touch the Master, they began taking the dust of his feet, crying, 'jai' (meaning 'hail to', or literally 'victory to') 'Sri Ramakrishna!' And now Ramakrishna began to touch them, one after another. Some became ecstatic. Others felt themselves endowed with a power for profound meditation. All said later that they felt Ramakrishna had that afternoon for the first time revealed himself as a divine incarnation.

It so happened that none of the young disciples were then present in the garden. Naren and several of the others were asleep inside the house, having attended the Master or meditated throughout the previous night. Latu and Sarat were on the roof of the house and saw what was going on. One of the devotees shouted to them ecstatically to come down without delay and share the Master's blessing. But the boys would not do so. They had seized this opportunity to sweep out his room and air his bedding in the sunshine, and – believing, as Naren had taught them, that service to the guru is more important than any individual mystical experience – they would not leave their work half done. Not long after this, Ramakrishna returned to normal consciousness. He then went back into the house.

Saradananda sums up the significance of this event as follows: 'The Master, by revealing his true nature to the devotees, set them free from fear.'

On January 2nd, Naren had an experience which he described, two days later, to M.: 'I was meditating here last Saturday when I suddenly felt a peculiar sensation in my heart. It was probably the awakening of the kundalini. I clearly perceived the ida and pingala nerves. Yesterday, I told the Master about it. I said to him, "The others have had their realization, please let me have it too. Am I the only one who has to stay unsatisfied?" He said, "Why don't you settle your family affairs first? Then you can have everything. . . . What is it you want?" I said, "I want to remain in samadhi for three or four days, only coming down to the sense-plane once in a while, to eat a little." Then he said to me, "You're a fool – there's a much higher state than that! You are fond of singing the song, 'All that exists art Thou' – well, after coming down from samadhi, one may see that it is God himself who has become the universe and all that exists. Only an ishwarakoti can reach that state. An ordinary man can only reach samadhi, at best. He can't go any farther.'

'So this morning, I went home. My family scolded me, saying "Why do you wander about like a vagabond? Your bar examination will soon be here, and you're not attending to your studies." I went to study at my grandmother's. But when I tried to begin reading, I was overcome by great fear. I felt that study was something terribly evil. I burst into tears – I've never cried so bitterly in my life before. I left my books and ran out of the house. I ran through the streets. My shoes flew off – I don't know where they went. I ran past a stack of straw and got straw all over me. I went on running until I got here.'

The slight improvement in Ramakrishna's condition came to an end, and now the disease made steady progress. His body became dreadfully emaciated, until it was almost a skeleton. He could speak only in hoarse whispers; sometimes he was reduced to making signs. The haemorrhages in his throat were frequent, and he was often in great pain. But, throughout these final months of physical deterioration, he remained essentially himself, a being of manifest spiritual power, selfless love and keen intuition. His mind never seemed at all clouded by his sufferings and his cheerfulness was astonishing. He would say, 'Oh my mind, remain in bliss; let the body and its pain look after each other.' He told Naren, 'I am leaving the boys in your care. See that they practise their meditation and worship. Don't let them go back home.' One day, he asked them all to take begging-bowls and beg their food in the streets, in the manner of wandering monks. They enjoyed doing this, and they brought back the various kinds of raw food they had been given, and cooked them. They offered some to the Master. He took a few grains of rice, saying, 'Well done! This food is very pure.'

During the night of March 14th, he whispered to M., 'I've gone on suffering like this because I'm afraid you'll shed so many tears if I leave you. But, if you all tell me, "That's enough suffering – let the body go," then I may give it up.'

The next morning, however, he was eager to speak of his spiritual experiences, although he could only do so in whispers. 'Do you know what I see at this moment? God has become everything. Men and women are just frameworks covered with skin – it is he who is moving their heads and limbs. I had a vision like this, once before – that the gardens and houses and roads and men and cattle were made of wax. I see that God himself has become the block and the executioner and the sacrificial victim. . . . Ah, what a vision!

'There sits Latu, resting his head on the palm of his hand. But I see that it's the Lord himself who rests his head on his hand.

'If this body were to be preserved a short while longer, many people would become spiritually awakened. . . . But, no – that won't happen. This time, the body will not be preserved . . . .

'There are two persons in this body – one is the Divine Mother – yes, the Mother is one of them – the other is her devotee. It's the devotee who broke his arm. It's the devotee who is now sick. . . . Do you understand? Alas – to whom shall I tell all this? Who'll understand me?

'God becomes man, an avatar, and comes to earth with his devotees. And the devotees leave the world with him when he leaves it –'

At this point, Rakhal, who was present in the room with Naren, M. and others, said, 'So we beg you not to go away and leave us behind!'

Ramakrishna smiled: 'A band of minstrels suddenly appears, dances and sings. Then, just as suddenly, it departs. They arrive and they leave, without anybody recognizing them.'

Presently, Naren said, 'Some people get angry with me when I talk to them about renunciation.'

'One *must* renounce!' said Ramakrishna. Then, pointing to his limbs, he went on, 'If one thing is placed upon another, you must take away the one to get at the other. How can you get at the second thing without removing the first? When you see everything filled with God and nothing but God, how can you see anything else?'

Naren asked, 'Must one renounce the world?'

'How can you see the world, if you see nothing but God? Didn't I just say that? But I'm talking about mental renunciation. Not one of those who have come here is a worldly person. Perhaps some of them had a little bit of desire – for woman, for instance —' (At this, both Rakhal and M. smiled) 'But the desire has been satisfied.'

Ramakrishna looked at them all with eyes that were full of love. Then he exclaimed, 'Grand!'

'What's grand?' Naren asked.

'I see that everything is being made ready for a grand renunciation!'

Although this remark sounds like a prophecy, the 'grand renunciation' had in fact already begun. In January 1886, Gopal Ghosh, who had just returned from a pilgrimage, told Ramakrishna that he wanted to present monastic ochre wearing-cloths and rosaries of rudraksha beads to some of the monks who were passing through Calcutta. 'Why not give them to these boys?' Ramakrishna asked, indicating Naren and some of the other disciples. 'They are full of the spirit of renunciation. You won't find any better monks anywhere.' Gopal had twelve pieces of cloth and twelve rosaries; these he handed over to the Master. One evening, Ramakrishna distributed them, putting the disciples who received them through a special ceremony and then giving them permission to accept food, like real monks, from anybody, regardless of caste or creed. These disciples were Naren, Rakhal, Jogindra, Baburam, Niranjan, Tarak, Sarat, Shashi, Gopal Ghosh, Kali and Latu. The twelfth cloth and rosary were put aside for Girish. In this sense it may be said that the Ramakrishna Order was founded by Ramakrishna himself, although it did not come into official existence until after his death.

Now that it became tragically obvious that medical science had failed and that Ramakrishna was dying, Sarada Devi made up her mind to try to save him by fasting and prayer. So she went to the Temple of Shiva at Tarakeshwar, and lay down before the shrine for two days without food or drink, begging for a miraculous cure. Speaking of this fast in her later years, she would describe how, 'during the night of the second day, I was startled to hear a crackling sound, as if a pile of earthenware pots were being broken by a single blow. I came out of the stupor in which I had been lying, and the idea flashed through my mind: "What is a husband? What is a wife? What are worldly relationships? Why am I about to kill myself?" All my ego-attachment to the Master disappeared. My mind was possessed by complete renunciation. I groped through the darkness and sprinkled my face with holy water from the small tank behind the temple. I also drank a little, as my throat was parched with thirst. I felt refreshed. The next morning, I came back to the Cossipore Garden. When the Master saw me, he seemed amused. He asked, "Well – did you get what you wanted?" Then he said, "You got nothing."'

One evening, while Naren was meditating, he felt as if a lamp had begun to burn behind his head. The light grew more and more intense, until it seemed that the lamp itself burst. Naren went into samadhi. When, after a while, he became partly aware of his surroundings, he felt that he had somehow lost his body and was nothing but a head. 'Where's my body?' he shouted. Gopal Ghosh heard him and came into the room. 'Where's my body?' Naren repeated. 'Why, it's here, Naren. Can't you feel it?' asked Gopal. But Naren continued to cry out for his body, until Gopal, in alarm, ran to tell Ramakrishna what had happened. Ramakrishna did not seem at all surprised. 'Let him stay like that for a while,' he said calmly. 'He's been bothering me long enough to put him into that state.'

As Naren's mind came slowly down to the normal plane, he felt a marvellous peace. He hastened to Ramakrishna's room. 'Now Mother has shown you everything,' Ramakrishna told him. 'But what she has shown will be hidden from you. It will be shut up in a box, like a jewel – and I'll keep the key. When you've finished doing Mother's work on earth, then the box will be unlocked and you'll know everything you knew just now.'

Later, Ramakrishna told the other disciples, 'Naren will give up his body of his own free will. When he knows who he really is, he'll refuse to stay on this earth. Very soon, he's going to shake the world with his intellect and his spiritual power. I've prayed to Mother to keep knowledge of the Absolute away from him and cover his eyes with a veil of maya, because he has so much work to do. But the veil is so thin, it may be torn at any moment.'

It has been said already that we have no continuous narrative of the last three and a half months of Ramakrishna's life. Saradananda's book ends with an account of the events of January 1st; M. takes us only to the last week in April. After that we have nothing but a few scattered reminiscences, passed down to us from Sarada, Naren, Rakhal and other disciples and devotees. Their proper chronological order is sometimes uncertain.

Once, while Ramakrishna was hardly able to speak, he wrote on a piece of paper, 'Naren will teach others.' When Naren protested, Ramakrishna said, 'You will have to. Your very bones will make you do it.' On another occasion, he told Naren, 'Rakhal has the keen intelligence of a king. If he chose, he could rule a kingdom.' Naren understood his Master's intention in saying this. Next time the disciples were all seated together, Naren spoke in praise of Rakhal's greatness and announced, 'From today, we shall call Rakhal our king.' Henceforward, Rakhal was known familiarly as 'Maharaj', Great Raja. Ramakrishna was delighted when they told him the new nickname. This was one of the many ways in which he strengthened those bonds of love which alone could hold the young monks together in their future time of trial.

Hari (Turiyananda) used in later years to tell the devotees an anecdote which illustrates the strange 'play-acting' aspect of Ramakrishna's illness.

'One day, I approached the Master's bed and asked him, "Sir, how are you?" The Master replied, "Oh, I am in great pain. I can't eat anything, and there's an unbearable burning in my throat." But I wasn't fooled. I saw that the Master was still testing my devotion. For I knew that the Upanishads declare that the play of the Atman is all "as if" – not actuality. The Atman never experiences any sickness or suffering. And a man of realization *is* the Atman.

'The more the Master complained, the clearer it was to me that I was being tested. Finally I couldn't control myself any longer. I burst out, "Sir – whatever you may say, I see you only as an infinite ocean of bliss!"

'At this, the Master said to himself with a smile, "This rascal has found me out!"'

During this terminal phase of the disease, Nag Mahashay visited Ramakrishna only occasionally, because he found it hard to bear the sight of the wasting body. On one of these visits, Ramakrishna welcomed him warmly, embraced him and then asked, 'Can *you* do anything to cure me? The doctors have failed.'

Nag Mahashay possessed a psychic power by which he was able, if he wished, to transfer a patient's disease to his own body. He hesitated only for a moment; then, in the greatness of his devotion, he found courage and said in a firm voice, 'Yes, sir, I can cure you. By your grace, I'll do it at once.' He stepped forward and was about to lay his hands on Ramakrishna. But Ramakrishna pushed him away, saying, 'Oh yes – I know you could do *that*.'

Early in August, Ramakrishna called Jogin and asked him to read aloud out of the Bengali almanac the days of the month Sravana, from the twenty-fifth (August 9th) onward. Jogin read on until he reached the last day of the month, which is August 15th in the Julian calendar. Ramakrishna then made a sign that he did not want to hear any more.

A few days later, Ramakrishna summoned Naren to him. There was no one else in the room. Gazing fixedly at Naren, he passed into samadhi. Naren felt that a force somewhat like an electric current was taking possession of his body; slowly, he lost consciousness. When he came to himself again, he found Ramakrishna weeping. 'Oh, Naren,' he said, 'I've just given you everything I have – and now I'm as poor as a beggar! But these powers I've handed over to you will make you able to do great things in the world. When all that is accomplished, you can go back where you came from.'

On August 13th, Naren was again in Ramakrishna's room, alone. The body on the bed seemed barely alive and quite preoccupied with its pain. Could this abjectly suffering creature be an incarnation of God? 'If he would declare his divinity now, in the presence of death,' Naren said to himself, 'I'd accept it.' He was instantly ashamed of the thought and put it from his mind. For some moments he stood watching the Master's face intently. Then, slowly, Ramakrishna's lips parted and he said in a distinct voice, 'Oh Naren – aren't you convinced *yet*? He who once was born as Rama, and again as Krishna, is now living as Ramakrishna within this body – and not in your Vedantic sense.'

By adding 'not in your Vedantic sense' Ramakrishna was, of course, emphasizing that he did not merely mean he was essentially the Atman, as is every being and object, according to Vedanta Philosophy. Ramakrishna was explicitly declaring himself to be an avatar and the reincarnation of former avatars.

Throughout Sunday, August 15th, Ramakrishna appeared to be sinking. His pulse was irregular and shortly before dusk he began to breathe with difficulty. Nevertheless, he had the strength to say a loving and reassuring farewell to Sarada, who had come with Lakshmi to his bedside. 'Listen,' he told her, 'it seems I'm to go away somewhere – all through water – to a place that's far off.' When Sarada began to weep, he continued, 'You mustn't be anxious. Your life will be just the same as it's been for so long. Naren and the others will look after you. They'll be as good to you as they've been to me. Take care of dear Lakshmi —'

During the evening, they tried to give him a little liquid food, but he could hardly swallow. While they were fanning him, he passed into samadhi and the body stiffened. The disciples feared that this must be the end. However, after midnight, he regained consciousness, said he was very hungry and, to their astonishment, took a full cup of porridge without apparent discomfort. He seemed refreshed by it. Naren now suggested that he should try to sleep. At this, Ramakrishna uttered the name of Kali three times, in a clear ringing tone of which they would have supposed him physically incapable. Then he lay down, as if to sleep. He seemed to be quite comfortable, so Naren went downstairs to rest for a while.

Then, suddenly, a thrill passed through Ramakrishna's body, making its hair stand on end. The eyes became fixed on the tip of the nose. The face smiled. Ramakrishna was in samadhi. This happened at two minutes after one o'clock, early on Monday morning, August 16, 1886.

It proved to be his *mahasamadhi* – that final samadhi in which a knower of Brahman leaves the physical body. But the devotees were unable, as well as unwilling, to recognize it as such. Throughout the rest of the night, they watched and waited, with gradually diminishing hope. Girish Ghosh and Ram Chandra Datta arrived; and, as morning dawned and the news spread around Calcutta, they were joined by many others. Vishwanath Upadhyaya refused to despair. He declared that there was still some heat in the body and began to rub the spine. When, at noon, Dr Sarkar came to make an examination, he said that, in his opinion, death had actually occurred only half an hour previously.

At five o'clock that afternoon, Ramakrishna's body was brought downstairs and laid on a cot. It had been dressed in an ochre cloth and decorated with sandal-paste and flowers. A photograph, to which I referred in the last chapter, was then taken, at the suggestion of Dr Sarkar. An hour later, to the accompaniment of devotional music, the body was carried to the near-by Baranagore ghat on the Ganges and there cremated – almost directly across the river from the spot on which the great temple of the Belur Math, Ramakrishna's monastery, would one day stand.

But the mourners that evening could not see that temple, or those other stately buildings, rising from the opposite bank to reassure them that the word and work of Ramakrishna would be carried on, from generation to generation, into the future. The last holy song was sung, the fire died down in the pit, the hot summer night fell on the unheeding city and the inconstant waters. Ramakrishna was gone from them in the flesh, leaving nothing tangible but these ashes which the devoted Shashi now collected in a copper urn. They were left alone with their loss.

Nevertheless, as the disciples walked back from the cremation-ground, they shed no tears. They all knew that their lives were committed, they could never desert each other now. They had nothing but their shared experience and their faith in the Master – and it was enough. So, with the courage of youth, they lifted up their voices and shouted, as if in triumph, *Jai Sri Ramakrishna!*

21

The Story Continues

That same evening, in accordance with Hindu custom, Sarada Devi sat down and began to remove her ornaments in token of her widowhood. Just as she was about to take off her gold bracelets, Ramakrishna appeared to her, looking as he had looked before his sickness came upon him. Taking her by the wrists, he asked, 'Why are you putting away the ornaments of a married woman? Do you really believe I'm dead?' Because of this vision, Sarada continued to wear her bracelets. Some days later Balaram Bose bought a piece of white cloth without a coloured border, such as a widow should traditionally wear, and asked Golap Ma, one of Sarada's woman friends and a great devotee, to give it to her. Golap Ma found this commission painful and embarrassing; it was, in effect, a blunt reminder to Sarada of her loss. But when Golap Ma went to visit her, she saw that Sarada had already torn away a strip from the broad red border of her own wearing-cloth, making it very thin. Throughout the rest of her life, Sarada wore cloths with thin red borders, never plain white ones.

About a week after Ramakrishna's death, Naren and a young house-holder devotee named Harish were standing near the pond in the garden of the Cossipore house. It was eight o'clock in the evening. Suddenly, Naren saw a draped and shining form approaching them along the path from the gate. He asked himself if this could be the Master, but said nothing to Harish, fearing that he was the victim of an hallucination. But, a moment later, Harish himself exclaimed in a hoarse whisper, 'What's that?' So Naren shouted, 'Who's there?' Hearing the shout, some other disciples ran out of the house. But the luminous form vanished near a jasmine bush, within ten yards of where they stood.

Such were the spiritual reassurances. But the material outlook was far from reassuring. The lease on the Cossipore house was due to expire at the end of August. Ram Chandra Datta and most of the older devotees saw no reason why it should be renewed. It was quite unnecessary, they said, to go to the expense of providing a house for the young disciples. Why need they live together? Why shouldn't they return to their own homes and lead good pious Hindu lives, fulfilling their family duties?

One should not blame this group of householders for their attitude. They had no way of knowing that Ramakrishna had intended to found an order of monks; his instructions to the young disciples and his distribution of the monastic ochre cloths had been kept strictly private. Besides, the very idea of a monastic organization was foreign to Bengalis of that period; monks were thought of as individuals who wandered alone from place to place, never co-operating with each other.

Ram Chandra and his group held a meeting on August 19th and made plans for the immediate future. Since the Cossipore house was to be given up, there was nowhere for Sarada Devi to live. It was decided that she should go on a pilgrimage, which might ease her grief. Meanwhile, Ramakrishna's ashes were to be deposited in a garden-house at Kankurgachi, a village on the eastern outskirts of Calcutta. This house had been bought by Ram Chandra, at Ramakrishna's suggestion, as a retreat for devotees who wished to meditate and perform kirtan; and it had been hallowed by visits from Ramakrishna himself. As for Ramakrishna's teaching, this was to be propagated in the conventional manner, by means of public lectures, books, and articles in magazines.

These plans were acceptable to the great majority of the devotees. They were not at all acceptable to Naren and the other disciples; nor to the small minority of householders who stood by them, including M., Girish Ghosh, Balaram Bose and Surendra Nath Mitra. These still wished to see the Master's ashes enshrined on the bank of the Ganges – a project which had been at first favoured by the majority and then given up because it would necessitate buying a plot of land. When it became certain that the ashes would be taken to Kankurgachi, Shashi and Niranjan determined on a trick. They secretly transferred most of the ashes to another vessel, leaving only enough in the original urn to allay suspicion. When the ceremony was held at Kankurgachi on August 23rd, the boys took part in it with apparent good will; Shashi himself carried the urn on his head. But meanwhile the rest of the ashes had been hidden in Balaram Bose's house. These ashes have now found their proper home beside the Ganges, within the shrine of the Temple of the Belur Math. A temple has also been built at Kankurgachi, to enshrine the copper urn.

Sarada Devi was unhappy when she heard of the dispute about the ashes; it seemed so trivial to her in the presence of death. She left for her pilgrimage to Vrindavan at the end of August, with Jogindra, Kali, Latu, Tarak, Golap Ma and some other women devotees. Rakhal went to live in Balaram's house. The rest of the boys had to return home temporarily, much against their will.

One evening early in September, while Surendra Nath Mitra was meditating in his household shrine, Ramakrishna appeared to him and said, 'What are you doing here? My boys are roaming about, without a place to live in. Attend to that, before anything else.' So Surendra hurried to Naren and promised to give as much money every month as he had given for the Cossipore house, provided that Naren could find a house where the Master's ashes and other relics could be worshipped regularly and where the monastic disciples could live, with the householder devotees visiting them from time to time.

After much hunting, Naren discovered a sufficiently cheap house near the Ganges at Baranagore. By the end of September, they had started using it. Gopal Ghosh was probably the first permanent inmate. The rest of the disciples came there during the daytime, and began to live there as soon as they were able to free themselves from family obligations.

The house had been deserted for some while before their arrival, because it was supposed to be haunted. It was said that many murders had been committed there. Cobras lived underneath it, and jackals were to be met with in the wilderness of the garden. The house itself was near to collapse. But the disciples were scarcely conscious of these disadvantages. For now they had their monastery and could live as their Master had taught them.

The boys slept on straw mats on the ground. Early in the morning, before daylight, Naren would get up and wake the others, singing, 'Awake, arise, all who would drink of the Divine Nectar!' Ramakrishna's bed was placed in the centre of their shrineroom with his picture upon it. At the foot of the bed, on a low stool, stood an urn containing the ashes they had hidden at Balaram's, together with a pair of the Master's slippers. Here, Shashi performed the daily worship.

The boys had no regular supply of money; sometimes they were near starvation. Often they ate nothing but boiled salt rice and bitter herbs. They had only one presentable set of clothes in common, to be worn by anyone who had to go into the city. They called themselves 'the *danas*' – the ghost-companions of Shiva – in token of their indifference to worldly ties and pleasures.

In the evenings, they would gather on the roof, where they argued eagerly for hours, about Ramakrishna, Shankara, Jesus of Nazareth, Hindu and European philosophy. Naren taught the others to sing and play musical instruments. The music would continue far into the night; and the neighbours complained without avail.

In December, Baburam was invited by his mother to come back for a short visit to his home in the village of Antpur, and to bring Naren with him. But, by the time they were to start, the party had grown to include Sarat, Shashi, Tarak, Kali, Niranjan, Gangadhar and Sarada Prasanna. They travelled down to Antpur by train, singing religious songs all the way. It will be remembered that Baburam's mother was herself a devotee of Ramakrishna; so she was delighted to have her son and his monastic brothers turn the visit into a retreat and devote many hours of every day to meditation.

One night, a fire of logs had been lighted in the compound. The disciples gathered around it and meditated for a long while. Then Naren began to tell them the story of Jesus, with emphasis on his great renunciation. He quoted the text from the Gospel according to St. Matthew: 'The foxes have holes, and the birds of the air have nests; but the Son of man hath not where to lay his head.' He spoke of the journeys of Christ's apostles. Then he called upon his brothers to become apostles likewise and to pledge themselves to renounce the world. This they all did, standing up in a body; taking the fire and the stars for their witnesses. Later, they discovered that this evening had been the Christian Christmas Eve, and they felt that a more propitious time for their vow could not have been chosen.

It was after their return to Baranagore that the disciples assumed their monastic names, while performing the appropriate fire ceremony. Thenceforward they wore the ochre cloth of the monk. Kali (Abhedananda) has left an autobiography in which he states that the ceremony took place in the third week of January 1887. This date is probably correct, although there is a letter from Tarak (Shivananda) which seems to imply that it is much too early. It must also be remarked that M's account in the *Gospel* of his various visits to the monastery (during the first five months of 1887) always refers to the disciples by their original names. This may be due, however, to M's long-standing familiarity with them.

The first of M's visits was on February 21st. As soon as M. arrived, Tarak and Rakhal began to sing a song in praise of Shiva which Naren had just composed:

> *See where Shiva dances – strikes both cheeks*
> *and they resound –* ba-ba-bom!
> *Dimi-dimi-dimi rolls his drum – his necklace swings,*
> *a rope of skulls!*
> *His wet locks are the Ganges waters – mighty*
> *his fire-darting trident!*
> *See his belt, a gleaming serpent – see the bright moon*
> *on his forehead!*

Rakhal and Tarak danced as they sang. M. notes that Naren, Niranjan, Sarat, Shashi, Kali, Baburam and Sarada Prasanna were also living at the monastery at that time.

Later in the day, Naren returned from Calcutta, where he had been attending to family business. 'How is your lawsuit going?' Kali asked him; and he replied sharply, 'Why should you bother about that?' He was in a sternly ascetic mood, disgusted with the world. 'Woman is the gateway to Hell,' he said. 'Everybody is under the control of Woman.' This was not an anti-feminist outburst. Naren was using the word, as Ramakrishna had often used it, to symbolize male lust.

That night, they celebrated the annual worship of Shiva, the Shiva-ratri, out-of-doors in the garden. The Shiva-ratri extends from sunset to sunrise, and consists of four periods of worship, during the four watches of the night. When it was over, they breakfasted on fruit and sweetmeats which Balaram had sent them.

Naren was now full of fun, and started to clown. Putting a sweet into his mouth, he stood motionless, mimicking Ramakrishna in samadhi. He fixed his eyes in an unblinking stare. One of the devotees, getting into the spirit of the joke, came forward and supported him, pretending to keep him from falling. Naren closed his eyes for a few moments, then opened them again. With the sweet still in his mouth, he drawled, like one who is just recovering consciousness, 'I – am – all – right.' The others laughed loudly.

One day, Rakhal's father came to the monastery and begged him to return home. 'Why do you take the trouble to come here?' Rakhal asked him, not unkindly. 'I'm very happy here. Please pray to God that you may forget me, and that I may forget you, too.'

On May 7th, Naren came to visit M. at his home in Calcutta. He told M.: 'I don't care about anything. You see, even now while I'm talking to you, I feel like getting up at this very moment and running away.' Then, after a short silence, he said, 'I'm going to fast until death, that I may realize God.' 'That is good,' said M., perhaps with some amusement at Naren's impetuosity. 'For God one can do anything.'

NAREN: But suppose I can't control my hunger?
M: Then eat something, and begin fasting again.

They drove out to Baranagore together, to find that Sarada Prasanna had left the monastery during Naren's absence. No one knew where he had gone. Naren was vexed and said that Rakhal should have forbidden him to leave. But Rakhal had been away when it happened, visiting the Dakshineswar Temple. So Naren scolded Harish, saying, 'I'm sure you must have been giving one of those lectures of yours, standing with your feet apart! Couldn't you have stopped him?' Harish said meekly that Tarak had asked Sarada Prasanna not to go, but without effect. 'You see what troubles I have!' Naren exclaimed to M., 'I'm involved in maya, even here! Who knows where this boy is?' However, it was later found that Sarada had left a letter behind him. He wrote that he was going to Vrindavan on foot. 'It is very dangerous for me to live here. My mind is going through a change. I used to dream about my parents and other relatives; then I dreamed about Woman, the embodiment of Maya. Twice I've been through the suffering of having to go back home. So I am taking myself far away. The Master once told me, "Your people at home are apt to do anything; never trust them."'

By this time, Rakhal had returned. Hearing the contents of Sarada's letter, he said, 'That's the real reason for his going away. He once told me, "Naren often goes home to look after his mother, brothers and sisters. And he directs the family lawsuit. I'm afraid I may follow his example, and start going home too."' At this, Naren remained silent, as if ashamed.

Then they began to talk of making pilgrimages. Rakhal was in favour of doing this. 'What have we achieved by staying here?' he said. 'Nothing!' But Naren disagreed, 'What will you achieve by wandering around? You're always talking about attaining knowledge of God through discrimination. As if one ever could!'

'Then why have you renounced the world?' a devotee asked Naren. 'Must we go on begetting children, just because we haven't realized God?' said Naren, 'What are you talking about?'

One of the other disciples, who was lying on the floor, started to pretend that he was in agony, because of his separation from God. He groaned, 'Why should I go on living? Oh – this pain – I can't stand it! Please – give me a knife!'

'There it is,' said Naren, pretending to take him quite seriously; 'just stretch out your hand.' And they all laughed.

Some days later, Sarada Prasanna reappeared as suddenly as he had left. His pilgrimage had not been a success, for he had gone no farther than Konnagar, a small town only a few miles distant. However, he had stopped a night at the Dakshineswar Temple and seen Pratap Chandra Hazra, who was giving himself the airs of a paramahamsa, now that he felt secure from Ramakrishna's ridicule. Hazra had even had the effrontery to ask Sarada Prasanna, 'What do you think of me?' When Sarada did not answer, Hazra demanded tobacco. He seemed to expect to be waited on.

Sarada told all this to M., with humorous simplicity. When M. asked him what he had taken with him on the journey, he answered, 'Oh, one or two pieces of cloth and a picture of the Master. . . . I didn't show the picture to anyone.'

Shashi's father came to the monastery, wanting to take him home. He had done this before. Shashi dreaded these scenes, for he loved his parents. On this occasion, he fled through another door and Shashi's father had to be content to talk to M.:

SHASHI'S FATHER: It's Naren who's the cause of all this trouble. He's the one who's in charge here.

M: No one is in charge here. They're all equals. What could Naren have to do with it? He couldn't make a man renounce home against his will. We householders – we haven't been able to renounce our homes, have we?

SHASHI'S FATHER: But what you are doing is the right thing. You are serving both God and the world. Why can't one practise religion in your way? That's just what we want Shashi to do. Let him live at home. He can still come here now and then. You have no idea how his mother weeps for him.

M. felt sad and said nothing.

One afternoon, a young devotee named Rabindra burst in upon them, wild-eyed, with a torn wearing-cloth, having run all the way from Calcutta barefoot. Ramakrishna had been fond of Rabindra but had told him, 'You will have to go through a few more experiences.' And now Rabindra had just discovered that the woman he was in love with was a prostitute. 'She's a traitor!' he kept repeating. 'I shall never go back. I shall stay with you here.'

They advised him to calm himself by bathing in the Ganges. Then one of them took him to a near-by cremation-ground to look at the corpses and meditate on the impermanence of the world.

Rabindra spent that night at the monastery. Next day, he bathed in the Ganges. When he returned from the river with his wearing-cloth wet, Naren whispered slyly to M.: 'It would be good to initiate him into sannyas, right at this moment.' Sarada Prasanna brought Rabindra a dry cloth to change into; it was ochre. 'Now he has put it on —' Naren exclaimed. 'The cloth of renunciation!'

But Rabindra did not become a sannyasin, after all.

Sometimes, Naren would seem to argue against the existence of God; then again, he would sing devotional songs and shed tears. The others told him he was inconsistent. He merely smiled.

M. describes an evening on which one of the disciples read from the life of Sri Chaitanya. Perhaps something in the language of the story struck him as antiquated and funny; his tone became sarcastic. At once, Naren snatched the book from his hand, crying, 'That's how you spoil the thing that really matters!' Then he read a chapter which told how Chaitanya gave his love to everyone, from brahmin down to untouchable.

A DISCIPLE: I say that one person can't give love to another.

NAREN: The Master gave it to me.

A DISCIPLE: Are you sure?

NAREN: What do you know about love? You belong to the servant class. You should all serve me and massage my feet – instead of flattering yourselves you can understand anything. Now go and get me a pipe.

A DISCIPLE: I'll do no such thing! (*General laughter.*)

M (*to himself*): The Master certainly endowed all these brothers with spirit. It's no monopoly of Naren's. Can one possibly renounce the world without it?

Meanwhile, at Vrindavan, Sarada Devi was becoming more and more completely the being whom everyone later was to address as Holy Mother. To call her 'Mother' was no mere expression of respect. All those who met her often became aware of a maternal quality in her. It was not only Ramakrishna's disciples who were her sons; as she grew older she seemed to inhabit a world made up entirely of her children, and to be genuinely unable, like a mother, to see faults in any of them. The shy young wife of Ramakrishna, who had hidden herself even from his devotees, now became accessible to all who needed her. Yet she acquired no air of authority, no imposing presence. It would even happen that a newcomer mistakenly prostrated herself before Golap Ma her companion, rather than before this ordinary-looking woman whom Ramakrishna himself had jokingly described as 'a cat hidden under the ashes'. But the Mother's devotees were overwhelmed by just this very simplicity. Nivedita writes, 'To myself, the stateliness of her courtesy and her great open mind are almost as wonderful as her sainthood.'

At first, the Holy Mother was most unwilling to assume the role of a spiritual teacher. She only began to do so after she had been repeatedly prompted by Ramakrishna in her visions. Again and again she was made conscious of his presence. He appeared at the window of the train carriage in which she was travelling to Vrindavan, and told her not to lose his gold amulet. He appeared after her arrival at Vrindavan, saying, 'Here I am – where did you think I'd gone to? I've only passed from one room into another.' She had not been long in Vrindavan before he told her to initiate Jogindra. She could not bring herself to do this, however, until he had appeared to her two more times, telling her the mantra she must use, and until she had found out that Jogindra had also been visited by Ramakrishna and been told to take initiation from her.

In August 1887, The Holy Mother returned to Calcutta. By now, the monks of Baranagore were setting out on the pilgrimages which were to separate them from each other for months and even years. Only a few of them were to be found at the monastery at any one time. The Holy Mother was worried about this restlessness of her sons; she feared that the Order would dissolve itself. That it did not do so was due, no doubt, to the extraordinarily strong bond of affection between the brothers, to the inspiration given them by Naren and Rakhal even when they were not present, and to the very bohemianism of their monastic life. Most organizations are held together by their rules and therefore dissolved when the rules are broken; but, in this case, there were no rules to break! Also the devotion of Shashi (Ramakrishnananda) to the Master's relics and his performance of the daily worship before them created a powerful spiritual focus at Baranagore; he, at least, never left the monastery. And, within the next few years, a group of new disciples gathered there; young men who had never known Ramakrishna and were to become, so to speak, the second-generation swamis of the Order. In November 1891, the monastery was moved to Alambazar, half-way between Baranagore and Dakshineswar. This house was in much better condition than the other, but it was also regarded as haunted and therefore also cheap.

Naren and Rakhal both wandered widely about India, sometimes together, more often alone. As was to have been expected, Rakhal had his greatest spiritual experiences in Vrindavan, the scene of Krishna's childhood. At the beginning of 1895, Rakhal finally returned to the monastery, because he felt that it was his duty to serve the Order. Naren had always praised Rakhal's loyalty. 'Others may desert me,' he used to say, 'but Raja will stand by me till death.'

In July 1890, Naren resolved to set out on a pilgrimage of indefinite length, even though this meant breaking the last ties of obligation to his family. He went to say good-bye to the Holy Mother and receive her blessing. 'If I can become a man in the true sense of the word, then I shall return,' he told her. 'Otherwise, never.' 'You must not say that!' the Mother exclaimed, in distress. So Naren, to reassure her, answered, 'By your grace I shall be back soon.' She urged him to say good-bye also to Bhuvaneswari, but he answered, 'You are my only mother now.' They were not destined to see each other again for seven years.

At first, Naren travelled with some of his brother monks; then he parted from them and went on alone to Delhi, using one of the names he assumed to avoid recognition. In Delhi he was recognized, nevertheless; so he left again hurriedly. This was the beginning of three years of wanderings which took him through Rajputana down into western India and then southward, by way of Bombay, Poona, Kolhapur and Bangalore. He mixed and talked and ate with all conditions of people: rajas, untouchables, college professors, peasant farmers, Moslems, Jains. He saw the abject poverty and filth and near-starvation in which the many lived, and the dazzling wealth of the very few. He saw crude superstition which disgusted him, true faith which inspired him, apathy and ignorance and laziness which made him furiously impatient, petty jealousies and feuds which drove him to despair. He saw a great people disunited and degraded; but he saw also the vast potential strength of that people and the possibility of a renaissance which would be more splendid than all the ancient splendours of its history. He saw, almost with clairvoyance, what India might one day be, and what she might have to offer to the rest of the world.

Naren knew no language but the truth. He spoke his mind fearlessly to everyone he met. He rebuked the Maharaja of Alwar for wasting his time shooting tigers with the English, neglecting his duties to his subjects. The Maharaja, who affected Western ideas, said to Naren that it was ridiculous to show reverence to images and pictures, which were nothing but stone, clay, metal or paint. Naren's reply was to tell the Prime Minister to take down the Maharaja's picture from the wall and spit on it. He told the Maharaja of Mysore that he was surrounded by flatterers. When some orthodox brahmins asked him what he considered the most glorious period in Hindu history, he answered,

'When five brahmins used to polish off one cow', and he went on to say that Indians ought to give up vegetarianism if they were to compete with other nations in this modern age.

Naren shocked and offended many, but his honesty won him many friends, some of them powerful. The Maharaja of Mysore and his Prime Minister begged him to choose any gift he fancied, the costlier the better. Naren took a tobacco pipe from one and a cigar from the other. The Raja of Ramnad and the Raja of Khetri both urged him to go and speak for Hinduism and India in the West; offering to pay his expenses. They told him about the Parliament of Religions which was to be held in Chicago in 1893 during the World's Columbian Exposition (commemorating the four-hundredth anniversary of the discovery of America by Columbus). They wanted Naren to attend the Parliament as the Hindu delegate. But Naren could give them no definite answer. He was not yet sure of his duty.

And so he continued his journey southward, usually on foot and sharing the food of the very poor, sometimes faint with hunger, until he reached the southernmost point of India, Cape Comorin. When he had worshipped in the temple there, he looked out over the sea and saw a rock. Something moved him to swim out to it, despite the danger of sharks, and there he sat for a long while, deep in thought. It was one of those occasions in life on which an individual pauses to take his bearings, to become conscious of his destiny, perhaps to accept decisions already subconsciously made but not yet recognized. If the individual is a Naren, such an occasion may later come to be regarded as historic. Looking ahead from that day at Cape Comorin – it was sometime in the winter of 1892 – we may see not only its direct relation to certain future events, Naren's two journeys to the West and the founding of the Ramakrishna Mission, but also its indirect influence on the thoughts and lives of India's future leaders, on Gandhi and on the men who followed him.

On the rock at Cape Comorin, Naren had a very powerful emotional experience; a vision of what he and his brothers could do to help India. This experience led him to some practical conclusions which governed his future actions. It will be best to present these conclusions here in non-emotional terms and as simply as possible:

India's greatness is fundamentally religious, but religion is not what India needs in her present state of weakness. India needs education, to enable her to help herself. However, this education will be worthless unless it is directed by people who are living in the spirit of Indian religion, as demonstrated by Ramakrishna; people who have trained themselves in the sciences of the West without losing that spirit; people who have renounced all worldly ties and advantages and dedicated themselves utterly to service. Such people must, obviously, be monks, working together within an organization. Who should provide the funds for this organization? The nations of the West – because India has something equally valuable to offer them in exchange; the spirit of her religion. The West is dangerously weakened by a lack of spirituality, just as India is weakened by a lack of food. The nations of the West must be persuaded that, if India collapses, they too will collapse. When once they truly believe this, they will stop trying to exploit India. The exchange of values will begin and the whole world will benefit from it.

On May 31, 1893, Naren sailed from Bombay on board a ship bound for Vancouver, via Colombo, Hong Kong and Japan. After some further hesitations, he had decided to attend the Parliament of Religions. Devotees had contributed money. The Raja of Khetri had given him an orange silk robe, an ochre turban and a first-class steamer ticket. The Raja had also suggested a new monastic name to him and he had agreed to assume it; henceforth he became Swami Vivekananda.

When Vivekananda arrived in Chicago in mid-July he found that the opening of the Parliament had been postponed until September. He had barely enough money to support him through this unforeseen interim; someone advised him that he would be able to live more cheaply in Boston, so he took a train on there. During the journey he met a lady who invited him to stay at her home, a farm near Holliston, Massachusetts. Here, he immediately became a local celebrity. He gave talks to church and social groups in the neighbourhood. He was taken for a raja, because of his commanding appearance. Children laughed at his turban. Newspapers misspelled his name; their weirdest version of it being 'Sivanei Vivcksnanda'. Another lady who met him at this time writes, 'On Sunday [he was] invited to speak in the church and they took up a collection for a heathen college to be carried on on strictly heathen principles – whereupon I retired to my corner and laughed until I cried. He [Vivekananda] is an educated gentleman, knows as much as anybody. Has been a monk since he was eighteen. Their vows are very much our vows, or rather the vows of a Christian monk. Only Poverty with them means poverty. . . . He is wonderfully clever and clear in putting his arguments. . . . You can't trip him up nor get ahead of him.'

From the first, Vivekananda seems to have adapted himself perfectly to his new surroundings. He inspired, charmed, shocked and amused his hearers; he never played down to them or spared their feelings by modifying his language. 'Ah, the English!' he would exclaim, 'Only just a little while ago they were savages. The vermin crawled on the ladies' bodices.' He answered criticisms of Hinduism with equally blunt criticisms of Christianity. Yet his attitude towards America was eagerly receptive. He was quick to learn and praise. When he had been taken to visit a prison near Boston, his reaction was as follows:

How benevolently the inmates are treated, how they are reformed and sent back as useful members of society – how grand, how beautiful, you must see to believe! And oh, how my heart ached to think of what we think of the poor, the low, in India. They have no chance, no escape, no way to climb up. They sink lower and lower every day.

When Vivekananda talked like this, he was not just being broad-minded. There was much in his nature which was akin to the American spirit; for this very reason he was India's ideal ambassador. He was later to write to a friend:

I love the Yankee land – I like to see new things. I do not care a fig to loaf about old ruins. . . . I have too much vigour in my blood for that. In America is the place, the people, the opportunity for everything new.

Early in September, his hosts paid his fare back to Chicago, giving him the address of the committee which was in charge of looking after the delegates to the Parliament. This address Vivekananda lost *en route* – he was extremely careless in such matters. Rather than hunt through a street directory, it seemed easier to him to revert to the natural behaviour of a monk in India; he slept in a boxcar in the railway freight yards, woke 'smelling fresh water' (as he put it), followed his nose down to the lakeside, knocked at the doors of some wealthy homes and was rebuffed, and finally reached Dearborn Avenue where he sat down, resigning himself to the will of God. Very soon, a front door opened and a lady came out to him – having already guessed from his clothes why he was in the city. She invited him in to shave and have breakfast and afterwards took him to the headquarters of the committee. 'What a romantic deliverance!' said Vivekananda. 'How strange are the ways of the Lord!'

When the Parliament opened, on the morning of September 11th, Vivekananda immediately attracted notice as one of the most striking figures seated on the platform. Though powerfully built, he was not above medium height, but he seems always to have created the effect of bigness, together with a masculine grace of movement, often compared to that of a lion or tiger. Others commented on his look of being 'inly-pleased'; there was a humorous watchful gleam in his eyes which suggested an amused detachment of spirit. Everyone responded to the deep bell-like beauty of his voice; certain vibrations of it caused a kind of psychic excitement among his hearers. But neither his appearance nor his voice can fully explain the astonishing reaction of the audience to his first speech.

During the first morning's session, when his turn came to speak, he had excused himself, asking for more time. (Later, in a letter to friends in India, he confessed that he had been suffering from stage fright.) But, that afternoon, he rose to his feet. In his deep voice, he began, 'Sisters and Brothers of America' – and the entire audience clapped and cheered wildly for two whole minutes. Hitherto, the audience had certainly been well disposed; some of the speakers – including an archbishop of the Greek Church, a member of the Brahmo Samaj, a Confucian and a Buddhist – had been greeted enthusiastically and all of them with adequate politeness. But nothing like this demonstration had taken place. Perhaps the majority of those present hardly knew why they had been so moved. A crowd has its own kind of telepathy and this one must have been somehow aware that it was in the presence of that most unusual of all beings, a man whose words express exactly what he means and is. When Vivekananda said, 'Sisters and Brothers of America' he literally meant that he regarded the American women and men in front of him as his sisters and brothers; the false old oratorical phrase became simple truth.

As soon as they would let him, the Swami continued his speech.

It was a short one, pleading for universal tolerance and stressing the common basis of all religions. When it was over, there was more thunderous applause. A lady who was present recalled later, 'I saw scores of women walking over the benches to get near him, and I said to myself, "Well, my lad, if you can resist that onslaught you are indeed a God!"' She need not have been anxious. Such onslaughts were resisted by Vivekananda almost daily during his subsequent two years of lecturing in America. By the time the Parliament had come to an end, he had become, beyond comparison, its most popular speaker. There was no longer any problem as to how he could continue his mission to the West; he was in demand everywhere, and a lecture bureau was ready to organize his tours.

In those days, when the Frontier was still a living memory, one did not have to go far from the great cities to find oneself in the pioneer world of the tent show. Politicians, philosophers, writers, the great Sarah Bernhardt herself – all were treated more or less as circus attractions. Vivekananda was a Hindu swami; therefore, in the eyes of the public, he was some kind of a freak. He might hope for applause, but he could expect no consideration for his privacy. He had to face the crudest publicity, the most brutal curiosity, hospitality which was lavish but ruthless and exhausting. This circus life exhausted him eventually and wrecked his health; but, for the time being, he was equal to it and even seemed to enjoy it.

He offended many by his outspokenness. 'I have emptied entire halls!' he used to say, with smiling satisfaction. And no wonder! To the ears of rigid fundamentalists, his teaching of Man's essential divinity must have sounded utterly blasphemous. His favourite story was of a lion who had been raised among sheep and who therefore imagined himself to be a sheep, until another lion showed him his true image reflected in a pool. 'And you are lions,' he would tell his hearers, 'you are pure, infinite and perfect souls. . . . He, for whom you have been weeping and praying in churches and temples, is your own Self.' He preached self-reliance, individual search and effort. He warned against too great dependence on the words of others, no matter how divinely inspired. 'Obey the Scriptures until you are strong enough to do without them. Every man in Christian countries has a huge cathedral on his head, and on top of that a book. The range of idols is from wood and stone to Jesus and Buddha. Show by your lives that religion does

321

not mean words, or names, or sects, but that it means spiritual realization. Only those who have attained to spirituality can communicate it
to others, can be great teachers of mankind. They alone are the powers
of light.'

He spoke little about the Hindu cults of Rama, Kali, Vishnu or Shiva,
and it was only occasionally that he revealed that he, too, had a personal
cult – of the Master whom he regarded as a divine incarnation. After
he had returned to India from America, he used to say, 'If I had
preached the personality of Ramakrishna, I might have converted half
the world; but that kind of conversion is short-lived. So instead I
preached Ramakrishna's principles. If people accept the principles,
they will eventually accept the personality.'

From 1893 to 1895, Vivekananda lectured in various parts of the eastern
and central United States, appearing frequently in Chicago, Detroit,
Boston and New York. By the spring of 1895, he was very tired and in
poor health; but he made light of it. 'Are you never serious?' one of his
students asked him, reproachfully. 'Oh yes,' he answered, 'when I
have the belly-ache.' He could even laugh at the many cranks and so-
called healers who unmercifully pestered him, hoping to profit by his
reflected glory. In his letters he refers to 'the sect of Mrs Whirpool'
and to a certain mental healer 'of metaphysical, chemico, physical-
religioso, whatnot'. At the same time, he met and made an impression
on people of a more serious kind; students who were prepared to
dedicate the rest of their lives to the practice of his teaching. In June
1895, he was invited to bring a dozen of these to a house in Thousand
Island Park on the St Lawrence River. Here, for nearly two months, he
taught them informally; and this was probably the happiest part of his
visit to America.

In August, he sailed for France and England, returning to New
York in December. In April 1896 he returned to England, on what was
to be the first stage of his journey home. Vivekananda later admitted
that he had arrived in England with very mixed feelings; this was the
stronghold of the exploiters of his country. But the England which he
personally experienced proved to have an altogether different spiritual
climate. Even after his first brief visit, he wrote that his work had been
successful beyond all expectations. 'Every enterprise in this country
takes some time to get started. But once John Bull sets his hand to a

thing, he will never let it go. The Americans are quick, but they are somewhat like straw on fire, ready to be extinguished.'

From England, Vivekananda took with him two of his most faithful and energetic disciples, Captain and Mrs Sevier; also J. J. Goodwin, an Englishman whom he had first met in America and who had become the recorder of his lectures and teachings. Later he was to be followed to India by Margaret Noble (Nivedita), whom he had met in London during his first visit. These Western disciples all worked devotedly, in their different ways, for Indian education and freedom.

After leaving England and travelling for a while through Europe, Vivekananda landed in Ceylon on January 15, 1897. From there on, his journey to Calcutta was a triumphal progress; he was received with flags, bands, incense, rose water, flowers and the cheers of thousands. The Raja of Ramnad helped to draw his carriage through the streets and erected a forty-foot column in his honour. At one station, where no stop was scheduled, his admirers threw themselves down on the tracks and would not move until they had seen him. Perhaps Vivekananda's countrymen exaggerated the extent of his material success in America and Europe. But they quite rightly regarded his visit to the West as a psychological triumph far exceeding in its proportions the mere amount of money he had collected for his cause or the number of disciples he had made. Indeed, one may claim that no Indian before Vivekananda had ever persuaded Americans and Englishmen to accept him on such terms – not as a subservient ally, not as an avowed opponent, but as a sincere well-wisher and a friend, equally ready to teach and to learn, to ask for and to offer help.

In the midst of all the adulation, Vivekananda never lost his emotional balance; never forgot who he was, the disciple of Ramakrishna and the equal brother of his fellow-monks. (When they had read about his American lectures in the newspapers, they had at first supposed this remarkable swami to be a stranger to them – for they did not know Naren's new monastic name!) Brahmananda was the first of the Order to welcome him, placing a garland of flowers around his neck. Vivekananda bowed and touched Brahmananda's feet, quoting a saying from the Scriptures, 'The son of the guru is to be regarded as the guru himself.' Brahmananda returned the act of reverence, with another quotation, 'One's elder brother is to be revered as one's father.' Vivekananda was then taken to the Alambazar monastery, where he handed over to Brahmananda all the money which had been given him for the work of the future Ramakrishna Mission. Having done this, he was obliged to ask for a few pennies in order to take the ferryboat back across the Ganges. Henceforward, he insisted on sharing the poverty of his brothers.

On May 1, 1897, Vivekananda addressed a meeting of the monks and householder devotees of Ramakrishna, putting before them his plans for an organized Ramakrishna Mission. In brief, they were as follows:

The Mission will preach the truths which Ramakrishna preached and demonstrated in his own life. It will help others to put these truths into practice in their own lives, for their temporal, mental and spiritual advancement. It will train men to teach such knowledge or sciences as are conducive to the material and spiritual welfare of the masses. It will establish centres for monastic training and social work in different parts of India. It will also send trained members of the Order to countries outside India, to bring a better relation and a closer understanding between them. Its aims will be purely spiritual and humanitarian; therefore it will have no connection with politics.

It will be seen that Vivekananda's concept of a Mission actually includes a Math (monastery); the two are interrelated. The Swami was fond of quoting Ramakrishna's words, 'Religion is not for empty stomachs'; but this never meant that he was exalting social service above spiritual training. The stomachs must first be filled, certainly; but the fillers of the stomachs must first be trained to fill them, and trained spiritually as well as technically. Vivekananda knew very well that no one can go on performing the tedious, discouraging tasks of social service unless he has a powerful ideal to sustain him.

Thus it has come about that the Ramakrishna Order has established its monasteries and social service centres – including hospitals, dispensaries, colleges, schools of agriculture and industry, libraries and publishing houses – side by side. The headquarters of the Math and the Mission are situated in the same compound, at Belur; and the trustees of both are the same. Legally, they are separate entities, but only for the convenience of administrative planning and the allotment of funds. The monks of the Order keep exchanging one way of life for the other, when this is possible; spending some time in meditation and solitude, and then taking up administrative duties at one of the Mission centres.

The Order has at the present time over a hundred centres in different parts of India and the neighbouring Asian lands. In addition, there are some centres in the West for the study and practice of Vedanta Philosophy and Ramakrishna's teachings; ten of them in the United States, one in England, one in France, and one in Argentina.

The Ramakrishna Order has always obeyed Vivekananda's injunction to keep itself politically uninvolved. During the 1920's, when the struggle with England had become acute, it nevertheless refused its official sanction to Gandhi's Non-Co-operation Movement – and this despite the fact that nearly all of its members must have had a strong sympathy for his cause. Many of Gandhi's followers criticized the Order harshly for its attitude; but Gandhi himself never did so. He understood that a religious body which supports a political cause – no matter how noble and just – can only compromise itself spiritually and thereby lose that very authority which is its justification for existence within human society. In 1921, Gandhi came to the Belur Math on the anniversary of Vivekananda's birthday and paid a moving tribute to him, saying that the Swami's writings had taught him how to love India even more.

In America and in England, Vivekananda had contrasted Indian spirituality with Western materialism. In India, we find him attacking Indian sloth and lack of unity, national pride and personal courage; and praising American efficiency and British tenacity and national spirit. Of the English, he would say that 'They are, of all nations, least jealous of each other and that is why they dominate the world. They have solved the secret of obedience without slavish cringing – great freedom with law-abidingness.' Turning on his Indian followers, he would cry, 'You have not the capacity to manufacture a needle and you dare to criticize the English! Fools! Sit at their feet and learn their arts and industries. Without the necessary preparation, what's the use of just shouting in Congress?' And again, 'What we want is strength, so believe in yourselves. It is a man-making religion we want. Nationalism of purely agitational pattern cannot carry us far; with patriotism must be associated a real feeling for others. We must not forget that we have also to teach a great lesson to the world. But the gift of India is the gift of religion and philosophy.'

Vivekananda was the last person to worry about formal consistency.

He almost always spoke extempore, fired by the circumstances of the moment, addressing himself to the condition of a particular group of listeners, reacting to the intent of a certain question. That was his nature, and he was supremely indifferent if his words of today seemed to contradict those of yesterday. As a man of enlightenment, he knew that the truth is never contained in arrangements of sentences. It is within the speaker himself. If what he is, is true, then words are unimportant. In this sense, Vivekananda is incapable of self-contradiction.

However, it is not at all surprising that he has been much misunderstood; that parts of his message, taken out of context, have been presented as the whole. Even some of his brother monks, at the time of the founding of the Mission, were afraid that he was deviating from Ramakrishna's aims. And there have been some, in much more recent times, who have claimed him as a socialist and a nationalist revolutionary. They wish, in all sincerity, to honour Vivekananda as a great Indian patriot, and they are right as far as they go. But their statue of him would have to be a headless torso; Vivekananda without Ramakrishna.

The Mission went into action as soon as it had been established, taking part in famine and plague relief and beginning to found hospitals and schools. Vivekananda became its General President and Brahmananda the head of the Calcutta centre. Then the first buildings were erected on the land which the Order had purchased at Belur, and the Math was opened there, in January 1899.

In June 1899, Vivekananda sailed for his second visit to the West. He spent most of it in America, training small groups in different parts of the country and opening centres at places where devotees had urgently requested him to do so. He returned to India in 1900, a sick and exhausted man. He said frequently that he did not expect to live much longer. But he seemed calmer and happier than he had ever been; quite released from the driving anxious energy of his earlier crusading years. His mood is beautifully described in a letter he wrote to one of his disciples, in April 1900:

> I am well, very well mentally. I feel the rest of the soul more than that of the body. The battles are lost and won. I have bundled my things and am waiting for the Great Deliverer. . . .

After all, Joe, I am only the boy who used to listen with rapt wonderment to the wonderful words of Ramakrishna under the banyan at Dakshineswar. That is my true nature – works and activities, doing good and so forth, are all superimpositions. Now I again hear his voice. . . . Now only the voice of the Master calling. – 'I come, Lord, I come.' . . .

I am glad I was born, glad I suffered so, glad I did make big blunders, glad to enter peace. I leave none bound, I take no bonds. Whether this body will fall and release me or I enter into freedom in the body, the old man is gone, gone forever, never to come back again!

The guide, the guru, the leader, the teacher, has passed away; the boy, the student, the servant, is left behind. . . .

Behind my work was ambition, behind my love was personality, behind my purity was fear, behind my guidance the thirst for power. Now they are vanishing and I drift. I come, Mother, I come. . . .

It is said that Vivekananda's departure from this life, on July 4, 1902, had the appearance of being a premeditated act. For several months previously, he had been releasing himself from his various duties, and training successors. But his health was better that day and he ate his noon meal with relish. He also talked philosophy with some of his brother monks, gave a Sanskrit lesson for three hours to a class of novices and went for a two-mile walk with Premananda during the afternoon. In the evening he went into his room and spent an hour in meditation. Then he called the disciple who was his personal attendant and asked him to open all the windows and to fan his head. Vivekananda lay down on his bed; the disciple thought he must be asleep or in deep meditation. Shortly after nine, his hands trembled a little and he breathed once, very deeply. A minute passed. Again he breathed deeply, in the same manner. Then his eyes and face became fixed in an expression of ecstasy. A little blood appeared around his mouth, in his nostrils and in his eyes.

When the doctors arrived, they thought at first that animation was only suspended. They tried artificial respiration for at least two hours. At midnight they had to admit that there was no more hope. They gave the cause of death as apoplexy or heart failure. But the brothers of the Order were convinced that he whom they had called Naren and

Vivekananda had at last, as Ramakrishna had predicted, become aware of his true identity.

If a successor to Vivekananda had had to be elected, none of the brothers would have hesitated; he could have been no other than their Raja, Ramakrishna's spiritual son. But no such choice was necessary. Among Vivekananda's many acts which later seemed to have been a preparation for his departure was his resignation from the presidency of the Mission, more than a year before he died. Brahmananda had succeeded him in February 1901, and was to remain in office as president of both Math and Mission for the next twenty-one years.

I have spoken already of the transformation of Sarada Devi from the shy young wife of Ramakrishna into the Holy Mother of the Order. An equally great transformation may be said to have taken place in Rakhal, the gentle and yielding boy who became the almost super-humanly wise and powerful Brahmananda. Under his direction the Ramakrishna Math and Mission were shaped and Vivekananda's plans translated into action.

Brahmananda was a great administrator of the Mission's activities, but he constantly reminded his disciples and fellow-workers that spirituality comes first, social service second. 'The only purpose of life is to know God,' he would tell them. 'Attain knowledge and devotion; then serve God in mankind. Work is not the end of life. Disinterested work is a means of attaining devotion. Keep at least three fourths of your mind in God. It is enough if you give one fourth to service.'

He was very particular about the source of any money that was offered to the Mission, and about the motives with which it was offered. A millionaire once came to them saying that he was ready to renounce the world; they could have his entire fortune. But Brahmananda refused. He was aware that the man, although quite sincere, was only acting on the impulse of the moment. He would have regretted his offer later.

Brahmananda was far more concerned for the spiritual growth of his disciples than for their practical efficiency. He once reprimanded a senior monk who had been put in charge of a novice: 'Did I send this young boy to you to make into a good clerk?' The success of a religious order, he said, must be judged by the inner life of each of its members, not by its achievements in social service.

As head of the Order he was of course empowered to make the final decision whether or not to expel a monk who had been guilty of serious misbehaviour. But he never made such decisions. Often he did not deal directly with the offence itself; instead, he would send for the culprit and have him meditate daily in his presence and render him personal service. On such occasions, the effect of his immense spiritual power and love would be witnessed by all. The culprit would become transformed. Brahmananda's care for others extended far beyond the ordinary human limits of compassion; indeed it was supernatural, for, as he occasionally admitted, he was at all times in mental communication with everybody in the Order and aware of all their problems. He knew that he could give spiritual help whenever it was needed, even at a long distance; and this knowledge made him magnificently unanxious and serene.

However, it should not be supposed that he was over-lenient with his disciples. He would even subject a monk to public humiliation and dismissal from his presence; especially if he regarded that monk as having exceptional qualities and if he wished to train him for some difficult duty. Often, the apparent offence was something quite trivial. For example, a young monk who was performing the ritual worship had used three matches instead of one to light the lamps before the shrine; Brahmananda scolded him severely for lack of concentration. This caused some of the disciples to suspect that Brahmananda's rebukes were not what they seemed to be, but perhaps a method of destroying the disciple's bad karma. As one of them has written, 'The chastening of a disciple never began until after he had enjoyed several years of love and kind words. These experiences were painful at the time but they were later treasured among the disciple's sweetest memories. It often happened that even while the disciple was being rebuked by Maharaj he would feel a strange undercurrent of joy. The indifference of Maharaj was the only thing we could not have borne, but Maharaj was never indifferent. The very fact that he could speak to us in this way proved that we were his children, his own.'

It has been said that Brahmananda was so entirely fearless that others could not feel fear in his presence. Once, when he was walking with two devotees in the woods of Bhubaneswar, a leopard appeared and came straight towards them. He stood still and confronted it calmly until it turned tail. Again, while he was going along a narrow lane in

Madras, attended by two monks, a maddened bull came charging to meet them. The young men tried to protect their guru, who was already an elderly man, by standing in front of him; but he pushed them behind him with extraordinary strength and fixed his eyes upon the bull. It stopped, shook its head from side to side, and then trotted quietly away.

Brahmananda was tall and well built, with eyes that were sometimes deeply searching and sometimes apparently unseeing, as though they were regarding an altogether different reality. His hands and feet were beautifully formed. His back strikingly resembled Ramakrishna's – to such a degree that Turiyananda once caught sight of Brahmananda walking ahead of him in the gardens of Belur and believed for a moment that he must be having a vision of the Master himself. Once, in a crowded railway station, one of his disciples overheard the conversation of two men who had been watching Brahmananda with great interest. One of them remarked that it was impossible to guess his nationality; he didn't seem to belong to any of the Indian races. The other man agreed, adding, 'but you can see very well that he's a man of God'.

Brahmananda did not have the eloquence of a Vivekananda. He inspired people by his silences quite as much as by his words. It is said that he could change the psychological atmosphere in a room, making the occupants feel talkative and gay and then inclining them to silent meditation, without himself saying anything. For the most part, his teachings were very simply expressed. 'Religion is a most practical thing. It doesn't matter whether one believes or not. It is like science. If one performs spiritual disciplines, the result is bound to come. Although one may be practising mechanically – if one persists one will get everything in time. . . . And if you go one step towards God, God will come a hundred steps towards you. . . . Why did God create us? So that we may love him.' When one of his disciples asked permission to practise some severe spiritual austerities, Brahmananda asked, 'Why need you do that? We have done it all for you.' He treated Ramlal, Ramakrishna's nephew, with the greatest respect and made the young disciples bow down before him, because he had the blood of the family into which the Master had been born. But Ramlal would protest that he himself had never truly recognized his uncle's greatness until his eyes had been opened to it by Brahmananda. Once, when a famous musician was performing, a devotee complained that he had played no devotional songs. Brahmananda, who loved music, replied, 'Don't you realize that sound itself is Brahman?'

'It's good to laugh every day,' he used to say, 'it relaxes the body and the mind.' There are many stories of his fondness for practical jokes. On one occasion, Akhandananda, who had been staying with Brahmananda, said that he must leave next morning and return to his own mission centre at Sargachi. Brahmananda pleaded with him to stay a little longer, but the Swami insisted; so a palanquin was hired to take him to the railway station, several miles away. As the train left very early, it was necessary to start in the small hours of the night. Akhandananda did not notice that Brahmananda had whispered some instructions to the palanquin bearers. Having said good-bye to Maharaj, he settled down to doze in the darkness, with the curtains of the palanquin drawn. The journey seemed very long and the stops were frequent. The Swami called anxiously to the bearers from behind the curtains; he was afraid that he would miss the train. They reassured him, saying that there was plenty of time. At last they put down the palanquin and asked him to alight. When he parted the curtains to do so, there stood Brahmananda, as if ready to welcome him back after months of absence. Then Akhandananda realized that he had simply been carried round and round the compound in the dark. Brahmananda embraced him and the two of them laughed like children.

Although the Holy Mother was not a member of the Order she was, in a sense, its real head. Any wish or opinion expressed by her was regarded by Brahmananda and his brothers as a command to be obeyed without question. To them, the Mother was one with the Mother of the Universe and thus as holy as Ramakrishna himself. There were times when the Mother would indirectly acknowledge the existence of this Presence within her. In her family there was a female relative who was insane. Once this unfortunate woman began to curse the Holy Mother, crying, 'Let her die!' The Mother commented quietly, 'She does not know that I am deathless.'

Towards the end of her life, she fell sick of a recurring fever; her flesh wasted away and she became very weak. It was decided to move her from Jayrambati to the house which had been built for her in Calcutta. She was now too weak to leave her bed, and those around her noticed that she showed a growing detachment from everything earthly. She, who had cared for them all as her own children – who had recently stopped an attendant who was fanning her, saying, 'I can't sleep, thinking how your hand will ache' – now received the news of her beloved brother's death without shedding a tear. 'Whatever work the Master wanted done by this body seems to be over,' she said, 'now my mind longs for him and wants nothing else.' She began dismissing her closest relatives, sending them away to Jayrambati and elsewhere, as if to spare them the pain of her departure. One of the devotees cried, 'Mother, what will become of us?' She answered, 'Why are you afraid? You have seen the Master.' Not long after midnight, on July 21, 1920, she passed into her mahasamadhi.

Brahmananda spent the last years of his life in a state of high spiritual consciousness, coming down from it only in order to help and teach others. He began to have the vision of Ramakrishna almost every day; not only seeing him but also talking with him. And yet, in conversation with strangers who came to visit the Mission, he would discuss a variety of worldly topics with intelligence and apparent interest; only his intimate disciples were aware that he remained completely detached.

In 1922, shortly after the celebrations of Ramakrishna's birthday, Brahmananda had a slight attack of cholera. This was followed by a serious diabetic condition. He suffered greatly for several days, but his mood was ecstatic; for he had visions of Ramakrishna, Vivekananda and other brothers who were no longer alive in the body. He heard Krishna calling him to dance, and he exclaimed, 'Put anklets on my feet – I want to dance with Krishna!'

There was no coma at the end, as is usual in cases of diabetes. He had clear consciousness of his surroundings. His eyes were brilliant. He was perfectly calm. His last words to his disciples were, 'Do not grieve, I shall be with you always.' On April 10, 1922, he left the body in samadhi.

Ramakrishnananda said of Brahmananda, while he was still alive, 'Maharaj's mind has become one with the mind of Ramakrishna.' Shivananda, speaking to a disciple of Brahmananda who was leaving to take up his duties as a resident swami at one of the centres in the United States, expressed himself even more strongly: 'Never forget that you have seen the Son of God. You have seen God.' That same disciple, writing many years later, says, 'He was our father, mother, and everything. After his passing away I felt no void. As long as Maharaj was in the physical body there was a barrier. Afterwards, the barrier was gone. I know that Maharaj is still living – and helping all of us.'

'A band of minstrels suddenly appears, dances and sings. Then, just as suddenly, it departs.' At this point, our story reaches its natural end.

The story that continues is that of a growing organization, and of the men and women who have helped to make Ramakrishna and his message more and more widely known throughout the world. But this book is about Ramakrishna the phenomenon; and a phenomenon has no concern with its after effects. If God does actually visit the earth from time to time in human form, is he any the more or the less God because of the number of his disciples or the size of the Church they later build for him?

The biographer of an ordinary 'great man' is expected to conclude his work by assessing his hero's achievements, comparing him with other important figures of his period who were active in the same field, and assigning him a 'place in history'. I hope it will be obvious that any such attempt here would be meaningless.

To the best of my ability, the phenomenon has been described. How should one interpret it? How react to it? Should it be dismissed from the mind, as something irrelevant and inconveniently out of line with everyday experience? Or should it be taken as the starting-point of a change in one's own ideas and life?

These questions I leave to each individual reader – just as Saradananda and M. and the other writers about Ramakrishna leave them to me.

Bibliography

ABOUT RAMAKRISHNA

Sri Ramakrishna The Great Master, by Swami Saradananda, translated by Swami Jagadananda, Sri Ramakrishna Math, Mylapore, Madras, 1952.

The Gospel of Sri Ramakrishna, by M., translated by Swami Nikhilananda, Ramakrishna–Vivekananda Centre, New York, 1942.

'Memories of Sri Ramakrishna,' by Girish Chandra Ghosh, translated by Swami Aseshananda, *Vedanta and the West*, March–April, 1953.

Life of Sri Ramakrishna, Advaita Ashrama, 1948.

Sri Ramakrishna and Spiritual Renaissance, by Swami Nirvedananda, Ramakrishna Mission Institute of Culture, Calcutta, 1940.

Ramakrishna: his life and sayings, by F. Max Müller, Advaita Ashrama, Mayavati, 1951.

Rammohan to Ramakrishna, by F. Max Müller, Susil Gupta, Calcutta, 1952.

The Life of Ramakrishna, by Romain Rolland, Advaita Ashrama, 1930.

Ramakrishna et la vitalité de l'hindouisme, by Solange Lemâitre, Editions de Seuil, 1959.

ABOUT SARADA DEVI

Holy Mother Shri Sarada Devi, by Swami Gambhirananda, Sri Ramakrishna Math, Mylapore, Madras, 1955.

Sri Sarada Devi The Holy Mother (Her life and conversations), by Swami Tapasyananda, conversations translated by Swami Nikhilananda, Sri Ramakrishna Math, Mylapore, Madras, 1958.

ABOUT RAMAKRISHNA'S DISCIPLES

The Disciples of Sri Ramakrishna, Advaita Ashrama, 1943.

The Eternal Companion: Brahmananda, records of his teaching with a biography by Swami Prabhavananda, Vedanta Press, Hollywood, 1947.

'With My Master, Swamiji and Maharaj,' by Swami Vijnanananda, *Vedanta and the West*, March–April, 1955.

The Life of Swami Vivekananda, by his Eastern and Western Disciples, Advaita Ashrama, Calcutta (6th ed.), 1960.

The Life of Vivekananda and the Universal Gospel, by Romain Rolland, Advaita Ashrama, Calcutta, 1931.

Vivekananda, a biography, by Swami Nikhilananda, Ramakrishna–Vivekananda Centre, New York, 1953.

Reminiscences of Swami Vivekananda, by his Eastern and Western Admirers, Advaita Ashrama, 1961.

Swami Vivekananda in America: New Discoveries, by Marie Louise Burke, Advaita Ashrama, Calcutta, 1958.

A Man of God (Glimpses into the life and work of Swami Shivananda, a great disciple of Sri Ramakrishna), by Swami Vividishananda, Sri Ramakrishna Math, Madras, 1957.

Swami Turiyananda, a biography, by Swami Ritajananda (serialized in *Vedanta and the West*, beginning with July–August, 1960).

Swami Akhandananda and His Memoirs of Sri Ramakrishna, by Swami Jagadiswarananda, Ramakrishna–Vivekananda Centre, Dadar, Bombay, 1948.

HISTORICAL BACKGROUND

History of the Ramakrishna Math and Mission, by Swami Gambhirananda, Advaita Ashrama, Calcutta, 1957.

An Advanced History of India, by R. C. Majumdar and H. C. Raychaudhuri, Kalikinkar Datta, Macmillan and Co., London, 1948.

The Oxford Student's History of India, by Vincent A. Smith and H. G. Rawlinson, Oxford University Press, 1951.

The Men Who Ruled India, Vol. I, The Founders, Vol. II, The Guardians, by Philip Woodruff, St. Martin's Press, New York, 1954.

Golden Interlude, The Edens in India 1836–42, by Janet Dunbar, Houghton Mifflin, Boston, 1956.

Autobiographic Memoirs, by Frederic Harrison, Macmillan, 1911.

India. Pictorial, descriptive and historical, Bell and Daldy, London, 1864.

Shadows from India, by Roderick Cameron, William Heinemann, London, 1958.

SOCIAL BACKGROUND

India and Her People, by Swami Abhedananda, Vedanta Society, New York, 1906.

A Yankee and the Swamis, by John Yale, George Allen and Unwin, London, 1961.

Hindu Customs in Bengal, by Basanta C. Bose, The Book Company, Calcutta.

Indian Village, by S. C. Dube, Cornell University Press, Ithaca, New York, 1955.

India Changes! by Taya Zinkin, Oxford University Press, New York, 1958.

PHILOSOPHICAL AND RELIGIOUS

The Complete Works of Swami Vivekananda, Advaita Ashrama, Calcutta

Kali The Mother, by Sister Nivedita, Advaita Ashrama, Mayavati, 1950.

The Spiritual Heritage of India, by Swami Prabhavananda, with the assistance of Fredrick Manchester, George Allen and Unwin, London, 1962; Doubleday, New York, 1963.

Bhagavad-Gita. The Song of God. Translated by Swami Prabhavananda and Christopher Isherwood, Vedanta Press, Hollywood; Phoenix House, London.

Srimad Bhagavatam. The Wisdom of God. Translated by Swami Prabhavananda, Vedanta Press, Hollywood, 1943.

REFERENCE BOOKS

Encyclopaedia of Religion and Religions, by E. Royston Pike, Meridian Books Inc., New York, 1958.

A Classical Dictionary of Hindu Mythology, by John Dowson, Routledge and Kegan Paul, Ltd., London (9th ed.), 1957.

A Ramakrishna–Vedanta Wordbook, by Brahmacharini Usha, Vedanta Press, Hollywood, 1962.

Notes on Illustrations

Frontispiece: this, the first of four photographs taken of Ramakrishna, was made on Sunday, September 21, 1879. The place was Keshab's house, the Lily Cottage, on Upper Circular Road, Calcutta. Ramakrishna was in samadhi, supported by Hriday. Brahmo devotees were sitting on the floor. Keshab seems to have had the photograph made for his own use, as it is known that afterwards he kept a copy in his room.

1. This, the second photograph of Ramakrishna, was taken on Saturday, December 10, 1881. Surendra arranged for the portrait to be made in the studio of the Bengal Photographers in the Radhabazar section of Calcutta. Ramakrishna had previously shown an interest in the mechanics of photography. Before the picture was taken he inquired into the photographic process and studied the equipment. Later he drew upon the knowledge he had acquired for examples to illustrate his teachings.

2. The third photograph was probably taken in 1883 or 1884. Bhavanath Chatterjee engaged a photographer to come to Dakshineswar to take the picture. Ramakrishna was seated in samadhi on the raised veranda outside the Radhakanta temple. Narendra was present. Later when Ramakrishna saw a print he remarked: 'A high yogic state is pictured here. As time goes on this photo will be worshipped in every home.' Some prints from the original negative are in the possession of the Ramakrishna Order, from which the great numbers of copies in circulation today were made.

3. This photo and No. 4 were taken on the same day in November 1898 at Nivedita's house in Calcutta.

4. Holy Mother was photographed for the first time twelve years after Ramakrishna's death, when she was forty-five years old.

5. The octagonal room on the ground floor is 7 ft. 9 in. in diameter. Originally the entrance door was only four feet high. This was Sarada Devi's residence at Dakshineswar for several years. Chandra occupied the second floor. This illustration was made from the roof of Ramakrishna's room, looking north. Beyond is the Panchavati.

6. Narendra Nath Datta (1863–1902) in 1892 at Belgaum in western India.

7. Rakhal Chandra Ghosh (1863–1922) became Swami Brahmananda, but to this day he is affectionately referred to as Raja Maharaj or simply Maharaj. This picture was taken on May 10, 1921, as Maharaj was on his way to open the permanent building of the Ramakrishna Mission Students' Home in Madras.

8. Taken in 1902 at Balaram's home in Calcutta, not long before Swami Vivekananda's death. Sadananda was Vivekananda's disciple.

9. Hari Nath Chatterjee (1863–1922) became Swami Turiyananda. Baburam Ghosh (1861–1918) became Swami Premananda. This photo was probably taken in 1910 or 1911.

10. Formerly Sarat Chandra Chakravarty (1865–1927). He is shown in characteristic pose sitting in the small room at the entrance of the Calcutta residence of the Holy Mother and *Udbodhan* office, where he wrote in Bengali *Sri Ramakrishna the Great Master*.

11. Most probably Tarak Nath Ghoshal was born in 1854. He died in 1934. He is still referred to as Mahapurush Maharaj, 'great soul'. This picture was taken in Madras, probably in 1924.

12. Formerly Sarada Prasanna Mitra (1865–1915). This photograph was taken in San Francisco.

13. Formerly Shashi Bhushan Chakravarty (1863–1911).

14. Latu (his full name and date of his birth are unknown to us) became Swami Adbhutananda. He died in 1920. Jogindra Nath Choudhury (1861–99) became Swami Yogananda. This picture was taken from a group photo made at the Alambazar Math in 1896.

15. Girish Chandra Ghosh (1844–1912) as he looked at about the time he met Sri Ramakrishna.

16. Mahendra Nath Gupta was born in 1854 and died in 1932. In 1928 he was photographed kneeling beside the bel tree at the north of the Dakshineswar temple grounds where more than forty years before some of his most memorable encounters with Ramakrishna had taken place.

17. Also known as Mathur Mohan Biswas and Mathur Babu. From a painting. The date of Mathur's birth is uncertain. But it is known that he was a classmate of Devendra Nath Tagore who was born in 1817. Hence Mathur would probably have been between thirty-five and forty

years old when he met Ramakrishna in 1855, and between fifty and fifty-five when he died in 1871.

18. Chanting and singing songs of their own composition formed an important part of the religious observances of the Brahmos. They frequently accompanied themselves on one-stringed musical instruments like the one Keshab is holding. The banner reads: New Dispensation.

19. This photograph after the death of Ramakrishna, was made at about 5 P.M. on Monday, August 16, 1886, outside the front door of the Cossipore Garden House. Twenty-four of the more than fifty devotees who were present are identified in the key.

20. This old photograph conveys the atmosphere of Kamarpukur as it was years ago. In the courtyard of Khudiram's house (*left*) formerly stood a shed, where Gadadhar was born. Across the lane from the house is the Shiva temple in front of which Chandra had a vision indicating the birth of a divine child.

21. Village scene near Khudiram's house. The colonnaded temple is one of a group of buildings which comprised the Laha estate. At the left can be seen a corner of the nat-mandap. On the right an old palanquin is stored.

22. Several terms used in the diagram are not mentioned in the text of this book, but are used in Swami Saradananda's biography of Ramakrishna and in M's Gospel. The chandni is the portico at the head of the main landing ghat. 'Natmandir' – its synonym 'nat-mandap' is used in this book – is an Indian term for the open-air meeting halls or audience chambers frequently to be found facing Hindu shrines. Chandra was placed in the Ganges at the Bakultala ghat at the time of her death.

23. Visitors are seen entering the southeast veranda, outside Ramakrishna's room.

24. Looking west. Through the open door the semi-circular porch is visible, with the Ganges behind. Narendra came in through this door on his first visit to Ramakrishna. Many of the events related in the Gospel occurred in this room. It is about twenty-four feet square.

25. Looking down the steps of the ghat, Sri Ramakrishna first saw the Bhairavi getting out of a boat, probably like the 'country boat' shown in the foreground. In the portico occurred the first meeting between Ramakrishna and Tota Puri.

26. Image of the Divine Mother of the Universe from the front. The image is 33½ in. high and made of black basalt.

27. Profile from the west. The bedstead of the deity, with its mosquito curtain, is visible beyond the altar. The shrineroom is 15 ft. by 15 ft. The Kali figure is generally partly covered by flower garlands brought as offerings by worshippers.

28. The kind of carriage used by Ramakrishna on his many trips from Dakshineswar into Calcutta. Such carriages are still in use today.

29. During Ramakrishna's time this sword hung on the wall of the Kali shrineroom. It was used to kill goats intended as offerings. The sword is now kept locked in a case in the quarters of the temple manager.

30. The courtyard is 220 ft. by 440 ft. The dimensions of the nat-mandap are 75 ft. by 50 ft. The Kali Temple is 50 ft. square, not including the platform which surrounds it, and more than a hundred feet high. The Kali image faces south, towards the nat-mandap. The vantage space inside the central arch, where devotees crowd to view the deity, is about seven feet square. A corner of the most southerly Shiva Temple appears in the left foreground.

31. Preserved at the Belur Math is a manuscript of some hundred pages, written by Sri Ramakrishna. The contents include copies of three playlets based on stories from the Mahabharata and Ramayana. The manuscript was probably written before 1852. It is inscribed with Ramakrishna's youthful name and address, which are shown in the illustration: Sri Gadadhar Chattopadhyaya (Chatterjee), Village Kamarpukur. Students who understand the Bengali of the period say that the writing in the manuscript is fairly correct.

32. An early photograph suggesting the dense, solitary character of the Panchavati as it existed at the time of Ramakrishna.

Index